THE I TATTI
RENAISSANCE LIBRARY

James Hankins, General Editor

MANUTIUS

THE GREEK CLASSICS

ITRL 70

ALDUS MANUTIUS
✦ ✦ ✦
THE GREEK CLASSICS

EDITED AND TRANSLATED BY

N. G. WILSON

THE I TATTI RENAISSANCE LIBRARY
HARVARD UNIVERSITY PRESS
CAMBRIDGE, MASSACHUSETTS
LONDON, ENGLAND
2016

Series design by Dean Bornstein

Library of Congress Cataloging-in-publication data

The Greek Classics / edited and translated by N. G. Wilson.
pages cm — (The I Tatti Renaissance library ; 70)
Includes bibliographical references and index.
ISBN 978-0-674-08867-2 (alk. paper)
1. Greek literature — Translations into English.
2. Manuzio, Aldo, 1449 or 1450–1515.
I. Wilson, N. G. (Nigel Guy), 1935–
II. Series: I Tatti Renaissance library ; 70.
PA3621.G66 2016
880.8'001 — dc23   2015010876

Contents

ॐ⁂ॐ

· CONTENTS ·

APPENDICES

Prefatory Note

ཚེརྩ

The present year, when we mark the fifth centenary of the death of Aldus Manutius, the greatest scholar-printer of the Renaissance, seems an auspicious moment to inaugurate a new subseries within the I Tatti Renaissance Library dedicated to the history of the book. This relatively new field has stimulated great interest in the older histories of typography, engraving, and publishing, activities whose origins, for Western regions of the world, may be traced back to the Renaissance. Several other volumes are currently in preparation. A complementary volume will appear in 2016, entitled *Humanism and the Latin Classics*, edited and translated by John N. Grant, containing Aldus' prefaces to the works in ancient Latin and Neo-Latin published by his house; that volume will include a more detailed introduction to Aldus' life and labors than does the present volume. In preparation also is a volume edited and translated by M. C. Davies, containing the prefaces to works printed by Konrad Sweynheym and Arnold Pannartz, the first masters of the art of printing in Italy, between 1465 and 1473.

James Hankins
General Editor
July 2015

δι' τοῦτ' ἀναλίῳ τ' ἐκδλώσομεν
πράσσειν· τὰ δ' ἐπ' ὀφρύϊ παρ-
νασία. ἐν ἀρ' γειθ', ὅς -
σα καὶ ἐν Θήβαις. ὅσα τ' ἀρ-
καίσιν ἀνάσσων. μαρτυρή-
σει λυκαίου βωμὸς ἄναξ.
πελλάνα τε, καὶ σικυών·

ἔπω   καὶ μέγαρ' αἰακιδᾶν τ' εὐερκὲς ἄλσος
δὸς·   ἅτ' ἐλευσίς· καὶ λιπαρὰ μαραθών
       τ' αἰθ' ὑπ' αἴτνασ' ὑψιλόφου
       καὶ λιπλουτοι πόλιες· ἅτ' εὔ-
       βοια· καὶ πᾶσαν κατὰ
       ἑλλάδ' εὑρήσεις ὀρδυνῶν
       μάσσον' ἢ ὡς ἰδέμεν.
       ἀλλὰ κούφοισιν ἐκνεῦσαι ποδὶ
       ζεῦ τέλειε. αἰδῶ τε δίδοι
       καὶ τύχαν τερπνῶν γλυκεῖαν·

At Pindar, Olympians 13.115 (see Pr 40), instead of αἰδῶ, "honor," this copy has ἀλδῶ, "to Aldus." "Zeus the accomplisher, grant to Aldus a sweet good fortune, full of delights." Photo: Bodleian Library.

Introduction

꒰ꕥ꒱

Any introduction to a book dealing with early editions of Greek texts has to begin with the statement of an important fact that could easily be overlooked. Whereas printing in Latin and the vernacular languages spread rapidly in western and central Europe — from ca. 1459 in Germany, from 1465 in Italy, from 1470 in France — Greek presented problems. Some printers managed to cope with the not infrequent Greek quotations in the Latin classics, but there was a fundamental difficulty: whereas every educated person had some knowledge of Latin, a good command of classical Greek remained a fairly rare accomplishment, partly at least because the initial enthusiasm of learners could easily fade owing to the lack of good grammars and other teaching material that we now take for granted, with the result that many humanists contented themselves with reading the classics in translation. Because of this the potential for sales of Greek texts was severely limited.

In the preface to the grammar by Constantine Lascaris issued in Milan in 1476, the printer Demetrius "the Cretan" expresses his hope of providing texts that will be easily obtainable and not too expensive. He also refers to the complexities of casting the type, but it should be noted that the type he designed was a good deal simpler than those used later by the Aldine press, and the same is true of the most important of the early publications of Greek texts, the Homer that appeared in Florence in 1488; the type in this volume was a revised version of that used for the grammar of 1476.[1] While Aldus was setting up his business in the early 1490s, a rival enterprise was being established in Florence by the talented Greek refugee Janus Lascaris. Acting on the instructions of Lorenzo de' Medici, he had traveled to Greece to collect manuscripts,

and in 1494 he set up his press in Florence. It was remarkable for a bold experiment: he rejected the current types, which were all based on contemporary handwriting, and devised a type based on ancient inscriptions. In his dedication of the edition of the *Greek Anthology* of 1494, addressed to Piero de Medici, he comments, "Having a fresh opportunity to print, which would be of great value to scholars, I decided to rescue Greek typography from its ugly and very unprepossessing inadequacy. Since I realised that the sorts now in use for printing cannot be cast easily or made to fit together neatly, I investigated carefully the ancient letter forms, long since abandoned, and after suitable adjustment for the technique of printing devised by type-casters and related craftsmen I passed them on to the type-setters."[2] Lascaris was not able to exploit his innovation fully: the amount of material in the commentaries that had to be printed in the margins was too great to permit the use of uppercase type, and so for marginal scholia he reverted to a lowercase font with ligatures and abbreviations. But his innovation deserved to be followed, and one is bound to ask why Aldus decided to use type based on the scripts of some of the best known professional copyists of the day. With some hesitation I offer a conjecture. Perhaps many members of the public still had a certain sympathy for the view attributed to Federico da Montefeltro — but the story is certainly *ben trovato* — who allegedly would not have printed books in his library;[3] as a result, they might have accepted, even if only grudgingly, the products of the new technology provided that they were made to resemble as far as possible the traditional handwritten book.

Aldus Manutius (ca. 1451–1515)[4] is one of the outstanding figures of the Italian Renaissance. By training a humanist, he earned his living for several years as tutor in the household of the rulers of Carpi, a small town a few miles north of Modena. His enthusiasm for the study of Greek was already apparent ca. 1490, when, as tutor to Alberto and Leonello, the sons of Caterina Pio, he remarked

in a letter to their mother, "How can anyone who does not know Greek emulate Greek authors, the most learned in every field?" Though he had not yet made a great name for himself as a scholar, he had the vision to see that the rapid development of the printing industry presented the opportunity for a second career. While a knowledge of Greek was recognized as a valuable attainment, only a few texts had so far been printed. Much the most important was the Homer that appeared in Florence in 1488. But since the 1470s, Venice had become the leading center of printing, and it is tempting to conclude that this was the determining factor in his decision to move there in 1489 or 1490. It is notable that the first Greek texts issued by his press did not appear until 1495, which suggests that the economic and technical difficulties he faced were probably much greater than he had foreseen. An additional obstacle may have been the fact that the great collection of Greek manuscripts bequeathed to the city by cardinal Bessarion, which he probably expected to be able to use, was not regularly accessible, and so far as is known Aldus never succeeded in exploiting its treasures.

In the remaining twenty-five years of his life, Aldus' achievements may be summarized under three headings. Whereas his predecessors in the book trade are correctly described as printers, Aldus was more than just a printer: thanks to his own scholarly background and the active circle of collaborators that gathered around him, which at one time included Erasmus, he can reasonably claim to be the first person to deserve the title of publisher. He popularized pocket-sized editions for wider circulation, with a print run of a thousand copies. Owing partly to political events, in particular the consequences of the French invasion of 1494, when the Medici were driven out of Florence, his press became the only significant provider of Greek texts; Janus Lascaris, whose press issued several important editions and might have provided serious competition if he had continued to work in Florence, decided to enter the service of the French king.

The prefaces to the Aldine editions of Greek texts deserve to be made more easily available to the English-speaking public. They were last printed in a handsome and valuable edition by Giovanni Orlandi,[5] which enjoyed limited circulation and is now out of print. It will be obvious that in my notes to the texts I owe a good deal to Orlandi, and I am happy to acknowledge the debt. As was inevitable in a substantial and complex publication, some slips occurred, and I have done what I can to eliminate them.

This volume aims to present Aldus both as scholar and as publisher. In order to give a full picture, the General Editor of the series and I both felt it appropriate to add various appendices, including two other prefaces by Aldus and three texts contributed to Aldine publications by the Greek refugee Marcus Musurus (1470–1517), who had a remarkable knowledge of the classical language and literature and was much the most eminent regular member of the circle that helped to make the publishing program so successful.

I am much indebted to James Hankins and Martin Davies for their helpful suggestions.

NOTES

1. The sorts needed for the types used in the early editions were analyzed by Robert Proctor, *The Printing of Greek in the Fifteenth Century* (Oxford: Oxford University Press for the Bibliographical Society, 1900; reprinted, Hildesheim: Georg Olms, 1966), 156–203 (this work is available via Google Books). For the Aldine types, see Nicolas Barker, *Aldus Manutius and the Development of Greek Script and Type in the Fifteenth Century*, 2nd ed. (New York: Fordham University Press, 1992).

2. Cited by Proctor, *The Printing of Greek*, 78–79.

3. Martin C. Davies, "*Non ve n'è ignuno a stampa*: The printed books of Federico da Montefeltro," in *Federico da Montefeltro and his Library*, ed.

Marcello Simonetta, 63–78 (Milan: Y Press, and Città del Vaticano: Biblioteca Apostolica Vaticana, 2007).

4. I take the date of birth from Martin Davies' entry on Aldus in the *Oxford Companion to the Book*, ed. Michael F. Suarez and H. R. Woudhuysen (Oxford: Oxford University Press, 2010), 456–57. Fletcher, *New Aldine Studies*, 27, put it between 1447 and 1452, with a preference for the latter. I have no further evidence to offer.

5. *Aldo Manuzio editore: Dediche, prefazioni, note ai testi*, introduction by Carlo Dionisotti, Latin text with Italian translation and notes by Giovanni Orlandi, 2 vols. (Milan: Edizioni Il Polifilo, 1975).

THE GREEK CLASSICS

: I :

A

Aldus Manutius Romanus studiosis s. d.

1 Constantini Lascaris, viri doctissimi, institutiones grammaticas, introducendis in litteras Graecas adolescentulis quam utilissimas, quoddam quasi praeludium esse summis nostris laboribus et impendiis tantoque apparatui ad imprimenda Graeca volumina omnis generis, fecit cum multitudo eorum qui Graecis erudiri litteris concupiscunt — nullae enim extabant impressae venales et petebantur a nobis frequenter — tum status et conditio horum temporum et bella ingentia, quae nunc totam Italiam infestant, irato Deo vitiis nostris, et mox totum orbem commotura ac potius concussura videntur, propter omnifariam hominum scelera multo plura maioraque iis, quae causa olim fuere ut totum humanum genus summergeret aquisque perderet iratus Deus. Valde quam vera est tua illa sententia, Valeri Maxime, ac aurea et memoratu digna: 'Lento enim gradu ad vindictam sui divina procedit ira, tarditatemque supplicii gravitate compensat.' Est tritum vulgari sermone proverbium: 'Peccato veteri recens poena.' Cuius est, sibi assumat — ut aiunt. Forte: 'Et tuum est,' dixerit quispiam. Audi (non imus inficias: fatemur enim ingenue): sumus homines; atque utinam homines et re et nomine, non nomine solum homines, et re ex numero pecudum. 'Sunt enim — ait Cicero — nonnulli homines non re sed nomine.' Sed de his hactenus; dabit Deus his quoque finem: et, ut spero, propediem.

Constantine Lascaris, Grammar
(*March 8, 1495*)

A

Aldus Manutius of Rome to students, greetings.

The textbook of grammar by Constantine Lascaris,[1] a man of   1
great learning, is extremely useful for young people being introduced to Greek studies. It is a kind of prelude, involving enormous
labor and expense on our part and much equipment for the printing of Greek texts of all kinds, and this for two reasons: firstly the
number of people wishing to learn Greek—there were no printed
copies on the market and we were frequently asked for one—secondly the current state of affairs, the great wars which now afflict
the whole of Italy,[2] since God is angry at our misdeeds, and which
look as if they will soon upset or indeed shatter the whole world,
on account of the multifarious crimes of humanity, far more numerous and serious than those which were once the reason for an
angry God to submerge and destroy in a flood the whole human
race. How very true, Valerius Maximus, is that remark of yours, a
golden saying which deserves to be quoted: "With slow steps divine anger moves to punish, and it compensates for its slow pace
by the gravity of the punishment."[3] There is a well known proverb
in the vernacular: "Ancient misdeed, recent punishment."[4] Whomever that fits should accept his culpability, as they say. Perhaps
someone will say, "It fits you as well." Let me say—we will not
deny it but confess it freely—we are human; would that we were
human in reality as well as in name, not just in name but in practice to be counted among the animals. Cicero says, "Some people
are men not in reality but in name."[5] But enough of this; God will
bring these matters also to an end,[6] and (I hope) soon.

2   Accipite interea, studiosi litterarum bonarum, Constantini Las-
careos rudimenta grammatices, longe correctiora iis, quae impressa
visuntur. Nam ea Constantinus ipse in locis circiter centum et
quinquaginta emendavit; quod facile cognoscet, si quis cum hisce
illa conferet. Nam deleta quaedam videbit, multa correcta, plurima
addita. Ita vero emendatum manu ipsius Constantini librum nobis
dedere commodo Petrus Bembus et Angelus Gabriel, patritii Veneti, adeo nobiles praestantique ingenio iuvenes, qui nuper in insula Sicilia Graecas litteras ab eo ipso Lascari didicerunt et nunc
Patavii incumbunt una liberalibus disciplinis. Interpretationem
vero Latinam e regione addidimus arbitratu nostro, rati commodius utiliusque futurum Graece discere incipientibus. Parcant velim qui haec sine interpretatione Latina desiderant: nam rudibus
et ignaris penitus litterarum Graecarum Lascaris institutiones imprimendas curavimus. Mox eruditis et doctis optimi quique Graecorum libri favente Christo Iesu imprimentur. Valete.

B

Aldus Manucius Romanus studiosis s. p. d.

3   Nihil praetermittere est animus, quod utile credamus futurum
iis, qui Graecas litteras discere concupiscunt optimeque scire Latine. Quamobrem Graecas litteras omnis ac diphthongos earum-
que nomina et potestatem ac quemadmodum in Latinum transfe-
rantur, cum exemplis ad id accommodatis annotavimus; addidimus
etiam abbreviationes scitu quidem pulcherrimas. Et quia operae
pretium existimavimus scire Graece adolescentulos salutationem
angeli ad beatissimam virginem, exulumque filiorum Evae ad eandem, nec non divi Ioannis evangelium 'In principio erat verbum,'
item symbolum apostolorum, haec omnia Graece curavimus imprimenda atque e regione Latinam interpretationem. Addidimus

In the meantime, students of literature, accept Constantine 2
Lascaris' elements of grammar in a much more accurate form than
in the printed copies available.[7] Constantine himself has corrected
the work in about 150 passages, which anyone who compares those
copies with these will recognize; he will find some deletions, many
corrections, and a great deal added. A copy so corrected by Constantine himself[8] was lent to me by Pietro Bembo and Angelo
Gabriele, Venetian patricians, young men of great nobility and
outstanding talents, who recently learned Greek with Lascaris
himself on the island of Sicily and are now studying the liberal
arts together in Padua.[9] We have added a Latin version on facing
pages on our own initiative, reckoning it would be more conve-
nient and helpful for beginners in Greek. I hope those who prefer
these texts without a Latin version will be sparing in their criticism, because we have seen to the printing of Lascaris' textbook
for the benefit of novices entirely ignorant of Greek. Soon, with
the goodwill of Jesus Christ, all the best books of the Greeks will
be printed for scholars and men of learning. Farewell.

B[10]

It is our intention not to omit anything which we think will be 3
useful to people who wish to learn Greek and acquire an excellent
knowledge of Latin. We have therefore made a note of all the
Greek letters and diphthongs, giving their names, pronunciation
and transliteration into Latin, with suitable examples. We have
also added the abbreviations, which it is very good to know.[11] And
because we think it worthwhile for young people to know the
Greek for the angel's greeting to the Blessed Virgin and the greeting of the exiled children of Eve to her, and from John's Gospel,
"In the beginning was the Word," then the Apostolic Symbola —
all these we have printed in Greek with a Latin translation facing.

carmina Pythagorae cognomento aurea ob ipsorum excellentiam et divinas admonitiones; item Phocylidis sapientissimi viri moralia, docta quidem et plena praeceptis sanctissimis et documentis. Quae si placuisse cognovero, habeo longe meliora maioraque, quae postea Deo favente condonabuntur.

4   Omnem enim vitam decrevimus ad hominum utilitatem consumere. Deus est mihi testis nihil me magis desyderare quam prodesse hominibus; quod et anteacta vita nostra ostendit, ubicunque viximus, et ostensuram speramus, quando id volumus, in dies magis quandiu vivimus in hac lachrymarum valle et plena miseriae. Dabo equidem operam ut, quantum in me est, semper prosim. Nam, etsi quietam ac tranquillam agere vitam possumus, negotiosam tamen eligimus et plenam laboribus: natus est enim homo non ad indignas bono viro et docto voluptates, sed ad laborem et ad agendum semper aliquid viro dignum. Non torpeamus igitur; non vitam in otio, ventri somnoque reliquisque voluptatibus indulgentes transeamus veluti pecora. Nam, ut inquit Cato: 'Vita hominis prope uti ferrum est: ferrum, si exerceas, conteritur, si non exerceas, tamen rubigo interficit; ita, si se homo exerceat, consumitur, si non exerceat, torpedo plus detrimenti affert quam exercitatio.' Sed his omissis de re dicere incipiamus. Haec tam multis verbis dixi amore incredibili erga omnis homines incitatus meo.

C

5   Habetis, ingenui adolescentes et studiosi bonarum litterarum, quae vobis in fronte libri sum pollicitus. Superest ut nobis habeatis quam plurimam gratiam; quam tamen vel cumulatissime relatam existimabo, si emeritis sine cunctatione lucubrationes nostras. Quod si, ut spero, facietis, erit vobis duplex bonum, quod et nunc discetis rudimenta litterarum Graecarum, et facietis me posthac

We have added the Pythagorean verses[12] that are known as Golden because of their excellence and their divine admonitions, also the moral teachings of the wise Phocylides,[13] very learned and full of venerable precepts and exemplifications. If I learn that these texts have been well received, I have far better and more important material, which will then be offered, if God wills.

We have decided to devote our whole life to benefiting mankind. God is my witness that I wish nothing more than to help humanity; which our past life, wherever we have lived,[14] demonstrates, and we hope will demonstrate still further, since that is our wish, as long as we live in this vale of tears full of misery. I shall certainly try to the best of my ability to be helpful at all times. For although we can lead a quiet and undisturbed life we have nevertheless chosen one that is busy and full of occupations, since man is not born for pleasures that are unworthy of the good and educated person, but to work[15] and to be engaged always in something worthy of man. So let us not be lazy, let us not pass our lives in idleness, indulging in greed, sleep and other pleasures like sheep.[16] For as Cato says: "A man's life is like an iron tool. If you use it, it gets worn; if you do not, still rust destroys it. So if a man exercises himself, he wears himself out; if he does not exercise himself, idleness does more damage than activity."[17] But let us leave this topic and begin to get down to business.[18] I have spoken of this at such length because I was spurred on by my great love for all men.

C[19]

Honorable youths and students of literature, you have what I promised you at the beginning of the volume; it remains for you to show us your gratitude, which I shall regard as handsomely rendered if you buy our product without delay. If, as I hope, you do, you will gain double benefit, because you will now acquire the rudiments of Greek and you will make me keener to publish in

4

5

ad caetera his multo maiora dignioraque edenda alacriorem. Valete.

Venetiis M.CCCC.LXXXXV octavo Martii.

D

6   Non fieri potuit quin impressores quaedam, ut assolent, inver-
terint depravarintque. Quare opus fuit ut totum librum percur-
rerem, quaeque alicuius esse momenti videbantur errata annota-
rem. Id quidem fecimus, ut exiret liber in manus studiosorum
quam emendatissimus. Sed ut facilius singuli quique emendari errores possent, scripsimus alphabeti litteram qua signatus est qua-
ternus, atque ibidem chartarum numerum et in charta numerum
versuum, sic.

: II :

Ἄλδος ὁ Ῥωμαῖος τοῖς σπουδαίοις εὖ πράττειν.

1 Μουσαῖον τὸν παλαιότατον ποιητὴν ἠθέλησα προοιμιά-
ζειν τῷ τε Ἀριστοτέλει καὶ τῶν σοφῶν τοῖς ἑτέροις
αὐτίκα δι' ἐμοῦ ἐντυπησομένοις, τῷ τε εἶναι αὐτὸν ἥδι-
στον ἅμα καὶ λογιώτατον, καὶ μάλιστα ὡς ἂν εἰδῆτε τὰ
παρὰ τούτου τῷ Οὐιδίῳ δανεισθέντα δαιμονίως τῷ ὄντι
καὶ εὐφυῶς, καὶ ὅπως αὐτὸν ἐμιμήσατο ἐν ταῖς Ἡροῦς
καὶ Λεάνδρου πρὸς ἀλλήλους ἐπιστολαῖς.

2 Λαμβάνετ' οὖν τουτὶ τὸ βιβλίδιον, οὐ προῖκα μέντοι,
δότε δὲ τὰ χρήματα, ἵν' ἔχω καὶ αὐτὸς πορίζεσθαι ὑμῖν

future the remaining works, which are much more substantial and more important. Farewell.

Venice, March 8, 1495.

D[20]

It was inevitable that the printers in the usual way would make 6 some alterations and mistakes. So I had to go through the whole book and make a note of mistakes which seemed to be of some importance. We did this so that the book should come into the hands of students as free from error as possible. To make it easier to correct all the errors we have written the letter which marks the quire, and alongside the page numbers and the numbers of the lines on the page, as follows.

: II :

Musaeus, Hero and Leander
(*ca. 1495/97*)

Aldus of Rome to students, greetings.

I wanted the very ancient poet Musaeus[21] to be a prelude to Aris- 1 totle and the other sages who will be printed forthwith by me, because he is very agreeable and at the same time very eloquent, and particularly so that you might know what was borrowed from him by Ovid in truly sublime and clever fashion,[22] and how Ovid imitated him in the letters exchanged between Hero and Leander.[23]

So accept this little book, though it is not free; but give me the 2 money so that for my part I may furnish you with all the best

9

πάσας τὰς τῶν Ἑλλήνων ἀρίστας βίβλους· καὶ ὄντως,
εἰ δώσετε, δώσω, ὅτι οὐκ ἔχω ἐντυποῦν ἄνευ χρημάτων
πολλῶν. Πιστεύετε τοῖς οὐκ ἀκινδύνως ἐμπειρασθεῖσι,
καὶ πάντων μάλιστα οὑτωσὶ λέγοντι Δημοσθένει· Ἀεῖ
δὴ χρημάτων, καὶ ἄνευ τούτων οὐδέν ἐστι γενέσθαι τῶν
δεόντων.' Οὐ μὴν φιλοχρημάτως ἔχων, μᾶλλον δὲ τοῖς
τοιούτοις ἀπεχθανόμενος ταῦτά γε εἴρηκα· καί τοι χρημάτων ἄνευ οὐ δυνατὸν εὐπορεῖν ὧν ὑμεῖς μὲν ὑπερ-
βαλόντως ἐφίεσθε, αὐτοὶ δὲ πολλῷ μόχθῳ καὶ δαπάνῃ
πεπονηκότες διατελοῦμεν. Ἔρρωσθε.

: III :

A

Ἄλδου Μανουκίου Βασιανέος εἰς φίλους.

1   Μουσάων φίλοι ἠδ᾽ ἀρετῆς, καὶ ἐμεῖο φίλ᾽ Ἄλδου,
      χαίρετ᾽· ἰδοῦ ὑμῖν δῖος Ἀριστοτέλης.
    Αὐτίκ᾽ Ἀλέξανδρος κἀμμώνιος εἰς ἄρα κεῖνον
      καί τοι Ἰωάννης ἔσσετ᾽ ὁ γραμματικός.
    Ἐνδόξους τ᾽ ἄλλους δώσω, φίλοι, εἴ ῥα φυλάσσει
      χρυσοῦν τ᾽ ἠδὲ πολύν μοι μίτον ἡ Λάχεσις.
              Ἔρρωσθε.

Greek books. If you give, I certainly will; I am unable to print without substantial funds. Put your trust in men engaged in an enterprise that is not without risk, and most of all in Demosthenes who says, "Money is needed, and without it nothing essential can be done."[24] I say this not as someone anxious to make money, but rather out of dislike for such people; yet without money it is not possible for you to have a good supply of what you particularly desire, and we for our part continue to work at with great toil and expense. Keep well.

: III :

Aristotle, Organon[25]
(November 1, 1495)

A

Aldus Manutius of Bassiano[26] *to his friends.*

Friends of the Muses and of virtue, and friends of Aldus,   1
   greetings. Here is the divine Aristotle for you.
Immediately after him will be Alexander and Ammonius,
   and indeed John the Grammarian.[27]
Other famous texts I will provide, my friends, if Lachesis[28]
   maintains a long golden thread for me.
    Farewell.

B

Aldus Manucius Romanus Alberto Pio principi Carpensi s. p. d.

2   Necessariam esse Graecarum litterarum cognitionem hominibus nostris ita iam omnes existimant, ut non modo adolescentuli,
quorum iam maximus numerus, verum et senes aetate nostra
Graece condiscant. Olim apud Romanos Catonem unum accepimus didicisse Graecas litteras in senectute; quod tanquam memo-
randum et scitu dignum cum plurimi doctissimi viri litteris prodi-
derunt tum in Catone M. Tullius his verbis: 'Qui si eruditius
videbitur disputare quam consuevit ipse in suis libris, attribuito
Graecis litteris, quarum constat eum perstudiosum fuisse in senectute.' Et in eodem: 'Quid, quod etiam addiscunt aliquid? ut Solo-
nem in versibus gloriantem vidimus, qui se quotidie addiscentem
aliquid, senem fieri dicit; ut ego feci, qui Graecas litteras senex
didici; quas quidem sic avide arripui, quasi diuturnam sitim ex-
plere cupiens, ut ea ipsa mihi nota essent, quibus me nunc exemplis uti videtis.'

3   Nostris vero temporibus multos licet videre Catones, hoc est,
senes in senectute Graece discere; nam adolescentulorum ac iuve-
num Graecis incumbentium litteris iam tantus fere est numerus,
quantus eorum qui Latinis. Et propterea Graeci libri vehementer
ab omnibus inquiruntur; quorum quia mira paucitas est, ego adiuvante Christo Iesu spero me brevi effecturum, ut consulam tantae
inopiae — nec tamen sine meo magno incommodo et labore et iactura temporis; sed succurrendum est studiosis bonarum litterarum. Et quanquam incidimus in turbulenta tempora et tumul-
tuosa ac misera, quibus magis arma quam libri tractantur, tamen
nisi facta bonorum librorum copia non conquiescam.

B

*Aldus Manutius of Rome sends warm greetings
to Alberto Pio, prince of Carpi.*[29]

That a knowledge of Greek is necessary for men of our time is 2
now so well recognized that not only the young, of whom there
are a very great number, but in our generation the elderly are
learning it. In ancient Rome, according to tradition, only Cato
learned Greek in old age; as a memorable and important fact this
was recorded by numerous men of learning and by Cicero in his
Cato as follows: "If he seems to be more sophisticated in discussion
than he was in his own writings, put it down to his Greek, which
he is known to have been very keen on in his old age."[30] And from
the same work: "Again, suppose they continue to learn. We see
Solon making a proud statement in his verses and saying that he
was learning something every day as he grew old — just as I have
done, since I learned Greek in my old age, taking it up as avidly as
if I had to satisfy a thirst that went back a long time, with the result that I acquired the factual knowledge which you see me now
exploiting."[31]

But in our own day one can see many Catos, that is, elderly 3
men learning Greek in old age; for[32] the number of adolescents
and young people is now almost as great as that of students of
Latin. And for that reason Greek books are much sought after by
everyone. As there is a surprising shortage of them, I hope, with
the help of Jesus Christ, to be able to remedy this great scarcity
soon — not however without great personal inconvenience, difficulty and expenditure of time; but one must support students of
literature. And although we have fallen on turbulent, violent and
unhappy times, in which there is more use for armaments than
books, still I shall not rest until a supply of good books has been
provided.

4   Aristoteles igitur, Graecorum facile princeps — quanquam ait Cicero: 'Platonem semper excipio' —, in manus tuas, princeps inclyte, et caeterorum studiosorum, ut doctrina primus, ita primo impressus prodit emendatissimus: hoc est logici ac dialectici Aristotelis libri, quod organon Graeci appellant (quod etiam ostenditur Graeco epigrammate comperto a me in antiquo codice, quod ideo in fronte libri imprimendum curavi), Latine instrumentum interpretatur. Est enim instrumentum ad omnes scientias pernecessarium: hoc enim genus et speciem cuiusque rei cernimus, hoc definiendo explicamus, hoc tribuere in partes, hoc quae vera, quae falsa sunt iudicare possumus, cernere item consequentia, repugnantia videre, ambigua distinguere.

5   Hos libros, Alberte princeps, tibi dicamus, tum quia es doctorum aetatis nostrae alter Mecoenas — nam ipse tibi quod Flaccus Mecoenati merito dixerim: 'O et praesidium et dulce decus meum': in mea enim hac dura provincia tua ope defensus sum maxime et adiutus, ita ut, si mihi debent, tibi aeque debeant necesse est studiosi litterarum Graecarum —, tum etiam quia novi te librorum Graecorum percupidum, quos ut tibi pares, nulli parcis impensae, imitatus Picum Mirandulanum avunculum tuum, hominem ingenio admirabili et summa doctrina, quem nobis mors invida nuper surripuit, comitem Hermolao Barbaro et Angelo Politiano, viris aetatis nostrae doctissimis, qui tres tanquam triumviri poterant cum antiquitate certare. Horum tu aemulus, docte adolescens, non dubito quin brevi sis plurimum profecturus. Nihil enim tibi deest: non ingenium, quo valde abundas; non eloquentia, qua tu praeditus; non libri nec Latinae nec Graecae neque Hebraicae disciplinae, quos tibi summo studio curaque perquiris; non doctissimi praeceptores, quos tu conductos habes multa pecunia. Incumbe

So Aristotle, the best of the Greeks by far—although Cicero   4
says, "I always make an exception for Plato"[33]—is now in your
hands, distinguished prince,[34] and those of other scholars. Just as
he is first on the score of his learning, so his first appearance in
print is fully free from faults. These are Aristotle's books on logic
and dialectic, which the Greeks call the *Organon* (which is also
demonstrated by a Greek epigram I found in an early manuscript,
which I therefore printed at the beginning of the volume); in
translation it means "a tool," since it is a tool essential for all
branches of knowledge. By means of it we distinguish genus and
species, with it we explain by means of definitions, with it we di-
vide into categories, with it we can judge what is true, what is
false, see what follows logically, observe inconsistency, resolve am-
biguity.

We dedicate these books to you, Prince Alberto. Firstly because   5
you are a new Maecenas to scholars of the present day—for I
could deservedly address you, as Horace did Maecenas, as "protection, glory and joy for me,"[35] since in this hard profession of mine
I have been greatly defended and helped by your resources. So if
students of Greek are indebted to me, they must equally be indebted to you. Secondly because I know that you spare no expense
in your eagerness to acquire Greek books, following the example
of your uncle Pico della Mirandola, a man of wonderful intellect
and great learning, whom cruel death recently took away from
us.[36] He was a companion of Ermolao Barbaro[37] and Angelo Poliziano, leading scholars of our time, who as a kind of triumvirate
could rival antiquity. In your emulation of them, as a young man
of learning, I have no doubt you will quickly make great progress.
You have everything you need: intellectual power in great abundance, eloquence, in which you are gifted, books for Latin, Greek
and Hebrew studies, which you take great pains and care to acquire, learned teachers whom you employ at considerable expense.

igitur, ut facis, bonis artibus; ego quidem tibi, siquid possum, nunquam deero.

6   Habes nunc a me libros Aristotelis logicae disciplinae. Habebis Deo favente et philosophicos tum morales tum physicos, et quoscunque ille divinus magister legendos posteritati reliquit, modo extent. Erunt deinde a me tibi et caeteris studiosis commentatores Aristotelis: Ammonius, Simplicius, Porphyrius, Alexander, Philoponus et Themistius paraphrastes. Imprimentur etiam grammatici, poetae, oratores, historici, et quicunque profuturi videbuntur studiosis consulturique periturae doctrinae et bonis litteris. Habeo complures coadiutores, viros doctissimos, quorum auxilio nostri libri exibunt in manus hominum quam emendatissimi; in quibus est Alexander Bondinus, artium et medicinae doctor egregius ac doctissimus litterarum Graecarum, cuius est Graeca epistola, quam post meam impressam vides.

7   Haec diximus verbosius, ut gauderent qui bonis artibus ornari se concupiscunt, sperarentque sibi quam optime fore in posterum propter bonorum librorum futuram copiam, quibus, ut speramus, fugabitur tandem omnis barbaries: non enim puto esse hominibus tantam perversitatem, ut etiam inventis frugibus glande vescantur. Vale.

: IV :

Aldus Manucius Romanus lectori s. d.

1 Non sum nescius, studiose lector, hanc Apollonii Theodorique grammaticen visum iri tibi primo duriusculam atque insuavem,

So continue your study of good letters as at present; I shall never fail to help you in whatever way I can.

You are now receiving from us Aristotle's works on logic. If 6
God wills, you will have his works of moral philosophy and physics and whatever else that divine master left for posterity to read,
provided that they are preserved. Then you and other students
will receive from me the commentators on Aristotle, Ammonius,
Simplicius, Porphyry, Alexander, Philoponus and Themistius the
paraphrast;[38] grammarians, poets, orators, historians and all other
authors who seem likely to be useful to students and to help endangered scholarship and literary studies. I have several assistants,
men of great learning, with whose help our books will reach the
public as free from error as possible.[39] One of them is Alessandro
Bondini,[40] a distinguished doctor of arts and medicine, very expert
in Greek, whose Greek letter you see printed after mine.

We have spoken of these matters at some length, for the enjoy- 7
ment of those who wish to excel in the liberal arts and hope to
benefit greatly in due course thanks to the forthcoming supply of
good books. By these, we hope, all barbarism will finally be swept
away, since I do not believe that men are perverse enough to eat
acorns after the discovery of grain.[41] Farewell.

: IV :

Theodore Gaza, Introduction to Grammar
Apollonius Dyscolus, On Syntax
(December 25, 1495)

Aldus Manutius of Rome, to the reader.

I am not unaware, studious reader, that this grammar of Apollo- 1
nius and Theodore will at first appear to you to be a trifle difficult

deinde, cum eam accurate relegeris, et facilem et iocundam. Nam Theodorus, si dictionem attenderis, videbitur tibi dulcis, eloquens et plane Atticus, nihilque praetermisisse quod sit necessarium volenti Graece discere; si vero doctrinam atque ordinem — pace aliorum dixerim — solus docere bonas litteras caeterorumque grammaticorum facile princeps. Quem si vel semel studiose perlegeris, non poteris non nocturna versare manu, versare diurna.

2   Incipiens nanque ab elementis, ad constructionem usque et figuras aliquot elocutionemque progreditur, grammaticamque concinna quadam brevitate inchoat ac pene perficit. Dividitur in libros quatuor. Primus litteras continet omnesque orationis partes, praeter praepositionem, de qua in quarto cumulate tractatur. Declinat nomina et verba, ingeniose quidem et perutiliter; ubi operae pretium est videre seorsum quae $\mu\acute{\varepsilon}\sigma\alpha$ appellantur ab activis passivisque inflecti; item quae $\pi\acute{\alpha}\theta\eta$ Graeci, passiones nos dicimus, et nominum et verborum quam brevissime explicari. Secundus item repetit octo orationis partes, quasi loca quaedam praedictorum denotans et plura exponens; praeterea, quemadmodum fit a Porphyrio, in quinque vocibus quae nos universalia dicimus, communia ac propria tam nominum quam verborum, et docte et copiose demonstrat, et, quod est utilissimum maximeque necessarium futuro grammatico, formationes verborum omnium doctissime docet. Qui vero est tertius tractat erudite de accentu et quantitate syllabae atque orthographia, ne, ut ipse dicit, barbarismus, quod est peccatum circa dictionem, eveniat, quotque modis fiat ostendit. Quartus autem de partium orationis constructione commemorat, cum figuris quibusdam elegantiisque dicendi.

3   Apollonio vero, si eum tibi legendo feceris familiarem, magnopere delectaberis ac proficies: est enim doctus, elegans, varius et

and dry, but later, when you have read it again carefully, easy and delightful. For Theodore,[42] if you pay attention to his style, will be found agreeable, eloquent and fully Attic;[43] he has not omitted anything you need if you want to learn Greek. Indeed, if you pay attention to his textbook and its arrangement—I would not wish to give offense to others—he alone will be found to give a good grounding, and is far superior to the other grammarians. If you read him carefully just once, you will be bound to turn his pages by night and by day.[44]

Beginning with the alphabet he progresses as far as syntax, 2 some rhetorical figures and eloquence. With stylish brevity he begins his grammar and almost exhausts the subject. It is divided into four books. The first deals with the letters and all the parts of speech apart from the preposition, which is dealt with comprehensively in the fourth. He gives the inflections of nouns and verbs cleverly and in the most useful fashion; there it is worth noting how what are called *mesa* (middle) are inflected differently from actives and passives; also how what the Greeks call *pathe* and we call *passiones* (inflections) in nouns and verbs are explained with great concision. The second book returns to the eight parts of speech, as if to emphasize some previous statements and giving further exposition; also, as in Porphyry,[45] with much erudition and detail he describes elements common to or characteristic of nouns and verbs which we call universals; and, most useful and absolutely necessary for the future grammarian, he gives a very well-informed account of the forms of all verbs. The third book is an erudite account of accents, quantity of syllables and orthography, to avoid, as he puts it himself, barbarism, i.e., faulty diction, and he shows in how many ways it comes about.[46] The fourth book deals with the construction of the parts of a discourse, with some figures and elegant features of style.

You will also derive great pleasure and profit from Apollonius if 3 you make close acquaintance through reading him, since he is

peracutus. Hic est de quo sic in prooemio meminit Priscianus: 'Quid enim Herodiani artibus certius? quid Apollonii scrupulosis quaestionibus enucleatius inveniri queat?' Et in eodem: 'Quamvis ad Herodiani scriptorum pelagus et ad eius patris Apollonii spaciosa volumina compendiosa existimanda sint scripta librorum meorum.' Eum vero esse, de quo Priscianus, potes ex eius vita colligere, quae impressa est in principio ipsius libri de constructione, in qua filii quoque Herodiani fit mentio. Edidit uterque de arte grammatica immensa volumina, quae legisse videtur Priscianus; nos autem, ut aliis plurimis in quavis scientia pretiosissimis libris, vel hominum incuria vel infoelicitate temporum his quoque caremus. Vix extant Apollonii quatuor libri de constructione, qui quales sint studendo tu ipse cognosces.

4   Illud non te fugiat: exemplaria habuisse me quam plurima, curasseque ut quam emendatissime imprimerentur, neque quicquam ausum aut addere aut diminuere. Sperabam enim cum caeteros Apollonii libros tum hos quoque de constructione habiturum nos aliquando correctiores, et quotcunque etiam scripsit Herodianus filius, si quo in carcere indigne et miserabiliter detenti latent squallidi fuliginosique et corrosi blattis.

5   Interim quos damus Apollonii Theodoriceque libros tibi non mediocriter profuturos studiose legas: quod si primo duriusculi videbuntur, memineris illius pertriti proverbii, nihil esse volenti arduum, nihil difficile, anteque virtutem esse a iustissimo Deo sudorem positum, et longum et arduum ad eam callem, ac primo asperum; verum, cum perveneris ad virtutem, nihil tibi illa iocundius, nihil dulcius. Nihil est, mihi crede, tam difficile, quod saepe et accurate legendo non fiat facile. Stude igitur assidue ac libenter, et proficies quantum voles; quoniam si studiosus fueris, erit tibi

learned, elegant, with stylistic variation, and very subtle.[47] He is
the man of whom Priscian[48] said in his preface: "What is more
reliable than the handbooks of Herodian? What could be found
that is better presented than the punctilious investigations of
Apollonius?" And in the same passage: "Yet my own writings must
be judged concise when compared with the ocean of Herodian's
work and the lengthy volumes of his father Apollonius." That he is
the man of whom Priscian speaks you can see from the biography
printed at the beginning of his text on syntax, where his son
Herodian is also mentioned. Both composed immense grammatical works, which Priscian appears to have read; we however, thanks
to neglect or the ill fortune of our times, do not have them, as is
the case of many other book of great value in all fields.[49] Apollonius' four books on syntax only just survived; their quality you will
see for yourself as you work through them.

Please take note: I obtained a great many copies[50] and took care 4
to have them printed as accurately as possible, without daring to
delete anything. I hoped that one day we might have Apollonius'
other works and less corrupt copies of those books on syntax, together with everything written by his son Herodian, if they undeservedly lie hidden like prisoners in some miserable dungeon, in
squalor, covered in soot and gnawed by insects.[51]

In the meantime you should read with care the works of Apol- 5
lonius and Theodore which we offer; they will be of no small
benefit. If at first they seem rather difficult, remember the well-
known proverb: for the man with a will nothing is arduous, nothing difficult, and God in his supreme justice has put sweat on the
path toward virtue, the road to which is long and arduous, and
initially rough; but when you reach virtue, there is nothing more
pleasant, nothing sweeter.[52] Believe me, there is nothing so difficult that does not become easy through frequent and attentive
reading. So study with application and goodwill, and you will
progress as far as you wish; if you are studious you will acquire

multa rerum cognitio, multa doctrina. Quod est Isocratis: Ἐὰν ᾖς φιλομαθής, ἔσῃ πολυμαθής. Vale.

: V :

Aldus Manucius Romanus Baptistae Guarino praeceptori suo s. p. d.

1   En tibi, magister doctissime, Theogonia Hesiodi, quam petis a nobis interpretaturus publice discipulis tuis. Addidimus eiusdem poetae scutum ac georgicorum libros, nec non Theocriti idyllia seu opuscula triginta; item moralia versu elego Theognidis, poetae antiquissimi, cuius et Plato in legibus et Isocrates meminit in orationibus. Nec deest Phocylides, quem antiquis ethographis annumerat Isocrates ad Demonicum. Operae pretium etiam visum est addere interpretationem Maximi Planudii eius libelli qui incipit: 'Cum ego animadverterem,' quem fama est fuisse Catonis cuiusdam; sed quicunque fuit, doctus fuit et lectu dignus. Cuius sententiae cum esset Planudius, Graecis quoque legendum tradidit versu hexametro, et docte quidem et eleganter. Hanc interpretationem in membrana abhinc trecentis annis et plus eo scriptam litteris prope exesis, ut vix dignosci possent, vidisse se retulit mihi Franciscus Roscius, iuvenis plenus fide et Graece et Latine apprime doctus. Nec mirum: est enim et ipse ex tua foelici Verona oriundus, quae mater et alumna est et semper fuit doctissimorum hominum. Inseruimus et alia quaedam profutura studiosis, quae in fronte libri impressa licet videre.

much information and learning. As Isocrates said: "If you are keen to learn, you will acquire wide erudition."[53] Farewell.

: V :

Theocritus, Hesiod, Theognis, Selected Works
(February 1496)

*Aldus Manutius of Rome to his teacher
Battista Guarino,*[54] *warm greetings.*

Here is Hesiod's *Theogony* for you, learned master, which you were   1
wanting from us because you are about to give public lectures to
your pupils. We have added the same poet's *Shield* and *Georgics,*[55]
plus thirty *Idylls* by Theocritus; also the advice on morals in elegiac
verse by Theognis, a very early poet, who is mentioned both by
Plato in his *Laws*[56] and Isocrates in his orations.[57] Phocylides is
included; Isocrates, *To Demonicus,* counts him as one of the early
moralists.[58] It seemed worthwhile also to add Maximus Planudes'
translation of the book which begins, "When I noticed"; this is
reputedly by someone called Cato—but whoever he was, he was
learned and worth reading.[59] Since Planudes took that view he
made it available for the Greeks to read as well, in hexameters,
quite skillfully and elegantly. Francesco Roscio[60] told me he had
seen a copy of this translation on parchment dating back three
hundred years or more, with the script worn away so that it could
hardly be read.[61] He is a thoroughly reliable young man and well
up in Greek and Latin—not surprisingly, since he comes from
your blessed city of Verona, which is and always has been mother
and nurse of scholars. We have added other texts useful for students; the titles may be seen printed on the first page.

2   Siqua tamen leges incastigata, magister doctissime, tam hic
quam in caeteris libris, quos ego ad communem studiosorum omnium utilitatem curo imprimendos (nam esse aliqua non eo inficias), non mihi imputes sed exemplaribus. Non enim recipio me
emendaturum libros — nam in quibusdam Oedipo coniectore opus
esset: ita enim mutilati quidam sunt et inversi, ut ne ille quidem
qui composuit, si revivisceret, emendare posset — sed curaturum
summo studio, ut vel ipso exemplari imprimantur correctiores. Sic
in Apollonio grammatico fecimus, sic in hoc libro in iis quas addidimus eclogis, rati satius esse aliquid habere quam nihil. Quod
incorrectum est, si lateat, raro vel potius nunquam emendatur; si
vero prodit in publicum, erunt multi qui castigent, saltem longa
die. Sic in Fabio Quintiliano, sic in C. Plinio nepote, sic in nonnullis aliis factum videmus, qui quotidie emendantur, quotidie
pristinae elegantiae et candori propius accedunt. Sed periniqui
sunt et ingrati, siqui sunt qui me accusent; his ego nihil impreca-
rer, nisi ut quemadmodum ego ita et ipsi curarent aliquando imprimendos Graecos libros: sentirent certe longe aliter. Sed haec
satis.

3   Hunc vero librum tibi dicamus, praeceptor excellentissime, tum
mea in Veronenses benivolentia (debeo enim plurimum Veronensi-
bus; nam a Gaspare Veronensi peregregio grammatico didici Romae Latinas litteras, a te vero Ferrariae et Latinas et Graecas), tum
quia totus fere hic liber est de moribus. Quid enim convenientius
quam de moribus scribere ad eum qui sit moribus omnium ornatissimus? Es tu quidem aetate nostra alter Socrates. Nec vereor me
tibi assentari putes: scis enim esse haec quam verissima. Sed tu
mihi parcas velim, quando de te ad te haec scripsimus, idque fecimus, ut qualem ipsi te esse scimus, omnes sciant. Vale mei memor.

If, learned master, you find errors, either here or in other books 2
which I am printing for the general benefit of the educated public — and I do not deny that there are some — do not put it down
to me but to the exemplars used. I do not undertake to correct the
texts; in some of them one would need Oedipus to make conjec-
tures,[62] because they are so damaged and corrupt that not even the
author, if he were returned to life, would be able to remove the
errors; but I do undertake to make every effort to ensure that the
printed texts are at least more correct than the exemplars. That is
what we did with Apollonius' grammar, and we have done it in
this book, in the *Eclogues* we included,[63] because we reckoned it
better to have something than nothing. An uncorrected text, if
unpublished, is rarely or indeed ever emended; if it reaches the
public there will be many people to correct it over a very long period. We have seen this with Quintilian, Pliny the Younger and
some others; every day they are corrected, every day they get closer
to their former elegance and purity.[64] But anyone who criticizes
me is quite unjust and ungrateful; I would not wish them anything worse than that they too should one day print Greek texts;
they would certainly change their minds. But enough of this.

This book we dedicate to you, excellent teacher, partly because 3
of my goodwill toward Verona (I owe a great deal to the Veronese,
since I learned Latin in Rome from an outstanding scholar, Gaspare da Verona,[65] and Latin and Greek in Ferrara from you),
partly because almost the whole of the book deals with moral
questions. What could be more appropriate than to write about
morals for someone who excels all others in his moral behavior.
For our times you are indeed a second Socrates. I am not worried
that you will think this flattery; you know it is absolutely true. I
hope you will excuse me for writing to you in this way about yourself; we have done so in order that everyone may know that you
are the kind of person we know you to be. Farewell, and think of
me.

: VI :

A

Aldus Manucius Basianas Romanus studiosis omnibus s. p. d.

1 Dura quidem provincia est, bonarum litterarum studiosi, emendate imprimere Latinos libros, durior accurate Graecos, durissima
non depravate vel hos vel illos duris temporibus. Quanam lingua
curem ipse imprimendos libros et quo tempore, videtis. Postquam
suscepi hanc duram provinciam (annus enim agitur iam septimus)
possem iureiurando affirmare me tot annos ne horam quidem soli-
dae habuisse quietis. Pulcherrimum utilissimumque esse inventum
nostrum omnes uno ore dicunt, laudant, praedicant; sit ita certe;
inveni tamen ipse quo excrucier modo, dum vobis prodesse cupio
bonosque libros suppeditare.

2 Quare qui me visunt amicis soleo dicere modo Graecum illud
proverbium: κίχλα χέζει αὐτῇ κακόν, hoc est 'turdella sibi malum cacat'; quod honestius Plautus: 'Ipsa sibi avis mortem creat'
(aiunt enim non nisi per avium alvum redditum nasci viscum,
maxime palumbis et turdis; 'haec enim est natura—inquit Plinius
in naturali historia—ut nisi maturatum in ventre avium non pro-
veniat'); modo illud: κακὰ ἐφ᾽ ἑαυτὸν ἕλκων ὡς ὁ καικίας
νέφος, nam ita flare Caecian scribit Aristoteles, ut non propellat
nubes, ut alii venti, sed ut ad sese vocet ac trahat. Sic mihi evenit:

: VI :

The Treasury
The Cornucopia of Amalthea *and*
The Gardens of Adonis
(*August 1496*)[66]

A

Aldus Manutius of Bassiano near Rome to all students, warm greetings.

It is a really difficult undertaking, students of literature, to print   1
Latin texts without errors; it is more difficult to print Greek accurately, and extremely difficult to print either without faults in
difficult times. You can see in which language and under what
circumstances I print books. Since I began this difficult undertaking—it is now in its seventh year[67]—I could swear on oath that in
all those years I have not had a single hour of true peace. That my
plan is splendid and of great value everyone declares in a chorus of
praise and enthusiasm. It may indeed be so; but I have found a
way to torture myself through my desire to help you and supply
good books.

So I am in the habit of quoting at times to friends who visit me   2
that Greek proverb κίχλα χέζει ἑαυτῇ κακόν, which means,
"The thrush shits trouble for itself";[68] Plautus more decently has,
"The bird herself creates her own death"[69] (for they say that bird-
lime is produced only in the entrails of birds, especially doves and
thrushes; "for that is its nature," says Pliny in his *Natural History*;
"it cannot be produced unless matured in the entrails of birds").[70]
At other times I quote κακὰ ἐφ' ἑαυτὸν ἕλκων ὡς ὁ καικίας
νέφος,[71] because Aristotle says that the Caecias[72] blows in such a
way that it does not disperse the clouds like other winds but pulls
and draws them toward itself.[73] That is what has happened to me;

mihi ipse malum peperi, immensa mihi paravi incommoda, immensos labores. Sed me ipse consolor, vel quod gratissimas esse video lucubrationes meas ac plurimum prodesse omnibus maiorique in dies emolumento futurum, vel quod multi ἐκ τῶν βιβλιοτάφων iam liberant e carceribus libros venalesque exponunt; quod ego brevi futurum interminatus sum, cum nullum a quoquam commodo vel horam accipere librum possem.

3 Sum equidem voti compos: iam passim offeruntur ultro Graeca volumina mittunturque venalia ad bibliopolas; ad me quoque plurima missa sunt. Spero fore et illud, ut, siqui sunt tam pravo ingenio, ut communi omnium bono moereant, aut rumpantur invidia aut succumbentes moerori misere conficiantur et denique suspendant se, quandoquidem quaecunque extant Aristotelis volumina videbunt brevi nostris excusa formis. Imprimentur propediem et commentarii: iam fere omnes coegi. Incumbite vos, quaeso, incumbite bonis litteris, quando ego vobis, adiuvante Christo Iesu, Deo optimo maximo, optimum quenque librum suppeditabo.

4 Ecce habetis opus oppido quam utile et necessarium, quem κέρας Ἀμαλθείας, quem κήπους Ἀδώνιδος, quem iure thesaurum appellaverim. In eo enim fere omnia reposita sunt, quae desiderare quis possit ad perfectam absolutamque cognitionem litterarum Graecarum, et eorum praecipue quae leguntur apud poetas, qui verba variis figuris ac linguis ita saepe immutant, ut facilius sit Nili caput quam alicuius temporis thema aut principium invenire.

5 Sed hoc libro quam facillima facta sunt omnia: nam docet et quo modo et qua lingua ununquodque immutatum sit, canonismata passim et regulas tradens per ordinem litterarum. Linguarum praeterea meminit Atticae, Ionicae, Aeolicae, Doricae, Boeticae, Cretensis, Cypriae, Macedonicae, Tessalae, Rheginae, Siculae,

I have made trouble for myself. I have brought upon myself immense inconvenience, immense labor. But I console myself with the thought either that I can see my productions are very well received and of great benefit to all, with increasing benefit in the future, or that many of the "book buriers"[74] are now releasing volumes from their prisons and offering them for sale—which, at a time when I could not borrow a book from anyone even for an hour, I threatened would soon happen.[75]

My wish has in fact been granted: Greek books are now on offer everywhere and are being sent for sale to the book dealers. Also many have been sent to me. I hope it will also turn out that if there are people mean enough to be dismayed to see a benefit shared by all, they will die of envy, succumb to grief and a miserable end, and finally hang themselves when in the near future they see all the work of Aristotle printed in our typeface. The commentaries too will soon be printed; I have collected almost all of them. Make an effort, I ask of you, make an effort to study good books, when I with the help of Jesus Christ, God who is best and greatest, provide all the best texts. 3

Here you have a thoroughly useful, essential work, which I could justifiably call the cornucopia of Amaltheia,[76] the gardens of Adonis,[77] a store of treasures. It includes almost everything you could wish for with a view to a full and complete knowledge of Greek, and especially with regard to what one reads in the poets, who so often alter words in their various forms and dialects that it would be easier to trace the source of the Nile than to find the stem or the root of a verb in some tenses. 4

But that is all made very easy by this book; it tells you how and in which dialect each verb alters, providing conjugations and rules throughout in alphabetical order. In addition it deals with the dialects of Attica, Ionic, Aeolic, of the Dorians, Boeotia, Crete, Cyprus, Macedonia, Thessaly, Reggio, Sicily, Taranto, Chalcidice, 5

Tarentinae, Chalcidicae, Argivae, Laconicae, Syracusanae, Pamphyliae, Atheniensis, quibus usi Graeci poetae inveniuntur, et Homerus praecipue.

6   His linguis ac figuris variis habent illi miram licentiam: addunt, detrahunt, transmutant, invertunt; quid non faciunt? denique utuntur dictionibus ut caera. Si poetae Graeci voluerint, ὁ ἄνθρωπος ἔσται ὄνος, ἵππος, βοῦς, κύων, longe melius ostendent hominem esse asinum, quam sophistae. Non potui aliquando non ridere legens hanc dictionum, ut sic dicam, μεταμόρφωσιν: verbi causa, ex ἅμα et ἴσος fit ἄμισυς et mutatione ἥμισυς; comparativum est ἡμισύτερος, secunda forma ἡμισίων, tertia ἥσσων, et Attice ἥττων: ecce ex ἄμισυς factum est ἥττων, ubi ne una quidem littera est primitivi. Quod nobis non licere sic conqueritur Marcialis: 'Dicunt εἰαρινὸς tamen poetae, Sed Graeci, quibus est nihil negatum. Nobis non licet esse tam disertis, Qui Musas colimus severiores.'

7   Imitamur tamen hanc linguarum varietatem et copiam lingua vulgari: non enim eadem est Romanis lingua, quae Parthenopaeis, quae Calabris, quae Siculis; aliter Florentini loquuntur, aliter Genuenses; Veneti a Mediolanensibus lingua et pronuntiatione multum intersunt; alius Brixianis, alius Bergomatibus sermo. Quod Latine caput, vulgo Romani capo appellant; Veneti vero abiectione p litterae per concisionem dicunt cao; at qui Padum accolunt, ex ao crasin facientes, co. Item cenato, cenao, cenò, et id genus innumera. Sic Graeci dicunt communiter τοῦ κέρατος, Iones vero, ἀποβολῇ τοῦ τ, κέραος, at Dores, κατὰ κρᾶσιν, κέρως. Quid, quod unaquaeque urbs peculiarem habet linguam, plerunque etiam in eodem oppido varie loquuntur? Utinam tantam copiam Latine haberemus: longe antecelleremus Graecos.

8   Sed ut ad librum redeam, quem copiae cornu hortosque Adonidis et thesaurum dicimus, propter summam, quae in eo est, rerum bonarum copiam: primus labor in eo fuit Guarini Camertis et

Argos, Laconia, Syracuse, Pamphylia, and Athens, as found in the usage of Greek poets, Homer in particular.

In these dialects with a variety of forms there is an astonishing 6 display of freedom: they add, delete, alter, transpose; they do everything: in fact they treat words like wax. If Greek poets wish, a man will become an ass, a horse, an ox, a dog;[78] they could prove that man is an ass far better than the sophists. Sometimes I could not help laughing as I read about this metamorphosis, if I may use the term, of words. For example from ἅμα and ἴσος ἅμισυς is formed and by mutation becomes ἥμισυς; the comparative is ἡμισύτερος,[79] with a second form ἡμισίων and a third ἥσσων, in Attic ἥττων. So ἥττων derives from ἅμισυς without having one single letter of the original form. We cannot do that, as Martial complains: "The poets however say εἰαρινός [of spring] but they are Greeks, for whom nothing is forbidden. We who cultivate stricter Muses cannot be so inventive."[80]

But we imitate their wealth and variety of dialects in the spoken 7 language. At Rome the dialect is not the same as in Naples, Calabria or Sicily; the speech of Florentines and Genoese is different; the Venetians are quite distinct from the Milanese in dialect and pronunciation; Brescia and Bergamo differ in language. The word which in Latin is *caput* in Roman speech is *capo*; the Venetians drop the *p* and with abbreviation say *cao*; those who live near the Po contract *ao*, giving *co*. Similarly, *cenato, cenao, cenò*; there is no end to this sort of thing. In the same way the Greeks generally say κέρατος, but the Ionians, losing the tau, κέραος, and the Dorians, with crasis, κέρως. Furthermore every city has its own dialect; frequently there are differences within the same town. I wish we had such riches in Latin; we would far outdo the Greeks.

But let me return to the book, which we call a cornucopia, the 8 gardens of Adonis and a treasury, because of the great store of good things in it. Guarino of Camerino[81] and Carlo Antinori of

Caroli Antenorei Florentini, hominum multi studii ac in Graecarum litterarum lectione frequentium. Hi simul ex Eustathio, Ety-
mologico et aliis dignis grammaticis accepere haec canonismata
digessereque per ordinem litterarum, nec sine adiumento et consilio Angeli Politiani, viri summo ingenio ac impense docti. Secundus vero labor meus fuit, qui ea omnia recognovi non parvo labore,
cum iis conferens unde excerpta voluminibus fuerant. Multa enim
addidi, plurima immutavi, adiuvante interdum Urbano, divi Francisci fratre optimo, a quo brevi habebitis quas summa cura ac
doctissime composuit in Graecam linguam introductiones. Sunt
etiam in hoc libro copiosae ac perutiles formationes τῶν εἰμὶ καὶ
εἶμι verborum; item quot sint verba quae esse significant, quot
item ire et quot sedere. Addidi ego libellum ex scriptis Herodiani,
quas magni verbi παρεκβολὰς dicunt, in quo multa profecto
sunt lectu dignissima, et quae in aliis grammaticis non temere leguntur, et praecipue quae de praeterito Attico conscribuntur, docte
sane et peracute; nec non et Choerobosci quaedam, in quibus
ostendit non in omnibus regulas et similitudines quaeri oportere;
eiusdem etiam quae ν litteram in contextu orationis ob maleso-
nantiam attrahant.

9   Hinc sequuntur inaequalia verba, per ordinem litterarum, quae
ἀνόμαλα Graeci appellant; quae idcirco addidimus, quoniam et
ipsa cum caeteris optime convenire videbantur. Addere etiam operae pretium duximus περὶ ἐγκλινομένων καὶ ἐγκλιτικῶν varia
opuscula, quorum usum apud nostros (de encliticis loquor) non
memini legere in pluribus quatuor quinqueve ad summum dictionibus (que ve ne et cum postposita, ut quibusdam placet, et versus); nam ἐγκλινόμενα, quae inclinata Latine placet dicere (ut
loco praesentis participii, praeteritum, deficiente praesenti in pas-
sivo verbo, accipiatur), ea dicuntur, quae admittunt in fine tonum
acutum convertuntque in gravem in contextu orationis; apud
Graecos vero encliticorum plurimus usus in quinque orationis

Florence,[82] men of much learning and regular readers of Greek, worked on it at first. They assembled these rules from Eustathius,[83] the *Etymologicum*,[84] and other sound grammarians, and arranged them alphabetically; at the same time they had help and advice from Angelo Poliziano, a man of the highest ability and great erudition.[85] The second part of the task was mine; with considerable effort I checked it all by comparison with the sources of the excerpts. I made many additions and innumerable alterations, with intermittent help from Urbano, an excellent Franciscan brother, from whom you will soon receive an introduction to the Greek language, composed with the greatest care and erudition.[86] In this book there are full and helpful conjugations of the verbs εἶμι and εἰμί, all the verbs which mean "to be," also "to go" and "to sit." I have added a short book written by Herodian, known as the *Excursus* on the great book about the verb,[87] in which there is a lot that is worth reading and not easily found in other grammars, especially the statement about the Attic aorist, very well informed and subtle; I have also added something from Choeroboscus,[88] in which he shows that rules and analogies do not need to be sought everywhere, plus what he says about words attracting the letter *nu* for reasons of euphony.

At this point follow irregular verbs, in alphabetical order, known in Greek as *anomala*.[89] I added them because they too seemed to fit in very well with the rest of the material. We also thought it worth adding some opuscula on enclitics and oxytone words. Their use in Latin—I refer to enclitics—I remember seeing in no more than four or five cases at the most (*que ve ne* and *cum*, attached as suffixes, and *versus*, as some people maintain). Oxytone words, generally known in Latin as *inclinata* (if the past participle can be accepted in place of the present, which is lacking in the passive) are those with an acute accent on the final syllable, which becomes grave in the context of the sentence; in Greek there is much use of enclitics in five parts of speech: noun,[90] pro-

9

partibus: nomine, pronomine, verbo, adverbio et coniunctione. Auctores sunt Herodianus, Ioannes grammaticus Charax, Choeroboscus, Aelius Dionysius. Et quoniam passim in hoc libro secundum varia idiomata leguntur crebrae mutationes, non ab re fuit quotquot ad manus nostras pervenerunt de idiomatis varios tractatus inserere.

10   Postremo illud nolo vos ignorare, bonarum litterarum amantissimi: notasse me asteriscis quae obscura, concisa et depravata visa sunt, obeliscis vero quae superflua iudicavi. Cur autem aliqua signo alterutro annotanda praetermiserim, habui multas causas, sed praecipua fuit angustia temporis. Peto igitur a vobis, siqua in tanto opere non placuerint, quod vel reprehendenda vel non plana videantur, ne mihi succenseatis, sed iis, si audebitis, unde accepta sunt, vel bellis potius exterarum gentium, quibus et Graecia et Italia semper obnoxia fuit. Mendosorum enim est exemplarium culpa, non mea: nihil magis depravatum grammaticis, fragmentata omnia, nihil absolutum, nihil integrum.

11   Quanquam hic liber, ut dixi, thesaurus est, κέρας τε Ἀμαλθείας καὶ κῆποι Ἀδώνιδος, quoniam in eo uno fere omnia congesta sunt, quae digna scitu in aliis leguntur. Itaque, si inter tot laudanda aliquid minus probandum legeritis, mementote illius Horatiani praecepti: 'Verum ubi plura nitent in carmine, non ego paucis Offendar maculis, quas aut incuria fudit Aut humana parum cavit natura.' Estote igitur impressionis nostrae aequi iudices affectique beneficio minime ingrati, et miseremini laborum nostrorum. Valete.

noun, verb, adverb, and conjunction. The authorities are Herodian, John Charax the grammarian,[91] Choeroboscus, Aelius Dionysius.[92] And since throughout this volume there are numerous mutations in the various dialects, it was not inappropriate to insert all the various treatises about dialects that came to hand.

Finally, enthusiasts for literature, I would not like you to be 10 unaware that I have marked with asterisks whatever seemed obscure, too concise or corrupt, and with *obeli*[93] whatever I judged to be superfluous. There are many reasons why I omitted to mark certain passages with either sign, the principal one being lack of time. So I would ask you not to criticize me if some things in this large work do not satisfy you or seem to be open to criticism or to be unclear; criticize, if you will, the sources from which they derive, or rather the invasions by foreign powers, to which Greece and Italy have always been exposed. The fault lies with corrupt exemplars, not with me; there is nothing more corrupt than grammatical texts, everything is in fragmentary form, nothing is complete, nothing is fully preserved.

Yet this book, as I said, is a treasury, the cornucopia of Amal- 11 theia and the gardens of Adonis, because almost everything worth knowing from other texts has been collected together in this one. And so, if you find in the midst of so much valuable material something that is less satisfactory, remember Horace's dictum: "But when most of a poem shines, I shall not be offended by a few blemishes which carelessness produced or human nature failed to avoid."[94] So be fair in your judgment of our printing; accept the benefit without any trace of ingratitude, and be sympathetic to our endeavors. Farewell.

B

12

Ἄλδου.

Λῆς γνῶσ᾽ Ἡσίοδον καὶ Σιμιχίδαν καὶ Ὅμηρον
ποιητάς τ᾽ ἄλλως; Τὰν λαβὲ πραξομέναν,
κεῖς γὰρ Λατοΐδα γλυκερὸν δῶ κεῖς τε πορεύσει
μεστά ῥ᾽ ἀηδονέων ἄλσεα Πιερίδων.

: VII :

Aldus Manutius Bassianas Romanus Alberto
Pio principi Carpensi s. p. d.

1 Pisistratus tyrannus, vir multa doctrina et eloquentia, liberalium
disciplinarum libros Athenis publice ad legendum praebuisse primus dicitur, ac duosdequinquaginta libros Homeri, Iliada et Odys-
seam, dispersos ac confusos, ut qui variis locis et temporibus a
poeta recitati effusique, cum vagaretur, fuerant, in eum qui nunc
est ordinem redegisse et quodammodo consuisse; unde ῥαψῳδία
et singulis libris et universo operi, ut quidam volunt, est inditum
nomen, παρὰ τὸ ῥάπτειν καὶ τὴν ᾠδήν. Proposuerat enim vir
ille de re litteraria optime meritus dignum praemium iis, qui
Homeri carmen aliquod attulissent; qua re facile fuit dispersum
carmen colligere aurum promittenti; quin immo—tanta est vis
nummorum—maioris spe muneris quam plurimi dati sunt subdi-
titii versus, quos postea Aristarchus, gravi iudicio grammaticus,
notavit atque obelisco transfixit. Utinam mihi idem liceret, iu-
cundissime princeps! Colligendis enim corrigendisque accurate

B

By Aldus.[95]

Do you wish to know Hesiod, Simichidas,[96] Homer
  and other poets? Take this book for study;[97]
it will transport you to the sweet home of the son of Leto
  and the groves of the Pierides,[98] full of nightingales.

: VII :

Aristotle, Natural Philosophy
(February 1497)

Aldus Manutius of Bassiano near Rome, to Alberto Pio,
prince of Carpi, warmest greetings.

The tyrant Peisistratus, a man of much learning and eloquence, is   1
said to have been the first to provide in Athens at public expense
books relating to the liberal arts; also to have put together somehow and arranged in their present order the forty-eight books of
Homer's *Iliad* and *Odyssey*, which had been recited at various times
and places by the poet as he traveled.[99] Hence the single books
and the work as a whole, as some people say, were given the name
rhapsodia, derived from *rhaptein* and *ode*. As a great patron of literature he offered a rich prize to anyone who brought in a poem by
Homer; so it was easy with the promise of money to collect the
scattered texts. What is more—such is the power of money—
many spurious verses were offered in the hope of a greater reward;
these were later identified and marked with an *obelus* by Aristarchus, a critic of sound judgment.[100] Would that I could do the
same, most friendly of princes! I would certainly spare no expense

omnibus Aristotelis et Theophrasti operibus parcerem certe nulli impensae. Non me voluntate et studio superavit Pisistratus, sed divitiis.

2   Verum, quia labor omnia vincit improbus, brevi spero futurum, ut pleraque omnia Aristotelis et Theophrasti veniant in manus studiosorum excusa typis nostris quatuor voluminibus. En primum absolvimus et, quod etiam in logicis fecimus, in tuo nomine publicamus, ut intelligant studiosi tibi etiam se debere, si mihi debent. Nam non modo assidue adiuvas provinciam nostram opibus tuis, sed agros quoque fertilissimos amplissimosque te mihi donaturum palam dicis; immo oppidum amoenum ex tuis ita meum futurum polliceris, ut in eo aeque ac tu iubere possim. Quod facis, ut bonorum librorum et Latine et Graece commodius faciliusque a me ibi fiat omnibus copia, constituatur etiam academia, in qua, relicta barbarie, bonis litteris bonisque artibus studeatur, ac tandem secentos annos et plus eo glandem depasti homines vescantur frugibus. Non sperno, princeps liberalissime, ingentia munera tua; veniam equidem non invitus quocunque iusseris, ac tecum, quem a teneris, ut aiunt, unguiculis educavi instituique, incumbam studio sapientiae, quam philosophian Graeco vocabulo appellamus. Sim plane rusticus et nullo iudicio, nisi tecum esse semper velim; et eo maxime, quod tu existimas nihil praestantius, nihil melius doctrina homini posse contingere, teque totum tradis studio sapientiae.

3   Utinam viveret ille Ioannes Picus avunculus tuus, quem immatura morte raptum semper deflebimus! Nam cum sua, quamvis magna, tamen adhuc crescenti doctrina, tum te sororis et Ioanne Francisco Pico Galeoti fratris filio acerrime, ut facitis, philosophantibus, superaret omnium fortunam. Quanquam illi optime

for the collation and accurate editing of all the works by Aristotle and Theophrastus. Peisistratus did not outdo me in desire and eagerness but in wealth.

But since hard work overcomes all obstacles[101] I hope that practically all the writings of Aristotle and Theophrastus, printed by me in four volumes, will soon reach students. Here we complete the first,[102] and as we did with the logic, we publish them with a dedication to you, so that students understand that they are indebted to you as well, if they are indebted to me. Not only do your resources provide regular assistance for our enterprise, but you have said in public that you will give me very fertile and extensive estates; indeed, you promise me for the future one of your agreeable castles, where I could be in command just as you are. This you do in order that I may more easily and conveniently put together there a stock of good books in Greek and Latin, and also set up an academy[103] in which, having left barbarism far behind, one may study good literature and the liberal arts, and men may at last, after six hundred years and more of a diet of acorns, feed on cereals.[104] I do not spurn, most generous prince, your huge generosity; I will come willingly whenever you order me; and with you, whom I have instructed and educated, as they say, from the cradle,[105] I will settle down to the study of the wisdom which we designate by the Greek word "philosophy." I would be utterly uncultivated and lacking in judgment if I did not wish to be with you always; and all the more so[106] because you believe nothing is nobler, nothing better for a man than education, and you devote yourself entirely to your enthusiasm for learning.

Would that your uncle Giovanni Pico[107] were still alive. We shall always lament his early death, With his already great but ever increasing learning, with you, the son of his sister, and Giovanni Francesco Pico,[108] son of his brother Galeotto, all keenly devoted to philosophy, as you are, he would surpass all men in good fortune. But his fate was for the best; he rests in happiness, in joy, in

2

3

accidit: quiescit enim laetus, gaudet, triumphat cum superis. Nam ob bene eius actam vitam et sanctos mores ad superos tanquam e custodia et vinculis corporis censeo quam expeditissime nostrum evolasse Picum; itaque sinamus illum in pace quiescere et frui divinis.

4   Tu nunc, princeps studiosissime, accipe Aristotelis hos naturalis philosophiae libros uno volumine comprehensos, hoc est: de auscultatione physica libros octo, quorum primi quinque sunt de principiis naturalibus, reliqui vero de motu — sic enim dividendos Themistius censet —; de coelo libros quatuor; de generatione et corruptione duos; meteorologicos quatuor; de mundo unum ad Alexandrum; de mundo item unum Philonis Iudaei, summa viri doctrina ac tanta eloquentia, ut cum Platone certare videatur — quod et tritum illud apud Graecos ostendit: ἢ Πλάτων φιλωνίζει ἢ Φίλων πλατωνίζει —; hinc sequuntur opuscula Theophrasti de igne, de ventis, de lapidibus ac de signis aquarum, ventorum, hyemis, ἀνωνύμου. Habes etiam ante physica vitas Aristotelis et Theophrasti compositas ab Laertio; rursum Aristotelis vitam ab Ioanne Philopono scriptam brevissime; et post has Galeni opusculum, qualecunque dare potuimus, de historia philosophorum. Illud nolui silentio praeterire: hos Theophrasti libellos idcirco post meteorologicos Aristotelis libros fuisse additos, quod derelictos a philosopho Theophrastum, ut alia pleraque, composuisse accepimus; quare quicquid extat Theophrasti congessimus una cum philosopho imprimendum digerendumque in suum locum, ut hic fecimus.

5   Sed illud vehementer dolendum: ex tot quae composuit Theophrastus — non pauciora enim quam Aristoteles scripsit, quod in eius vita licet videre — hos tantummodo, eosque non integros et correctos, sed mutilatos ac mendosos, cum inscitia librariorum hominumque incuria, tum praecipue dura gravique offensa temporum, inveniri, atque adeo raros, ut eorum quae hic legis unum duntaxat exemplar habere potuerim in tota Italia. Qualescunque

triumph with those above. I think our Pico ascended to the world above, freed from the custody and bonds of the body, as quickly as possible because of his good life and saintly character. So let us allow him to rest in peace and enjoy divine favor.

Now, learned prince, receive these works of natural philosophy 4 by Aristotle in one volume. They are eight books on physics, of which the first five deal with the principles underlying nature, the remainder with motion (that is the division recommended by Themistius),[109] four books on the heavens, two on generation and decay, four on meteorology, one on the universe, addressed to Alexander, another single book on the universe by Philo Judaeus, a man of good learning and such eloquence that he seems to compete with Plato, as is shown by that well-known saying of the Greeks: "Either Plato is like Philo or Philo is like Plato."[110] There follow minor works by Theophrastus, on fire, winds and minerals, and an anonymous work on weather signs, winds and storms. Preceding the *Physics* you have the biographies of Aristotle and Theophrastus by Laertius,[111] then a very brief life of Aristotle by John Philoponus;[112] after these a short work by Galen, in the best form we can manage, on the history of philosophy.[113] I do not wish to pass over in silence the fact that the essays by Theophrastus are added after Aristotle's *Meteorology* because we have gathered that it was left incomplete by the philosopher, like much else, and put into shape by Theophrastus. So we have assembled everything by Theophrastus that is extant,[114] to be printed and given its proper place alongside the philosopher's works, as we have done here.

But there is one thing much to be regretted. Of the numerous 5 works of Theophrastus — for, as one can see from his biography, he wrote as much as Aristotle — it was only possible to find these; and they are not complete and in good order but mutilated and faulty. And they are so rare that I was able to find only one copy of what you read here in the whole of Italy. So I have printed

igitur habere potui, imprimendos curavi, sperans, sicubi latent meliores, in lucem aliquando exituros, a studiosis, qui mendosos hos legerint, quaesitos perdiligenter. Aristotelis vero et quae nunc legenda damus et quae mox Deo favente daturi sumus, multum certe elaboravi ut, tum quaerendis optimis et antiquis libris atque eadem in re multiplicibus, tum conferendis castigandisque exemplaribus, quae dilaceranda impressoribus traderentur perirentque ut pariens vipera, in manus hominum venirent emendatissima.

6   Id ita sit necne, sunt mihi gravissimi testes in tota fere Italia, et praecipue Venetiis Thomas Anglicus, homo et Graece et Latine peritissimus praecellensque in doctrinarum omnium disciplinis, et Gabriel meus, Brassicellae natus, vir impense doctus ac rei litterariae censor acerrimus alterque Quintilius; Iustinus etiam Corcyraeus, miro ingenio adolescens Graeceque sane quam eruditus; Ferrariae vero Nicolaus Leonicenus et Laurentius Maiolus Genuensis: quorum alter, philosophorum aetatis nostrae medicorumque omnium facile princeps, librorum Aristotelis, quos ipse haberet, mihi copiam humanissime fecit; alter, praestanti vir ingenio et maturo iudicio ac omnibus bonis artibus praeditus, omnes prope Aristotelis libros summa cura summoque studio contulit cum libris Leoniceni nostri meo rogatu. Idem et ipse Venetiis accuratissime feci, non sine adiumento virorum doctorum, qui et Venetiis sunt et Patavii.

7   Quanquam minus fieri potuit, nequid his libris desideraretur; quod non mea quidem culpa factum est — nam hoc vere queo dicere: quicquid meo labore formis excuditur, ipsis exemplaribus longe correctius ac magis perfectum exire ex aedibus nostris —, verum tum hominum, qui ante nos fuerunt, tum edacium temporum, quae tandem cuncta immutant, consumunt, abolent. Hinc illud:

whatever texts I could obtain, in the hope that, if better copies lie
hidden somewhere, they will eventually come to light, after a careful search by scholars who have read these faulty texts. I have done
a great deal of work on Aristotle, both on the texts now offered to
the reader and on those which we shall shortly offer, if God favors.
In order that they should reach the public in as correct a state as
possible, the best early manuscripts were sought, several copies of
the same text were collated and corrected, and they were handed
over to the printer to be taken apart, perishing like the viper that
gives birth.

For the truth of what I say I have the most reliable witnesses, 6
from almost every part of Italy, especially Venice: Thomas the
Englishman,[115] a great expert in Greek and Latin and outstanding
in all subjects, and my friend Gabriele,[116] born in Brisighella, a
man of extraordinary learning and a severe critic of literature, a
new Quintilius;[117] also Justin from Corfu,[118] a young man of wonderful intelligence and pretty expert in Greek. But in Ferrara there
are Niccolò Leoniceno[119] and Lorenzo Maioli[120] from Genoa. The
former is by far the leading philosopher and doctor of our age and
very kindly lent me his manuscripts of Aristotle; the latter, a man
of great ability, mature judgment and knowledgeable in all the
liberal arts, with great care and attention collated at my request all
the Aristotelian texts with my friend Leoniceno's manuscripts. I
have done the same in Venice with the utmost care, assisted by
scholars in Venice and Padua.

It was not possible to ensure that nothing should be found 7
wanting in these books. That is not my fault — I can truthfully say
that whatever I take the trouble to print emerges from our house
in far better and more correct form than it exhibited in the exemplars — it is the fault of earlier generations and the destructiveness
of time which in the end change, consume and destroy everything.
Hence,

Tempus edax rerum, tuque, invidiosa vetustas,
omnia destruitis, vitiataque dentibus aevi
paulatim lenta consumitis omnia morte.

Et illud:

Omnia fert aetas, animum quoque.

Hinc illa acclamatio:

Quid non longa dies, quid non consumitis, anni?

8   Quapropter improbe et inique faciet, siquis nos accusabit. Nonne est omnium ingratissimus, qui, donatus nummo aureo ab amico, qui ne illum quidem dare nisi summis laboribus poterat, queritur, maledicit, accusat, quod non dederit centum?

9   Tu vero, optime princeps, hos libros, qualescunque sunt, accipe, quo vultu caetera, quae a me proficiscuntur, soles. Non multo post publicabimus caetera Aristotelis et Theophrasti in tuo nomine; hinc omnis commentarios in Aristotelem dabimus; praeterea divini Platonis omnia opera et quotquot in illum extant commentaria. Dabimus etiam et Hippocratis et Galeni omnia et caeterorum illustrium, qui in medicina scripserunt. Condonabimus deinceps mathematicos omnis. Quid quaeris? Efficiam profecto, si diu vixero, ne desint boni libri bonarum litterarum et liberalium artium studiosis. Vale.

Time that eats away the world, and you, jealous antiquity,
you destroy everything, and slowly with a lingering death
you consume all things, already spoiled by the teeth of
    aging.[121]

And this:

Age carries off all things, the mind as well.[122]

Hence this pronouncement:

Length of days, and years, what is there that you do not
    destroy?[123]

So it will be improper and unfair for anyone to blame us. If a 8
man is given a single gold coin by a friend who could only give it
with very great difficulty, he is the most ungrateful of men if he
complains, curses, or criticizes because the friend did not give him
a hundred.

Best of princes, accept these books, such as they are, with the 9
same good grace as you accept my other productions. It will not
be long before we publish with a dedication to you all the rest of
Aristotle and Theophrastus; then we will offer all the commentaries on Aristotle, followed by the complete works of the divine
Plato and all the commentaries on him. We will also offer Hippocrates, the whole of Galen and all the other eminent medical
writers. After that we shall give you all the mathematicians. What
else do you want? I will certainly make sure, if I live long enough,
that there is no lack of good books for students off literature and
the liberal arts. Farewell.

: VIII :

A

Aldus Manutius Romanus Alberto Pio principi Carpensi s. d.

1   Sperabam fore aliquando, inclyte princeps, ut possem rerum causis cognoscendis omni studio curaque incumbere, ac optima philosophorum praecepta nocturna versare manu, versare diurna; sed multo aliter quam existimaram evenire intelligo, quandoquidem sic impedior in dies magis, ut nesciam de quo verius quam de me dici queat Ovidianum illud: 'Qui non est hodie, cras minus aptus erit.' Quod nisi tanta mea incommoda bonarum literarum studiosis scirem prodesse plurimum, vitam mihi esse acerbam putarem. Quare illo me hemistichio solor: 'Unum pro cunctis dabitur caput,' sperans tamen adhuc futurum aliquando quod cupio, ac mecum saepe dicens:

θαρσεῖν χρή, φίλος Ἄλδε· τάχ᾽ αὔριον ἔσσετ᾽ ἄμεινον.

2   Verum accipe nunc, mi Alberte, hos de animalibus Aristotelis libros, quibus legendis et tu multum proficies et quicunque clarus in liberalibus disciplinis evadere concupiscit, tum copia et varietate rerum, tum foelici et eleganti stilo divini Aristotelis. Quod si hos de animalibus libros cum iis conferes, quos miro successu Theodorus Gaza, licet Graecus homo, tamen et Latine et Graece eruditorum omnium aetatis suae facile princeps, fecit Latinos, brevi quantum profeceris non poenitebit: ibi enim utriusque linguae

: VIII :

Aristotle, Zoological Works
(*June 1, 1497*)

A

Aldus Manutius of Rome to Alberto Pio, prince of Carpi, greetings.

I had hoped, distinguished prince, that I would one day be able to   1
devote all my care and energy to the study of the nature of
things,[124] to study night and day the best teachings of the philosophers; but I realize that matters are turning out quite contrary to
expectation, since I suffer ever-increasing obstacles and do not
know of anyone to whom that remark of Ovid, "Whoever is not
capable today will be less so tomorrow,"[125] could be more aptly applied. If I did not know that my great hardships are of substantial
benefit to students of literature, I would reckon my life was bitter.
So I console myself with the half-line, "One will be sacrificed for
all,"[126] while still hoping that my wishes will be realized one day,
and saying to myself,

> One must have courage, dear Aldus, perhaps tomorrow will
> be better.[127]

But now, dear Alberto, accept these books by Aristotle, *De ani-*   2
malibus.[128] You and anyone else who wishes to achieve distinction
in the liberal arts will gain a great deal by reading them, both from
the quantity of diverse subject matter[129] and the elegant stylistic
felicity of the divine Aristotle.[130] For if you compare this text of *De*
animalibus with the one rendered into Latin with remarkable success by Theodore Gaza—although he was Greek, he was easily
the best of all the scholars of his time in Latin and Greek—you
will have no cause to be dissatisfied with the progress you can

proprietatem licet cognoscere, quod et nobis et Graecis est apprime necessarium. Nullus est, mihi crede, Graecus liber in quo facilius disci Graeca lingua possit ab hominibus nostris propter Theodorum. Sic Graece didicit Hermolaus Barbarus, sic Picus Mirandula avunculus tuus, sic Hieronymus Donatus, sic Angelus Politianus, summo viri iudicio, summo ingenio ac undecumque doctissimi; sic denique quicunque Graecas literas callet temporibus nostris. Idem et tibi, mi Alberte, censeo faciendum, ut, cum et tu non mediocri sis ingenio, iis quos praedixi et eloquio par fias et scientia rerum.

3   Quare vero hos Aristotelis in philosophia libros hoc ordine curarimus imprimendos, ut praeposuerimus physica cum caeteris in eodem volumine, hos dein libros de animalibus, hinc de plantis Theophrasti libros atque Aristotelis et problemata καὶ τὰ μετὰ τὰ φυσικά, statueram ad te hac epistola scribere quam possem brevissime, cum scirem non defuturos qui hunc ordinem accusarent: nam magna inter doctos hac de re semper fuit controversia et adhuc sub iudice lis est. Sed consuluit labori nostro Franciscus Caballus, multi homo studii philosophusque doctissimus ac excellens Venetiis medicus. Is enim libellum de ordine librorum Aristotelis in philosophia, accurate quidem et erudite composuit, quem ipsi brevi excusum formis publicabimus. Libellos praeterea Theophrasti, nec non Aristotelis quosdam, qualescunque habere potuimus, dedimus. Vale.

B

4   En tibi, lector carissime, fragmenta ea, quae Gaza in prooemio de animalibus in nonnullis codicibus tum Graecis tum Latinis inveniri ait; quae suo fortasse loco impressa legeres, si suo tempore

soon make. In that work you can appreciate the characteristics of each language, which is absolutely essential for us and for the Greeks, Believe me, there is no Greek text from which Greek can be more easily learned by our fellow countrymen, thanks to Theodore. That is how Ermolao Barbaro, your uncle Pico della Mirandola, Girolamo Donà[131] and Angelo Poliziano, men of great judgment, great ability and all-round erudition learned Greek; so also everyone who is good at Greek today.[132] So I think, dear Alberto, you should do the same, so that, being a person of no small ability, you match those men I have mentioned in eloquence and knowledge.

My reason for printing Aristotle's philosophical works in this order — first *Physics* and the rest in the same volume, then this work *De animalibus*, then Theophrastus *On Plants* with Aristotle's *Problemata* and *Metaphysics*[133] — I decided to explain to you as briefly as possible in this letter, since I knew that there would be no lack of critics of this order; there has always been much controversy on this subject among scholars and the matter is still not settled.[134] But Francesco Cavalli[135] helped us in this difficulty — he is a man of deep learning, a great expert in philosophy and an outstanding doctor in Venice. He wrote a short essay, very precise and learned, on the order of Aristotle's philosophical works, which we will issue in print shortly. In addition we have printed minor works of Theophrastus, and some by Aristotle, in whatever state of preservation we could find them.[136] Farewell.

3

B

Here, dear reader, are the fragments which Gaza in the preface of his *De animalibus* says are to be found in some Greek and Latin manuscripts. You would perhaps have had them printed where

4

in manus nostras venissent. Nunc vero hoc loco adiecta maluimus, quam te iisdem qualibuscunque fraudari. Vale.

: IX :

Aldus Manutius Alberto Pio principi illustrissimo s. p. d.

1   Plato philosophus, interrogatus, Alberte princeps illustrissime, πῶς ἂν ἄριστα διοικῶνται αἱ πόλεις, respondit: ἐὰν οἱ φιλόσοφοι βασιλεύσωσιν ἢ οἱ βασιλεῖς φιλοσοφήσωσιν: verum ac sapiens responsum et Platone dignum principe Academicorum. Optime enim gubernarentur respublicae, si aut philosophi regnarent aut principes philosopharentur: non tot rapinas, tot caedes, non foedissimam tetramque luxuriem, non caetera nefanda flagitia impune aspiceremus. Nec dubito quin, cum dico philosophos, eos intelligas, qui sancte, qui vere, qui integerrime, ut tu facis, philosophantur; non quosdam indoctos primum, hinc pravos et haereticos ac potius nulli addictos religioni, qui nomine tantum sunt, non etiam re philosophi, quique de virtute locuti . . . at caetera non nobis, sed satyro liceant. Nec mirum tales, ex pecudum magis quam ex hominum genere, non posse candidas disciplinas aureamque virtutem attingere. Μὴ καθαρῷ γὰρ καθαροῦ ἐφάπτεσθαι, οὐχὶ θεμιτόν, ut ait Plato.

2   Cum tu igitur, princeps, unus ex paucis, quos aequus amavit Iupiter, acerrime philosopheris, hos etiam de philosophia libros in tuo nomine publicare constitui; hoc est: Theophrasti περὶ φυτῶν

they belong if they had reached me in time. But as it is, we preferred to add them here rather than deprive you of them, for what they are worth. Farewell.

: IX :

Aristotle, Metaphysics, Mechanics, *and* Problems
Theophrastus, Botanical Writings
(June 1, 1497)[137]

Aldus Manutius to Alberto Pio, most illustrious prince, warmest greetings.

Most illustrious prince Alberto, when the philosopher Plato was asked how cities might be best governed, he replied: "If philosophers are kings and kings are philosophers"[138] — a true and wise reply, worthy of Plato as head of the Academy. Cities would be governed best if philosophers ruled or princes were philosophers; we would not witness so much plunder, so much slaughter, utterly disgusting and sordid luxury, nor all the other unspeakable unpunished crimes. And I have no doubt that when I speak of philosophers, you understand them to be men who piously, genuinely and in all honesty, like yourself, study philosophy — and not certain ignoramuses and wicked heretics, adherents of no religion, who are merely philosophers in name but not in practice, who talk about virtue — but the rest is not our business and should be left to a satirist.[139] It is no wonder that such people, who are more like cattle than human beings, cannot aspire to honorable disciplines and golden virtue. As Plato says: "For the impure to lay hands on the pure is not right."[140]

Since you, prince, as one of the few favored by Jupiter in his justice,[141] are a very keen philosopher, I determined to publish these philosophical texts as well with a dedication to you — that is,

1

2

ἱστορίας libros novem — nam decimi perpauca quaedam, ut erant in exemplaribus, imprimenda iussimus; reliqua vel non extant vel in nono, ut ibi etiam diximus, confusa et immista sunt — ; eiusdem περὶ φυτῶν αἰτιῶν libros sex; hinc et Aristotelis et Alexandri Aphrodisiensis problemata; sequuntur deinde Aristotelis μηχανικά eiusdemque τῶν μετὰ τὰ φυσικά quatuordecim libri, et postremo opusculum τῶν μετὰ τὰ φυσικά Theophrasti. Quibus imprimendis ea usus sum cura, ut, si cui alius atque ego feci constituendus ordo videbitur, facile id queat pro arbitrio suo. Quare autem nos hoc ordine usi sumus, alibi cognosces. Illud certo scias cum caeteris studiosis: omnia a nobis in dura hac et sumptuosa provincia fieri accuratissime.

3   Quod sicubi non factum videbitur, quod quaedam dari meliora potuerint, videte ne sitis ingrati, cum nocte dieque vel supra vires vobis laborem. Quod tamen facio perlibenter; nec ab incoepto unquam desistam, nisi effecero quod sum pollicitus. Nullis profecto parcam sumptibus quamvis magnis; parvifaciam labores omnis, etiamsi in voluptate vivere et in ocio esse semper possim. Es enim tu mihi optimus testis, an potiores Herculis erumnas credam saevosque labores et Venere et coenis et plumis Sardanapalli. Natus enim homo est ad laborem et ad agendum semper aliquid viro dignum, non ad voluptatem, quae beluarum est ac pecudum.

4   Optime tu igitur, princeps, Herculem Iovis satu editum imitaris, qui, cum primum pubesceret, quod tempus a natura ad deligendum quam quisque viam sit ingressurus datum est, duas cernens vias, unam virtutis, alteram voluptatis, virtutum ingressus est viam. Quare perge tu philosophari, ut coepisti, sisque exemplo caeteris: ὡς, φιλοσοφούντων τῶν βασιλέων, ἄριστα διοικοῖντ' ἂν αἱ πόλεις. Ἔρρωσο.

nine books of *Historia Plantarum* by Theophrastus, and we gave
instructions to print a very small amount of the tenth, as found in
the manuscripts, the rest of it being either lost, as we stated there,
or confusingly muddled up with the ninth; the same author's six
books *De causis plantarum*; then the *Problems* of Aristotle and Alexander of Aphrodisias; then follow Aristotle's *Mechanica* and fourteen books of his *Metaphysics*, and finally Theophrastus' short work
on *Metaphysics*. In printing I have taken care that, if anyone thinks
the sequence should be different from the one I have adopted, they
could easily arrange it to suit themselves. You will learn elsewhere
why we have adopted the present sequence.[142] Like other scholars
you may be quite sure that the whole of this difficult and expensive enterprise is managed with the highest standards of accuracy.

If at any point this appears not to be the case, because some- 3
thing could have been better presented, try not to be ungrateful,
because I labor for you night and day to the limit of my strength
and beyond. But I do it very willingly, and having begun I shall
not give up until I have made good my promise. I will definitely
spare no expense, however substantial; I shall make light of all the
effort, even if I could live a life of pleasure and permanent relaxation. You are the best witness to judge whether I prefer the labors
of Hercules and his demanding tasks to erotic pleasure, the banquets and the featherbeds of Sardanapalus.[143] Man is born to
toil,[144] always to perform tasks worthy of human beings, not for
pleasure, which is for wild beasts and cattle.

So you, prince, do very well to follow the example of Hercules, 4
offspring of Jupiter, who in his first youth, the time when nature
allows us to choose which path each of us will follow, saw two
roads, one leading to virtue, the other to pleasure, and chose the
road toward virtue.[145] So continue the study of philosophy as you
have begun, and set an example to others, because if kings are
philosophers, cities would have the best government. Keep well.

: X :

A

Aldus Manutius Romanus studiosis omnibus s. p. d.

1 Constitueram τὰ τῶν Ἑλλήνων λεξικά, quae dictionaria Latine possumus dicere, non prius publicare excusa typis nostris quam copiosissima emendatissimaque haberem. Verum, cum id perquam difficile esse cognoscerem non mihi solum, negociis familiaribus impedito et re impressoria, sed etiam expeditissimo cuique atque utriusque linguae et liberalium artium medicinaeque et scientiarum omnium doctissimo, mutavi sententiam, quandoquidem et nosse cuncta oportet et dictiones omneis κατὰ κυριότητα interpretari; quod nescio an quisquam praestare nostro tempore praeter unum aut alterum possit, quo et Graecae et Latinae literae, licet meliuscule sese habeant quam multis anteactis annis, tamen adhuc iacent. Quis enim bene novit liberales artes? quis est simplicium rerum, quibus in medicina opus est, doctissimus? Heu heu pudet dicere: vix lactucas, brassicas, et quae vel caecis seipsam ostendit herbam cognoscimus. Quod ego cum cogito, etsi non possum non dolere vehementer, tamen non solum non succumbo dolori, sed sic accingor nocte dieque ad succurrendum, nullo devitato labore, ut sperem brevi futurum, quo et bonas artes omneis et medicinam ipsam calleant homines aetatis nostrae, valeatque studiosissimus quisque, nisi sibi ipse defuerit, cum antiquitate contendere. Doleant, maledicant, obstent, et quantum et quandiu velint, si qui sunt invidi, indocti et barbari; ἔσται ἔσται καλῶς.

: X :

Joannes Crastonus, Greek Dictionary
(*December 1497*)

A

Aldus Manutius of Rome to all students, warmest greetings.

I had decided not to issue in print from our house the lexica of the 1
Greeks, which we can call *dictionaria* in Latin, until I had them in
very full and correct form. But when I realized that it was extremely difficult, not only for me, hindered as I am by problems in
the family and in the printing shop, but even for anyone entirely
unhindered and fully qualified in both languages, the liberal arts,
medicine and all the sciences, I changed my mind. In fact one
needs to know everything and define each word according to its
primary meaning, which I doubt if anyone, apart from one or two
exceptions, can do in our own times, when Greek and Latin studies, though a little better off than for many years in the past, are
still depressed. Who is really proficient in the liberal arts? Who is
a master of the simple facts that are needed in medicine? Also,
alas — one is ashamed to say it — we scarcely distinguish lettuce,
cabbage and the plant that even the blind recognize. When I think
of this I cannot help feeling very sorry, but I do not give way to
grief. I also prepare myself to help night and day, with no pains
spared, with the result that I hope there will soon come a time
when men of our generation will be skilled in all the liberal arts
and medicine itself; and all the best scholars, unless they let themselves down, will have the strength to challenge antiquity. If there
are any jealous, uncivilized ignoramuses, let them feel pain, curse
us, obstruct us as much and as long as they like. It will turn out
well, it will.

2   Accipite nunc igitur, quod pro tempore damus, duplex uno
volumine dictionarium, ubi quid sit additum, in fronte libri licet
videre. Si qua item facta sint meliora, legentes cognoscite; et expectate magnum etymologicum, Sudam, Pollucem, Pausaniam,
Stephanum et caeteros bonos, quos cura nostra impressos brevi
publicare est animus; expectate deinceps optimos quosque Graecos. Nunc aere nostro decem Aristophanis comoediae cum optimis commentariis excuduntur, Sudas item, omnesque in uno volumine doctissimorum epistolae. Mox aggrediemur Hermogenis
rhetorica et Aphthonii progymnasmata, et in eos ipsos et in Aristotelem commentarios, necnon Galeni quaecunque extant in medicina.

3   Sed quanquam certo scio dicturos plerosque, cum nostras has
pollicitationes legerint, Ovidianum illud: 'Pollicitis dives quilibet
esse potest,' id tamen fero aequo animo, quandoquidem, volente
Christo Iesu Deo nostro optimo maximo, et haec et multo maiora
videbunt, quae paro, quae molior.

4   Vestrum est interea, studiosi et amici fautoresque provinciae
nostrae, si cupitis Aldum vestrum opem vobis et pereunti doctrinae impressorio aere facilius allaturum, aere vestro emere libros
nostros. Ne parcite impensae: sic enim brevi omnia dabimus. Et
mementote quod praecepit optimus poeta Hesiodus:

Καὶ δόμεν ὅς κεν δῷ, καὶ μὴ δόμεν ὅς κεν μὴ δῷ.
δώτῃ μέν τις ἔδωκεν, ἀδώτῃ δ' οὔτις ἔδωκεν.

So now receive what we offer for the time being, a double dic- 2
tionary in one volume;[146] from the first page you can see what additions have been made; ascertain as you read what improvements
there are, and look forward to the *Etymologicum Magnum*, Suidas,
Pollux, Pausanias,[147] Stephanus and the other good authorities,
which it is our intention to issue soon, edited and printed by ourselves. After that, look forward to all the best Greek authors. At
present ten plays of Aristophanes[148] with excellent commentaries
are being printed at our expense, likewise Suidas, and all the correspondence of cultivated writers in a single volume. Next we shall
tackle Hermogenes' rhetorical treatises and the introductory course
book by Aphthonius, the commentaries on them and on Aristotle,
plus all that has survived of Galen on medicine.[149]

But though I am sure most people, on reading these promises 3
of ours, will quote Ovid's line: "Anyone can be rich in promises,"[150]
I shall take it calmly, since with the goodwill of Jesus Christ our
Lord, the best and greatest, they will see both these books and
others much more substantial, which I am preparing and planning.

In the meantime it is up to you, students, friends and support- 4
ers of our profession, if you want your Aldus to find it easier to
help you and our endangered culture by means of the money in-
vested in printing, to purchase our books. Do not spare expense,
because then we will quickly provide everything. And remember
the saying of the excellent poet Hesiod:

Καὶ δόμεν ὅς κεν δῷ, καὶ μὴ δόμεν ὅς κεν μὴ δῷ.
δώτῃ μέν τις ἔδωκεν, ἀδώτῃ δ᾽ οὔτις ἔδωκεν.

Hoc est:

> Da tibi qui dederit, qui non dederit tibi ne da;
> danti aliquis dedit, at non danti non dedit ullus.

Ἔρρωσθε.

B

Ad lectorem.

5   Cum indicem istum, quem impressum vides, studiose lector, componere cogitarem, etsi nec impensae parum nec laboris mihi futurum sciebam, tamen, ut te et caeteros, qui Graecas literas discere concupiscitis, quocunque possem modo iuvarem, contempsi utrunque. Hinc enim, cum dicere Graece aliquid voles, discere facile poteris, et multa etiam multis modis. Quod siquid tam in dictionario Graeco quam in hoc indice frustra a te quaesitum fuerit, quia videlicet plurima desint, id aequo animo ferre debes, tum quia multo plures res esse quam vocabula non es nescius, tum etiam quoniam infinitas prope Graecas dictiones in unum cogere est cuivis magis arduum quam vitium nomina recensere Virgilio fuerit, qui sic in *Georgicis:*

> Sed neque quam multae species nec nomina quae sint
> est numerus; neque enim numero comprendere refert.
> Quem qui scire velit, Libyci velit aequoris idem
> discere quam multae zephyro turbentur arenae,
> aut ubi navigiis violentior incidit eurus,
> nosse quot Ionii veniant ad littora fluctus.

6   Sed quo facilius quod quaeris invenire possis, nota tibi in extremitate libri arithmeticis numeris singulas chartas; et scias c. literam in indice significare chartam, et numerum statim post c. esse

That is:

> Give to him who gives, do not give to him who does not;
> people give to a donor, no one gives to the nondonor.[151]

Keep well.

B

To the reader.[152]

When I was thinking of compiling this index which you see 5
printed, studious reader, although I knew there would be no small
expense and labor for me, nevertheless, in order to help you and
all the others anxious to learn Greek in whatever way possible, I
made light of both factors. When you want to say something in
Greek—and many things in many ways—you will easily learn
how to do it with this book. If you fail to find something in the
Greek dictionary and in this index, because obviously there are
many gaps, you must acquiesce with a good grace, partly because
you know that there are many more objects than words, partly
because collecting the almost infinite Greek vocabulary in one
work is harder for anyone than it was for Vergil to name all varie-
ties of grapes, as he puts it in the *Georgics*:

> There is no number for their variety or their names,
> nor is it important to enumerate them.
> Anyone who wished to know should wish to learn how many
> grains of sand on the Libyan shore are disturbed by the west
> wind,
> or when the more violent east wind falls upon ships,
> to know how many waves in Ionia beat on the shore.[153]

But to make it easier to find what you need, take note of indi- 6
vidually numbered leaves at the end of the volume. Note that the
letter *c* in the index means *charta*, and the numeral immediately

chartarum numerum, et qui post illum sequitur ostendere versiculum, ac omnes reliquos deinceps versiculum significare, si forte
post numerum versiculi, antequam iterum c. literae occurras, sit
alius numerus: nam saepe accidit ut idem vocabulum quonam
modo Graece dicatur, bis et ter in eadem charta inveniri queat.
Chartam vero intellige totum quod patens vides aperto libro, hoc
est columnas quatuor; et primos quatuor versiculos columnarum,
unum versum; secundos item quatuor, unum, et deinceps caeteros:
semper quatuor unum accipe. Cum igitur mitteris ad primum
versum, vide an sit quod quaeris in primo versu primae columnae;
quod si ibi non fuerit, vide singulos primos caeterarum columnarum, et sic in caeteris.

7   Sed quod diximus fiat exemplo manifestius. Prudens dicitur
Graece in dictionario modis quinque et triginta; quae dictio sic est
⟨in⟩ indice: Prudens c. 3. 39 [. . .]. Et similiter in caeteris. Vale.

: XI :

Aldus Manutius Romanus Ioanni Francisco Pico Mirandulae s. d.

1 Cogitanti mihi iandiu, Ioannes Francisce Pice, aliquem ex libris
nostra cura impressis in tuo nomine publicare, tum ut ostenderem
te, quem puerum olim ob egregiam indolem diligebam, nunc
virum et doctum et sanctis ornatum moribus amari a nobis co-
lique ac observari plurimum, tum quod Picus meus tibi patruus
fuerit, ille ille inquam Picus, quem ob singularem doctrinam phoe-
nicem omnes uno ore appellabant, visum est ab istis optimis in

after the *c* is the leaf number; the number which follows indicates
the line, and all the rest indicate the number of the line if after the
line number there is another numeral before the next *c*. For it often turns out that the rendering of a word into Greek in two or
three ways can be found on the same leaf. By leaf you must understand the whole of what you see when the book lies open, that is
to say four columns. The first four lines at the top form one "line,"
the second four another, and so on; always take the four as a unit.
So when you are referred to "line 1" see if what you are looking for
is in the first line of the first column; if it is not, look at the first
lines of the remaining columns, and similarly for the rest.

What we have said may be made clearer by an example. Ac-   7
cording to the dictionary *prudens* is expressed in Greek in thirty-
five ways. The word is given as follows in the index: *prudens* 3.39
[. . .].[154] Similarly for the remainder. Farewell.

: XI :

Urbano da Belluno, Greek Grammar
(January 1498)

*Aldus Manutius of Rome to Giovanni Francesco
Pico della Mirandola, greetings.*

I had been thinking for some time of dedicating one of our   1
printed books to you, Giovanni Francesco Pico. This was partly to
prove that the child for whose great talent I showed affection in
the past is now an adult,[155] educated and endowed with blameless
character, and is greatly loved, respected and revered by us, partly
because my friend Pico was your uncle—I mean the Pico whom
the public with one accord called "the phoenix" on account of his

Graecam linguam introductionibus incipere. Nam, cum scirem te Graecas literas discendi percupidum idemque acciperem ab Alexandro Sarcio Bononiensi, integerrimo viro ac optimo, ut aiunt, amici amico et tui quam studiosissimo, hunc optimum fore librum existimavi, ubi facile ac brevi quod cupis queas efficere.

2   In eo enim de nomine et verbo et caeteris orationis partibus sic copiose tractatur, ut nihil quod necessarium Graece discere incipientibus videretur praetermiserit Urbanus meus, divi Francisci sacerdos optimus ac integerrimus, qui ad communem omnium et Latinorum maxime utilitatem istas institutiones meo rogatu, ac impulsu potius, composuit. Accipe igitur munusculum nostrum qua fronte cuncta literatorum soles, non quod te dignum sit, sed quia tu humanissimus. Vale.

: XII :

Aldus Manutius Romanus Alberto Pio Carporum
principi s. p. d.

1   Iure quidem, Alberte princeps inclyte, logicos physicosque Aristotelis libros cura nostra formis excusos sub tuo nomine publicavimus, quoniam tu illis assidue sic das operam, ut iam excellas iudicio doctorum hominum. Sed longe convenientius morales hos oeconomicosque ac politicos Aristotelis libros tibi dicamus, cum sis et princeps, et ad regendum natus princeps, atque optimis moribus et doctrina praeditus. Accipe igitur et hos, qua fronte

unique learning.[156] I have decided to begin with this excellent text-book of Greek grammar. Since I knew that you were very keen to learn Greek and heard the same from Alessandro Sarti of Bologna,[157] a most honorable man and very loyal as a friend to his friends, as they say, besides being a great admirer of yours. I decided this would be the best book, from which you could quickly and easily satisfy your wishes.

In it there is a full treatment of the noun, verb and other parts 2 of speech, so that nothing which seemed essential for beginners in Greek has been omitted by my friend Urbano, an excellent and most honorable Franciscan.[158] He has composed at my request, or rather at my urging, this textbook for the general benefit of everyone, and especially speakers of Latin. So give this modest gift the same reception as you grant to all the works of the educated, not because it is worthy of you but out of your great kindness. Farewell.

: XII :

Aristotle, Moral Philosophy
(June 1498)

*Aldus Manutius of Rome to Alberto Pio, prince of Carpi,
warmest greetings.*

It was right, noble prince Alberto, to dedicate to you our printed 1 edition of Aristotle's books on logic and physics, since your continuous study of them has now made you an expert in the opinion of scholars. But it is much more appropriate to dedicate to you these works by Aristotle on ethics, economics and politics, since you are a prince, a prince born to reign, and of excellent character and education. So accept these as well, with the same goodwill as

caeteros philosophi libros sub tuo editos nomine accepisti. His enim libris quonam modo se quisque optime regat triplici editione Aristoteles docet; item quemadmodum res privata et familia, res publica et civitas gubernanda sit, docte et prudenter ostendit. Haec omnia nos summa cura et diligentia compressa tradimus; quanquam ad Eudemum moralia, quia unum duntaxat exemplar habere potuimus, offendent nonnunquam et tuas et aliorum doctissimas aures; item oeconomica potius fragmenta quaedam quam liber integer et absolutus videbuntur.

2   Atque utinam id omne, quod est a Leonardo Aretino in Latinum traductum, dare potuissem! quod ut haberemus, Romam, Florentiam, Mediolanum, in Graeciam, ad ipsos quoque divisos toto orbe Britannos — et quo non? — misimus, nec nisi quod etiam Venetiis habebatur accepimus. Atque hic est sextus mensis ex quo pene absolutos hos libros, dum id, quod deerat, expectaremus, non sine magno incommodo intermisimus: hoc est secundum a Leonardo tralatum librum, qui Latine incipit: 'Probam mulierem.' Qui cum a nobis nusquam inveniretur, in eius locum aliud quoddam, etsi ad politica magis quam ad oeconomica spectare videtur, studiosis damus, daturi et id parum quod deest, cum primum haberi poterit.

3   Videant igitur quidam vel ingrati vel invidi vel malevoli, quam sit difficile qualescunque, nedum emendatos, imprimendos curare Aristotelis libros caeterorumque illustrium perraros inventu. Sed semper mundus fuit malus, semper ingratus benefactoribus. Non miror itaque, si in mundi odium evectus Sotades in haec carmina erupit:

Αὐτὸς γὰρ ἐὼν παντογενὴς ὁ πάντα γεννῶν
οὐ κρίνει δικαίως τὰ κατ᾽ ἄνθρωπον ἕκαστον·
καὶ γὰρ κατὰ γαῖαν τὰ κακὰ πέφυκεν αἰεί,
καὶ τοῖς μεγάλοις ἀεὶ κακοῖς γέγηθ᾽ ὁ κόσμος,

you accepted the philosopher's other works dedicated to you. In them Aristotle gives instruction in three different forms on how each of us should behave; and in well-informed and judicious manner he shows how private and family life, how the state and the city should be governed. All this we offer, assembled with great care and attention. However, the *Eudemian Ethics* will in some places offend your ears, and those of other scholars, because we were only able to find a single exemplar; and the *Oeconomica* will look more like fragments than a complete fully preserved text.[159]

I wish I had been able to offer everything that was translated by   2
Leonardo Bruni into Latin.[160] To obtain it we wrote to Rome, Florence, Milan, Greece, even to the Britons who are separated from the whole world[161] — and where did we not write to? But we received only what was available in Venice.[162] It is now five months since we put aside this almost finished edition, which was very inconvenient, while we waited for the missing material; it is the second book translated by Bruni, which begins in Latin *Probam mulierem*.[163] Since we could not trace it anywhere, in its place we offer students something else, even if it seems more concerned with politics than economics;[164] we shall provide the small amount that is missing as soon as it can be found.

So let certain ungrateful, jealous and malicious people under-   3
stand how hard it is to print in any form, let alone without faults, books by Aristotle and other famous writers that are very rarely to be found. But it has always been a wicked world, always ungrateful to benefactors. So I am not surprised that Sotades broke into verse to express his hatred of the world.[165]

> The creator of all, who himself gives life to everything,
> is not just in his judgments of individual men.
> In fact there has always been evil on earth,
> and the cosmos for ever takes delight in great evils,

ὅτι πάντες ὅσοι περισσὸν ἠθέλησαν εὑρεῖν
ἢ μηχανικὸν πόνημ' ἢ σοφὸν μάθημα,
οὗτοι κακὸν εἰς τὸν θάνατον τέλος ἐποίησαν,
ὑπὸ τοῦ γεννήτορος κόσμου κακῶς παθόντες.
Σωκράτην ὁ κόσμος πεποίηκε σοφὸν εἶναι,
καὶ κακῶς ἀνεῖλε τὸν Σωκράτην ὁ κόσμος,
ἐν τῇ φυλακῇ κώνειον ὅτι πιὼν τέθνηκεν.
Πουλύποδα φαγὼν ὁ Διογένης ὠμὸν τέθνηκεν.
Αἰσχύλῳ γράφοντι ἐπιπέπτωκε χελώνη.
Σοφοκλῆς ῥᾶγα φαγὼν σταφυλῆς πνιγεὶς τέθνηκε.
Κύνες οἱ κατὰ Θράκην Εὐριπίδην ἔτρωγον.
Τὸν θεῖον Ὅμηρον λιμὸς κατεδαπάνησεν.

4   Quanquam mihi, in tanto odio et invidia improborum hominum, id valde gaudendum est, quod industria nostra potissimum
maximisque laboribus effectum est quod maxime cupiebamus: ut
scilicet reiiciendas ineptias et barbariem Graecisque auctoribus et
bonis artibus dandam operam iam omnes, qui recto sunt iudicio,
censeant coeperintque plurimi exemplaria Graeca nocturna versare
manu versare diurna. Gaudendumque vel id plurimum mihi est,
cum tu praeclarus ac doctus princeps de hac provincia nos multum
ames, fortiter tuearis, pie foveas. Vale, decus et praesidium nostrum.

because all who have wished to make advances,
either with a mechanical device or a wise doctrine,
all came to a bad end in death, suffering badly
from the cosmos that had created them.
The cosmos made Socrates a wise man,
and the cosmos destroyed Socrates in evil fashion,
because he died in prison after drinking hemlock.
Diogenes died after eating raw octopus,
a tortoise landed on Aeschylus as he was writing,
Sophocles died when he choked on a grape from a bunch,
the dogs of Thrace ate Euripides,
hunger consumed the divine Homer.

Yet in the midst of such hatred and jealousy on the part of the   4
wicked I take great delight in the fact that our main ambition has
been achieved, thanks principally to our industry and hard work: I
mean that all men of good judgment now understand the need to
reject trivialities and lack of culture, to give attention to Greek
authors and the liberal arts; that very many people are beginning
to turn the pages of Greek texts night and day.[166] It is a particular
source of pleasure to me that you, a distinguished and learned
prince, display toward us great affection, powerful protection and
devoted support for this enterprise. Farewell, source of fame and
protection for me.[167]

: XIII :

Aldus Manutius Romanus Danieli Clario Parmensi s. p. d.

1 Perbeati illi mihi videntur, Clari, vir doctissime, qui hoc tempore in summa bonorum librorum copia liberalibus disciplinis operam daturi Graece discunt. Facile enim ac brevi Graecam linguam, nisi ipsi sibi defuerint, consequentur, in qua multis saeculis nullus fere ex Latinis, culpa magis temporum quam ingeniorum, excelluit; facillime, Graecis literis adiutricibus, omnium laudatarum artium procreatricem philosophiam callebunt, nec medicinam minus.

2 Errant meo iudicio multum, qui se bonos philosophos medicosque evasuros hoc tempore existimant, si expertes fuerint literarum Graecarum: quibus et Aristoteles quicquid ad dialecticen, ad philosophiam et naturalem et transnaturalem et moralem, quicquid ad rhetoricen et poeticen pertinet, doctissime scripsit; et Ammonius, Simplicius, Themistius, Alexander Aphrodisieus, Philoponus, Eustrathius, et caeteri peripateticae sectae eruditissimi viri, omnia quaecunque vel scientiae pervestigatione vel disserendi ratione comprehenderat Aristoteles, optime ac luculentissime commentati sunt; quibus item Hippocrates, Galenus, Paulus, et alii in medicina excellentissimi viri, omnia quae ad medicae artis spectant cognitionem, copiosissime verissimeque literis commendarunt. Non aliis quam Graecis literis ii, qui mathematici vocantur, artem suam obscuram, reconditam, multiplicem subtilemque facillimam cognitu posteris tradiderunt; quo in genere permulti, ut Architas, Ptolemaeus, Nicomachus, Porphyrius, Euclides, perfecti homines

: XIII :

Aristophanes, Nine Comedies
(*July 13, 1498*)

*Aldus Manutius of Rome to Daniele Clario of Parma,
warmest greetings.*[168]

Extremely fortunate in my opinion, most learned Clario, are those 1
who now have a full supply of good books and learn Greek when
they are about to devote themselves to the liberal arts. With ease
and speed, unless they fail to do justice to themselves, they will
learn Greek, in which practically no Latin speaker excelled for
many centuries, owing to the circumstances rather than any lack of
ability; with the aid of Greek literature they will easily become
proficient in philosophy, the mother of all reputable arts, and
equally in medicine.

In my opinion those who think they can nowadays become 2
good philosophers and doctors without knowledge of Greek are
making a serious mistake. Aristotle wrote very learnedly in Greek
about all matters of dialectic, philosophy — natural, metaphysical
and moral —, rhetoric and poetry. Excellent and clear commentary
on everything Aristotle dealt with in his scientific investigations or
his method of reasoning has been written by Ammonius, Simplicius, Themistius, Alexander of Aphrodisias, Philoponus, Eustratius and the other erudite members of the Peripatetic school.[169]
Similarly Hippocrates, Galen, Paul[170] and other outstanding doctors have given a full and accurate account of all topics required for
a knowledge of medicine. It was in Greek, not in other languages,
that those who are called mathematicians handed down to future
generations their obscure, recondite, complex and subtle art, not
making it easy to acquire. In this field a great many, such as Ar-
chytas, Ptolemy, Nicomachus, Porphyry[171] and Euclid attained

extiterunt. Quae omnia quam depravate et corrupte, quam muti-
late et perperam, ut taceam etiam quam barbare et inepte Latinis
scripta sint, quis vel mediocriter eruditus ignorat?

3   Sed brevi spero futurum ut, explosa barbarie reiectisque inep-
tiis, bonis literis verisque disciplinis non, ut nunc, a paucissimis,
sed uno consensu ab omnibus incumbatur. En erit tandem ut,
glande neglecta, inventis vescamur frugibus.

4   Optime igitur tu, mi Clari, in praestanti ista et opulenta urbe
Ragusio iuventuti consulis, qui eam et Graece et Latine simul, ut
praecipit Quintilianus, summo studio ac fide iam multos annos
publico conductus stipendio doces. Quod ut tibi factu facilius sit,
mitto ad te Aristophanem, ut illum non modo legendum, sed ediscendum quoque discipulis praebeas tuis; quem etiam in tuo nomine publicare voluimus, ut coniunctionem studiorum amorisque
nostri quo possem munere declararem, et praesertim cum tu, etsi
de facie nos non novimus, assiduis tamen me afficias beneficiis.
Essem profecto ingratissimus, si te valde amantem non redama-
rem.

5   Accipe igitur novem Aristophanis fabulas: nam decimam, Ly-
sistraten, ideo pratermisimus, quia vix dimidiata haberi a nobis
potuit. Sint satis hae novem cum optimis et antiquis, ut vides,
commentariis; quibus Graece discere cupientibus nihil aptius, nihil melius legi potest, non meo solum iudicio, quod non magnifa-
cio, sed etiam Theodori Gazae, viri undecunque doctissimi, qui,
interrogatus quis ex Graecis auctoribus assidue legendus foret
Graecas literas discere volentibus, respondit: 'Solus Aristophanes,'
quod esset sane quam acutus, copiosus, doctus et merus Atticus.
Hunc item Ioannes Chrysostomus tanti fecisse dicitur, ut duode-
triginta comoedias Aristophanis semper haberet in manibus, adeo
ut pro pulvillo dormiens uteretur; hinc itaque et eloquentiam et

perfection. Anyone with even a little knowledge is aware of how all these texts have degenerated and been corrupted and mutilated, how they have been faultily, not to say barbarously and incompetently, rendered into Latin.

But I hope it will soon be the case that barbarism will be banished and incompetence rejected, with good literature and serious disciplines cultivated universally by general agreement, not just by the few as at present. Then at last the result will be to give up acorns and feed on the crops we have discovered.[172]

So, my dear Clario, you are performing a great service for the young people of that important and rich city Ragusa[173] by teaching them Greek and Latin, as Quintilian recommends.[174] You have taught there for many years, paid by the city, with enthusiasm and loyalty. To make your task easier I am sending you Aristophanes so that you can present him to your pupils, not merely to be read but to be studied thoroughly.[175] We wished to dedicate it to you, in order to declare, by means of the gift I could offer, our shared interests and mutual respect,[176] especially since you do me regular favors even though we have not met. I should indeed be most ungrateful if I did not reciprocate your great friendship.

Here therefore are nine plays by Aristophanes; the tenth, *Lysistrata*, we omitted because barely half of it could be obtained.[177] Let these nine be sufficient, with ancient and excellent commentaries, as you can see.[178] For people wishing to learn Greek there is nothing more suitable, nothing better to read. And that is not simply my opinion, but that of Theodore Gaza,[179] a man of much learning in all fields. When he was asked which Greek author should be read assiduously by people wishing to learn Greek he said: "Only Aristophanes," because he was very witty, rich, erudite and pure in his Attic language. John Chrysostom is said to have had such a high opinion of him that he always had twenty-eight comedies of Aristophanes to hand and used them as a pillow when sleeping; which is how he is said to have acquired the

severitatem, quibus est mirabilis, didicisse dicitur. Ego sic assidue legendum a Graecis censeo Aristophanem, ut a nostris Terentium: quem quod semper legeret, M. Tullius familiarem suum appellabat. Vale.

Venetiis tertio idus Iulias M.IID.

: XIV :

Aldus Manutius Romanus Antonio Codro Urceo s. p. d.

1 Collegimus nuper, Codre doctissime, quotquot habere potuimus Graecas epistolas, easque typis nostris excusas duobus libris publicamus, praeter multas illas Basilii, Gregorii et Libanii, quas, cum primum fuerit facultas, imprimendas domi servamus. Auctores vero, quorum epistolas damus, sunt numero circiter quinque et triginta, ut in ipsis libris licet videre. Has ad te, qui et Latinas et Graecas litteras in celeberrimo Bononiensi gymnasio publice profiteris, muneri mittimus, tum ut a te discipulis ostendantur tuis, quo ad cultiores litteras capessendas incendantur magis, tum ut apud te sint Aldi tui μνημόσυνον et pignus amoris. Vale.

Venetiis quintodecimo calendas Maias M.ID.

elegance and solemnity for which he is remarkable.[180] I think Greeks ought to read Aristophanes as assiduously as we read Terence, whom Cicero termed a close friend because he was always reading him.[181] Farewell.

Venice, July 13, 1498.

: XIV :

The Greek Epistolographers[182]
(April 17, 1499)

Aldus Manutius of Rome to Antonio Codro Urceo,[183] warmest greetings.

We have recently collected, learned Codro, all the Greek letters we   1
could find and we now issue them from our press in two volumes, with the exception of the numerous letters of Basil, Gregory and Libanius, which we retain in house, to be printed as soon as occasion offers.[184] But the authors whose letters we offer number about thirty-five, as can be seen from the volumes themselves. We send them as a present to you as the holder of the official chair of Greek and Latin in the distinguished university of Bologna, so that you may show them to your pupils, thus further encouraging them to pursue their literary studies to a higher level, and so that the volumes may remind you of your friend Aldus and serve as a sign of his affection. Farewell.

Venice, April 17, 1499.

: XV :

Aldus Manutius Romanus Hieronymo Donato patritio Veneto s. d.

1 Nescio quid sit, Donate, vir integerrime, addo etiam doctissime,
quod ex eo tempore, quo non parvo meo incommodo et labore
renascentibus in Italia bonis litteris quocunque potui modo coepi
opem afferre, omnia mihi adversa, nunc hominum perfidia, nunc
temporum infelicitate, contigerint; nisi id Graecorum infortunio
adscribendum est, quod erumnosi futuri sint quicunque ex nostris
Graecitati opitulantur. Quod etsi quidam ioco solent dicere, multis tamen id ita esse probari exemplis potest.

2 Quod vero maiore in dies animo perstiterim in proposito et
nunc maxime perstem, illud saepe commemorans: 'Tu ne cede
malis, sed contra audentior ito,' mecum ipse demiror, atque eo magis, cum excrucier ac pene opprimar laboribus, et iuvet op⟨p⟩rimi,
iuvet esse miserum. 'Video meliora proboque, deteriora sequor':
nam tempus, rem quam carissimam, perdens, mihi obsum, ut aliis
prosim; sed feram aequo animo mea damna, dum prosim, nec, si
vixero, ab incoeptis unquam desistam, donec quod semel statutum
mihi est perfecero. Et quanquam maiora viribus aggressi sumus,
cum domi nostrae ea ad Latinam Graecamque et Hebraicam
linguam formis publicandam summo studio assiduoque labore
cudantur, quae admirationi omnibus futura speremus, tamen —
faveat Deus — bene ac pulchre omnia perficientur.

: XV :

Dioscorides, The Materials of Medicine
Nicander, Theriaca and Alexipharmaca
(*July 8, 1499*)

Aldus Manutius of Rome to Girolamo Donà,[185]
Venetian patrician, greetings.

I do not know why, most honorable (and I would add most   1
learned) Donà, but since I began to assist as best I could the revival of literary studies in Italy, with no small inconvenience and
effort, everything has been against me, partly because of human
dishonesty, partly because of the disasters of the age — unless it is
to be put down to the fortunes of the Greeks that anyone who
helps Greek interests will be unlucky. Although some people say
this in jest, it can be demonstrated by many facts.

With ever-increasing determination I persevere in my aim, and   2
now especially I persist, regularly bearing in mind, "Do not give
way to adversity, but oppose it with greater courage."[186] I am surprised at myself, all the more since I am hard pressed and almost
overwhelmed by my labors, content to be oppressed, content to be
unhappy. "I can see the better course and I applaud it, but I follow
the inferior."[187] Losing time, the most precious thing of all, I hurt
myself in order to be of benefit to others; but provided I am of
benefit I will accept my losses with a good grace; and, if I survive,
I will never, having begun, give up before completing what was
originally planned. Although I have taken on more than I can
manage, since type is being cast in my house for printing Latin,
Greek and Hebrew,[188] with great enthusiasm and continuous labor — we hope it will be admired by all — nevertheless everything
(may God favor us) will be brought to completion in good and
elegant form.

3   Interea Dioscoridem ac Nicandrum damus, rati gratissimos atque utilissimos fore studiosis omnibus, atque iis maxime, qui sunt
in Pliniana lectione versati. Scis enim plurima esse in Dioscoride,
quae mutuatus videtur Plinius, quod utrunque saepe legeris al-
terumque cum altero accurate contuleris. Hunc igitur librum, quo
plus auctoritatis foret hisce laboribus nostris, in tuo nomine aere
nostro excusum publicare voluimus, quod tibi humanissimo omnium non ingratum fore existimabamus. Quare velim hunc etiam
benigna fronte suscipias, meque de hoc quoque labore, ut facis,
ames.

4   Quanquam illud fortasse in Dioscoride displicebit: simplicia
quaedam, quae aliis quam Graecis appellantur nominibus, in contextu esse inserta; eaque in margine potius imprimenda fuisse
censebis. Sed id nos idcirco fecimus, quoniam in contextu in omnibus ea legimus exemplaribus; praeterea quia non absurdum videbatur, etiam quo apud alias gentes nomine simplicia appellarentur,
Dioscoridem voluisse docere: et praesertim cum ipse militem se
fuisse ac multam terram peragrasse dicat in prooemio. Sed in con-
textune an in margine legantur, parvi referre existimo. Illud magis
puto dolendum: nonnulla ex iis nominibus esse incorrecta; quae
tamen unusquisque sibi, correctius nactus exemplar, emendare
poterit. Nos, quae habere potuimus, dedimus. Vale.

Venetiis octavo idus Iulias M.ID.

In the meantime we offer Dioscorides and Nicander, reckoning   3
they will be most useful to all scholars, and particularly those who
are well versed in Pliny. You know that there is a great deal in
Dioscorides which Pliny seems to have taken over;[189] you should
read both of them repeatedly and carefully, comparing one with
the other. So we decided to dedicate this book, printed at our expense, to you, in order to lend greater authority to these labors of
ours; we reckoned that to you, as a person of great humanity, it
would not be unwelcome. So I should like you to give a kind reception to it and display your customary affection for me on account of this effort as well.

Yet one feature in Dioscorides may disappoint: some substances   4
with non-Greek names are inserted in the text, and you may think
that they should have been printed in the margin.[190] But we did
this because we found them in the text in all the manuscripts; besides which it did not seem absurd that Dioscorides should have
wished to state additionally the names by which substances are
known in other nations, especially as he tells us in his preface that
he was a soldier and had traveled to many parts of the world. But
I do not think it matters much whether they are read in the text or
in the margin. However, I do think it regrettable that some of the
names are incorrect; but each reader, finding a better copy, will be
able to correct them for himself. We have provided what we could
find. Farewell.

Venice, July 8, 1499.

: XVI :

Aldus Manutius Romanus Alberto Pio Carporum principi s. p. d.

1 Etsi scio a plerisque me tarditatis crimine accusari, Alberte, praesidium meum, quod plurimum differre videar, quae toties pollicitus sum studiosis dare, tamen has literatorum querelas aequo
animo ferendas ducimus, tum quia possum vel graviora perferre,
dum prosim, tum etiam quod sum ipse mihi optimus testis me
semper habere comites, ut oportere aiunt, delphinum et ancoram.
Nam et dedimus multa cunctando et damus assidue.

2   Cum igitur superioribus diebus curassem imprimenda Arati
phaenomena cum Theonis enarratione, visum est illis adiungere
Procli sphaeram, et eo magis quod eam Thomas Linacrus Britannus docte et eleganter Latinam nuper fecerit ad meque nostris ex-
cudenda formis miserit. Est enim opusculum iis, qui in astrono-
miam induci atque imbui cupiunt, utilissimum. Quod cum ipse
Linacrus noster, acri vir iudicio, percenseret, Arcturo principi suo
hoc a se tralatum opusculum nuncupavit, quod adolescens ille bonarum literarum studiosus astrologiae operam daret. Quamobrem
et nos id ipsum opusculum nostra cura impressum ad te legendum
mittimus, quod iam peripateticus mathematicis disciplinis navare

: XVI :

Julius Firmicus Maternus, Astronomica
Marcus Manilius, Astronomica
Aratus, Phaenomena
Proclus, Sphaera[191]
(October 14, 1499)

Aldus Manutius of Rome to Alberto Pio,
prince of Carpi, warmest greetings.

Although I am aware, Alberto — you are my great defender — of   1
being criticized by most people for tardiness, because I seem to
create long delay after frequent promises to provide for scholars,
nevertheless we feel it right to bear these complaints from the educated with equanimity, partly because I can endure worse provided
that I am giving help, partly because I am perfectly aware of having as my companions the dolphin and anchor,[192] as they say one
ought. In fact despite delays we have produced plenty and we
produce regularly.

So having seen to the printing of Aratus' *Phaenomena* with   2
Theon's commentary in the last few days, I took the decision to
add Proclus' *Sphaera,* particularly because the Englishman Thomas
Linacre had recently made a learned and stylish version in Latin
and sent it to me to be printed by our press. It is a short work of
great value to anyone wishing to be introduced to and immersed in
astronomy. Since our friend Linacre[193] himself took this view — he
is a man of acute judgment — he dedicated the version to his
prince Arthur,[194] because the young man, a student of good literature, was interested in astrology. Hence we too send you this short
work, which we have printed for you to read, since you have
now, like a Peripatetic philosopher, begun to devote attention to

operam coeperis. Quod eo etiam libentius leges, quod sit a Thoma Linacro summa tibi familiaritate coniuncto interpretatum.

3   Utinam et Simplicium in Aristotelis physica, et in eiusdem meteora Alexandrum, quos nunc summa cura Latinos facit, ad me dedisset, ut et illos una cum Proclo ad te mitterem! quanquam, ut spero, eosque et alios in philosophia medicinaque perutiles libros aliquando dabit, ut ex eadem Britannia, unde olim barbarae et indoctae literae ad nos profectae Italiam occuparunt et adhuc arces tenent, Latine et docte loquentes bonas artis accipiamus, ac Britannis adiutoribus fugata barbarie arces nostras recipiamus, ut eadem hasta sanetur, a qua illatum est, vulnus.

Horum ego Latinitatem et eloquentiam admiratus, Gulielmi Grocini, viri Graece etiam, nedum Latine peritissimi, atque undecunque doctissimi, quam ad me doctam quidem et elegantem dedit epistolam subiungere placuit, ut pudeat philosophos nostros barbare et inepte scribere, aemulatique Britannos, non dico grandaevi — γερόντιον γὰρ ψιττακὸς ἀμελεῖ σκυτάλην —, sed caeteri omnes Latine et docte philosophentur. Sed quod in ea me plurimum laudat, facit amice.

Venetiis, pridie idus Octobres M.ID.

mathematical subjects. You will enjoy reading it all the more because the translation is by your close friend Thomas Linacre.

I wish he had also given me Simplicius, *On Aristotle's Physics* and 3
Alexander on the same author's *Meteorologica*, which he is now rendering into Latin with great care.[195] I could have sent them to you along with Proclus. But in due course, I hope, he will produce these books and others of great value for philosophy and medicine. The result will be that from Britain, once the source of barbarian and ignorant attitudes that made their way in our direction, occupied Italy, and still possess our strongholds,[196] we may now acquire the liberal arts in scholarly and stylish Latin, so that with the help of Britons barbarism is banished and we recover our strongholds; the wound is cured by the same spear that caused it.[197]

Out of admiration for their Latinity and eloquence I decided to 4
add a learned and stylish letter sent to me by William Grocyn,[198] a great expert in Greek, not to mention Latin — to make our philosophers ashamed of writing in their barbarous and incompetent way; they should imitate Britons. I do not address this to the elderly — the aged parrot disregards the cane[199] — but everyone else should take up philosophy in stylish Latin. That he is exceedingly complimentary to me in his letter is a mark of friendship.

Venice, October 14, 1499.

: XVII :

A

Aldus Manutius Romanus Angelo Gabrieli patritio Veneto s. p. d.

1 Cum plurimis in rebus, Angele humanissime, novi te plenissimum amoris, humanitatis, officii, diligentiae, tum praecipue tua in Constantinum Lascarem Byzantinum, praeceptorem tuum, pietate, quem aeque semper amasti, coluisti, observasti ac patrem, non nescius longe magis praeceptoribus debere nos quam parentibus, quod a magno Alexandro dictum memorant. Nam, ex quo Messana, ad quam erudiendi gratia profectus fueras, rediisti Venetias linguae Graecae peritissimus—erat enim eo tempore Messana studiosis literarum Graecarum Athenae alterae propter Constantinum—, me nunquam destitisti rogare, ut secundum de constructione librum, et de nomine et verbo tertium, necnon de pronominibus κατὰ πᾶσαν διάλεκτον καὶ ποιητικὴν χρῆσιν opusculum Constantini nostri, nunquam ante impressos, typis nostris excudendos curarem. Quapropter, quod saepe me recepi facturum, en exeunt tandem in publicum tuo rogatu et ii quos volebas, secundus et tertius, et primus ter ante impressus. Interpretationem etiam Latinam sic addidimus, ut et amoveri a Graeco et insertari eidem facile possit pro uniuscuiusque arbitrio.

2 Sed illud non possum non dolere: non licuisse Constantino lucubrationes suas omnes cura nostra impressas ante videre quam e vita discederet; quod si accidisset, visus sibi fuisset superare omnium fortunas. Id ego et ex epistolis, quas ad me super ea re scripsit, facile perspexi, et quia librum tertium περὶ ὀνόματος καὶ

: XVII :

Constantine Lascaris, The Eight Parts of Speech
(*December 1501?*)

A

Aldus Manutius of Rome to Angelo Gabriele,[200]
patrician of Venice, warmest greetings.

In many affairs, most civilized Angelo, I have experienced your   1
great affection, kindness, sense of obligation and diligence, but especially your loyalty to your tutor Constantine Lascaris of Byzantium,[201] whom you have always loved, cultivated and respected as
much as a father, since you are not unaware that we owe far more
to our teachers than to our parents; that is recorded as a saying
of Alexander the Great.[202] Ever since you, already an expert in
Greek, returned to Venice from Messina, where you had gone to
be educated — Messina was then a second Athens for students of
Greek on account of Constantine — you have never ceased to ask
me to ensure the printing of the second book on syntax, his third
on nouns and verbs, and the short work by our friend Constantine
on pronouns in all dialects and in poetic usage. So now, as I promised on frequent occasions, here they are in print as you requested:
both the second and third books you asked for and the first, previously printed three times.[203] We have added a Latin version in
such a way that it can be separated from the Greek or easily inserted according to the wishes of the individual.

But there is one fact I am bound to regret, that Constantine   2
could not see all his works as printed by us before he passed
away;[204] if that had happened he would have thought himself the
happiest of men. That was plain to me from his letters to me on
the subject, and also because he concluded the third book on the

ῥήματος sic finivit: εἴη εὐτυχὲς ὥσπερ τὸ πρῶτον, quasi prae-
sagiens futurum ne non secundum et tertium libros suos, ante
quam moreretur, impressos videret, ut primum vidit. Atque hoc
illud est, quod mihi maxime dolet; etsi quicquid in illius interitu
mali accidit, non ipsi, sed nobis accidit, orbatis viro optimo et parente literarum Graecarum; quandoquidem haudquaquam dubito
quin, cum bene semper beateque vixerit, quiescat cum superis
fruaturque aeternum divinis.

3   Tu vero, mi Angele, ignoscas mihi velim, si grammaticos hosce
Constantini libros, apprime utiles studiosis futuros, non tam cito,
ut optabas et ipse volebam, imprimendos curarim. Non enim te
fugit, ne id facere possem, multa mihi fuisse impedimento, et praeter caetera dura haec tempora, quibus longe magis studetur armis
quam literis. Vale et me, ut facis, ama.

B

Aldus lectori s.

4   Si forte nescieris, studiose lector, quonam modo quae Graece
imprimenda curavimus cum interpretatione Latina ordinanda sint,
ut pagina paginae respondeat et versus versui, utpote qui videas
separatos quinterniones Graecos ab iis, qui Latinam ipsorum
continent tralationem, sic accipe: posse te pro arbitrio tuo Latinum Graeco insertare et ex duobus quinternionibus unum et ex
uno duos facere, si prius tamen adverteris, ut Latina pagina semper Graecae opponatur. Et quia binae eae quae in singulorum
quinternionum medio sitae sunt paginae abundabant, quoniam
nullas habebant oppositas Graecas, quas Latinas ostenderent, operae pretium duximus aliquid Graece lectu dignum cum Latino e
regione in ipsis, ne perirent, imprimendum curare. Quod si evenerit, ut ibi esse non potuerit quod Graece imprimebatur, quaeren-
dum reliquum in sequentium quinternionum medio. Cur vero

noun and the verb by saying, "May this have the same good fortune as the first," as if he foresaw that he would not see the second and third books in print, as he had seen the first. And this is what is especially painful for me. Yet whatever misfortune there was in his death affected us, not him, since we are deprived of an excellent man and the father of Greek studies. But I have no doubt at all that, as his life was always honorable and virtuous, he is resting in heaven and enjoying eternal blessings.

I hope you will excuse me, my dear Angelo, for not having 3 printed these grammatical treatises by Constantine, which will be so useful to students, as soon as you asked and I myself wished. You will realize that there were many obstacles preventing me — apart from everything else the difficult times we live in, in which wars receive far more attention than literature. Farewell, and love me as ever.

B

Aldus to the reader.[205]

In case you do not know, studious reader, how the Greek we 4 have printed is to be coordinated with the Latin translation, so that the pages and lines match (since you can see that the Greek quires are separate from those containing the Latin version of the same), here is the answer; you can insert the Greek into the Latin as you wish and make one quire from two or two from one, provided you first ensure that a Latin page always faces one in Greek. And since there were two spare pages in the middle of each quire because they had no Greek facing to match the Latin,[206] we thought it worthwhile to print something useful in Greek with Latin opposite, so that they should not be wasted. If it turns out that what was printed in Greek cannot[207] stand there, the remainder has to be sought in the middle of the following quires. You

curarimus, ut Latinum a Graeco separari queat, non te fugiat a
nobis ob id factum, ut et doctis, qui nullo egent adiumento legendis Graecis, et Graecarum literarum rudibus, qui, nisi Latinum e
regione in Graecis operibus viderint, a Graecorum librorum lectione deterrentur, satisfaceremus. Vale.

C

Aldus Manutius Romanus lectori salutem.

5   Etsi eram typicis literariisque negociis impeditus, ac immersus
potius, tamen, si Constantini Lascaris grammaticos libros in Latinum traducerem, non putaram multum difficultatis laborisque futurum. Sed plurimum certe fuit; quandoquidem, dum Constantini
Graecae linguae compendiarium facere Latinum studeo, adverti
et Theodori Gazae introductionem grammaticam et Apollonii
cognomento Difficilis et caeterorum pleraque, a quibus Constantinus accepit, in linguam nostram transferre me oportere. Adde
quod et nostri grammatici evolvendi fuerunt, et Priscianus praecipue, quem Latinum dicere Apollonium possumus. Nam, si cum
Prisciano Apollonium conferes, ubi de constructione tractavit —
caetera enim Prisciani non poteris, quia non extat integer Apollonius —, ad verbum fere tralatum a Prisciano Apollonium eleganter
quidem et erudite cognosces. Quod, dum in academia nostra Scipio Carteromachus Pistoriensis, homo et Graece et Latine doctissimus, quibusdam Apollonium interpretaretur, Nicolaus Zudecus,
gravis philosophus ac medicus et acuto vir ingenio, deprehendit.

6   Habere igitur in manibus inter traducendum Priscianum maxime oportuit, ut quibus nominibus Graecas quasdam dictiones
Latinas ille dixisset, et ipse dicerem. Sed me nullius unquam, dum
prosim, pigebit laboris.

should be aware of our reason for making it possible to separate the Latin from the Greek: it was to satisfy both the experts, who need no help in reading Greek, and beginners in Greek, who are deterred from reading Greek books if they do not see Latin facing the Greek texts. Farewell.

C

Aldus Manutius of Rome, to the reader.

Although I was occupied, or rather submerged by, literary and 5 typographical business, I had thought it would not be very difficult or laborious to translate Constantine Lascaris' books on grammar into Latin. But it really was extremely so. While I was trying to turn Constantine's short guide to the Greek language into Latin, I realized that I ought to translate into our language Theodore Gaza's introductory grammar, and the one by Apollonius who was known as Difficult,[208] plus many works by others on whom Constantine drew. In addition our grammarians needed to be read through, especially Priscian, whom we may call the Latin Apollonius. If you compare Apollonius with Priscian where he deals with syntax — the rest of Priscian you will not be able to compare, because Apollonius does not survive entire — you will see that Apollonius was translated almost word for word by Priscian in elegant and scholarly fashion. This fact was noticed by Niccolò Zudeco,[209] a sound philosopher, doctor and man of acute intelligence, at a time when Scipio Carteromachus[210] of Pistoia, an expert in both Greek and Latin, was interpreting Apollonius for some people in our Academy.

So while translating it was essential to have Priscian to hand so 6 that I too could use the Latin words he employed for certain Greek terms. But I shall never regret any labor if it serves a purpose.

87

7   Habes praeterea Cebetis Thebani tabulam et Graece et Latine
in singulorum quaternionum medio cura nostra impressam, opusculum lectu dignissimum et perquam utile, ⟨in quo vitae humanae
conditio ingeniose describitur, ostenditurque viam ad virtutem
angustam esse arduamque et laboris plenam, eumque qui ad eam
velit accedere, abstinentem in primis et constantem fore oportere,
ac tandem cum ad eam pervenerit, perpetua felicitate fruiturum;
contrariam, quae ducit ad vitia, latam esse quidem et planam ac
voluptatum plenam, sed tandem ducere in praecipitium atque ad
aeternam miseriam et infelicitatem.⟩ Id vero addidimus, tum ut
prodessem studiosis, tum ne charta, quae in singulorum quaternionum medio abundabat, periret. Vale.

D

Aldus studiosis s.

8   Quoniam Hebraicam linguam necessariam esse existimamus ad
sacrae scripturae cognitionem, nunc alphabetum et literarum com-
binationes et alia quaedam damus, quo legere Hebraice condisca-
tis. Deinceps institutiones grammaticas, dictionarium et sacros
libros, si haec placuisse cognovero, Deo volente, dabimus. Valete.

⁝ XVIII ⁝

Aldus Romanus salutem dicit Ioanni Taberio Brixiensi.

1   Quantum voluptatis ceperim, Taberi, cum in ista urbe populosis-
sima nobilissimaque Brixia plurimos summo studio incumbere literis Graecis te magistro accepi, non facile dixerim. Video enim

In addition you get the *Picture* by Cebes of Thebes,[211] in both 7
Greek and Latin, printed in the middle of each quire; it is a short
work, very well worth reading and extremely valuable. ⟨In it the
human condition is cleverly described; the path to virtue is shown
to be narrow, steep and full of toil; the man who wishes to take it
has to be ascetic above all and determined; when he finally arrives
he will enjoy perpetual happiness. The other path, leading to vice,
is broad, flat and full of pleasures, but in the end leads to a preci-
pice, to eternal misery and unhappiness.⟩[212] We added it for the
benefit of students and to avoid wasting the spare leaf in the middle of each quire. Farewell.

D

Aldus to students, greetings.

Since we consider the Hebrew language essential for the under- 8
standing of Holy Scripture, we now provide an alphabet, the
combinations of letters and some other material, so that you can
now learn to read Hebrew. In due course, God willing, we will
provide, if I find that these items have given satisfaction, a textbook of grammar, a dictionary and the sacred texts.[213] Farewell.

: XVIII :

Stephanus Byzantius, On Cities
(*March 18, 1502*)

Aldus of Rome to Giovanni Taberio of Brescia,[214] *greetings.*

I cannot easily say how pleased I was, Taberio, to hear that a great 1
many people in the populous and noble city of Brescia are studying Greek under your tuition. I see that events are turning out

longe melius, quam sperabam cum imprimendis Graecis libris navare operam coepi, evenire. In quo illud saepe cum amicis admirari
soleo: cum iam tot annos omnia ardeant armis et Christianorum
et infidelium—eodem enim anno, quo vexari bello coepit Italia,
difficillimam hanc ego imprimendorum librorum provinciam profuturus studiosis accepi—, sic incensos homines ad studia bonarum literarum, incendique in dies magis, ut invitis bellis et inter
arma literae, quae tot saecula obrutae iacuere, emergant. Nam non
in Italia solum, sed etiam in Germania, Gallia, Pannonia, Britannia, Hispania et ubique fere, ubi Romana lingua legitur, non modo
ab adulescentibus iuvenibusque, sed a senibus quoque summa
aviditate studetur literis Graecis. Quamobrem, etsi pene opprimor
laboribus, mirifice tamen illis delector; tum et gratulor studiosis
omnibus, et maxime adulescentibus, quod eo tempore nati sint,
quo bonae literae reviviscunt; et mihi admodum gaudeo, quod non
frustra tantum laboris tandiu sustinuerim atque eo sim animo, ut
nullo labore, nulla quamvis magna impensa perterritus, ad longe
maiora in dies magis magisque accingar, succedantque omnia, Iesu
Christo favente, feliciter.

2   Cum itaque tu istic summa laude et Graece et Latine publice
quam plurimos doceas, scripserisque ad me superioribus diebus,
ut quosdam Graecos libros, quod esset eis opus discipulis tuis, ad
te mitterem, et tunc illos misi libenter, et nunc Stephanum, qui de
urbibus scripsit, damus libentissime: est enim opus perquam utile
maximeque necessarium iis, qui humanitati incumbunt, ob historiarum poetarumque, in quibus assidue versantur, lectionem. Nam
et urbes fere omnes, quae apud eos ipsos historicos poetasque
leguntur, κατὰ στοιχεῖον eleganter docet, et quonam modo gen-
tilia ab ipsis nomina deducantur, ostendit. Adde quod eorum

much better than I could hope when I began to devote my energies to printing books in Greek. In this context I and my friends are often surprised by the following fact: although the whole world for so many years has been afflicted by wars of Christians and unbelievers — in fact in the very year when Italy began to suffer from war I undertook the extremely difficult enterprise of printing for the benefit of students — people are so keen on the study of literature, and indeed increasingly enthusiastic, that despite the wars literary studies, submerged and at a low ebb for so many centuries, are reviving. Not just in Italy, but also in Germany, France, Hungary, Britain, Spain, and in almost every place where the language of the Romans is read, there is great eagerness to study Greek, and not only among adolescents and young people, but also among the elderly. And so, although I am almost worn out by my labors, I still take great delight in them. I also congratulate all students, especially the young, on having been born in an age of literary revival, and I am quite pleased for myself that I have not labored so much and for so long in vain. I am determined to devote myself with ever-increasing energy to far greater tasks, undeterred by the effort and the expense, however great, so that by the grace of Jesus Christ all will turn out well.

And so, since you are the official and highly-praised teacher 2 there of many pupils in Greek and Latin, and you wrote to me some days ago to ask me to send you some Greek books needed for your pupils, I was happy to send them; and now we are delighted to send you Stephanus, who wrote about cities. It is a text of great value and absolutely essential for students of the humanities in their reading of history and poetry, in which they are regularly occupied. He gives in elegant form and in alphabetical order information about almost all the cities named in those same historians and poets, and he shows how the adjectives are derived from them. In addition it is worth learning from him the correct

nominum orthographiam, in qua plurimum errare solent Graecarum literarum rudes, ex eo operae pretium est discere.

3   Quanquam illud doleo, non extare totum τῶν ἐθνικῶν Στεφάνου opus: nam et abbreviatio est id quod nos excudendum curavimus—sic enim de Stephano apud Sudam:

Ἑρμόλαος γραμματικὸς Κωνσταντινουπόλεως γράψας τὴν ἐπιτομὴν τῶν ἐθνικῶν Στεφάνου γραμματικοῦ προσφωνηθεῖσαν Ἰουστινιανῷ τῷ βασιλεῖ

—et deest etiam in ea κ. μετὰ τῶν ε. a fine, item η, ι, λ, ν, o a principio; quapropter locus relictus est, ut, si forte aliquando inveniatur, insertari operi commode possit.

4   Eum librum tibi dicamus, Taberi suavissime, munerique mittimus, ut, cum sanctissimis moribus optimisque literis in ista urbe dignissima opulentissimaque Brixia iuventutem instituas, cognoscas te propterea a nobis amari plurimum, sitque hic liber apud te μνημόσυνον amoris summi erga te mei perpetuum. Expecta brevi Iulium Pollucem et Thucydidem μετὰ τῶν παραλειπομένων Ξενοφῶντος et alios quosdam. Vale.

Venetiis XV calendas Apriles M.DII.

: XIX :

Aldus Manutius Romanus Heliae Capreolo Brixiano
bonarum literarum studiosissimo s.

1   Iulius Pollux Naucratita scripsit vocabularium et de synonymis, quae a nostris univoca dicuntur, et de singulis dictionibus, varium,

spelling of the names, in which beginners in Greek often make mistakes.

Yet I regret that Stephanus' *Ethnica* is not extant entire; what we 3 have printed is an abridgment.[215] This is the entry about Stephanus in the *Suda*:[216]

> Hermolaus, a grammarian in Constantinople, wrote the epitome of the *Ethnica* by Stephanus the grammarian dedicated to the emperor Justinian.

The end of entries beginning κε is missing, as are those in κη κι κλ κν and the first part of those in κο. Therefore a space has been left, so that if the missing text should be found, it can be inserted conveniently.

We dedicate this book to you, my dear Taberio, and send it as 4 a gift, so that you may be assured of our great affection for you, since as a person of excellent character and great culture you teach the young in that highly regarded and wealthy city of Brescia. This book is to be a reminder for you, in perpetuity, of my great affection for you. You should expect soon Julius Pollux, Thucydides with the *Paralipomena* of Xenophon and some others.[217] Farewell.

Venice, March 18, 1502.

: XIX :

Julius Pollux of Naucratis, Onomasticon
(April 11, 1502)

Aldus Manutius of Rome to Elia Caprioli of Brescia,[218]
a great student of literature, greetings.

Julius Pollux of Naucratis wrote a dictionary of synonyms, which 1 our authors call 'univocal terms,' and of individual terms. It has

copiosum, elegans, doctum et perutile, quod ὀνομαστικόν inscribitur, quod sic ipse in epistola ad Commodum Caesarem, cui dicatur opus:

> Ὀνομαστικὸν μὲν οὖν ἐστι τῷ βιβλίῳ τὸ ἐπί-
> γραμμα· μηνύει δὲ ὅσα τε συνώνυμα ὡς ὑπαλλάτ-
> τειν δύνασθαι καὶ οἷς ἕκαστα ἂν δηλωθείη. Πεφι-
> λοτίμηται γὰρ οὐ τοσοῦτον εἰς πλῆθος ὁπόσον εἰς
> κάλλους ἐκλογήν. Οὐ μέντοι πάντα ὀνόματα περι-
> είληφε τουτὶ τὸ βιβλίον· οὐδὲ γὰρ ἦν πάντα ῥάδιον
> ἑνὶ βιβλίῳ συλλαβεῖν.

Hoc est, ne verbum verbo reddamus:

> Vocabularium igitur huic libro inditum est nomen; indicat autem et multa de eodem dici, et quonam modo singula ap⟨p⟩ellemus. Nititur enim non tam multitudine quam pulchri delectu. Nec tamen omnia nomina complexus hic est liber; neque enim facile erat uno libro omnia comprehendere.

2   Totum vero opus dividitur in decem libros; nec per ordinem literarum vocabula denotantur, sed sunt praeposita capita rerum omnium summatim ante singulos libros. Quanquam ego, ut facilius omnia inveniri queant, quae libris singulis ante id ipsum volumen pertractantur, copiosiusque et dilucidius et Latine et Graece imprimenda curavi arithmeticis numeris annotata, quibus ad columnulam, in qua est id quod quaeritur, studiosus lector remittitur; quandoquidem singulas quasque libri totius columnulas iisdem numeris signandas curavimus.

3   Sudas de Polluce haec:

> Πολυδεύκης Ναυκρατίτης, τινὲς δὲ Ἀρδονέννας σο-
> φιστὴν γράφουσι παίζοντες (πόλις δὲ Φοινίκης ἡ

variety, is full, elegant, learned and very valuable. The title is *Onomasticon*, as he himself says in the letter to the emperor Commodus, to whom the work is dedicated.

Ὀνομαστικὸν μὲν οὖν ἐστι τῷ βιβλίῳ τὸ ἐπί-
γραμμα· μηνύει δὲ ὅσα τε συνώνυμα ὡς ὑπαλλάτ-
τειν δύνασθαι καὶ οἷς ἕκαστα ἂν δηλωθείη. Πεφι-
λοτίμηται γὰρ οὐ τοσοῦτον εἰς πλῆθος ὁπόσον εἰς
κάλλους ἐκλογήν. Οὐ μέντοι πάντα ὀνόματα περι-
είληφε τουτὶ τὸ βιβλίον· οὐδὲ γὰρ ἦν πάντα ῥάδιον
ἑνὶ βιβλίῳ συλλαβεῖν.

Translated freely, that is:

This book is therefore called a vocabulary. It shows that many words are used for the same object and how we designate individual objects. It depends not so much on quantity as on choice of what is elegant. But this book does not deal with every word, because it was not easy to include them all in one work.

The work as a whole is divided into ten books. Words are not 2 listed in alphabetical order, but at the beginning of each book there are summary headings of all the material. But to make it easier to find everything I have printed at the front of the volume itself what is dealt with in each book, in fuller and clearer form, both in Latin and in Greek, adding numbers by which the attentive reader is directed to the column containing what he is looking for; we have ensured that all the columns throughout the book are marked with corresponding numerals.

Suidas says this about Pollux: 3

Πολυδεύκης Ναυκρατίτης, τινὲς δὲ Ἀρδουέννας σο-
φιστὴν γράφουσι παίζοντες (πόλις δὲ Φοινίκης ἡ

Ἀρδούεννα). Ἐπαίδευσε δὲ ἐν Ἀθήναις ἐπὶ Κομμό-
δου τοῦ βασιλέως· καὶ ἐτελεύτησε βιοὺς ἔτη ν΄ καὶ
η΄, συντάξας βιβλία ταῦτα. Ὀνομαστικὸν ἐν βιβλί-
οις δέκα, ἔστι δὲ συναγωγὴ τῶν διαφόρων κατὰ τοῦ
αὐτοῦ λεγομένων· διαλέξεις ἤτοι λαλίας· μελέτας·
εἰς Κόμμοδον Καίσαρα ἐπιθαλάμιον· Ῥωμαϊκὸν λό-
γον· σαλπιγκτὴν ἢ ἀγῶνα μουσικόν· κατὰ Σωκρά-
τους· κατὰ Σινωπέων· Πανελλήνιον· Ἀρκαδικόν· καὶ
ἕτερα.

Hoc est:

Pollux Naucratita, sed quidam Arduennae oriundum io-
cantes scribunt (Phoeniciae vero urbs Arduenna). Docuit
autem Athenis imperatore Commodo. Vitam obiit annos
natus octo et quinquaginta, cum scripsisset hos libros: vocabularium decem libris — est autem collectio eorum, quae de
eodem dicuntur variis modis —, dissertationes sive loquelas,
declamationes, epithalamium ad Commodum Caesarem, in
laudem Urbis orationem, tubicinem vel certamen musicum,
contra Socratem, contra Sinopeos, in laudem totius Graeciae, in laudem Arcadiae, et alia.

4   Haec Latina fecimus non tua causa, cum et ipse pro tua doctrina id queas et Taberium istic habeas et Graece et Latine doctissimum, quicum sic coniunctissime et amantissime vivis, ut de vobis tritum illud apud Graecos vere dici possit: σώματα μὲν δύο,
ψυχὴ δὲ μία — sed eorum, quibus legendis Graecis auxilio et interprete opus est. Scribimus enim sub tuo nomine studiosis omnibus.

5   Pollucem vero ipsum, mi Helia, in tuo nomine editum muneri
tibi mittimus, quia tibi, cum propter eruditionem tuam, tum

Ἀρδούεννα). Ἐπαίδευσε δὲ ἐν Ἀθήναις ἐπὶ Κομμό-
δου τοῦ βασιλέως· καὶ ἐτελεύτησε βιοὺς ἔτη ν' καὶ
η', συντάξας βιβλία ταῦτα. Ὀνομαστικὸν ἐν βιβλί-
οις δέκα, ἔστι δὲ συναγωγὴ τῶν διαφόρων κατὰ τοῦ
αὐτοῦ λεγομένων· διαλέξεις ἤτοι λαλίας· μελέτας·
εἰς Κόμμοδον Καίσαρα ἐπιθαλάμιον· Ῥωμαϊκὸν λό-
γον· σαλπιγκτὴν ἢ ἀγῶνα μουσικόν· κατὰ Σωκρά-
τους· κατὰ Σινωπέων· Πανελλήνιον· Ἀρκαδικόν· καὶ
ἕτερα.

which means:

Pollux of Naucratis—but some people as a joke write that
he came from Arduenna (Arduenna is a city in Phoenicia).[219] But he taught in Athens when Commodus was emperor. He died at the age of fifty-eight, having written the
following books: a dictionary in ten books—but it is a collection of the various ways of describing the same object—
addresses or informal talks, declamations, an epithalamium
for the emperor Commodus, an oration in praise of the City,
The Trumpeter or musical competition, Against Socrates,
Against the inhabitants of Sinope, an encomium on the
whole of Greece, an encomium of Arcadia, etc.

We have turned this into Latin, not for your sake, since you 4
know enough to do it for yourself, and you have with you Taberio,
an expert in Greek and Latin; you live close to him and on the
best of terms, so that the Greek adage could be applied to you—
two bodies but one soul;[220] I translated for the benefit of those
who need help and a translation for reading Greek. While naming
you we address all scholars.

Pollux himself we send as a gift, printed and dedicated to you, 5
my dear Elia, because I feel great friendship for you on account of

propter temperatos moderatosque mores, quibus te praeditum esse
audio, sum amicissimus; praeterea quia, cum superioribus diebus
Ioanni Taberio nostro Stephanum de urbibus dicarimus — quem
cum Polluce a compluribus una colligatum iri, ob eam quae est
inter ipsos convenientiam, certo scio — volui vos et hoc in libro
esse coniunctos, ut animo estis. Adde etiam quia, quoties eum ipsum librum in bibliotheca tua videbis, nominis nostri memineris;
nam faciei non poteris, cum nos de facie non cognorimus: quod
tamen ipsum aliquando futurum et cupimus et speramus. Vale.

Venetiis III idus Apriles M.DII.

: XX :

Aldus Manutius Romanus Danieli Rainero patritio Veneto s. d.

1 Si quisquam est in hac inclyta republica Veneta, Daniel Rainere,
qui ex hac nostra provincia publicandi vel potius e duris ac tetris
carceribus liberandi bonos libros maximam voluptatem capiat, in
his te esse sum ipse optimus testis: nam non solum in via, quoties
tibi fio obviam, hortaris me, ut nec duris hisce temporibus cedens
nec laboribus ullis succumbens constanter ac fortiter ut coepi pergam, sed etiam confers te saepe in aedes nostras, quidnam vel Latine vel Graece vel etiam Hebraice — in tribus enim his linguis
edoctus es — excudatur visurus. Taceo quanto mihi adiumento sis,
tuos et Graecos et Latinos commodando libros, admonendoque ut
id maxime imprimendum curem, quod studiosis summae utilitati

your learning and the restrained and moderate character which I know you are endowed with. Furthermore, as we had dedicated Stephanus *On Cities* a few days ago to our friend Giovanni Taberio — and I am quite sure people will have it bound with Pollux because of the affinity between them — I wanted you to be united by this book as well as you are united in spirit. A further reason is that each time you see the book itself in your library you will remember us by name; you will not be able to recall my face because we have not met face to face; but we wish and hope that will happen one day. Farewell.

Venice, April 11, 1502.

: XX :

Thucydides, Histories
(May 14, 1502)

Aldus Manutius of Rome to Daniele Renier,
patrician of Venice,[221] *greetings.*

If there is anyone in this celebrated Venetian republic, Daniel Renier, who derives great pleasure from our enterprise of publishing — or rather liberating good books from their harsh and gloomy prisons — I am the best witness to the fact that you encourage me not to make concessions to hard times or to give up in the face of any awkward tasks, but to continue as I have begun with determination and courage. Not only that; you often come to our house to see what is being printed in Latin, Greek or even Hebrew, since you are well versed in these three languages. I need not say how much you have helped me by lending me your Greek and Latin books and by recommending that I concentrate on printing what you reckon will be of the greatest value to students. Nor have I

1

futurum putes. Nec quivi unquam in te vel minimum invidiae deprehendere, quod mea opera et labore bonae literae publicantur, ut quosdam pusillanimes et bibliotaphos notavi. Contra quos sic Plinius in prooemio quinti et vigesimi naturalis historiae libri:

> Ipsa quae nunc dicetur herbarum claritas, medicinae tantum gratia gignente eas tellure, in admirationem curae priscorum diligentiaeque animum agit. Nihil ergo intentatum inexpertumque illis fuit, nihil deinde occultatum, quod non prodesse posteris vellent. At nos elaborata iis abscondere ac supprimere cupimus et fraudare vitam etiam alienis bonis. Ita certe recondunt, qui pauca aliqua novere invidentes aliis. Et neminem docere in autoritatem scientiae est. Tantum ab excogitandis bonis ac adiuvanda vita mores absunt; summumque opus ingeniorum diu in hoc fuit, ut intra ununquenque recte facta veterum perirent. At hercle singula quosdam inventa deorum numero addidere, omniumque vitam clariorem fecere cognominibus herbarum, tam benigne gratiam memoria referente.

2 Sed de his hactenus; non enim dubito quin brevi rumpantur invidia, quandoquidem, vivam modo, quicquid est lectu dignum, Christo Iesu favente, exibit in publicum; et praesertim cum longe plures sint ex doctis qui nobis et consilio et libris et opera amore literarum summo studio adiuvent, quam qui contra, quique nos de hac provincia ubique locorum adament, quam qui oderint; quod indicant ad me a doctissimis fere quibusque epistolae, quo pergam in dies audentius.

3 Tu vero, Daniel doctissime, sic nos assidue protegis, ut facile appareat gaudere te mirum in modum communi reipublicae literariae bono. Quapropter Thucydidem nuper cura nostra excusum

detected in you the slightest trace of jealousy because good books are published through my energy and labor, as I have noticed in the case of some small-minded people and "buriers of books."[222] Pliny has this criticism of them in preface to Book XXV of the *Natural History*:

> The value of plants grown in the soil exclusively for medical use, which will now be described, leads me to admire the care and diligence of the ancients. They in fact left nothing untried and untested, and nothing was concealed; they wished everything to be beneficial to posterity. But we try to hide and suppress what they worked out, to deprive humanity of benefits that others invented. That is the form of concealment practiced by those who have learned a little and are jealous of others. To teach no one adds to the prestige of their learning. So far are their habits from inventing what is good and improving life. For a long time the supreme intellectual task was to nullify the achievements of the ancients by keeping them to oneself. But I swear that individual inventions have elevated some men to the company of the gods. Added distinction came to all through the names they gave to plants. History recorded its grateful thanks.

But enough of this. I have no doubt they will soon die of jeal- 2 ousy, since everything worth reading will be published, provided I survive, with the favor of Jesus Christ; especially since among the learned there are far more people who help us actively with their advice, their books and their love of letters than those who do the opposite; there are more people everywhere who appreciate our undertaking than those who dislike it. Letters to me from almost every scholar suggest I should go forward ever more boldly.

You, learned Daniel, give us such consistent protection as to 3 make it clear that you rejoice greatly in the progress of the republic of letters. So with a dedication to you we offer Thucydides for

sub tuo nomine studiosis damus, ut, si quam mihi ob eam rem habituri sunt gratiam, et tibi habeant, cuius hortatu ac potius favore edendis Graecis autoribus, iisque doctissimis, in dies sumus alacriores.

4   Quantus autem et qualis autor fuerit Thucydides, quamque fide plenus, putavi supervacaneum scribere, tum quia id in eius vita, quam Graece hoc ipso in libro imprimendam curavimus, abunde tractatur, tum etiam quod satis notum esse arbitramur hominibus nostris. Illo tamen argumento summae autoritatis vel apud antiquissimos probatur fuisse Thucydidem, quod eum Demosthenes octies sua manu scripsisse dicitur, quo magis magisque sibi familiarem faceret. Quod Lucianus ad indoctum et multos ementem libros sic scribit:

’Αλλ’ ἐνὶ τούτῳ μόνῳ πάντα ἐκεῖνα ἀναδραμεῖσθαι νῦν ἐλπίζεις, τῷ κτᾶσθαι πολλὰ βιβλία, κᾆτα δὴ ταῦτα ἔχε συλλαβὼν ἐκεῖνα τὰ τοῦ Δημοσθένους, ὅσα τῇ χειρὶ τῇ αὑτοῦ ὁ ῥήτωρ ἔγραψε· καὶ τὰ τοῦ Θουκυδίδου, ὅσα παρὰ τοῦ Δημοσθένους καὶ αὐτὰ ὀκτάκις μεταγεγραμμένα εὑρέθη καλῶς.

5   Eram daturus una cum Thucydide τά τε Ξενοφῶντος καὶ Πλήθωνος Γεμιστοῦ παραλειπόμενα; sed quia non habebam minimum tria exemplaria, distulimus in aliud tempus. Interea, cum haec scriberem, erat sub incude Herodotus et Sophocles cum commentariis. Vale, et provinciae nostrae, ut soles, fave.

Venetiis pridie idus Maias M.DII.

students, fresh from our press. If they show any gratitude to me on this account, they should also be grateful to you, since it is through your encouragement and indeed support that we became increasingly active in the printing of Greek texts, and indeed the most informative ones.

The greatness of Thucydides, his qualities and his reliability, I thought it unnecessary to set out; the matter is treated at length in the Greek life printed in this volume;[223] and we reckon in any case that it is sufficiently well known to our public. But it is clear that Thucydides enjoyed the highest reputation in antiquity from the following proof: Demosthenes wrote out the text eight times to increase his familiarity with it. Lucian reports this in his work against the ignoramus who bought many books.[224]

> But you now expect all that to accrue by simply acquiring many books. Accordingly you must gather up into your possession all the books of Demosthenes that the orator wrote in his own hand, and the copies of Thucydides made by Demosthenes, transcribed eight times, a great find.

With Thucydides I was going to provide Xenophon and Gemistos Plethon's *Paralipomena*,[225] but not having at least three copies I have put it off until another occasion. Meanwhile, as I write this, Herodotus and Sophocles with scholia are in the press. Farewell, and continue to support our enterprise.

Venice, May 14, 1502.

: XXI :

Aldus Romanus Ioanni Lascari viro praeclaro ac doctissimo s. d.

1 Sedentibus nobis his brumae frigoribus in hemicyclo ad ignem
cum Neacademicis nostris, forteque esset una Marcus Musurus
noster, post multa variaque vicissim, ut solet, dicta inter nos, in tui
incidimus mentionem. Tum Marcus, ut est studiosissimus tui ac
perquam gratus discipulus — nam quantum bonis literis moribus-
que profecit (profecit autem plurimum) id omne tibi acceptum
refert —, cum longo sermone de te honorifice multa narrasset, te
proximis Iulio et Augusto mensibus et Mediolani et Ticini vidisse
addidit, deque renascentibus Graecis literis plurimum tibi secum
fuisse sermonem, necnon, ob communem studiosorum omnium
utilitatem, nostra hac provincia gaudere te mirum in modum maximeque laudare labores nostros.

2 Quamobrem, cum septem tragoedias Sophoclis nuper imprimendas parva forma curassem, eas sub tuo nomine volui ex Neaca-
demeia nostra prodire in publicum, tibique muneri mittere εἰς
μνημόσυνον summi amoris erga te mei. Τὰ δὲ εἰς αὐτὰς
εὑρισκόμενα σχόλια οὔπω μὲν ἐτυπώθη· τυπωθήσεται δέ,
θεοῦ σώζοντος, ὅσον οὐκ ἤδη· πρὸς δὲ καὶ ὅσα ἐς ἀνάπτυξιν
μέτρων ἥκει. Atque utinam id ante habuissem quam ipsae tragoediae excusae forent: nam, etsi res est quam laboriosissima, tamen singulos quosque versus, in choris praesertim, siqui perperam
digesti sunt, curassem in suum locum restituendos. Quod quia
non licuit, id sibi quisque curato, si placuerit. Tu vero, mi Lascaris,
sis velim meus, quantum ego sum tuus. Vale.

: XXI :

Sophocles, Seven Tragedies
(August 1502)

*Aldus of Rome to the distinguished and learned
Janus Lascaris,[226] greetings.*

As we sat in a semicircle round the fire with our members of the 1
Neacademia in this cold winter weather, and our friend Marcus
Musurus[227] happened to be with us, after the usual lengthy and
varied exchanges, your name was mentioned. Then Marcus, being
a great admirer of yours and a thoroughly grateful pupil—his
progress in literary studies and development of character, which
has been great, he thinks entirely due to you—talked at length
about you and with high praise, and said he had seen you last July
and August in Milan and Pavia, and you had a long conversation
with him about the revival of Greek studies. Furthermore, you
were remarkably enthusiastic about this enterprise of ours for the
general benefit of scholars, and you had high praise for our efforts.

So having recently arranged to set up in type Sophocles' seven 2
tragedies in small format,[228] I wanted them to be issued by our
Neacademia with a dedication to you, and to send them as a gift
in recognition of your great affection for me. The scholia that can
be found have not yet been printed; but they will be printed, if
God preserves us, almost at once, together with everything to do
with the explanation of meters.[229] I wish I had had this material
before printing the tragedies themselves; for although it is an exceedingly laborious business, I would have seen to the correct restoration of individual lines, especially in the choruses.[230] Since that
was not possible, each reader should do it for himself if he wishes.
As for you, my dear Lascaris, I wish your friendship to be as great
toward me as mine is toward you.[231] Farewell.

⁖ XXII ⁖

Aldus Manutius Romanus Ioanni Calpurnio Brixiano s. d.

1 Non immemor triti illius sermone proverbii apud Graecos: χεὶρ χεῖρα νίπτει, Calpurni, vir doctissime ac Patavini gymnasii, in quo summa cum laude profiteris publice et Graecas et Latinas literas, magnum decus, cupiebam ad te aliquid muneri mittere, quo et benevolentiam erga te meam ostenderem studiosis, et publice testarer te admodum quam humanum esse et liberalem. Nam, cum nullum unquam a te petierim beneficium, quod non libenter in me contuleris, idque vel maxime superioribus diebus in bibliotheca tua ostenderis, cum a te M. Tullii epistolas ad Atticum, Pausaniamque Graecum, quos accurate et summo iudicio castigatos enarras auditoribus, petiissem—recepisti enim tum eos tum caeteros libros tuos daturum te mihi, cum velim, non invitum, ut publicentur prosintque hominibus excusi characteribus nostris—, cum igitur nullum unquam a te petierim beneficium, quod non libenter in me contuleris, has novem Musas Herodoti in aedibus nostris nuper impressas tibi dicatas dono damus.

2 Quas eo gratiores tibi fore existimamus, quoniam multis exemplaribus castigatae emittuntur ex Academia nostra in manus studiosorum. Nam Clio abundat, a caeteris quibuscum contulimus exemplar nostrum, decem prope chartis, quae et in ea desunt, quae a Laurentio Valla tralata habetur.

3 Nec puto apud te, integerrimum ac summa aequitate virum, ideo minus autoritatis habituras, quod mendaces in historia a nostris habeantur, atque ita ut propter Herodotum vel ipsa Graecia,

⁝ XXII ⁝

Herodotus, Histories

(September 1502)

Aldus Manutius of Rome to Giovanni Calpurnio of Brescia,[232] *greetings.*

I have not forgotten, Calpurnio, that Greek proverb much used in   1
conversation, "One hand washes another."[233] You are a learned
member of the Paduan school, where your public lectures on
Greek and Latin win high praise, a great distinction. I wanted to
send you a gift, to demonstrate to scholars my goodwill toward
you and to testify before the public to your notable kindness, humanity and liberality. Though I have never asked for a favor which
you would not have granted willingly — and you showed this the
other day in your library, when I asked you for Cicero's letters to
Atticus and Pausanias in Greek, texts corrected accurately and
with acumen on which you lecture to your audience, and you
agreed with a good grace to give me these and your other books
when I need them, to be published by our press for the benefit of
the world — so since I never asked a favor which you did not willingly grant, we give you the nine Muses of Herodotus, printed
recently in our house and dedicated to you.

I think you will appreciate them all the more because they have   2
been checked against many exemplars and are issued by our Academy for students. Clio is longer by almost ten pages than in the
other copies against which we collated our own; these are also
missing in the version which we possess from the pen of Lorenzo
Valla.[234]

Since you are a man of absolute integrity and fair-minded I do   3
not suppose you will regard the Muses as lacking in authority because they are today thought to be mendacious as history, to such
an extent that on account of Herodotus Greece itself, the mother

virtutum omnium parens et alumna disciplinarum, mendax a nonnullis dicatur; quando id errore potius factum, quam quod ita sit,
cum accurate Musas ipsas perlegeris, facile cognosces. Nam, quoties indignum quid creditu scribit Herodotus, se fere semper excu-
sat, vel οὕτω λέγουσι dicens vel ὡς ἀκήκοα vel ὅπερ ἐμοὶ οὐ
πιστόν vel ἅγ᾽ ἐμοὶ ἄπιστα et id genus quid aliud. Sed solet
accidere ut, cum quis de aliquo vel iniuria maledixerit, sequantur
alii temere et inconsulte, nulla habita ratione.

4   Quemadmodum de Cretensibus vel nunc obloquuntur plurimi,
ψευστάς eos et ἀπατεῶνας immerito appellantes, ita ut κρητίζειν ἐπὶ τοῦ ψεύδεσθαι καὶ ἀπατᾶν accipiant, natumque sit
inde proverbium: κρητίζειν πρὸς Κρῆτας. Cuius calumniae
duae causae traduntur. Altera quia, cum Idomeneus rex Cretensis,
orta dissensione inter Graecos bellantes ad Troiam de principatu
in dividenda praeda, ab omnibus iudex electus, primum se omnium constituerit, propterea dictum esse κρητίζειν mentiri et
decipere. Quod quam iuste factum fuerit, consyderent velim docti.
Primum, si ex unius ignominia tota urbs patriave infamis habenda
est, quis in toto orbe terrarum locus expers erit infamiae, cum non
unum, sed multos unaquaeque urbs gignat pravos et vitiosos?
Praeterea, qui magis propter unum Idomeneum tota insula Creta
mendax dicenda est, quam propter Minoem et Rhadamanthum,
viros Cretenses quam optimos verissimosque, proba ac verax, qui
ob eorum integerrimam vitam iudices apud inferos puniendis ani-
mis esse traduntur? Deinde potuit Idomeneus illum principatus
honorem sibi suo iure vendicare, quod et fortissimus et prudentis-
simus et rex esset, ut ait Homerus.

5   Altera vero causa fuisse dicitur, quod Iovi sepulchrum Cretenses in Creta fabricati sint, in eoque scripserint Ζεὺς Κρόνου,

of all virtue and nurse of disciplines, is declared by some people to be mendacious.[235] If you read with care the Muses you will soon see that this is the result of a misunderstanding rather than a reality. For whenever Herodotus records something which does not deserve to be credited, he almost always excuses himself by saying, "As they say" or "as I have heard" or "which for me is not credible" or "what to me is incredible" or something else of the same sort. But it tends to happen that if someone makes nasty remarks about a man, even undeservedly, others follow rashly and without consideration, giving no thought to the matter.

In this way many people are now abusive about Cretans, calling them liars and cheats undeservedly, so that they take the expression "to be a Cretan" to refer to lies and deceit, which is the origin of the proverb "to be a Cretan among Cretans."[236] For this two causes are on record. The first is that, when the Greeks fighting at Troy quarreled about precedence in the division of booty, Idomeneus the Cretan king, having been chosen by all as arbiter, assigned first place to himself. For that reason lying and deception was called Cretan behavior. I invite the educated to consider what justice there was in that. First of all, if a whole city or country is to be considered infamous because of the bad behavior of an individual, what place in the whole world will avoid infamy, given that each and every city produces not just one but many evil men? Besides, why should the whole island of Crete be termed mendacious on account of Idomeneus alone, rather than honest and truthful on account of Minos and Rhadamanthus, Cretans of great honesty and truthfulness, who are said to have been appointed judges for the punishment of souls in the underworld because of their integrity? Again, Idomeneus, being very brave and prudent and a king, as Homer says,[237] could reasonably claim for himself the honor of precedence.

The other cause is said to be that the Cretans fabricated the tomb of Zeus in Crete and inscribed it "Zeus, son of Kronos,"

cum nunquam Iupiter obierit mortem, sed perpetuo sit; atque hinc Callimachus: σὺ δ᾽ οὐ θάνες, ἐσσὶ γὰρ αἰεί. Sed miror sic temere solere homines iudicare: nam, si fabulis credimus, vani et mendaces, si historiis, graves et veri sumus. Iovem in Creta natum et educatum fingunt poetae, eumque nec interiisse unquam nec interiturum fabulantur; historici vero hominem illum fuisse conscribunt et Saturni regis filium. Quod cum ita sit, quis negabit Iovem occidisse? Omnia enim orta occidunt. Quare mendaces dicendi sunt qui Iovem nunquam mortuum esse asserunt, non Cretenses, qui sepulchrum ei fabricati sunt. Praeterea, si propter illum Epimenidis Cretensis versiculum: Κρῆτες ἀεὶ ψεῦσται, κακὰ θηρία, γαστέρες ἀργοί, quem et Callimachus et apostolus secutus est, mendaces habendi sunt Cretenses, et ipse Epimenides fuit mendax, quia Cretensis; mentitur igitur Epimenides, et sic veri sunt Cretenses; qui si veri, verus et Epimenides, quia Cretensis; sic rursus mendaces illi — atque ita nihil concludi potest, cum sit dialecticorum ψευδόμενον et fallacia. Vides itaque in Cretenses manifestam calumniam, quod Iovi sepulchrum fabricati sint; quanquam in Callimachi enarratiunculis non Iovis, sed Minois illud sepulchrum fuisse legitur, atque inibi epigramma inscriptum Μίνωος Διὸς τάφος, ac vetustate deletum Μίνωος et relictum Διὸς τάφος, atque hinc natum errorem, ut Iovis esse sepulchrum putaretur.

6   Sed ut ad propositum revertamur, non recte mendacii arguitur Herodotus, quandoquidem res pure et simpliciter, ut accepit, posteritati tradidit. De quo, ut nosti, et Thucydide haec Fabius Quintilianus:

> Historiam multi scripsere praeclare; sed nemo dubitat longe duos caeteris praeferendos, quorum diversa virtus laudem pene est parem consecuta: densus et brevis et semper instans

although Jupiter never died and exists for ever. Hence Callimachus: "But you did not die, since you exist for ever."[238] But I am amazed that men make judgments so hastily. If we believe in fables, we are stupid and untruthful; if in history, we are serious and truthful. According to the fictions of poets Jupiter was born and brought up in Crete; in their fables he never died, nor will he. Historians, however, report he was a man, the son of King Saturnus.[239] That being so, who will deny that Jupiter died? All things that are born die. So it is those who assert that Jupiter never died who are mendacious, not the Cretans who fabricated a tomb for him. Besides, if Cretans are to be regarded as liars because of that line of Epimenides the Cretan, "Cretans are always liars, evil beasts, lazy potbellies," cited by Callimachus and the Apostle,[240] Epimenides too, as a Cretan, was himself a liar; so Epimenides is lying and thus the Cretans are truthful. If they are truthful, Epimenides as a Cretan is also truthful; so they once again are mendacious—and no conclusion can be drawn, because this is a trick of the logicians and a fallacy. Hence you can see clearly the insult to the Cretans because they constructed a tomb for Jupiter. However, in commentaries on Callimachus[241] it is stated that the tomb was not for Jupiter but for Minos, and the inscription carved on it read, "The tomb of Minos, son of Zeus." With the passing of time the word "Minos" was lost and "tomb of Zeus" remained, which caused the error that it was thought to be the tomb of Jupiter.

But to get back to our theme: Herodotus is not fairly accused 6 of lying, since he recorded facts for posterity in a straightforward and simple way, as he learned of them. Of him, as you know, Fabius Quintilian has this to say:[242]

> Many have written splendid histories, but no one doubts that two are to be placed far above the rest, their different qualities having brought them almost equal fame. Thucydides is dense, succinct and always pressing forward,

sibi Thucydides, dulcis et candidus et effusus Herodotus; ille concitatis, hic remissis affectibus melior; ille concionibus, hic sermonibus; ille vi, hic voluptate.

Ecce summis effertur laudibus a Quintiliano Herodotus, nec aliqua mendacii nota arguitur.

7   Haec in Herodoti et Cretensium defensionem scripsimus, tum quia dolebamus falso eos mendaces vocari ab hominibus nostris, tum etiam ut, visis diligenter rationibus nostris, iudicent studiosi, falsone an vere et habiti olim fuerint et nunc habeantur mendaces. Te vero nostrae sententiae facile accessurum certo scio, quia, si quisquam est aetate nostra verus ac iustus, is tu es. Munus autem hoc nostrum gratissimum tibi futurum non dubitamus, tum ipso munere, tum quia ostendit nos accepti beneficii non esse immemores. Vale.

: XXIII :

Aldus Romanus Demetrio Chalcondylae viro clarissimo s. p. d.

1   Si starent Athenae illae olim virtutum omnium domicilium, Demetri doctissime, deflerem una cum illis bonorum librorum et factam abhinc mille annos et fieri assidue iacturam plurimam et miserabilem. Nam, ut taceam tot librorum millia in illa Ptolemaei Philadelphi bibliotheca, omnium quae unquam fuerunt longe maxima, quo tempore C. Caesar, ut totum sibi terrarum orbem subigeret, et humana et divina iura pervertebat, infelicissime

Herodotus is charming, clear and discursive. One is superior
in strong, the other in calm emotions; one in speeches, the
other in conversations; one in forcefulness, the other in his
will to please.[243]

Here Herodotus is given the highest praise by Quintilian and not
subjected to any charges of lying.

We have composed this defense of Herodotus and the Cretans   7
partly because we were upset that they are called liars by our contemporaries,[244] partly so that students can weigh our arguments
carefully and decide whether the charge of mendacity has been
true or false, then or now. I am sure you will readily agree with my
view, since if there is today any man truthful and just, it is you.
We have no doubt that this gift of ours will be most welcome to
you, not just as a gift but as a proof that we have not forgotten a
favor received. Farewell.

∴ XXIII ∴

Euripides, Seventeen Tragedies
(February 1503)

*Aldus of Rome, to the illustrious Demetrius
Chalcondyles,[245] warmest greetings.*

If that famous city Athens, once the home of all the virtues, still   1
existed, learned Demetrius, I would join it in lamenting the great
and deplorable losses of good books that took place a thousand
years ago and are continuing all the time.[246] I need not mention
the many thousands of books in the famous library of Ptolemy
Philadephus, far the greatest that ever existed, and most unfortu-
nately burnt[247] at the time when Caesar disregarded human and
divine law in his attempt to dominate the whole world;[248] I need

conflagrasse; ut taceam citra annos sexaginta et libros in tota Graecia καὶ αὐτὴν τὴν Ἑλλάδα deperditam; nonne in Italia tempestate nostra maximas bonorum librorum bibliothecas vel direptas
paucis annis vidimus? vel nescio quo infortunio conclusas ac tineis
et blattis destinatas videmus? Sed quoniam Athenae iandiu nullae
sunt, tecum, qui solus tua doctrina nobis illas repraesentas, hanc
visum est deflere calamitatem.

2   Quanquam consultum est optime a Deo studiosis omnibus ex-
cudendi librorum invento et laboribus nostris, quandoquidem
mille et amplius boni alicuius autoris volumina singulo quoque
mense emittimus ex Academia nostra. Et nunc decem et octo Euripidis tragoedias tibi, qui es Graecorum omnium aetatis nostrae
facile princeps, nuncupatas damus, non multo post in septem pri-
mas daturi et commentarios. Vale.

: XXIV :

Aldus Pius Manutius Romanus Alberto Pio
inclyto Carporum principi s. p. d.

1   Si verum illud est, Alberte, princeps doctissime, quod vulgo dici
assolet, deberi quodcunque promissum fuerit, debere me ingenue
fateor in libros Aristotelis commentarios ex Neacademia nostra in
manus studiosorum et tuas praesertim emittere, quandoquidem id
me persaepe recepi facturum. Quod autem sero promissa ipsa
nostra appareant, fateor id quoque, si duntaxat annos enumeres;
verum, si et qui anni fuerint quamque pleni malorum omnium
consyderes, non modo non sero dari videbuntur, sed et nunc dari

not mention books lost in the whole of Greece less than sixty years ago and the destruction of Greece itself.[249] Have we not seen in our own time in Italy very large libraries of good books dispersed within a few years, do we not see them closed because of some disaster and consigned to moths and bookworms? But as Athens ceased to exist long ago, I decided to lament this tragedy with you, since you alone through your learning stand for Athens among us.

God, however, has greatly served the interests of all students 2 through the invention of printing and our labors, since we issue every month from our Academy a thousand and more copies of some good author. And now, dedicated to you as by far the leading scholar among all the Greeks of our time, we offer eighteen tragedies by Euripides;[250] soon we shall also provide commentaries on the first seven.[251] Farewell.

: XXIV :

Ammonius of Alexandria, On Aristotle's
"De interpretatione"[252]
(October 17, 1503)

*Aldus Pius Manutius of Rome to Alberto Pio,
prince of Carpi, warmest greetings.*

If it is true, learned prince Alberto, as is commonly asserted, that 1 all promises are duties, I readily admit my duty to issue from our Neacademia commentaries on the works of Aristotle for scholars and especially for you; I had often promised to do it. That our promises are slow to be realized is another admission, if you simply count the years; but if you consider what years they were and how full of every misfortune, it will not only be seen that they are not late in being made good, but you will be amazed that they

potuisse, meque inter tot mala et publica et privata semper auden-
tiorem in proposito perstitisse, miraberis. Non enim te fugit, quot
et quae incommoda privatim etiam, et domi et foris, et in Italia et
extra, ex quo duram hanc accepi provinciam, passus semper fuerim, et nunc maxime patiar, dum quidam, qui ex alienis incommodis student ut sua comparent commoda, interturbant avari omnia,
meque manibus pedibusque a proposito dimovere conantur. Et
conentur quandiu placet! eo enim me constantiorem sentient, quo
magis magisque institerint; idque Iesu Dei optimi maximi auxilio:
qui si pro nobis, quis contra?

2   Damus igitur nunc Ammonii commentaria in decem praedica-
menta et librum de interpretatione Aristotelis, necnon Magentini
Mitylenaei archiepiscopi in eundem non inutilia quaedam, atque
etiam Pselli paraphrasin; tibique, quod polliciti olim fuerimus,
nuncupamus; simulque ut nos abhinc triennium non parvis dona-
tos a te opibus familiaeque tuae gentilitio perornatos nomine hisce
ad te literis publice fateamur, quo sciant omnes, qui haec legerint,
quantum tibi debemus; tum ne mirentur, si me cognomento Pium
posthac appellatum vel legerint vel audierint. Id vero a nobis antea
propterea non est factum, ne quod honori datum est, levitati novo
assumpto cognomento adscriberetur. Expectabam igitur, ut aliquem sub tuo nomine ex aedibus nostris emitterem librum, ubi
tuam hanc in me liberalitatem ostenderem: id quod hic est factum.

3   Reliquos in Aristotelem commentarios deinceps Deo volente
dabimus, tibi omneis nuncupaturi, quandoquidem, cui plus debea-
mus quam tibi, habemus neminem. Vale, ingens praesidium nostrum et decus principum.

Venetiis XVI calendas Novembres M.D.III.

could now be performed and that I persisted in my aims with ever-increasing courage despite numerous difficulties, private and public. You are aware of the many and various obstacles I have always had to deal with in my private life, at home and elsewhere, in Italy and abroad, ever since I took up this demanding profession. You are aware of how I am suffering especially now, when some people, seeking their own advantage from the difficulties of others, are trying by every means to deter me from my aims.[253] And let them try as long as they like; the more they persist, they will find me all the more determined, thanks to the help of Jesus, God who is best and greatest; and if he is on our side, who can be against?[254]

So now we offer Ammonius' commentaries on the ten categories[255] and on Aristotle's book *De interpretatione*, plus some not unuseful material on the same work by Magentinus, archbishop of Mytilene,[256] together with Psellus' paraphrase;[257] and we dedicate them to you, as promised some time ago. At the same time, by the present letter, we announce to the public that three years ago we received a substantial donation from you and the honor of using your family name; so that anyone who reads this may realize how much we owe to you and not be surprised if in future they read or hear that I have the additional name Pio. We took no action previously in case it might be treated as frivolity on the assumption of a new name which had been given me as an honor. So I waited until I published a book dedicated to you, in which I could report your kindness to me in this regard; which now has been done.

God willing, we will provide the remaining commentaries on Aristotle, all to be dedicated to you, since there is no one to whom we owe more than you. Farewell, our mighty source of protection and glorious prince.

Venice, October 17, 1503.

: XXV :

Ἄλδος ὁ Ῥωμαῖος Γουΐδῳ τῷ Φερετρίῳ Οὐρβινέων
ἡγεμόνι εὖ πράττειν.

1 Ὦ παῖ πατρὸς ἀγαθοῦ παρ᾽ Ἰουλίου Πολυδεύκους
ἐγράφη πρὸς Κόμμοδον παῖδ᾽ ἔτι ὄντα, περιόντος ἔτι
Μάρκου τοῦ πατρός, ὃς τά τε ἄλλα καλὸς κἀγαθὸς ἦν
ἀνὴρ καὶ φιλόσοφος. Ἀτὰρ διατί οὐ καὶ Ὦ παῖ ἀγαθὲ
ἔγραφεν ὁ Πολυδεύκης; ἢ ὅτι ἐν παισὶ γνῶναι τὴν ἀγα-
θότητα οὐ δυνάμεθα, κωλυόντων, οἶμαι, τριῶν τουτωνί,
ἡλικίας φημὶ καὶ φόβου καὶ διδασκάλου; Καὶ μὴν εἴπερ
τις ἄλλος παῖς ἀγαθὸς ἐγένετό ποτε, ἦν Κόμμοδος οὗτος, μὴ μόνον πατρός γε ζῶντος, ἀλλὰ καὶ τεθνηκότος,
ἐν τῇ ἀρχῇ δὲ μόνον τῆς βασιλείας, ὁπότε πᾶσιν ἐδόκει
λίαν ἄξιος εἶναι καὶ πατρὸς καὶ τῆς τῶν πραγμάτων
διαδοχῆς· καὶ γὰρ οὐ πολλοῦ χρόνου παρεληλυθότος, ἐς
τοσοῦτον ἧκε κακίας, ὥστε τῶν τε τότε ἀνδρῶν καὶ τῶν
πάλαι ἁπάντων, καθ᾽ ἃ ἱστόρηται Ἡρωδιανῷ, γενέσθαι
κάκιστος, ἐπειδὴ τῇ ἐξουσίᾳ πάντες, καὶ ταῦτα τρυφῶν-
τες, εἰώθαμεν χείρονές τε γενέσθαι καὶ ἀτεχνῶς ὑπερ-
βάλλειν τῇ μοχθηρίᾳ. Ἀλλ᾽ ἔγωγε πρὸς σὲ οὕτως ἂν
γράψαιμι· Ὦ ἀγαθὲ υἱὲ πατρὸς ἀγαθοῦ, ἐπεὶ οὐ μόνον
πατρῷόν ἐστί σοι κτῆμα βασιλεία τε καὶ σοφία, ἀλλὰ

: XXV :

Xenophon, Hellenica
Pletho, Events in Greece after the Battle of Mantinea
Herodian, History from the Death of Marcus Aurelius
Greek Scholia on Thucydides
(*November 14, 1503*)

Aldus of Rome to Guido da Montefeltro, duke of Urbino, greetings.[258]

"Son of a good father" was Julius Pollux's address to Commodus,   1
still a child, at a time when his father Marcus, a man of other
good qualities and a philosopher,[259] was still alive. But why did
Pollux not write "Good son"? Was it because in childhood we cannot know what is good, hindered I suppose by the following three
factors, youth, fear and the teacher? And yet if ever there was a
good child, it was this Commodus, not just during his father's
lifetime but after his death as well, though only at the beginning of
his rule, when everyone thought him fully worthy to succeed his
father and take up office. Not much time elapsed, according to the
historian Herodian,[260] and he became the worst of men in his own
generation and the whole of antiquity, since all of us with power,
and as a result proud,[261] tend to deteriorate and simply commit
excesses of misbehavior. But I would address you as "Good son of
a good father,"[262] since kingship and wisdom are a paternal gift

καὶ ἡ ἀγαθότης, οἷς πᾶσι κεκόσμησαι καὶ παῖς καὶ νεα-
νίας καὶ νέος καὶ νῦν ἐς ἄνδρας τελῶν. Ἀληθὲς ἄρα τὸ
τῆς τραγῳδίας ἐκεῖνο·

Δεινὸς χαρακτὴρ κἀπίσημος ἐν βροτοῖς
ἐσθλῶν γενέσθαι, κἀπὶ μεῖζον ἔρχεται
τῆς εὐγενείας τοὔνομα τοῖσιν ἀξίοις.

2 Οὐκοῦν ἐξέστω αὖθις εἰπεῖν, ὦ ἀγαθὲ υἱὲ πατρὸς ἀγαθοῦ·

Αἲ γάρ, Ζεῦ τε πάτερ καὶ Ἀθηναίη καὶ Ἄπολλον!
τοιοῦτοι δέκα μοι βασιλεῖς καὶ κοίρανοι εἶεν,

ὅτι ἐν τοῖς χαλεπωτάτοις τουτοισὶ χρόνοις καλῶς ἂν
εἶχε τὰ καθ᾽ ἡμᾶς ὑπὸ βασιλέων φιλοσοφούντων κατὰ
τὸν θεῖον Πλάτωνα διοικουμένων τῶν πόλεων, ὅστις ἐρω-
τηθείς ποτε πῶς ἂν ἄριστα διοικοῖντο αἱ πόλεις, εἶπεν·
Ἐὰν οἱ φιλόσοφοι βασιλεύσωσιν, ἢ οἱ βασιλεῖς φιλο-
σοφήσωσι. Σὺ τοίνυν τοιοῦτος ὢν ἐπιθυμεῖς ἄλλου μὲν
οὐδενὸς τοῦ ποιῆσαι δέ τι τούς τε ἀνθρώπους καὶ τὰς
πόλεις ἀγαθόν, τοῦτο δ᾽ ἄντικρυς εἰδότες οἱ λαοί σου δίς
σε βίᾳ τῶν πολεμίων τῆς ἀρχῆς ἐξωθούμενον, δὶς ἀπαξ-
άπαντες ὁμοφωνοῦντές τε καὶ ἀγαλλόμενοι, οὐκ ἀκινδύνως ἐς τὴν σὴν ἐπεσπάσαντο βασιλείαν· ἰδοὺ δή τι
καλόν τε καὶ ὠφέλιμον φιλόσοφον εἶναι καὶ βασιλέα
τὸν αὐτόν. Ἀλλὰ μικρὸν τοῦτ᾽ ἂν εἴη, εἰ μὴ ἀλλ᾽ ἄττ᾽
ἔχοι πολὺ μείζω πορίσαι ἡμῖν ἀγαθά· τουτέστιν, ἵνα μὴ
καθ᾽ ἕκαστα λέγων διατρίβω, ἀνδρείαν ἐν πᾶσι με-
γίστην. Φερέτωσαν οἵ τε καιροὶ καὶ αἱ τύχαι ὡς ἂν
βούλοιντο ἄνω καὶ κάτω τὰ τῶν ἀνθρώπων πράγματα,
καὶ αὐτὰ νῦν μὲν οὕτως ἐχέτω νῦν δ᾽ ἑτέρως· οὐ φροντὶς

for you, as is also goodness — by all of which you have been distinguished as child, adolescent, young man and now as a mature adult. So that quotation from tragedy is true:

> It is a marvelous stamp of distinction in mankind
> to be of fine descent, and the repute of high birth
> grows greater for those who are worthy of it.[263]

So let me say again, "Good son of a good father," 2

> Father Zeus, Athena and Apollo,
> may I have ten such kings and rulers,[264]

because in these extremely difficult times our affairs would prosper if philosopher kings governed cities as the divine Plato proposed. Once when asked how cities might be best governed he said "If philosophers are kings or kings philosophers."[265] And so, given your character, you have no wish to do anything other than good for men and their cities. Knowing that full well, your people have twice seen you driven from office by enemy force and twice with universal agreement and delight restored to your kingdom, not without risk. There we see how fine and beneficial it is to be philosopher and king.[266] That would not amount to much if it did not have the power to confer some other benefits of much greater value; by which I mean (I will not waste time by going into detail) the greatest bravery in all circumstances. Let chance and fate raise or depress human affairs as they will, and let them be at one moment as they are, and at another different — it is of no concern to

Ἱπποκλείδη. Οὐδὲν δήπου ἑαυτοῦ δυστυχοῦντος διοίσε-
ται εὐτυχῶν ἀνὴρ φιλόσοφος. Τοιούτους μέν τινας τῶν
παλαιῶν γενομένους, καὶ ἀκηκόαμεν παρὰ σοφῶν καὶ
ἀνέγνωμεν αὐτοὶ ἐν ἱστορίαις. Σὲ δὲ εἴδομεν ἐν ἑκατέρᾳ
τῇ τύχῃ θαυμαστόν· καὶ γὰρ ἐν τῇ εὐδαιμονίᾳ, πρὸς τῷ
δίκαιος εἶναι, καὶ ἀεὶ ὁμοιοτρόπως ἀγαθὸς καὶ πρᾷος εἶ
καὶ φιλάνθρωπος καὶ δὴ τὰ πάντα χαριέστατος· ἀλλ᾽
ὁπόταν τὰ παρὰ τῆς τύχης οὐ συναντᾷ σοι κατὰ τὸ
πρέπον καὶ κατὰ τὴν ἀξίαν τὴν σήν, τοιοῦτος ὢν τυγχάνεις, ὥστε δοκεῖν οὐδὲν ὅλως πάσχειν κακόν. Ἵνα δὲ
μὴ πόρρωθεν ἀνιχνεύωμεν παραδείγματα, ἐπιδείξω αὐτὸς
σαφέστατα τὴν σὴν ἀνδρείαν τε καὶ φρόνησιν· ἠκούσα-
μεν γὰρ οἷα μὲν ἔπαθες τοὺς ἐχθρούς σου φεύγων καὶ
τὴν δουλείαν, καὶ ὡς τέλος ἔσωσέ σε ὁ Θεός, ὅπως δ᾽
ἐνεκαρτέρησας τύχης ἀνεχόμενος ἐναντιούσης, ἐσμὲν
καὶ ἡμεῖς μάρτυρες σὺν ἄλλοις ὅτι πλείστοις τοῦτ᾽ αὐτὸ
ἑωρακότες Ἐνετίῃσι καὶ τεθαυμακότες, ὃ δὴ τῆς ἱερᾶς
δῶρόν ἐστι φιλοσοφίας.

3   Ταῦτα μὲν οὖν λογιζόμενος περὶ σοῦ, ἠθέλησα μίκρ᾽
ἄττα χαρίζεσθαί σοι, τοῦτο δὲ ποιεῖν ἄν μοι ἐδόκουν, εἰ
πρὸς σὲ πέμποιμι τὴν Ξενοφῶντος Ἑλληνικὴν ἱστορίαν,
ἅτινα λέγεται παραλειπόμενα τῆς Θουκυδίδου ξυγγρα-
φῆς, ἄρτι δὴ παρ᾽ ἡμῖν ἐντετυπωμένην, διὰ τὸ πάμπαν
εἶναι χαρίεσσαν, καὶ αὐτὸν τὸν συνθέντα οὕτω λόγιον,
οὕτω τοῦ Ἀττικοῦ πνέοντα θυμοῦ, ὥστε ὑπὸ τῶν παλαιῶν Ἑλλήνων καλεῖσθαι μέλισσαν Ἀττικήν· ἔτι δὲ
καὶ τῷ ἐοικέναι σοι τά τ᾽ ἄλλα καὶ τὴν ἡγεμονείαν·
ἡγεμὼν γὰρ ἦν ὁ Ξενοφῶν, τυγχάνεις δὲ ὢν καὶ αὐτός·
ἐκεῖνος καὶ σοφὸς ἦν τὴν παιδείαν καὶ τοὺς τρόπους

Hippocleides.[267] A philosopher enjoying good fortune will not be different from himself in misfortune. Some of the ancients were such men, as we have heard from scholars and read for ourselves in histories. We have seen that you are admirable in both extremes of fortune. In happy circumstances, apart from being just, you are always consistently noble, gentle, kind, and you display great charm in all matters. But when fortune does not treat you as it should and in accordance with your merits, you are the kind of person who seems not to be suffering in any way at all. Without making a search for more distant evidence I will myself demonstrate in full clarity your bravery and wisdom. For we have heard how you suffered in escaping from your enemies and from slavery, how in the end God saved you, how you were steadfast in your acceptance of hostile fate. We are also admiring eyewitnesses, along with many others, of those same qualities in Venice, and that is the gift of sacred philosophy.

This being my opinion of you, I wanted to do you some small 3 favor, and I thought I could do it by sending you Xenophon's *Hellenica*, which is said to be matter omitted by Thucydides. It was recently printed by us because it is thoroughly charming, and the author himself so intelligent, so perfumed by Attic thyme, that the ancients called him the Attic bee.[268] In addition it suits you because of the military events described and in other ways. Xenophon was a commander and so are you. He was well educated and

κόσμιος, γέγονας καὶ αὐτὸς θαυμαστὸς τὰ τοιαῦτα.
Ἀλλὰ περὶ τῆς σῆς ἀρετῆς νυνὶ ταῦτα.

4 Ἐτυπώθη δ' ὁμοῦ Ἡρωδιανὸς περὶ τῆς μετὰ Μάρκον
βασιλείας, καὶ Πλήθωνος τὰ παραλειπόμενα, καὶ σχόλιά
τινα πάνυ ἀναγκαῖα ἐς Θουκυδίδην, ὧν χωρὶς μικροῦ
δεῖν ἀξύνετος ὁ συγγραφεύς.

5 Ταῦτα δὴ οὖν σοι ἐδωρησάμην, ἀρεστὰ καὶ κεχα-
ρισμένα ποιεῖσθαί σοι νομίζων, καὶ ὅπως εἴη παρὰ σοὶ
μνημεῖον ἧς ἔχων ἀεὶ διατετέλεκα πρός τέ σε καὶ τὴν
σὴν βασιλείαν εὐνοίας. Ἔρρωσο.
Ἐνετίῃσιν Ἀνθεστηριῶνος τετάρτῃ καὶ δέκα. ͵α. φ. γ.

: XXVI :

Aldus Pius Manutius Romanus Alberto Pio Carpensium principi s. p. d.

1 Ioannis grammatici, cui ob labores assiduos, quorum constat eum
fuisse perstudiosum (φιλόπονος γὰρ φιλεργός, περὶ τὸ πονεῖν
πρόθυμος), Philopono inditum est cognomentum, in priora philosophi resolutoria commentarios statim post Ammonium in
librum de interpretatione, ut par erat et librorum Aristotelis ordo
exigebat, excusos cura nostra publicare constitueram; sed quia
quos is ipse Philoponus in resolutoria posteriora composuit, para-
tiores correctioresque haberentur, illos nunc damus, daturi deinceps, Deo favente, et reliquos.

of sober character, and you too are remarkable in such respects. But let that suffice for now on the subject of your virtues.

In the same volume Herodian on the empire after Marcus and   4
Plethon's *Supplement*[269] are printed, together with some absolutely essential scholia on Thucydides, without which that author is almost unintelligible.

So I offer you this gift, reckoning to do something welcome and   5
pleasing, in the hope it may remind you of the loyalty I have always felt toward you and your kingdom. Farewell.

Venice, Anthesterion[270] *14, 1503.*

: XXVI :

John Philoponus, Commentary on the Posterior Analytics
Anonymous, Commentary on the Posterior Analytics[271]
(March 1504)

Aldus Pius Manutius of Rome to Alberto Pio,
prince of Carpi, warmest greetings.

John the grammarian was nicknamed Philoponus on account of   1
his unremitting activity, since it is clear that he was most industrious (*philoponos* is equivalent to *philergos*, "eager to work hard").[272] I had decided that we should print his commentaries on the *Prior Analytics* immediately after Ammonius on the *De interpretatione*, as was reasonable and required by the sequence of Aristotle's works.[273] But as Philoponus' own commentary on the *Posterior Analytics* was easier to obtain and in more correct copies,[274] we publish it now, with subsequent publication, God willing, of the remainder.

2   Quoniam vero inter imprimendum varia nobis fuere exemplaria, nihil aut addere aut diminuere aut commutare audentes (temerarium enim id quidem), quae varia visa sunt, asteriscis signanda curavimus, inde operi absoluto addenda, quo unicuique pro arbitrio suo de illis liceret diiudicare. In secundum etiam resolutoriorum librum duplicem nacti expositionem, utranque iussimus informandam: nihil enim praeterire est animus, quod utile fore studiosis visum fuerit. Quodsi evenerit quod speramus (ἐλπίδες γὰρ ἐν ζωοῖσιν), tanquam praeludium quae dedimus fuisse dicent omnes prae iis, quae Iesu Deo optimo maximo annuente sumus daturi.

3   Sub tuo vero haec iucundo mihi nomine, Alberte Pie doctissime, ex Neacademia nostra in studiosorum manus emittimus. Tu nanque es et praesidium et dulce decus meum.

   Venetiis mense Martio MDIIII.

: XXVII :

A

Aldus Pius Manutius Romanus Matthaeo Longio, Caesareae
maiestatis a secretis ac praeposito Augustensi, s. p. d.

1   Magnam vim esse probitatis, praesul dignissime, ut eam vel in eis, quos nunquam vidimus, diligamus, cum saepe alias experiendo

Since we found variation in the exemplars while printing, not 2
venturing to add, delete or alter anything (that would be rash), we
have marked with asterisks passages where variants were found;
these are added at the end of the volume, so that everyone can
exercise his own judgment about them. Having found an alternative exposition of the second book of the *Analytics*, we gave instructions to print both; my aim is not to omit anything that looks
as if it will be useful to scholars. If this turns out as we hope (for
there is hope among the living),[275] everyone will say that what we
have produced is a kind of prelude to what we will provide, with
the help of Jesus, the God who is best and greatest.

We issue this work from our Neacademia for scholars; it is is- 3
sued in your name, most learned Alberto Pio, a name dear to me.
For you are my defense and my sweet source of fame.[276]

Venice, March 1504.

: XXVII :

Aristotle and Theophrastus,
Zoological and Botanical Writings;
Pseudo-Aristotle and Alexander of Aphrodisias, Problemata,
translated into Latin by Theodore Gaza[277]
(March 27, 1504)

A

Aldus Pius Manutius to Matthaeus Lang,[278] *private secretary to his
Imperial Majesty and provost of Augsburg, warmest greetings.*

On many other occasions, and especially this year, most venerable 1
prelate, I have learned by experience how great the power of integrity is, it being such that we appreciate it even in people we have

cognovi, tum hoc anno maxime. Nam, licet te de facie non cognoscam, tamen, ex quo scripsit ad me Vienna Cuspinianus, doctus homo et fidei plenus, de moribus, de doctrina, de probitate tua, cumque idem saepe Ioannes Fruticenus mihi, cum mecum viveret, dixerit, ita sum factus tuus, ut non possim magis. Addebat Fruticenus te a divo Maximiliano Caesare ad hunc, in quo nunc es, dignitatis gradum tua virtute et probitate evectum, solereque Caesarem id genus homines amplecti, fovere, extollere. Qua in re et illius maiestas plurimum laudanda est, et tu, qui viam ad astra virtute affectes, ac doctrina et integritate carissimus factus sis Caesari. Ex qua re licet inferre doctrina et illum esse et probitate ornatum:

αἰεὶ γὰρ τὸν ὅμοιον ἄγει θεὸς ὡς τὸν ὅμοιον.

2   Tot tuis igitur laudibus desyderabam aliqua in re gratificari tibi, qua observantiam in te meam cognosceres. Quapropter, cum nuper Aristotelis de animalibus et Theophrasti de plantis libros una cum eiusdem Aristotelis et Alexandri problematis imprimendos curassem, quae omnia Theodorus Gaza, suae aetatis eruditorum facile princeps, et feliciter et erudite Latinitate donavit, tibi eos dicare constitui ac muneri mittere, ut benevolentiam in te meam apud te perpetuo contestarentur, efficerentque sua praesentia, quo saepenumero Aldi memor esses tui.

3   En igitur eos ad te libros misimus, rati dignitati tuae, tum multarum rerum, quibus referti sunt, cognitione, tum correctione nostra, fore gratissimos. Quantum vero ipsis corrigendis elaborarimus, legens ac conferens cum Graecis exemplaribus tu ipse cognosces et miseresces laborum nostrorum.

Venetiis sexto calendas Apriles M.D.IIII.

never set eyes on. For although I do not know you from a meeting face to face, nevertheless, ever since the learned and trustworthy Cuspinianus[279] wrote to me from Vienna about your character, erudition and integrity—and since Giovanni Fruticeno,[280] when he lived with me, often told me the same—my loyalty to you has been so complete that I cannot do more. Fruticeno added that thanks to your ability and integrity you had been elevated by the divine[281] Emperor Maximilian to the high rank you now hold, and that the Emperor makes it his practice to welcome, encourage and promote men of this kind. In this matter his Majesty is greatly to be applauded, and you, by your merits taking the path to reach the stars,[282] have made yourself the Emperor's very close friend, thanks to your learning and honesty. From this fact it is possible to infer that he too is learned and honorable.

For God always joins like to like.[283]

I therefore wished to offer you a favor of some kind in recogni-　2 tion of your numerous merits, so that you could be aware of my high regard for you. That being so, since I had lately seen to the printing of Aristotle's zoological and Theophrastus' botanical works, along with Aristotle's and Alexander's *Problemata*, all rendered elegantly and with learning by Theodore Gaza,[284] certainly the leading scholar of his generation, I decided to dedicate them to you and send them as a gift, a possession to bear lasting witness to my goodwill toward you, ensuring by their presence that you would frequently be reminded of your friend Aldus.

Look, then: we've sent these books to you, reckoning that they　3 would be most welcome to Your Worthiness, both because of the multifarious knowledge they contain and because we've corrected them. How much effort we expended in correcting them you will see for yourself by reading and comparing them with the Greek text, and you will take pity on our labors.

Venice, March 27, 1504.

B

4   In toto hoc emendanda volumine, quae alicuius sunt visa momenti, haec sunt. Sed nota, lector, ad versuum inveniendum numerum scriptos tantum esse connumerandos.

5   Haec in summis occupationibus, ut potuimus, volumine cursim recognito, adnotavimus. Nec imus inficias multa nos, quae emendare oportuit, praeteriisse; sed ea inter studendum emendent quibus plus quam nobis ocii fuerit. Ego enim solus non possum omnia; atque utinam id eveniat, quod speramus, quod molimur; quandoquidem et pulchriora omnia et correctiora dabuntur. Quod si non licuerit, vel voluisse non poenitebit.

Venetiis mense Martio M.D.IIII.

: XXVIII :

Aldus Pius Manutius Romanus Zenobio Florentino
ordinis praedicatorum s.

1   Sperabam, Zenobi doctissime, in libris Philostrati de Apollonii Tyanensis vita me quam plurima et digna scitu et praeclara lecturum; sed longe aliter certe evenit. Nihil enim unquam memini me legere deterius lectuque minus dignum: nam non modo fabulosa omnia et anicularum narrationibus persimilia visa sunt, sed insulsa quoque et perinepta. Qua re quanta inter legendum molestia, quanto taedio affectus fuerim, non facile dixerim. Sed quid facerem? Desistere ab incoeptis turpe existimabam: receperam enim me et Graece et Latine eum librum studiosis daturum. Tum, quia

B[285]

Here are the errata in the whole of this volume that seemed to be of some importance. But note, reader, that in order to find the line number only full lines are to be counted.[286]   4

We have made these notes as we could, editing the volume rapidly in the midst of important business. And we are not going to deny that we've passed over a lot of things that should be corrected; but those who have more time than we do should correct them in the course of their studies. I can't do everything by myself. Would that what we hoped and planned will turn out to be the case, seeing that everything will be produced in a more beautiful and correct form. If that is not made possible, we won't be sorry for having wished it so.   5

: XXVIII :

Philostratus, Life of Apollonius of Tyana
Eusebius of Caesarea, Against Hierocles
(*May 1504*)

*Aldus Pius Manutius of Rome, to Zanobi the
Dominican of Florence,*[287] *greetings.*

I had hoped, most learned Zanobi, to read in Philostratus' books about the life of Apollonius of Tyana a great many important things worth knowing, but it really turned out quite otherwise. I cannot recall ever reading anything worse or less deserving attention; not only did it all seem fantasy and like old wives' tales, but it was tasteless and very stupid. So I cannot easily describe the annoyance and boredom I felt while reading it. But what was I to do? I thought it improper to give up, having once started, because I had promised to produce this text in Greek and Latin for   1

iam ter Latine excusus tanquam venenum sine antidoto vagaba-
tur—deerat enim Eusebii opusculum, quod illum moderaretur et
redargueret falsumque ostenderet—, operae pretium videbatur, si
et Philostrati libros et in illos id ipsum Eusebii opusculum, tum
Graecum tum Latinum docte a te eleganterque tralatum, emitterem ex aedibus nostris, ut, si quispiam ex Philostrati libris veneni
aliquid imbibisset, haberet Eusebium, quo ut mustella ad rutam a
serpente demorsa confugeret.

2   Quoniam vero divus Hieronymus octo Philostrati de vita Apollonii libris habere fidem videtur, cum in epistola ad Paulinum
presbyterum de divinae historiae libris sic dicit: 'Apollonius ille,
sive magus, ut vulgus loquitur, sive philosophus, ut Pythagorici
tradunt, intravit Persas, pertransivit Caucasum, Albanos, Scythas,
Massagetas, opulentissima Indiae regna penetravit, et ad extremum, latissimo Phison amne transmisso, pervenit ad Bragmanas,
ut Iarcham in throno sedentem aureo et de Tantali fonte po-
tantem, inter paucos discipulos de natura, de moribus ac de cursu
dierum et syderum audiret docentem. Inde per Elamitas, Babylo-
nios, Chaldaeos, Medos, Assyrios, Parthos, Syros, Phoenices, Ara-
bas, Palaestinos reversus ad Alexandriam, perrexit ad Aethiopiam,
ut Gymnosophistas et famosissimam solis mensam videret in sabulo. Invenit ille vir ubique quod disceret et, semper proficiens,
semper se melior fieret. Scripsit super hoc plenissime octo voluminibus Philostratus'—quoniam igitur his verbis confirmare videtur
divus Hieronymus scripta Philostrati, non modo librum, quem
Hierocles scripsit, quo ex nugis Philostrati Apollonium Iesu
Christo humani generis redemptori temere comparavit, aut Eusebii apologiam non vidisse eum arbitror, sed ne octo quidem
Philostrati de vita Apollonii libros accurate legisse. Nunquam

students.[288] Then, since the work had been printed in Latin three times and circulated as a poison without antidote—it lacked the essay by Eusebius[289] to discuss and refute him, proving him false —it seemed a good idea for us to publish Philostratus' work and that essay by Eusebius directed at it, both in Greek and in your competent and elegant Latin version; thus anyone who imbibed some poison from Philostratus' book could have Eusebius, to whom he might turn as a weasel bitten by a snake has recourse to rue.

But St. Jerome seems to give credit to Philostratus' eight books   2
On the Life of Apollonius, when in a letter to the presbyter Paulinus [of Nola] about books on sacred history he says:[290] "That man Apollonius, whether he was a magician as popular belief has it, or a philosopher as the Pythagoreans report, crossed into Persia, traveled through the Caucasus, among Albanians, Scythians and the Massagetae, reached the wealthy realms of India, and finally after crossing the broad river Phison, came to the Brahmins, with the result that he heard Iarchas. He was seated on a golden throne and drinking from the fountain of Tantalus, lecturing to a few students about nature, ethics, the passing of time and the movement of the stars. Then he returned to Alexandria via the Elamites, Babylonians, Chaldaeans, Medes, Assyrians, Parthians, Syrians, Phoenicians, Arabs, and Palestinians. He went as far as Ethiopia to see the Gymnosophists and the celebrated table of the sun in the sand.[291] Everywhere he went he found something to learn so as to improve himself, with continuous progress all the time. Philostratus wrote a very full account of him in eight books." Since Jerome seems by these remarks to lend authority to Philostratus' work, I think he had not seen Hierocles' book,[292] with its comparison of Apollonius to Jesus Christ, the redeemer of humanity, on the basis of nonsense from Philostratus, nor the *Apologia* by Eusebius, and I think he had not even read Philostratus' eight books *On the Life of Apollonius* attentively. As a vigorous

enim acerrimus ille Christiani nominis propugnator in Hieroclis scripta non invehi nedum non scribere potuisset aut saltem in ea ipsa epistola ad Paulinum aliove in loco temerarii illius conatus non meminisse. Nam nec ipse id legi apud Hieronymum nec audivi qui legerit: multos enim Hieronymi studiosos consuluimus.

3   Tum, ubi de sede Iarchae meminit, auream illam fuisse scribit, cum Philostratus ex aere nigro aureis imagunculis distinctam fuisse dicat his verbis:

Ὁ δὲ Ἰάρχας ἐκάθητο μὲν ἐπὶ δίφρου ὑψηλοῦ, χαλ-
κοῦ δὲ μέλανος ἦν, καὶ πεποίκιλτο χρυσοῖς ἀγάλμα-
σιν, οἱ δὲ τῶν ἄλλων δίφροι χαλκοὶ μέν, ἄσημοι δὲ
ἦσαν, ὑψηλοὶ δὲ ἧττον· ἐπεκάθηντο γὰρ τῷ Ἰάρχᾳ.

4   Praeterea in Aethiopiam profectum ait Apollonium, ut Gymnosophistas et famosissimam solis mensam videret in sabulo. At de mensa solis apud Philostratum nulla est mentio, nec quicquam admiratione dignum in Aethiopia vidisse Apollonium refert praeter Memnonis Aurorae filii statuam, de qua haec scribit:

Τὸ δὲ ἄγαλμα τεθράφθαι πρὸς ἀκτῖνα μήπω γενει-
άσκον, λίθου δὲ εἶναι μέλανος, ξυμβεβηκέναι δὲ τὼ
πόδε ἄμφω κατὰ τὴν ἀγαλματοποιίαν τὴν ἐπὶ Δαι-
δάλου, καὶ τὰς χεῖρας ἀπερείδειν ὀρθὰς ἐπὶ τὸν θά-
κον· καθῆσθαι γὰρ ἐν ὁρμῇ τοῦ ὑπανίστασθαι τὸ
σχῆμα τοῦτο, καὶ τὸν τῶν ὀφθαλμῶν νοῦν, καὶ
ὁπόσα τοῦ στόματος ὡς φθεγξαμένου ᾄδουσι· καὶ
τὸν μὲν ἄλλον χρόνον ἧττον θαυμάσαι φασίν· οὔπω γὰρ ἐνεργὰ φαίνεσθαι. Προσβαλούσης δὲ τὸ
ἄγαλμα τῆς ἀκτῖνος—τουτὶ δὲ γίγνεσθαι περὶ ἡλίου
ἐπιτολάς—μὴ κατασχεῖν τὸ θαῦμα· φθέγξασθαι

defender of Christianity he could not have failed, not just to attack the works of Hierocles, but to lambaste them; nor indeed could he have failed, either in that same letter to Paulinus or in some other place, to mention that insolent suggestion. I have not read any such thing in Jerome nor heard of anyone who has, despite consulting many students of Jerome.

At the point where he mentions Iarchas' seat he says it was 3 golden, whereas Philostratus tells us as follows: that it was made of black bronze and decorated with small figures in gold.

> Iarchas sat on a high chair; it was of black bronze and decorated with figures in gold. The others had bronze chairs but they were not decorated and they were not as tall, because they sat below Iarchas.[293]

Besides that he says Apollonius went to Ethiopia to see the 4 Gymnosophists and the celebrated table of the sun in the sand. But Philostratus says nothing about the table of the sun, and he does not report Apollonius having seen anything worthy of note in Ethiopia except the statue of Memnon, the son of Aurora, about which he says:[294]

> Τὸ δὲ ἄγαλμα τετράφθαι πρὸς ἀκτῖνα μήπω γενει-
> άσκον, λίθου δὲ εἶναι μέλανος, ξυμβεβηκέναι δὲ τὼ
> πόδε ἄμφω κατὰ τὴν ἀγαλματοποιίαν τὴν ἐπὶ Δαι-
> δάλου, καὶ τὰς χεῖρας ἀπερείδειν ὀρθὰς ἐπὶ τὸν θά-
> κον· καθῆσθαι γὰρ ἐν ὁρμῇ τοῦ ὑπανίστασθαι τὸ
> σχῆμα τοῦτο, καὶ τὸν τῶν ὀφθαλμῶν νοῦν, καὶ
> ὁπόσα τοῦ στόματος ὡς φθεγξαμένου ᾄδουσι· καὶ
> τὸν μὲν ἄλλον χρόνον ἧττον θαυμάσαι φασίν· οὔ-
> πω γὰρ ἐνεργὰ φαίνεσθαι. Προσβαλούσης δὲ τὸ
> ἄγαλμα τῆς ἀκτῖνος—τουτὶ δὲ γίγνεσθαι περὶ ἡλίου
> ἐπιτολάς—μὴ κατασχεῖν τὸ θαῦμα· φθέγξασθαι

μὲν γὰρ παραχρῆμα τῆς ἀκτῖνος ἐλθούσης αὐτῷ
ἐπὶ στόμα· φαιδροὺς δὲ ἱστάναι τοὺς ὀφθαλμοὺς
δόξαι πρὸς τὸ φῶς, οἷα τῶν ἀνθρώπων οἱ εὐήλιοι.
Τότε ξυνεῖναι λέγουσιν, ὅτι τῷ ἡλίῳ δοκεῖ ὑπανίστασθαι, καθάπερ οἱ τὸ κρεῖττον ὀρθοὶ θεραπεύοντες.

Hoc est, ut, siqui haec Graecarum literarum rudes legerint, et ipsi
intelligant:

Statuam vero (Memnonis scilicet, scribit Damis) ad solis
versam fuisse radios impuberemque et ex nigro lapide, ac
pedes ambos, secundum quae Daedali fuit temporibus sta-
tuariam, coiisse; manus praeterea inniti rectas ad sedem:
nam surgere volentis habitu sedere illam, oculorumque men-
tem et quaecunque locuti oris praedicant. Atque alio quidem
tempore minus eos admiratos dicunt, quod nihil quicquam
agere videretur; at cum solis radius statuam tetigit, quod
fiebat oriente sole, non potuisse aiunt non demirari: nam
cum primum solis radius ad illius os pervenit, locutam memorant, hilaresque oculos velut puros hominum visus stetisse ad lucem. Tunc aiunt intellexisse nascenti soli, quemadmodum qui Deum recti adorant, statuam videri assurgere.

De hac statua Iuvenalis satyra penultima:

Dimidio magicae resonant ubi Memnone chordae;

de eadem quoque et Plinius et Strabo meminerunt.

5   Cum igitur ad hanc famosissimam statuam plurimi accederent
videndi gratia, et Apollonium accessisse scribit Philostratus; de
mensa vero solis, ut dixi, nusquam meminit. Esse tamen eam in

μὲν γὰρ παραχρῆμα τῆς ἀκτῖνος ἐλθούσης αὐτῷ
ἐπὶ στόμα· φαιδροὺς δὲ ἱστάναι τοὺς ὀφθαλμοὺς
δόξαι πρὸς τὸ φῶς, οἷα τῶν ἀνθρώπων οἱ εὐήλιοι.
Τότε ξυνεῖναι λέγουσιν, ὅτι τῷ ἡλίῳ δοκεῖ ὑπανίστασθαι, καθάπερ οἱ τὸ κρεῖττον ὀρθοὶ θεραπεύοντες.

That is (so that if there are any readers without knowledge of
Greek, they too may follow),

> But the statue ⟨of Memnon, that is, writes Damis⟩ faces the
> rays of the sun, it does not yet have a beard, and is made of
> black stone. Its feet are joined together, in the style of statu-
> ary in the age of Daedalus; the hands press straight down on
> the seat; the pose was of someone about to get up; people
> comment on the intelligence in the eyes and on the lips that
> are saying something.[295] At most times, they say, it was less
> remarkable because it seemed completely inert; but when the
> rays of the sun hit the statue, which happened at sunrise,
> they say one could not fail to be astonished; as soon as the
> sun's rays reached its mouth, they say the statue spoke, and
> its eyes, as if with clear human gaze, look up happily toward
> the light. Then they claim to have understood that the statue
> was getting up in honor of the rising sun, in the same way as
> men stand to worship God.

In his penultimate satire Juvenal says of this statue:

> when magical chords resound in the half-preserved Mem-
> non.[296]

Pliny[297] and Strabo[298] also mention it.

Since a great many people traveled to that famous statue, Phi-   5
lostratus says that Apollonius also went; but as I said, he never
mentions the table of the sun. Solinus, however, in chapter 40

Aethiopia sic Solinus capite xxxx: 'Locus apud eos est Heliotrapeza, opiparis epulis semper refertus, quibus indiscrete omnes vescuntur: nam etiam divinitus eas augeri ferunt.' Sic item Herodotus libro tertio, cui Thaliae nomen:

Ἡ δὲ τράπεζα τοῦ ἡλίου τοιήδε τις λέγεται εἶναι·
λειμών ἐστιν ἐν τῷ προαστείῳ ἐπίπλεος κρεῶν
ἑφθῶν πάντων τῶν τετραπόδων, ἐς τὸν τὰς μὲν
νύκτας ἐπιτηδεύοντας τιθέναι τὰ κρέα τοὺς ἐν τέλεϊ
ἑκάστους ἐόντας τῶν ἀστῶν, τὰς δὲ ἡμέρας δαίνυσθαι προσιόντα τὸν βουλόμενον. Φάναι δὲ τοὺς ἐπιχωρίους ταῦτα τὴν γῆν αὐτὴν ἀναδιδόναι ἑκάστοτε.
Ἡ μὲν δὴ τράπεζα τοῦ ἡλίου καλεομένη λέγεται
εἶναι τοιήδε.

Solis autem mensam fuisse aiunt huiusmodi. Est in suburbano pratum decoctarum carnium plenum quadrupedum omnium, quo magistratus urbium singulos perhibent nocte quidem certatim carnes adferre, die vero licere eas quicunque adcesserit epulari, atque ab ipsa terra undique has elargiri praedicare indigenas. Solis igitur quae adpellatur mensa huiusmodi fuisse dicitur.

Haec apud Herodotum legisse Hieronymum arbitror, ac alterum pro altero, hoc est pro Memnonis statua solis mensam per errorem posuisse: utraque enim erat in Aethiopia.

6   Sic item pro Indo amne Fison scripsisse eundem existimo, ubi ait: 'Et ad extremum, latissimo Fison amne transmisso, pervenit ad Bragmanas.' Nam de Fison nusquam meminit Philostratus, sed de Tigri, Euphrate, Cophino, Indo, Hydraote, Hyphaside, qui antequam veniatur ad Bragmanas inveniuntur; estque Indus latissimus omnium. De quo sic Philostratus:

places it in Ethiopia, as follows: "There is a locality there called Heliotrapeza, always loaded with rich banquet food, consumed by all without distinction; they say it is kept supplied by divine agency." Similarly Herodotus in Book III.[299]

'Η δὲ τράπεζα τοῦ ἡλίου τοιήδε τις λέγεται εἶναι·
λειμών ἐστιν ἐν τῷ προαστείῳ ἐπίπλεος κρεῶν
ἑφθῶν πάντων τῶν τετραπόδων, ἐς τὸν τὰς μὲν
νύκτας ἐπιτηδεύοντας τιθέναι τὰ κρέα τοὺς ἐν τέλεϊ
ἑκάστους ἐόντας τῶν ἀστῶν, τὰς δὲ ἡμέρας δαίνυσθαι προσιόντα τὸν βουλόμενον. Φάναι δὲ τοὺς ἐπιχωρίους ταῦτα τὴν γῆν αὐτὴν ἀναδιδόναι ἑκάστοτε.
'Η μὲν δὴ τράπεζα τοῦ ἡλίου καλεομένη λέγεται
εἶναι τοιήδε.

The table of the sun is described as follows: in a suburb there is a meadow full of cooked meats from every kind of quadruped. At night all the citizens who are officeholders regularly put out the meat, and during the day anyone who wishes comes to enjoy a feast. The natives say that the earth itself is always the provider. That is what the table of the sun is said to be like.

I think Jerome read this in Herodotus and confused one thing with another, mistakenly mentioning the table of the sun instead of the statue of Memnon, since both were in Ethiopia.

In the same way I think he wrote Fison by mistake for the river 6 Indus, when he says: "And at the end, crossing the very broad river Fison, he reached the Brahmins." Philostratus never speaks of Fison, but of the Tigris, Euphrates, Cophinus, Indus, Hydraotes and Hyphasides, which are located before he reaches the Brahmins, and the Indus is the widest of them all, of which Philostratus has this to say:[300]

Τὸν μὲν δὴ Ἰνδὸν ὧδε ἐπεραιώθησαν σταδίους μάλιστα τεσσαράκοντα· τὸ γὰρ πλόϊμον αὐτοῦ τοσοῦ-
τον· περὶ δὲ τοῦ ποταμοῦ τούτου τάδε γράφουσι,
τὸν Ἰνδὸν ἄρχεσθαι μὲν ἐκ τοῦ Καυκάσου, μεῖζον᾽
αὐτόθεν ἢ οἱ κατὰ τὴν Ἀσίαν ποταμοὶ πάντες, προ-
χωρεῖν δὲ πολλοὺς τῶν ναυσιπόρων ἑαυτοῦ ποιού-
μενον.

Sic itaque Indum praetervecti sunt stadiis maxime quadraginta: tantum enim in eo navigabile est. Sed de amne hoc sic
scribunt: Indum oriri quidem a Caucaso, maiorem inde
quam omnes qui per Asiam fluvii; navigabiles vero ex se multos facere.

Et licet non hunc ad extremum, antequam pervenisset ad Bragmanas, transierit Apollonius, sed Hydraotem — nam ad Hyphasidem
pervenisse quidem scribit eum Philostratus, sed non transmisisse
etiam: potuit enim secundum flumen iter facere —, tamen, quia
Indus maximus est fluviorum omnium, quos traiecit Apollonius,
quemadmodum et Philostratus tradit, et quia ab Indo flumine
Indi dicti — sic enim Stephanus: Ἰνδὸς ποταμός, ἀφ᾽ οὗ Ἰν-
δοί —, verisimilius videtur pro Fison latissimo amne Indum quam
Hydraotem aut alium intelligi.

7   Quod vero pro Indo Fison scripserit Hieronymus, quoniam
apud Hebraeos sic appellatus sit Indus, mihi non videtur, tum
quia Indus a Caucaso nascitur, Fison vero a delitiarum hortis, qui
ἐπίγειος παράδεισος Graece dicuntur, tum etiam quia ipse in
Genesim, ubi dicitur nomen uni Fison, ait: 'Hunc esse Indiae flu-
vium Gangem putant.' Quod item pro Gange acceperit, negatur,
quia nunquam traiecisse Gangem scribitur Apollonius; praeterea
perabsurdum videtur maluisse illum Hebraica dictione quam

Τὸν μὲν δὴ Ἰνδὸν ὧδε ἐπεραιώθησαν σταδίους μάλιστα τεσσαράκοντα· τὸ γὰρ πλόϊμον αὐτοῦ τοσοῦ-
τον· περὶ δὲ τοῦ ποταμοῦ τούτου τάδε γράφουσι,
τὸν Ἰνδὸν ἄρχεσθαι μὲν ἐκ τοῦ Καυκάσου, μείζον᾽
αὐτόθεν ἢ οἱ κατὰ τὴν Ἀσίαν ποταμοὶ πάντες, προ-
χωρεῖν δὲ πολλοὺς τῶν ναυσιπόρων ἑαυτοῦ ποιού-
μενον.

And so they crossed the Indus like that, about forty stades,[301]
since it is navigable up to that point. But this is what they
say about the river: the Indus rises in the Caucasus and is
immediately bigger than all the rivers in Asia, and it creates
from its own waters many that are navigable.

And though Apollonius did not cross this river last before reaching the Brahmins, but the Hydraotes (for Philostratus says he
reached the Hyphasides and did not cross it because he could
travel with the current), still, as the Indus is the biggest of all the
rivers that Apollonius crossed, as Philostratus also reports, and
because the Indians are named after the Indus (Stephanus says
"The Indus river, hence Indians"[302]), it seems more likely that instead of the broad river Fison one should understand the Indus,
rather than the Hydraotes or another.

The idea that Jerome wrote Fison instead of Indus because that   7
is the Hebrew name for the Indus does not seem plausible to me,
because the Indus rises in the Caucasus, whereas Fison derives
from the gardens of pleasure, termed in Greek "paradise on
earth";[303] also commenting on *Genesis*, where Fison[304] is the name
of one of the rivers, he says: "Some people think Fison is the Ganges in India." But that he took it for the Ganges is refuted by the
fact that Apollonius is nowhere reported to have crossed the Ganges — apart from which it seems quite absurd for him to have preferred a Hebrew name to a Greek one, which we have adopted,

Graeca, quae et nostra facta est, uti, praesertim cum ad Latinum scriberet. Quamobrem non advertisse illum potius dixerim, quandoquidem parum huiuscemodi rerum satagebat ac invitus potius meminerat; quod et ipse in Danielem sic testatur:

> Et si quando cogimur literarum secularium recordari et aliqua ex iis dicere, quae olim omisimus, non est nostrae voluntatis, sed, ut ita dicam, gravissimae necessitatis.

8   Nec mirum sic errare Hieronymum potuisse: homo enim fuit, et transferendis componendisque sacris libris semper occupatissimus. Idem cum aliis tum et M. Tullio evenisse legimus: quod et Gellius in noctibus et Politianus in miscellaneis attestantur, et ipse in epistolis ad Atticum μνημονικὸν ἁμάρτημα fuisse fatetur, id est erratum memoriae.

9   Quod si dixerit quispiam Hieronymum apud alios, qui de vita Apollonii conscripserunt, Apollonium ipsum in Aethiopiam profectum, ut et solis mensam videret in sabulo, legere potuisse, id ego propterea negaverim, quia Philostratus omnes, quicunque ante se scripserunt aliquid de Apollonio, collegit in unum, ut in eo ipso contra Hieroclem libello his verbis tradit Eusebius:

> Δάμις μὲν οὖν ὁ πολλὰ ξυνδιατρίψας τῷ Ἀπολλωνίῳ ἀπὸ τῆς Ἀσσυρίων γῆς ὁρμώμενος αὐτόθι τε πρῶτον ἐπὶ τῆς ἰδίας χώρας αὐτῷ ξυμμίξας τὴν ἐξ ἐκείνου μετὰ τοῦ ἀνδρὸς αὐτῷ γενομένην ξυνουσίαν ἱστόρησεν. Ὁ δὲ Μάξιμος κομιδῇ βραχέα τῶν κατὰ μέρος αὐτῷ πεπραγμένων ἀνεγράψατο. Ὅ γε μὴν Ἀθηναῖος Φιλόστρατος τὰ φερόμενα πάντα ὁμοῦ, ἀπό τε τῶν Μαξίμου καὶ αὐτοῦ Δάμιδος καὶ ἄλλων συναγαγεῖν ἑαυτὸν φήσας, πάντων μάλιστα

especially as he was writing to a Latin speaker. So I think it more likely that he did not notice, as he was not very interested in such matters and presumably dealt with them unwillingly, as he himself says in his commentary on *Daniel*:[305]

> And if we are sometimes obliged to refer to secular literature and to quote from it—something we gave up long ago—it is not of our own volition but, as I may say, from direst necessity.

That Jerome made such a mistake is not surprising; he was human and always very busy with translating or writing religious works. We have read that this happened to others including Cicero. This is attested by both Gellius in his *Attic Nights*[306] and Poliziano in his *Miscellanea*,[307] and he himself in letters to Atticus admits a μνημονικὸν ἁμάρτημα, that is a lapse of memory.[308]

If anyone says that Jerome could have read in other authors describing the life of Apollonius that Apollonius himself went to Ethiopia to see the table of the sun, I would deny it on the ground that Philostratus assembled in one work all the authorities who had previously written anything about Apollonius, as Eusebius says in that same pamphlet refuting Hierocles, as follows:

> Δάμις μὲν οὖν ὁ πολλὰ ξυνδιατρίψας τῷ Ἀπολ-
> λωνίῳ ἀπὸ τῆς Ἀσσυρίων γῆς ὁρμώμενος αὐτόθι
> τε πρῶτον ἐπὶ τῆς ἰδίας χώρας αὐτῷ ξυμμίξας τὴν
> ἐξ ἐκείνου μετὰ τοῦ ἀνδρὸς αὐτῷ γενομένην ξυ-
> νουσίαν ἱστόρησεν. Ὁ δὲ Μάξιμος κομιδῇ βραχέα
> τῶν κατὰ μέρος αὐτῷ πεπραγμένων ἀνεγράψατο. Ὁ
> γε μὴν Ἀθηναῖος Φιλόστρατος τὰ φερόμενα πάντα
> ὁμοῦ, ἀπό τε τῶν Μαξίμου καὶ αὐτοῦ Δάμιδος καὶ
> ἄλλων συναγαγεῖν ἑαυτὸν φήσας, πάντων μάλιστα

ἐντελῆ τὴν ἀπὸ γενέσεως καὶ μέχρι τελευτῆς ἱστορίαν τοῦ κατὰ τὸν ἄνδρα βίου πεποίηται.

Damis igitur ab Assyria oriundus, quod diu cum Apollonio
vixerit quodque in propria regione primum se ei coniunxerit,
suam ab eo tempore cum illo peregrinationem historiae tradidit. Maximus vero pauca admodum, quae ab illo singilla-
tim gesta sunt, perscripsit. At Philostratus Atheniensis, qui
omnia, quae Tyanensis gessit, ex Maximi ipsiusque Damidis
et aliorum scriptis in unum collegisse se refert, absolutissi-
mam a nativitate ad interitum usque de eius hominis vita
historiam contexuit.

Quod et ipse Philostratus in principio primi libri ita testatur:

Ἐνέτυχον δὲ καὶ Μαξίμου τοῦ Αἰγιέως βιβλίῳ ξυν-
ειληφότι τὰ ἐν Αἰγαῖς Ἀπολλωνίου πάντα· καὶ δια-
θῆκαι δὲ τῷ Ἀπολλωνίῳ γεγράφανται, παρ' ὧν
ὑπάρχει μαθεῖν, ὡς ὑποθειάζων τὴν φιλοσοφίαν
ἐγένετο. Οὐ γὰρ Μοιραγένει γε προσεκτέον βιβλία
μὲν ξυντιθέντι ἐς Ἀπολλώνιον τέτταρα, πολλὰ δὲ
τῶν περὶ τὸν ἄνδρα ἀγνοήσαντι. Ὡς μὲν οὖν ξυν-
ήγαγον ταῦτα διεσπαρμένα καὶ ὡς ἐπεμελήθην τοῦ
ξυνθεῖναι αὐτὰ εἴρηκα.

Legi et Maximi Aegiensis librum de gestis in Aegis ab Apollonio. Ex testamento autem, quod Apollonius scripsit, colu-
isse eum philosophiam licet cognoscere. Neque enim Moera-
geni, qui quatuor contra Apollonium composuit libros,
habenda est fides: nam multa, quae ad eum virum pertinent,
ignoravit. Quod itaque haec dispersa in unum coegerim stu-
duerimque componere, diximus.

ἐντελῆ τὴν ἀπὸ γενέσεως καὶ μέχρι τελευτῆς ἱστορίαν τοῦ κατὰ τὸν ἄνδρα βίου πεποίηται.

So Damis, a native of Assyria, since he had lived a long time
with Apollonius and had first become acquainted with him
in his native land, wrote an account of travels with him from
that moment onward. Maximus on the other hand wrote a
rather brief account of individual acts he performed. But
Philostratus the Athenian states that he put together in one
work, drawing on Maximus, Damis himself and other
sources, every act of the man from Tyana; he composed a
very complete account of the man's life from his birth right
up to his death.

Philostratus himself testifies to this at the beginning of Book I.[309]

Ἐνέτυχον δὲ καὶ Μαξίμου τοῦ Αἰγιέως βιβλίῳ ξυν-
ειληφότι τὰ ἐν Αἰγαῖς Ἀπολλωνίου πάντα· καὶ δια-
θῆκαι δὲ τῷ Ἀπολλωνίῳ γεγράφανται, παρ' ὧν
ὑπάρχει μαθεῖν, ὡς ὑποθειάζων τὴν φιλοσοφίαν
ἐγένετο. Οὐ γὰρ Μοιραγένει γε προσεκτέον βιβλία
μὲν ξυντιθέντι ἐς Ἀπολλώνιον τέτταρα, πολλὰ δὲ
τῶν περὶ τὸν ἄνδρα ἀγνοήσαντι. Ὡς μὲν οὖν ξυν-
ήγαγον ταῦτα διεσπαρμένα καὶ ὡς ἐπεμελήθην τοῦ
ξυνθεῖναι αὐτὰ εἴρηκα.

I also read the book by Maximus of Aegae which recounts
Apollonius' activities in Aegae. From the will composed by
Apollonius it is possible to see that he studied philosophy,
since one should not trust Moiragenes,[310] the author of four
books against Apollonius, because he was unaware of many
relevant facts. Hence my statement that I have put together
scattered sources and tried to reconcile them.

10   At quorsum tot in ea Hieronymi de Apollonio? Ut, siquis ob
illa libris Philostrati de Apollonio credit, desinat credere; immo
potius et mendacem Philostratum et temerarium Hieroclem et
vanissimum circulatoremque Apollonium iisque simillimum fuisse
credat, qui per fora et areas, accita plebe ac decepta simplici turba,
super tripodibus et tabulatis stipem garriendo aucupantur; Dami-
dem vero, Apollonii socium, eum illi egisse puerum, qui circulatori
magistro, e regione scamno conscenso aut tripode, arrespondet.
Lactantius libro quinto magum fuisse scribit Apollonium; inibique
in Hieroclem cum aliis tum his invehitur verbis:

> Cum igitur talia ignorantiae suae deliramenta fudisset, cum
> veritatem penitus exci[n]dere connixus esset, ausus est libros
> suos nefarios ac Dei hostes φιλαλήθεις idest veritatis ama-
> tores annotare. O caecum pectus! o mentem Cimmeriis, ut
> aiunt, tenebris atriorem! Discipulus hic fortasse Anaxagorae
> fuit, cui nives atramentum fuerunt. Atqui eadem caecitas est,
> et vero falsitatis et mendacio veritatis nomen imponere. Vi-
> delicet homo subdolus voluit lupum sub ovis pelle c[a]elare,
> ut fallaci titulo posset irretire lectorem. Verum esto: insania
> hoc, non malitia feceris. Quam tandem nobis attulisti verita-
> tem, nisi quod, assertor deorum, eos ipsos ad ultimum per-
> didisti? Prosecutus enim summi dei laudes, quem regem,
> quem maximum opificem rerum, quem fontem deorum,
> quem parentem omnium altoremque viventium confessus es,
> ademisti Iovi tuo regnum, eumque summa potestate depul-
> sum in ministrorum numerum redegisti. Epilogus itaque te
> tuus arguit stultitiae, vanitatis, erroris. Affirmas deos esse, et

But why so much criticism of Jerome's remarks on the subject 10 of Apollonius? So that if, because of them, anyone gives credit to Philostratus' work about Apollonius, he should cease to do so; he should rather treat Philostratus as a liar, Hierocles as insolent, Apollonius as a charlatan and a fraud, very like the people who go to markets and squares, attracting the mob and deceiving the simpleminded, sitting on a chair or a platform and collecting money with some patter. Damis, the companion of Apollonius, acted for him, like the boy who sits on a chair or a stool opposite his master the charlatan and gives the answers. Lactantius in Book V[311] says that Apollonius was a magician and in the same passage attacks Hierocles in various ways as follows:

> So when he had poured forth such insane demonstrations of his ignorance, when he had attempted to abolish the truth, he had the audacity to entitle his books, which are wicked and hostile to God, Φιλαληθεῖς, [that is, "Lovers of truth"].[312] What blindness! A mind enveloped in something worse than the so-called Cimmerian darkness. Perhaps he was a pupil of Anaxagoras, for whom snow was the color of ink.[313] Yet it is the same form of blindness whether you call the true false or the false true. Obviously the devious man wished to hide a wolf in a sheep's skin, to attract the reader by a misleading title. Let us suppose you did this out of madness, not out of malice. Whatever kind of truth did you offer us, except that as a believer in gods you utterly destroyed those very gods? By detailing the merits of the highest god, whom you admit to be king, the greatest creator of all things, source of goods,[314] parent of all and nourisher of the living, you have deprived your Jupiter of his kingdom, deposed him from supreme power and relegated him to the rank of servant. So your conclusion proves your stupidity, vacuity and error. You affirm the existence of gods, yet you

illos tamen subiicis et mancipas ei Deo, cuius religionem
conaris evertere.

Haec Lactantius.

11 Legendis praeterea Philostrati mendaciis auxit mihi fastidium
interpretatio, quae non solum plerisque in locis barbara est, sed et
infida. Qua re libuit quaedam adnotare studiosorum admonendi
gratia. Illud primi libri: Οἱ τὸν Σάμιον Πυθαγόραν ἐπαινοῦντες τάδε ἐπ᾽ αὐτῷ φασιν, ὡς Ἴων μὲν οὔπω εἴη, γένοιτο δὲ
ἐν Τροίᾳ ποτὲ Εὔφορβος, interpres sic traduxit: 'Quicunque
Samium Pythagoram laudant, narrare solent in primis ipsum
priusquam in Ionia nasceretur fuisse Troianum Euphorbum'; ubi
sic potius dicendum aut tale quid: 'Qui Samium Pythagoram laudant, non Ionem sed Troianum Euphorbum fuisse eum memorant.' Οὔπω enim ἀντὶ τοῦ οὐ accipitur a Philostrato. Et paulo
post, illud: Καὶ ἐτίμων αὐτὸν ὡς ἐκ Διὸς ἥκοντα, καὶ ἡ σιωπὴ
δὲ ὑπὲρ τοῦ θείου σφίσιν ἐπήσκητο, ita transtulit: 'Quod in
cunctis ita eum colerent ac si ex Iove genitus ortusque esset, silentium insuper ab eo indictum originem a diis traxisse arbitrantur';
quod sic vertendum potius: 'Ipsumque tanquam ab Iove profectum
venerabantur; at silentium pro re divina ab ipsis exercebatur.' Illud
item ibidem: ὅτι καὶ τὸ σιωπᾶν λόγος, vertit: 'Ex hoc tacendi
rationem ab ipso inventam arbitrantur'; quod sic potius: 'Quoniam
et ipsum tacere oratio est.' Et in eadem charta illud: Οὔτε
διακείμενοι πρὸς τοὺς ἀνθρώπους, vertit: 'Neque ea quae dicunt temporibus locisve accommodate dicentes'; quod sic potius:
'Neque ob earum in homines benevolentiam.' Pagina item quarta
illud: Δώσω, ἔφη, ζυμήτας τε ἄρτους καὶ φοίνικος βαλάνους
ἠλεκτρώδεις τε καὶ μεγάλους, vertit: 'Dabo—inquit ille—fermentatos panes et mirandae magnitudinis rubras nuces'; quod sic
potius: 'Dabo—inquit—fermentatos panes ac palmae fructus

make them subjects and servants of the god whose religion you try to subvert.

That is from Lactantius.

While reading Philostratus' lies my annoyance was increased   11
further by the translation, which in many places is not only barbarous but unfaithful. So I should like to warn scholars by noting a few examples. This from the first book:[315] Οἱ τὸν Σάμιον Πυθαγόραν ἐπαινοῦντες τάδε ἐπ᾽ αὐτῷ φασιν, ὡς Ἴων μὲν οὔπω εἴη, γένοιτο δὲ ἐν Τροίᾳ ποτὲ Εὔφορβος. The translator has the following: "Those who praise Pythagoras of Samos tend to say first of all that before he was born in Ionia he had been the Trojan Euphorbus,"[316] where he should instead have said something like this: "Those who praise Pythagoras of Samos record that he was not Ionian but the Trojan Euphorbus," since in Philostratus οὔπω is equivalent to οὐ.[317] A little further on:[318] Καὶ ἐτίμων αὐτὸν ὡς ἐκ Διὸς ἥκοντα, καὶ ἡ σιωπὴ δὲ ὑπὲρ τοῦ θείου σφίσιν ἐπήσκητο, he translates as follows: "Because they treated him in all respects as if he were the child begotten by Jupiter, they think in addition the silence imposed by him had divine origin," which ought instead to have been rendered, "They revered him as if he were the son of Jupiter, but silence was their rule because of the divine connection." This again from the same passage:[319] ὅτι καὶ τὸ σιωπᾶν λόγος, he translated as, "Hence they think the practice of silence was his own invention," which should be, "Because even silence is a discourse." Again, on the same page:[320] Οὔτε διακείμενοι πρὸς τοὺς ἀνθρώπους, he translates, "Nor saying what people say at the right time and place," which should be, "Nor on account of their benefit to humanity." On page 4:[321] Δώσω, ἔφη, ζυμήτας τε ἄρτους καὶ φοίνικος βαλάνους ἠλεκτρώδεις τε καὶ μεγάλους, he translates, "I will give, he says, leavened bread and red nuts of wondrous size," which should be, "I will give, he says, leavened bread and fruits of the palm

succineosque et praegrandes.' Charta vero sexta multa deerant, quae nos traduximus addidimusque, in quibus est et epigramma de Eretriis.

12   Charta item decimasexta primo versu illud: Καὶ τοῦτ᾽ ἴσως ἦν τὸ μελαμπύγου τυχεῖν, vertit: 'Sed tamen id ipsum perinde iucundissimum est ac si dulcis aquae fontem invenissemus,' pro eo aut simili: 'Atque hoc fortasse fuerit in Clunatrum incidere' hoc est in Herculem. Est autem proverbium: μελαμπύγου τύχοις, in clunatrum incidas. Ubi haec Sudas:

Μελάμπυγοι ἐγένοντο πέρπεροι, Λίμνης υἱοί· ἀκολασταινόντων δὲ αὐτῶν πολλά, ἡ μήτηρ ἔλεγε φυλάσσεσθαι μήποτε ἐμπέσωσιν εἰς δασύπρωκτον. Ἐμπεσόντες οὖν εἰς Ἡρακλέα, ἐν ἀναφόρῳ ἐδέθησαν· εἶτα ὁρῶν αὐτοὺς γελῶντας καὶ κατακύπτοντας, ἐπυνθάνετο τὴν αἰτίαν· οἱ δὲ ἔλεγον ὅτι λόγιον ἦν τὸ τῆς μητρός, ἐμπεσεῖσθαι ἡμᾶς εἰς δασύπρωκτον. Καὶ γελάσαντα τὸν Ἡρακλέα ἀφεῖναι αὐτοὺς τῶν δεσμῶν, ὅτι τοὺς λευκοπύγους ὡς γυναικώδεις ἐκωμῴδουν.

Clunatri fuerunt mollicie elati Limnes filii, quos perlascivientes, ne in eum, qui hirsuto esset podice, inciderent, admonuit mater. Inciderunt igitur in Herculem, qui eos baculo incurvo adligavit; deinde, ridentes incurvantesque eos videns, petivit causam. At illi dixerunt: 'In eum, qui hirsuto esset podice, casuros nos vaticinata est mater.' Quo responso ridens Hercules vinculis solutos eos dimisit, quoniam tanquam molles et effoeminatos clunalbos reprehendebant.

tree,[322] amber-like and exceptionally large." On page 6 much was left out, which we have translated and inserted, including an epigram about the Eretrians.

In the first line of page 16[323] Καὶ τοῦτ᾽ ἴσως ἦν τὸ μελαμ- 12 πύγου τυχεῖν, he translates, "But this very thing is extremely welcome, as if we had found a spring of pure water," instead of the following or something like it: "And this perhaps was to meet Blackbuttocks," i.e., Hercules. There is a proverb Μελαμπύγου τύχοις, "May you meet Blackbuttocks," on which Suidas has this:[324]

Μελάμπυγοι ἐγένοντο πέρπεροι, Λίμνης υἱοί· ἀκολασταινόντων δὲ αὐτῶν πολλά, ἡ μήτηρ ἔλεγε φυλάσσεσθαι μήποτε ἐμπέσωσιν εἰς δασύπρωκτον.
Ἐμπεσόντες οὖν εἰς Ἡρακλέα, ἐν ἀναφόρῳ ἐδέθη-
σαν· εἶτα ὁρῶν αὐτοὺς γελῶντας καὶ κατακύπτοντας, ἐπυνθάνετο τὴν αἰτίαν· οἱ δὲ ἔλεγον ὅτι λόγιον
ἦν τὸ τῆς μητρός, ἐμπεσεῖσθαι ἡμᾶς εἰς δασύπρωκτον. Καὶ γελάσαντα τὸν Ἡρακλέα ἀφεῖναι αὐτοὺς
τῶν δεσμῶν, ὅτι τοὺς λευκοπύγους ὡς γυναικώδεις
ἐκωμῴδουν.

Blackbuttocks were effeminate sons of Limne. As they misbehaved a great deal, their mother told them not to have dealings with a man with a hirsute fundament. So they met Hercules who captured them with a bent staff; then, seeing them laugh and bend over, he asked them why. They said: "Our mother prophesied that we would meet someone with a hirsute fundament." Laughing at this reply Hercules freed them and sent them on their way, because they ridiculed as effeminate persons with a white fundament.

Quanquam illud: μελάμπυγοι ἐγένοντο πέρπεροι Λίμνης
υἱοί, perperam scriptum esse puto pro: δύο τινὲς ἀδελφοὶ
ἐγένοντο Κέρκωπες, Σεμνονίδος υἱοί. Nam in dictione Κέρκωπες sic idem Sudas:

Κέρκωπες δύο ἀδελφοὶ ἦσαν ἐπὶ τῆς γῆς πᾶσαν
ἀδικίαν ἐπιδεικνύμενοι· καὶ ἐλέγοντο Κέρκωπες ἐκ
τῆς τῶν ἔργων δεινότητος ὄντως ἐπονομαζόμενοι· ὁ
μὲν γὰρ αὐτῶν Πάσσαλος ἐγένετο, ὁ δὲ Ἀκλήμων.
Ἡ δὲ μήτηρ Σεμνονὶς ταῦτα ὁρῶσα ἔλεγε, μὴ περιτυχεῖν μελαμπύγῳ, τουτέστι τῷ Ἡρακλεῖ.

Cercopes duo fratres fuerunt iniustissimi super terra, ac Cercopes ob gravia facinora cognominati sunt; quorum alter
Passalus, alter Aclemon fuit. His visis mater Semnonis admonuit ne inciderent in clunatrum, hoc est in Herculem.

Praeterea in enarratione historiarum, quae in libris Gregorii habentur, sic legitur:

Δύο τινὲς ἀδελφοί, κατὰ γῆν πᾶσαν ἀδικίαν ἐν-
δεικνύμενοι, ἐλέγοντο Κέρκωπες ἐκ τῆς τῶν ἔργων
δριμύτητος, τὴν ἐπωνυμίαν λαχόντες. Ὁ μὲν γὰρ
αὐτῶν ἐλέγετο Πάσσαλος, ὁ δὲ ἕτερος Ἀκλήμων, ὥς
φησι Δίος ὁ ὑπομνηματιστής. Τούτοις δὲ ἡ μήτηρ,
Σεμνονὶς τῷ ὀνόματι, ἑωρακυῖα κατὰ γῆν πολλὰ
δεινὰ ἐργαζομένους αὐτούς, εἶπε μὴ περιτυχεῖν μελαμπύγῳ. Καί ποτε τοῦ Ἡρακλέους ὑπὸ δένδρου
κοιμωμένου καὶ τῶν ἑαυτοῦ ὅπλων ὑποκεκλιμένων
τῷ φυτῷ, πλησιάζοντες οὗτοι τοῖς ὅπλοις, ἐπιχει-

But the words μελάμπυγοι ἐγένοντο πέρπεροι Λίμνης υἱοί, are, I think, a mistake for δύο τινὲς ἀδελφοὶ ἐγένοντο Κέρκωπες, Σεμνονίδος υἱοί, because Suidas in the entry Κέρκωπες has,[325]

Κέρκωπες δύο ἀδελφοὶ ἦσαν ἐπὶ τῆς γῆς πᾶσαν ἀδικίαν ἐπιδεικνύμενοι· καὶ ἐλέγοντο Κέρκωπες ἐκ τῆς τῶν ἔργων δεινότητος ὄντως ἐπονομαζόμενοι· ὁ μὲν γὰρ αὐτῶν Πάσσαλος ἐγένετο, ὁ δὲ Ἀκλήμων. Ἡ δὲ μήτηρ Σεμνονὶς ταῦτα ὁρῶσα ἔλεγε, μὴ περι- τυχεῖν μελαμπύγῳ, τουτέστι τῷ Ἡρακλεῖ.

The Cercopes were two brothers who committed every kind of crime on earth and were nicknamed Cercopes on account of the gravity of their wrongdoing; one was Passalus, the other Aclemon. When their mother, whose name was Sem- nonis, saw their serious crimes, she told them not to meet Blackbuttocks, that is Hercules.

In addition we read in the account of the myths found in the works of Gregory the following:[326]

Δύο τινὲς ἀδελφοί, κατὰ γῆν πᾶσαν ἀδικίαν ἐν- δεικνύμενοι, ἐλέγοντο Κέρκωπες ἐκ τῆς τῶν ἔργων δριμύτητος, τὴν ἐπωνυμίαν λαχόντες. Ὁ μὲν γὰρ αὐτῶν ἐλέγετο Πάσσαλος, ὁ δὲ ἕτερος Ἀκλήμων, ὥς φησι Δῖος ὁ ὑπομνηματιστής. Τούτοις δὲ ἡ μήτηρ, Σεμνονὶς τῷ ὀνόματι, ἑωρακυῖα κατὰ γῆν πολλὰ δεινὰ ἐργαζομένους αὐτούς, εἶπε μὴ περιτυχεῖν με- λαμπύγῳ. Καί ποτε τοῦ Ἡρακλέους ὑπὸ δένδρου κοιμωμένου καὶ τῶν ἑαυτοῦ ὅπλων ὑποκεκλιμένων τῷ φυτῷ, πλησιάζοντες οὗτοι τοῖς ὅπλοις, ἐπιχει-

ρῆσαι ἠβουλήθησαν· εὐθὺς δὲ ὁ Ἡρακλῆς αἰσθόμε-
νος, λαβὼν αὐτούς, δεσμεύσας καὶ κατακέφαλα κρε-
μάσας, ἐβάστασεν ἐξόπισθεν. Καὶ τότε ἐκεῖνοι τῆς
ἐντολῆς τῆς ἑαυτῶν μητρὸς ἐμνήσθησαν κρεμάμε-
νοι, τοῦ Ἡρακλέους τὴν πυγὴν μέλαιναν ἐκ τῆς
τῶν τριχῶν δασύτητος θεωρήσαντες, πρὸς ἀλλήλους
αὐτὸ τοῦτο διαλεγόμενοι, γέλωτα πολὺν προῆψαν
τῷ Ἡρακλεῖ, καὶ εὐθὺς αὐτοὺς κατὰ τοῦτο τῶν
δεσμῶν ἐλυτρώσατο καὶ ἀπέλυσεν.

Duo quidam germani fratres, iniqua in terris agentes, cognomentum ex asperitate facinorum sortiti, Cercopes diceban-
tur. Ex ipsis, ut tradit commentator Dius, Passalus alter fuit,
Aclemon alter. His cum eorum mater, Semnonis nomine,
gravia videret facinora, ait ne in clunatrum inciderent. Atque
Hercule sub arbore aliquando dormiente, plantaeque ipsius
armis acclinatis, hi, cum armis propinquassent, aggredi vo-
luerunt. Statim vero sentiens, Hercules comprehensos, liga-
tos ac suspensos in caput post terga gestabat. Tuncque illi,
cum nigras Herculis nates ex pilorum hirsutie suspexissent,
matris praeceptum meminere suspensi, atque id ipsum di-
cendo ad invicem, cachinnum Herculi commoverunt; illi-
coque propterea eos ex vinculis liberavit dissolvitque.

13 Quaedam etiam, quae maxime displicebant, non potui non im-
mutare; in quibus et illud in libro octavo:

Εἰ δὲ καὶ μὴ τοιάδε ἦν τὰ τῶν Ἀρκάδων, ἀλλ᾽ εἶχον
ὥσπερ ἕτεροι προσαποδίδοσθαι τοὺς αὐτῶν δού-
λους, τί τῇ θρυλλουμένῃ σοφίᾳ ξυνεβάλετο, τὸ ἐξ
Ἀρκαδίας εἶναι τὸ σφαττόμενον;

ρῆσαι ἠβουλήθησαν· εὐθὺς δὲ ὁ Ἡρακλῆς αἰσθόμε-
νος, λαβὼν αὐτούς, δεσμεύσας καὶ κατακέφαλα κρε-
μάσας, ἐβάστασεν ἐξόπισθεν. Καὶ τότε ἐκεῖνοι τῆς
ἐντολῆς τῆς ἑαυτῶν μητρὸς ἐμνήσθησαν κρεμάμε-
νοι, τοῦ Ἡρακλέους τὴν πυγὴν μέλαιναν ἐκ τῆς
τῶν τριχῶν δασύτητος θεωρήσαντες, πρὸς ἀλλήλους
αὐτὸ τοῦτο διαλεγόμενοι, γέλωτα πολὺν προῆψαν
τῷ Ἡρακλεῖ, καὶ εὐθὺς αὐτοὺς κατὰ τοῦτο τῶν
δεσμῶν ἐλυτρώσατο καὶ ἀπέλυσεν.

Two brothers who committed crimes all over the earth were
known as Cercopes, acquiring the nickname because of the
gravity of their offenses. As Dius the commentator reports,
one was Passalos, the other Aclemon. When their mother,
Semnonis by name, noticed their serious crimes she told
them not to encounter Blackbuttocks. One day Hercules was
sleeping under a tree, with his weapons leaning against its
trunk.[327] They approached the weapons and tried to attack
him. But Hercules heard them at once, caught them, bound
them, hung them head down and carried them on his back.
They then saw Hercules' black buttocks with thick hair,
and as they hung they recalled their mother's advice. As
they mentioned it to each other Hercules was moved to
laughter, and as a result released them from their bonds and
let them go.

And some things which were particularly unsatisfactory I could 13
not avoid changing, among them the following in Book VIII.[328]

Εἰ δὲ καὶ μὴ τοιάδε ἦν τὰ τῶν Ἀρκάδων, ἀλλ᾽ εἶχον
ὥσπερ ἕτεροι προσαποδίδοσθαι τοὺς αὐτῶν δού-
λους, τί τῇ θρυλλουμένῃ σοφίᾳ ξυνεβάλετο, τὸ ἐξ
Ἀρκαδίας εἶναι τὸ σφαττόμενον;

sic traductum:

> Quod si Arcades ita non essent, sed ut caeteri servos lu-
> crandi causa venderent, quis tam vulgatum sacrificium audi-
> visset ex Arcadia esse qui iugulandus erat?

nos, quia ne construi quidem poterat, sic immutavimus:

> Quod si Arcades tales non essent, sed ut caeteri servos suos
> venderent, quid ad divulgatam sapientiam conferret, esse ex
> Arcadia quod mactaretur?

Nam, quid ξυνεβάλετο significaret, non videtur intellexisse.

14   Quot vero alia immutata sint, quot item addita, conferendo facile erit volenti cognoscere. Haec non corripiendi interpretis gratia
annotavimus: nam, ut Aristotelis ex secundo metaphysicorum
utamur verbis:

> Οὐ μόνον δὲ χάριν ἔχειν δίκαιον τούτοις, ὧν ἄν τις
> κοινωνήσαι τῆς δόξης, ἀλλὰ καὶ τοῖς ἔτι ἐπιπολαι-
> ότερον ἀποφηναμένοις· καὶ γὰρ οὗτοι συμβάλλον-
> ταί τι· τὴν γὰρ ἕξιν προήσκησαν ἡμῶν.

> Non solum vero iis, quorum quis accedet opinioni, habere
> aequum est gratiam, sed iis quoque, qui superficie tenus ali-
> quid tradiderunt: sunt enim et hi quodam modo utiles, nam
> nostrum exacuerunt ingenium.

Non igitur interpretis carpendi gratia haec diximus, sed ut studiosos, si cum Graecis velint Latina coniungere, admoneremus neque
huic neque id genus caeteris, qui abhinc circiter mille annos aliquid e Graeco in Latinum, paucis admodum quibusdam exceptis,
traduxerunt, fidem esse habendam, incumbendumque esse propterea literis Graecis. Quod ne pluribus admoneamus, facit Scipio

It was translated,

> But if the Arcadians were not like that, but sold slaves for profit like everyone else, who[329] would have heard of a well-known sacrifice, the victim to be slaughtered coming from Arcadia?

Since this could not even be construed we altered it to read:

> But if the Arcadians were not like that, but sold their slaves like everyone else, what would it contribute to received wisdom that the object sacrificed came from Arcadia?

He does not seem to have understood the meaning of ξυνεβάλετο.

How many other things have been altered and how many [14] added will easily be found by comparison if one wishes. We have not noted them in order to denigrate the translator; for, to quote Aristotle's words in Book II of the Metaphysics,[330]

> Οὐ μόνον δὲ χάριν ἔχειν δίκαιον τούτοις, ὧν ἄν τις κοινωνῆσαι τῆς δόξης, ἀλλὰ καὶ τοῖς ἔτι ἐπιπολαιότερον ἀποφηναμένοις· καὶ γὰρ οὗτοι συμβάλλονταί τι· τὴν γὰρ ἕξιν προήσκησαν ἡμῶν.

> It is right to be grateful not only to those whose opinion one shares but also to those who have explained something superficially, for they too make some contribution, since they have stimulated our mental skills.

So we have not said all this in order to criticize the translator, but to advise scholars, if they are willing to compare the Latin with the Greek, not to rely on this translation, nor, with just a few exceptions, the others like him, who over the last thousand years or so have rendered something from Greek into Latin. For this reason one must study Greek. We need not give this advice at greater length, because our friend Scipio Carteromachus, giving public

Carteromachus noster, qui hoc anno Venetiis, cum Demosthenis orationes publice enarraret, quantum Graecae literae necessariae sint hominibus nostris, pulcherrima ostendit oratione, quam ad studiosorum utilitatem cusam typis nostris nuper edidimus; quantum vero iis quos diximus credendum sit traductoribus, alia docebit oratione.

15   A te autem, Zenobi doctissime, huic rei consultum est optime, tum quia Eusebii libellum non inerudite et barbare, sed docte et Latine traduxisti, tum etiam quia per nostrorum hominum manus Philostrati mendacia vagari incognita non es passus, id ipsum Eusebii opusculum indicem et redargutorem καὶ ὡς ἀντιφάρμακον opponendo. Merito itaque hic liber sub tuo nomine ex Neacademia nostra exit in publicum meo iussu. Es enim tempestate hac nostra ex iis unus, quos aequus amavit Iupiter. Vale.

    Venetiis mense Maio M.D.IIII.

: XXIX :

A

Aldus Romanus omnibus una cum Graecis literis sanctos
etiam mores discere cupientibus s. p. d.

1   Gregorii episcopi Nazanzeni carmina ad bene beateque vivendum utilissima nuper e Graeco in Latinum ad verbum fere tralata imprimenda curavimus, studiosi adolescentes, rati non parum emolumenti vobis futurum, si id genus tralationis cum Graeco diligenter conferatis: nam et Graece simul discetis et Christiane vivere,

lectures in Venice this year on Demosthenes' orations, demonstrated in a very fine lecture, which we published recently for the
benefit of students, how important Greek is for people of our
generation. In another lecture he will show how far one can trust
the translators I mentioned.[331]

You, most learned Zanobi, have served this cause very well,   15
partly by a Latin version of Eusebius' pamphlet which is the fruit
of erudition and in good Latin, not ignorant and barbaric, partly
by not allowing Philostratus' untruths to circulate undetected by
the public. Eusebius' short work is in itself a warning and a refuta-
tion, an antidote which you have prepared. So it is right that this
volume, dedicated to you, is issued to the public on my instructions by our New Academy. In our generation you are one of the
few to be loved by Jupiter, who is just.[332] Farewell.

Venice, May 1504.

: XXIX :

Gregory of Nazianzus, Poetry[333]
(June 1504)

A

*Aldus of Rome to all those who wish to learn about Greek literature and
moral principles at the same time, warmest greetings.*

We have printed the poems of Gregory, bishop of Nazianzus, very   1
conducive to the good and pious life, recently translated from
Greek into Latin almost word for word; we reckoned, young
students, it would be quite beneficial for you to make careful
comparison of this kind of translation with the Greek, because
you would learn Greek and at the same time how to live as a

quandoquidem summa in illis et doctrina est et gratia, et sanctis moribus mire instituunt adolescentes. Id vero ita sit necne, conferendo cognoscite. Valete.

B

2   Impressis Gregorii Nazianzeni carminibus, nactus alium codicem, quaedam sic emendavi.

3   In Latina tralatione horum Gregorii Nazianzeni carminum essent et alia corrigenda; sed nos duo, quae ad manus erant, emendanda signavimus; caetera sibi quisque studendo corrigat. Nam mihi tantum assidue negocii est, ut vix resistam laboribus. Arduam enim nec aequam viribus accepi provinciam. Quare, nisi semper sperarem brevi quod desydero affuturum, desisterem ab incoeptis. Sed et spero et sic mecum saepe:

Θαρσεῖν χρή, φίλος Ἄλδε· τάχ' αὔριον ἔσσετ' ἄμεινον.

Ἐλπίδες ἐν ζωοῖσιν, ἀνέλπιστοι δὲ θανόντες·
χ' ὦ Ζεὺς ἄλλοκα μὲν πέλει αἴθριος, ἄλλοκα δ' ὕει.

Cras melius fortassis erit: confide, Manuti.
Viventes sperant; non est spes ulla sepultis;
et quandoque pluit deus et quandoque serenat.

C

4   Sunt vero carminum tria millia ac septem et quadraginta, quae circiter abhinc triennium imprimenda quidem curavimus; sed quia propter summas occupationes nostras non unquam ea potuimus in Latinum traducere, adhuc premuntur.

Christian. In these poems there is great learning and elegance, and they give the young wonderful instruction in good moral principles. Discover by comparison whether this is so or not. Farewell.

B

Having printed the poems of Gregory of Nazianzus I found 2 another codex[334] and made a few changes as follows: [. . .][335]

In the Latin version of these poems of Gregory of Nazian- 3 zus some other corrections should have been made; but we have marked two obvious things that needed improvement. The rest any studious reader should correct for himself, because I am so busy all the time that I am scarcely equal to the strain. I have undertaken an enterprise which is demanding and beyond my powers; hence if I did not maintain hope of soon achieving my aims I would abandon what I have begun. But I do have hope and often say to myself,

Dear Aldus, one must have courage; perhaps tomorrow will be better. There is hope among the living; the dead are without hope. And Zeus sometimes brings clear sky, at other times rain.

Perhaps tomorrow will be better; be confident, Manutius. The living hope; there is no hope among the dead. God sometimes rains, sometimes clears the sky.

C

There are 3,047 poems which I printed about three years ago;[336] 4 but because of overwhelming pressure of business we were never able to translate them into Latin, and they are still held back.[337]

: XXX :

Aldus Pius Manutius Romanus Hieronymo Aleandro Motensi s. p. d.

1   Si quisquam est, qui nos, quod alienos libros huic et illi pro arbitrio nostro nuncupamus, accusat, etsi cur id meo iure mihi quodammodo facere videor, alia epistola memini scribere, ut inde causam posset cognoscere, tamen et hic, si libuerit, legat, et desinat maledicere. Cum enim renasci quodammodo videantur libri summa cura, summis laboribus informati in aedibus nostris, licere mihi arbitror διὰ τὴν τοιαύτην παλιγγενεσίαν eos, cui libuerit, dedicare.

2   Quare Homeri Iliadem Ulysseamque, cum caeteris quae extant eiusdem poetae, sub tuo nomine, mi Aleander, exire ex Neacademia nostra voluimus, non ut hac dicatura te ad bonarum literarum studia redderemus alacriorem, cum tibi freno magis sit opus quam calcaribus, sed ut summa benevolentia in te mea, ob divinum ingenium tuum ac plurifariam doctrinam multarumque linguarum cognitionem, hac epistola omnibus innotescat. Tu enim, nondum quartum et vigesimum annum agens, es humanorum studiorum utriusque linguae doctissimus, nec minus Hebraicam calles, nuncque et Chaldeae et Arabicae tanto incumbis studio, ut quinque te habentem corda brevi sint homines admiraturi: nam tria, ut olim grandis de se Ennius dixit, tu hac ratione vel nunc habes. Tanta praeterea linguae volubilitate verba Graeca pronuntias, tantaque aptitudine et facilitate inspiras Hebraica, ac si mediis Athenis mediaque Israelitarum urbe, quo stabant tempore, natus et educatus esses.

: XXX :

Homer, Iliad
(October 31, 1504)

Aldus Pius Manutius of Rome to Girolamo
Aleandro of Motta,[338] warmest greetings.

If anyone criticizes us for dedicating other authors' works to vari-   1
ous people as we think fit, although I recall stating in another letter, so that the reasons could be known, why I feel myself to have
some right to do so, nevertheless the critic may like to read them
here as well—and stop slandering me. Since books seem to enjoy
a kind of rebirth when they are produced with great care and great
effort in our house, I think I am entitled to dedicate them, after
such a rebirth, to whomever I please.

So since we wished, dear Aleandro, Homer's *Iliad* and *Odyssey*,   2
together with other works of the same sort, to be issued from our
Neacademia with a dedication to you—not intending by the dedication to enhance your enthusiasm for the study of literature, since
you need reins rather than spurs, but so that my great goodwill
toward you on account of your sublime intellect, wide learning and
knowledge of many languages might be made known to all by the
present letter. For although you are not yet in your twenty-fourth
year, you are very expert in both the languages of the humanities,
together with equal competence in Hebrew; and now you are also
actively studying Syriac and Arabic so that people will soon marvel
at you as a man with five hearts. By this reckoning you already
have three, as the great Ennius once said of himself.[339] In addition
you pronounce Greek words with such fluency, you produce the
aspirates of Hebrew with such ease and accuracy, as if you had
been born and brought up in Athens itself or the city of the Isra-
elites when those cities flourished.

3   Quid de nostra, idest Latina lingua, dixerim? in qua adeo prae-
cellis, ut equestri oratione lyricorum, sylvarum, epigrammatum,
iambicorum, omne genus carminum iam magnos et doctos libros,
pedestri vero epistolas, orationes, dialogos, et pleraque alia felici
stilo absolveris; quae omnia an doctissimi cuiusque probatione
digna sint, iudicabunt ii, quorum propediem in manus venerint.
Omitto musices et mathematicarum artium, quae tibi inest, cognitionem; omitto liberalium disciplinarum omnium ipsiusque universae, ut Graeci dicunt, ἐγκυκλοπαιδίας studium, cui nunc una
cum Maphaeo Leone patritio Veneto, excellentis ingenii adoles-
cente bonarumque literarum perstudioso, die noctuque indissolu-
bili amore et cura Patavii navas operam. Sed, quod est omnium
maxime laude dignum, es moribus ornatissimus, es Christianissi-
mus, nec imitandos ducis levissimos quosdam, qui, ut excellenti
nimisque delicato esse ingenio videantur, communem bonorum
viam quasi fastidientes, vix olfactis, ut sic dixerim, doctrinis, infideles evadunt et, quod inde sequitur, vitiosissimi.

4   Cum igitur haec nemini adhuc videam contigisse ex hominibus
nostris, merito poetarum principem omniumque doctrinarum
fontem poetae etiam ingeniosissimo et omnium pariter doctrinarum studiosissimo tibi dedicaverim. Et quamvis eum ipsum Ma-
phaeum Leonem, Mecoenatem tuum, nunquam tibi deesse videam, quem parcis his temporibus liberalissimum esse mirabile
est, tamen de me etiam tibi queas volo omnia constantissime polliceri; itaque tibi persuadeas velim, me eum esse, cui ob ingenteis
virtutes, ob sanctissimos mores tuos aeque carus sis ac fuisti patri.
Vale.

What should I say of our own language, Latin? In it you are   3
now so skilled that you have already composed successfully substantial and learned works in poetry[340] — lyrics, pastorals, epigrams, iambic verse, every kind of poem — and in prose letters,
orations, dialogues and much else. To what extent all these earn
the approval of scholars will be judged by those whom they will
shortly reach. I leave out of account your knowledge of music and
the mathematical arts; I leave out of account your enthusiasm for
all the liberal arts and the whole range of what the Greeks term
encyclopedia;[341] this you are now studying with unfailing enthusiasm and attention in Padua, in the company of Maffeo Leoni, patrician of Venice, a young man of outstanding intellect and devo-
tion to literary studies.[342] But what is particularly laudable is the
honesty of your character and your Christian faith, your refusal to
follow the example of certain superficial people who, in order to
create the appearance of a superior and very refined intellect, as if
disdaining the path which good men share[343] and having acquired
a mere whiff of education, if I may put it like that, turn out to be
infidels and as a consequence riddled with faults.

Since I have not seen anyone in our generation to possess such   4
gifts, I should like to dedicate to you, as a poet of talent and keen
student of all branches of knowledge, the prince of poets and
source of all learning, as you deserve. And while I see that Maffeo
Leoni himself, your Maecenas, never fails you — his great generosity in these hard times is admirable — nevertheless I wish you to be
able to count on me for every form of loyal help; and so I should
like you to believe that I am the person to whom, by reason of
your outstanding virtues and impeccable character, you are as dear
as you were to your father. Farewell.

: XXXI :

Aldus Pius Manutius Romanus Hieronymo Aleandro Motensi s.

1 Curare oportere parenteis, quaenam statim natis infantibus indantur nomina, multis rationibus adducor ut credam, Hieronyme suavissime; sed praecipua est, quod non sapientibus solum hominibus, sed et ipsi Deo optimo maximo curae id fuerit. Hebraeae enim puellae semper virgini, redemptorem concepturae humani generis, ab angelo nuntiatum in Euangelio legimus: 'Et vocabis nomen eius Iesus'; et paucis ante mensibus Zachariae sacerdoti: 'Uxor tua pariet tibi filium, et vocabis nomen eius Ioannes.' Praeterea τετραγράμματον, Dei omnipotentis nomen incomprehensibile, infinitae virtutis esse commemorant, idque per Iesum, scin litera interposita, factum comprehensibile, quemadmodum per eum ipsum visibilis Deus apparuit, a doctis accepimus. Optime igitur a patre tuo, excellenti philosopho ac medico perinsigni, factum censeo, cum divo Hieronymo voluit te esse cognominem, quo illius fores et doctrinae aemulus et probitatis; id quod a te factum videmus miro successu. Perge igitur, mi Aleander, una cum Maphaeo Leone, Mecoenate tuo: sic itur ad astra, sic petitur coelum. Sed de his nunc satis; non enim dubito quin nostrae et caeterorum, qui te amant, expectationi respondeas.

2 Exigebat hic locus, ut de Batrachomyomachia et hymnis Homeri aliquid dicerem; sed satis esse duxi, quae super his a Demetrio Chalcondyle, viro aetatis nostrae doctissimo, in epistola

: XXXI :

Homer, Odyssey
Batrachomyomachia, Hymns
(October 31, 1504)

Aldus Pius Manutius of Rome to Girolamo Aleandro of Motta, greetings.

Many reasons lead me to believe, my dear Girolamo, that parents 1
should take care when naming their newborn children; but chief
among them is one that concerned not just wise men but God, the
best and greatest, himself. We read in the Gospel of the angel's
announcement to the Jewish girl who remained a virgin and was to
conceive the redeemer of the human race: "And you shall call him
Jesus," and a few months before that it was announced to the
priest Zacharias: "Your wife will bear a son, and you will call him
John."[344] In addition they say that the tetragrammaton,[345] the in-
comprehensible name of the almighty God, has infinite power,
and scholars have told us that through Jesus, with the insertion of
the letter *shin*, it is made comprehensible, just as it was through
him that God became visible. So I think your father, an excellent
philosopher and distinguished doctor, did well in wishing you to
share your name with St. Jerome, so that you might aspire to his
learning and honesty; and we can see you have been remarkably
successful in that. Therefore, my dear Aleandro, continue in company of your Maecenas Maffeo Leoni; this is the path to the
stars,[346] in this way heaven is sought. But enough of this, since I
have no doubt you will match our expectations and those of all the
other people who are devoted to you.

This is the point at which I should say something about the 2
Batrachomyomachia and the Homeric hymns; but I have thought
it sufficient to cite what Demetrius Chalcondyles, the greatest
scholar among our contemporaries, wrote on the subject in his

olim in fronte Homeri excusa Florentiae pereleganter ac docte his
scripta sunt verbis:

Δεῖ μέντοι μὴ ἀγνοεῖν ὡς ἔν τε τῇ Βατραχομυο-
μαχίᾳ καὶ τοῖς ὕμνοις ἐνιαχοῦ διὰ τὴν τῶν ἀντι-
γράφων διαφθορὰν οὔτε ὁ τῶν ἐπῶν εἱρμὸς οὔτε
μὴν τὸ τῆς διανοίας ὑγιὲς ἀπαρτίζεται, παραπλη-
σίως δὲ κἂν τῷ Δίωνος συγγράμματι· οὐ μὴν ἀλλὰ
τά τε τῆς Βατραχομυομαχίας καὶ τῶν ὕμνων ὁλό-
κληρά γε τυγχάνοντα οὐ φαύλως ἂν ἴσως εἶχε· δι-
εφθαρμένα δὲ ὑπὸ τοῦ τοσούτου χρόνου καὶ τῆς
περὶ ταῦτα τῶν λογίων ἀμελείας, οὐκ ἂν πολλὴν
τὴν ζημίαν ἐπιφέροιεν τοῖς φιλομαθέσι. Τὰ δὲ ὑφ᾽
ἡμῶν παροφθέντα κἂν ὁ βραχέα πεπαιδευμένος ἐν
τούτοις οὐ χαλεπῶς συνίδοι. Ἡμῖν μὲν οὖν καὶ τοῖς
ἐνθυμηθεῖσι τοιοῦτον ἔργον εἰς τέλος ἀγαγεῖν ἐς
τοσοῦτον ἐσπούδασται, καὶ πάνυ ὠφελίμως οἶμαι
τοῖς περὶ λόγους σπουδαίοις τῶν νέων. Ὅπου γὰρ
ἡ τῶν βιβλίων σπάνις οὐ μόνον τοὺς ἐφιεμένους
Ἑλληνικῶν γεύσασθαι λόγων, ἀλλὰ καὶ τοὺς ἤδη
τούτων ἡμμένους ἀπέτρεπέ τε καὶ διέσπα, ὡς οὐκ
ἐνὸν οὔτε ῥᾳδίως μαθεῖν, οὔτε μαθόντας ἐν μνήμῃ
κατέχειν μὴ ἰδίων εὐπορο ῦντας βιβλίων, ᾗ που νῦν
γε ἡ τοσούτου τε καὶ τοιούτου ποιητοῦ σύμπασα
πραγματεία εὐπόριστος γενομένη, οὐ σμικρὸν ἔρω-
τα πρὸς τὴν Ἑλληνικὴν παιδείαν τοῖς φιλολόγοις
εἰκότως ἂν ἐμποιοῖ· οὐδέ γε τὴν τυχοῦσαν ὠφέλειαν
παρέχοιτ᾽ ἂν τοῖς πάντα τὰ Ὁμήρῳ συντεταγμένα
ἀκριβῶς συνιεῖσιν, ὃν ὥσπερ πηγήν τινα τῆς
Ἑλληνικῆς διαλέκτου, τοῦ τε ἀνθρωπίνου βίου

most elegant and learned way, in a letter prefacing his Homer printed in Florence some time ago.[347]

One must recognize that in some passages of the *Batracho-* 3 *myomachia* and the *Hymns*, owing to the corruption of the manuscripts, neither the sequence of the verses nor the true meaning is preserved; similarly in the essay by Dio.[348] But the fully preserved parts of the *Batrachomyomachia* and *Hymns* may perhaps not be in a bad state; though damaged by the long passage of time and lack of interest in such things on the part of the educated, they may not cause much difficulty to scholars. Anything we have overlooked can easily be spotted even by someone not very expert in these matters. We and others concerned have taken great care to bring the enterprise to conclusion, I believe to the substantial benefit of young people interested in literature. Since the lack of books discouraged and distracted not just those who want to sample Greek literature but also those who had already approached it, when it was not easy to learn, nor having learned it to retain it in the memory without a good supply of one's own books,[349] now at least I suspect the easy availability of all the works of such a great poet may reasonably be expected to instill a great love of Greek culture among the educated. And this would be of no small benefit for those who acquire an accurate knowledge of all Homer's works. It is agreed by almost all who have studied him closely that he is

παράδειγμα καὶ οἷον φωστῆρα τῶν ἄλλων ποιητῶν
Ἑλλήνων τε καὶ Λατίνων, τῆς τε ἄλλης περὶ λόγους
παιδείας ἡγεμόνα γενέσθαι, ὑπὸ πάντων σχεδὸν
ὡμολόγηται τῶν τὰ ἐκείνου ἠκριβωκότων.

Vale.

Venetiis secundo calendas Novembres M.D.IIII.

: XXXII :

Aldus Pius Manutius Romanus Danieli Clario Parmensi s. p. d.

1 Summum locum in oratoria tenere apud Graecos Demosthenem
et in poetica Homerum, nemo est qui ambigat; sic apud Latinos in
oratoria Marcum Tullium esse facile principem, in poetica vero
Mantuanum poetam. Quod ita mihi esse verum videtur, ut non
modo non futurum unquam putem qui hos superet adaequetve,
sed ne accedat quidem propius. Et quanquam duo haec admirabi-
lium ingeniorum paria successu adeo felici suos elucubrarunt libros
et tradiderunt posteris, ut aeternos reliquerint, non tamen eodem
successu aut vitam vixerunt aut oppetierunt mortem. Nam poetae
et quietiorem egerunt vitam et sua morte mortui sunt, oratores
vero in summis semper vixerunt molestiis et tandem crudeliter
occubuerunt, quippe qui rebuspublicis regendis incubuere; in

as it were a source of the Greek language, a model for human life, a kind of beacon to the other Greek and Latin poets, and a guide for literary education in general.

Farewell.

Venice October 31, 1504.

: XXXII :

Demosthenes, Sixty-two Speeches
Libanius, Life of Demosthenes *and summaries of his speeches*
Plutarch, Life of Demosthenes
(*October 1504*)

Aldus Pius Manutius of Rome to Daniele Clario of Parma,[350] *warmest greetings.*

No one contests that among the Greeks Demosthenes is foremost   1
in oratory and Homer in poetry, just as among the Romans Cicero
is easily best for oratory and the poet of Mantua[351] for poetry.
This seems to me to be so clear that I think not only will there be
no one in future to surpass or equal them, but no one even to
come close. And although these two pairs of outstanding intellects
had such success in composing their works and transmitting them
to posterity, they did not have equal success in their lives and their
deaths. For poets have led a quieter life and died a natural death,
whereas orators always suffered great vexations and met a cruel
end, since they had involved themselves in the government of
states; in which if you are a novice and incompetent, you live

quibus si rudis es et ineptus, abiectus vivis et inglorius atque publicorum munerum omnino expers, sin vero aptus ac paulo quam caeteris ingeniosior, adtrahis ad te erumnas ὡς κακίας νέφος, adisque plerunque periculum capitis, quemadmodum accidisse Demostheni et Marco Tullio legimus.

2   Verum ex duobus his infelicior Demosthenes fuit. Nam et cum vitiis quibusdam natus est, quae industria non mediocri tolli oportuit—unde Valerius Maximus: 'Alterum Demosthenem natura, alterum industria fecit'—, et puer admodum privatus patre, sub infidis et avaris tutoribus educatus est; quos male administrata tutela in ius vocare coactus, non sine labore immodico ac periculo, deperdita etiam ablatorum parte, evicit. De eo sic in eius vita Libanius:

> Ὀρφανὸς δὲ καταλειφθεὶς ὑπὸ τοῦ πατρὸς κομιδῆ
> νέος, ἦν μέν, ὥς φασιν, ἀσθενὴς τῷ σώματι καὶ
> νοσώδης, ὥστε μηδὲ εἰς παλαίστραν φοιτῆσαι,
> καθάπερ πάντες οἱ τῶν Ἀθηναίων παῖδες εἰώθεσαν·
> ὅθεν καὶ ἀνδρωθεὶς ὑπὸ τῶν ἐχθρῶν εἰς μαλακίαν
> ἐσκώπτετο καὶ βάταλος ἐπωνυμίαν ἔσχεν.

Hoc est, ut et Graecarum literarum rudes intelligant:

> Privatus autem patre admodum iuvenis, fertur imbecilli fuisse corpore et valetudinario adeo, ut neque ad palaestram accederet, quemadmodum omnibus Atheniensium pueris moris erat. Quapropter, vir factus, ab inimicis in molliciem mordebatur, appellabaturque cognomento Batalus.

Et paulo inferius:

> Εἰς ἄνδρας ἐγγραφεὶς εὐθὺς ἀγῶνα κατὰ τῶν ἐπι-
> τρόπων ἐνεστήσατο, κακῶς διῳκηκότων τὴν οὐσίαν

miserably and without glory, not holding any public office, whereas if you have aptitude and a little more intelligence than others, you bring trouble upon yourself, as the Caecias wind brings clouds,[352] and you generally risk your life, as we read in the cases of Demosthenes and Cicero.

But of these two, Demosthenes was the more unlucky. He was 2 born with some disadvantages, which needed to be removed with no little effort (so Valerius Maximus says: "Nature produced one Demosthenes, hard work another").[353] When not much more than a child he lost his father and was brought up by unreliable and greedy guardians. He had to bring them to court for wrongful administration as guardians and defeated them, not without enormous difficulty and danger, also losing part of what had been embezzled. In his biography Libanius writes of him as follows.[354]

Ὀρφανὸς δὲ καταλειφθεὶς ὑπὸ τοῦ πατρὸς κομιδῇ νέος, ἦν μέν, ὥς φασιν, ἀσθενὴς τῷ σώματι καὶ νοσώδης, ὥστε μηδὲ εἰς παλαίστραν φοιτῆσαι, καθάπερ πάντες οἱ τῶν Ἀθηναίων παῖδες εἰώθεσαν· ὅθεν καὶ ἀνδρωθεὶς ὑπὸ τῶν ἐχθρῶν εἰς μαλακίαν ἐσκώπτετο καὶ βάταλος ἐπωνυμίαν ἔσχεν.

This means, so that persons not expert in Greek may understand:

Having lost his father when quite young, he is said to have been physically weak and in such poor health that he did not go to the gymnasium, as was the custom for all Athenian boys. For this reason in adulthood he was accused of effeminacy by his enemies and nicknamed Battalos.

A little further on:

Εἰς ἄνδρας ἐγγραφεὶς εὐθὺς ἀγῶνα κατὰ τῶν ἐπιτρόπων ἐνεστήσατο, κακῶς διῳκηκότων τὴν οὐσίαν

αὐτοῦ, καὶ εἷλε μὲν αὐτούς, οὐ μὴν ἠδυνήθη πάντα ἀπολαβεῖν ὅσα ἀπολώλεκε.

Idest:

Cum primum adscitus est inter viros, statim tutoribus male ipsius facultatibus administratis diem dixit; et evicit quidem eos, sed non omnia potuit, quae amiserat, recuperare.

Et in [in] eadem:

Ἔτι κἀκείνων μνημονευτέον ὅτι τραυλὸς μὲν ἦν τὴν γλῶτταν ἐκ φύσεως, τὸ δὲ πνεῦμα ἀτονώτερος.

Hoc est:

Ad haec et illa commemoranda: Demosthenem et lingua balbum et imbecillis fuisse lateribus.

Item in eadem:

Καὶ γὰρ δειλὸς ἦν τὸ πρῶτον πρὸς τοὺς τοῦ δήμου θορύβους καὶ εὐκατάπληκτος, ὥστε εὐθὺς ἐξίστασθαι. Διὰ δὲ τοῦτό φασιν αὐτὸν ἄνεμον ῥαγδαῖον τηροῦντα καὶ κινουμένην σφοδρῶς τὴν θάλατταν, παρὰ τοὺς αἰγιαλοὺς βαδίζοντα λέγειν καὶ τῷ τῆς θαλάττης ἤχῳ συνεθίζεσθαι φέρειν τὰς τοῦ δήμου καταβοάς.

Hoc est:

Etenim primo timidus ad concionum strepitus fuit et consternabundus, ut statim deficeret. Propterea vero aiunt ipsum, vehementem ventum commotumque admodum mare

αὐτοῦ, καὶ εἷλε μὲν αὐτούς, οὐ μὴν ἠδυνήθη πάντα ἀπολαβεῖν ὅσα ἀπολώλεκε.

That is:

When first registered as an adult he took his guardians to court because of their faulty administration of his property, and he won his case against them but could not recover everything that he had lost.

And in the same biography:

Ἔτι κἀκείνων μνημονευτέον ὅτι τραυλὸς μὲν ἦν τὴν γλῶτταν ἐκ φύσεως, τὸ δὲ πνεῦμα ἀτονώτερος.

Which is:

In addition it should be recorded that Demosthenes had a stammer and weak lungs.

Again from this source:

Καὶ γὰρ δειλὸς ἦν τὸ πρῶτον πρὸς τοὺς τοῦ δήμου θορύβους καὶ εὐκατάπληκτος, ὥστε εὐθὺς ἐξίστασθαι. Διὰ δὲ τοῦτό φασιν αὐτὸν ἄνεμον ῥαγδαῖον τηροῦντα καὶ κινουμένην σφοδρῶς τὴν θάλατταν, παρὰ τοὺς αἰγιαλοὺς βαδίζοντα λέγειν καὶ τῷ τῆς θαλάττης ἤχῳ συνεθίζεσθαι φέρειν τὰς τοῦ δήμου καταβοάς.

That is:

For at first he was nervous of the noise of the public meetings and easily put off, so that he immediately gave up. For that reason they say he waited for a stormy wind and very rough sea, and spoke as he walked along the shore; thanks to

observando, ad litora accedere et recitare sonituque maris
populi clamores ferre consuevisse.

Item in eadem:

Παρειλήφαμεν δὲ κᾳκεῖνο, ὡς καὶ ξίφος ποτὲ ἐκ τῆς
ὀροφῆς ἀπήρτησε, καὶ ἱστάμενος ὑπὸ τούτου ἔλε-
γεν. Ἐποίει δὲ τοῦτο δι᾽ αἰτίαν τοιαύτην· ἐν τῷ
λέγειν ἀπρεπῶς τὸν ὦμον εἰώθει κινεῖν, ὑπερεκρέμα-
σεν οὖν τοῦ ὤμου τὸ ξίφος ἐν χρῷ, καὶ οὕτω τῷ
δέει τῆς πληγῆς ἠδυνήθη κατασχεῖν ἑαυτὸν ἐπὶ τοῦ
πρέποντος σχήματος.

Hoc est:

Accepimus vero et illud: suspensum ab eo ensem fuisse de
tecto, atque sub ipso stetisse, cum recitaret. Quod hanc ob
causam fecisse dicitur: inter dicendum movere indecenter
humerum assolebat; suspendit igitur ensem ad cutem hu-
mero imminentem, atque ita metu plagae in decenti se forma
continuit.

3   Praeterea, cum maxime in patria floreret, nunc invidia civium,
nunc Philippi Alexandrive Macedonum maximorum regum perse-
cutione nunquam quievit; immo, a Philippo in pugna victus,
magna cum ignominia fugit. Tum bis exulavit: primo in Aegina et
Troezene, quinquaginta etiam talentis ab areopagitis damnatus
Alexandro rege; secundo autem, Antipatro imperante, capitis
damnatus a populo, autore Demade, in Neptuni templum, quod
erat in Calaurea insula, non tam salutis gratia, quam ut inde quotidie patriam prospiceret, e Troezeniorum urbe confugit; inibique

the noise of the sea he accustomed himself to tolerate the
noise of the crowd.

Again:

Παρειλήφαμεν δὲ κἀκεῖνο, ὡς καὶ ξίφος ποτὲ ἐκ τῆς
ὀροφῆς ἀπήρτησε, καὶ ἱστάμενος ὑπὸ τούτου ἔλε-
γεν. Ἐποίει δὲ τοῦτο δι᾽ αἰτίαν τοιαύτην· ἐν τῷ
λέγειν ἀπρεπῶς τὸν ὦμον εἰώθει κινεῖν, ὑπερεκρέμα-
σεν οὖν τοῦ ὤμου τὸ ξίφος ἐν χρῷ, καὶ οὕτω τῷ
δέει τῆς πληγῆς ἠδυνήθη κατασχεῖν ἑαυτὸν ἐπὶ τοῦ
πρέποντος σχήματος.

That is:

We have also heard the following: he hung a sword from the
ceiling and stood under it when speaking. This he is said to
have done because he was in the habit of moving his shoulders inappropriately while speaking; so he hung the sword
with the blade close to his skin, and thus through fear of
being cut he controlled his movements suitably.

Furthermore, though he had great influence in his country, he 3
was never able to rest owing to the jealousy of his fellow citizens at
some times, and the persecution by Philip and Alexander, the
great kings of Macedonia, at others; indeed, after defeat in battle
with Philip he fled in great ignominy. Then he was twice in exile,
first in Aegina and Troizen, condemned by the Areopagus to pay a
fine of fifty talents during Alexander's rule; secondly, when Antipater was in power, he was condemned to death by the people on
the proposal of Demades and left the city of Troizen for a temple
of Neptune on the island of Calauria, not so much for safety's
sake but so that he could set eyes on his native land every day.

hausto veneno, cum a satellitibus traheretur, excessit e vita, quemadmodum in eius vita Plutarchus meminit.

4 Operae pretium autem visum est quaedam ex eius epistola ad magistratus populumque Atheniensium hic inserere. Sunt enim huiusmodi:

Ἀλλὰ περὶ μὲν τούτων παύομαι, πολλὰ γράφειν ἔχων· τὸ γὰρ μηδὲν ἐμαυτῷ συνειδέναι πεῖράν μοι δέδωκεν εἰς μὲν ὠφέλειαν ἀσθενὲς ὄν, εἰς δὲ τὸ μᾶλλον λυπεῖσθαι πάντων ὀδυνηρότατον. Ἐπειδὴ δὲ καλῶς ποιοῦντες πᾶσι τοῖς ἐν ταῖς αἰτίαις διήλλαχθε, καὶ ἐμοὶ διαλλάγητε, ὦ ἄνδρες Ἀθηναῖοι· οὔτε γὰρ ἠδίκηχ᾽ ὑμᾶς οὐδένα (ὡς ἴστωσαν οἱ θεοὶ καὶ ἥρωες, μαρτυρεῖ δέ μοι πᾶς ὁ πρόσθεν παρεληλυθὼς χρόνος, ὃς δικαιότερον ἂν πιστεύοιθ᾽ ὑφ᾽ ὑμῶν τῆς ἀνεγκλήτου νῦν ἐπενεχθείσης αἰτίας) οὔτ᾽ ἐγὼ χείριστος οὔτ᾽ ἀπιστότατος φανήσομαι τῶν διαβληθέντων. Καὶ μὴν τὸ ἀπελθεῖν οὐκ ἂν εἰκότως ὀργὴν πρός με ποιήσειεν· οὐ γὰρ ἀπεγνωκὼς ὑμᾶς οὐδ᾽ ἑτέρωσε βλέπων οὐδαμοῦ μετέστην, ἀλλὰ πρῶτον μὲν τοὔνειδος τῆς εἱρκτῆς χαλεπῶς τῷ λογισμῷ φέρων, εἶτα διὰ τὴν ἡλικίαν οὐκ ἂν οἷός τ᾽ ὢν τῷ σώματι τὴν κακοπάθειαν ὑπενεγκεῖν. Ἔτι δ᾽ οὐδ᾽ ὑμᾶς ἐνόμιζον ἀβουλεῖν ἔξω με προπηλακισμοῦ γενέσθαι, ὃς οὐδὲν ὑμᾶς ὠφελῶν ἐμὲ ἀπώλλυεν. Ἔπειθ᾽ ὅτι γε ὑμῖν προσεῖναι τὸν νοῦν καὶ οὐδέσιν ἄλλοις, πολλὰ ἂν ἴδοιτε σημεῖα. Εἴς τε γὰρ πόλιν ἦλθον, οὐκ ἐν ᾗ μέγιστα πράξειν αὐτὸς ἔμελλον, ἀλλ᾽ εἰς ἣν καὶ τοὺς προγόνους ἐλθόντας ᾔδειν, ὅτε ὁ πρὸς τὸν Πέρσην κατελάμβανεν αὐτοὺς

And there, being dragged away by the ruler's henchmen, he took
poison and died, as Plutarch relates in his *Life*.[355]

It seemed worthwhile to insert here some parts of his letter to   4
the magistrates and people of Athens; they are as follows:[356]

Ἀλλὰ περὶ μὲν τούτων παύομαι, πολλὰ γράφειν
ἔχων· τὸ γὰρ μηδὲν ἐμαυτῷ συνειδέναι πεῖράν μοι
δέδωκεν εἰς μὲν ὠφέλειαν ἀσθενὲς ὄν, εἰς δὲ τὸ
μᾶλλον λυπεῖσθαι πάντων ὀδυνηρότατον. Ἐπειδὴ δὲ
καλῶς ποιοῦντες πᾶσι τοῖς ἐν ταῖς αἰτίαις διήλλαχθε, καὶ ἐμοὶ διαλλάγητε, ὦ ἄνδρες Ἀθηναῖοι· οὔτε
γὰρ ἠδίκηχ᾽ ὑμᾶς οὐδένα (ὡς ἴστωσαν οἱ θεοὶ καὶ
ἥρωες, μαρτυρεῖ δέ μοι πᾶς ὁ πρόσθεν παρεληλυθὼς χρόνος, ὃς δικαιότερον ἂν πιστεύοιθ᾽ ὑφ᾽
ὑμῶν τῆς ἀνεγκλήτου νῦν ἐπενεχθείσης αἰτίας) οὔτ᾽
ἐγὼ χείριστος οὔτ᾽ ἀπιστότατος φανήσομαι τῶν
διαβληθέντων. Καὶ μὴν τὸ ἀπελθεῖν οὐκ ἂν εἰκότως
ὀργὴν πρός με ποιήσειεν· οὐ γὰρ ἀπεγνωκὼς ὑμᾶς
οὐδ᾽ ἑτέρωσε βλέπων οὐδαμοῦ μετέστην, ἀλλὰ πρῶτον μὲν τοὔνειδος τῆς εἰρκτῆς χαλεπῶς τῷ λογισμῷ φέρων, εἶτα διὰ τὴν ἡλικίαν οὐκ ἂν οἷός τ᾽
ὢν τῷ σώματι τὴν κακοπάθειαν ὑπενεγκεῖν. Ἔτι δ᾽
οὐδ᾽ ὑμᾶς ἐνόμιζον ἀβουλεῖν ἔξω με προπηλακισμοῦ γενέσθαι, ὃς οὐδὲν ὑμᾶς ὠφελῶν ἐμὲ ἀπώλλυεν. Ἔπειθ᾽ ὅτι γε ὑμῖν προσεῖναι τὸν νοῦν καὶ
οὐδέσιν ἄλλοις, πολλὰ ἂν ἴδοιτε σημεῖα. Εἴς τε γὰρ
πόλιν ἦλθον, οὐκ ἐν ᾗ μέγιστα πράξειν αὐτὸς ἔμελλον, ἀλλ᾽ εἰς ἣν καὶ τοὺς προγόνους ἐλθόντας ᾔδειν,
ὅτε ὁ πρὸς τὸν Πέρσην κατελάμβανεν αὐτοὺς

κίνδυνος, καὶ παρ' ἣν πλείστην εὔνοιαν ὑπάρχου-
σαν ὑμῖν ἠπιστάμην· ἔστι δὲ Τροιζηνίων αὕτη, ἧ
μάλιστα μὲν οἱ θεοί, καὶ τῆς πρὸς ὑμᾶς εὐνοίας
ἕνεκα καὶ τῆς πρὸς ἐμὲ εὐεργεσίας, εὖνοι πάντες
εἴησαν, εἶτα σωθεὶς ὑφ' ὑμῶν δυνηθείην ἀποδοῦναι
χάριτας. Ἔν τε ταύτῃ τινῶν, ὡς ἐμοὶ χαριζομένων,
ἐπιτιμᾶν ὑμῖν τι πειρωμένων τῇ κατ' ἐμὲ ἀγνοίᾳ,
ἐγὼ πᾶσαν εὐφημίαν ὥσπερ ἐμοὶ προσῆκε παρει-
χόμην· ἐξ ὧν καὶ μάλιστα νομίζω πάντας ἀγασθέν-
τας δημοσίᾳ τιμῆσαι. Ὁρῶν δὲ τὴν μὲν εὔνοιαν
τῶν ἀνδρῶν μεγάλην, τὴν δὲ εἰς τὸ παρὸν δύναμιν
καταδεεστέραν, μετελθὼν εἰς τὸ τοῦ Ποσειδῶνος
ἱερὸν ἐν Καλαυρείᾳ κάθημαι, οὐ μόνον τῆς ἀσφα-
λείας ἕνεκα, ἣν διὰ τὸν θεὸν ἐλπίζω μοι ὑπάρχειν
(οὐ γὰρ εὖ οἶδά γε, ἃ γὰρ ἐφ' ἑτέροις ἐστίν, ὡς ἂν
βούλωνται πρᾶξαι, λεπτὴν καὶ ἄδηλον ἔχει τῷ κιν-
δυνεύοντι τὴν ἀσφάλειαν), ἀλλ' ὅτι καὶ τὴν πατρίδα
ἐνθένδε ἑκάστης ἡμέρας ἀφορῶ, εἰς ἣν τοσαύτην
εὔνοιαν ἐμαυτῷ σύνοιδα, ὅσης παρ' ὑμῶν εὔχομαι
τυχεῖν. Ὅπως οὖν, ὦ ἄνδρες Ἀθηναῖοι, μηκέτι πλείω
χρόνον τοῖς παροῦσι κακοῖς συνέχωμαι, ψηφίσασθέ
μοι ταῦτα, ἃ καὶ ἄλλοις τισὶν ἤδη, ἵνα μήτε ἀνάξιον
ὑμῶν μηδέν μοι συμβῇ, μήτε ἱκέτης ἑτέρων ἀναγ-
κασθῶ γενέσθαι· οὐδὲ γὰρ ὑμῖν τοῦτο γένοιτ' ἂν
καλόν. Ἐπεὶ εἴ γέ μοι τὰ πρὸς ὑμᾶς ἀδιάλλακτα
ὑπάρχει, τεθνάναι με κρεῖττον ἦν.

Hoc est:

Sed de his cum multa possim, scribere praetermitto. Nullius
enim me conscium esse culpae, ad utilitatem quidem

κίνδυνος, καὶ παρ᾽ ἣν πλείστην εὔνοιαν ὑπάρχου-
σαν ὑμῖν ἠπιστάμην· ἔστι δὲ Τροιζηνίων αὕτη, ᾗ
μάλιστα μὲν οἱ θεοί, καὶ τῆς πρὸς ὑμᾶς εὐνοίας
ἕνεκα καὶ τῆς πρὸς ἐμὲ εὐεργεσίας, εὖνοι πάντες
εἴησαν, εἶτα σωθεὶς ὑφ᾽ ὑμῶν δυνηθείην ἀποδοῦναι
χάριτας. Ἔν τε ταύτῃ τινῶν, ὡς ἐμοὶ χαριζομένων,
ἐπιτιμᾶν ὑμῖν τι πειρωμένων τῇ κατ᾽ ἐμὲ ἀγνοίᾳ,
ἐγὼ πᾶσαν εὐφημίαν ὥσπερ ἐμοὶ προσῆκε παρει-
χόμην· ἐξ ὧν καὶ μάλιστα νομίζω πάντας ἀγασθέν-
τας δημοσίᾳ τιμῆσαι. Ὁρῶν δὲ τὴν μὲν εὔνοιαν
τῶν ἀνδρῶν μεγάλην, τὴν δὲ εἰς τὸ παρὸν δύναμιν
καταδεεστέραν, μετελθὼν εἰς τὸ τοῦ Ποσειδῶνος
ἱερὸν ἐν Καλαυρείᾳ κάθημαι, οὐ μόνον τῆς ἀσφα-
λείας ἕνεκα, ἣν διὰ τὸν θεὸν ἐλπίζω μοι ὑπάρχειν
(οὐ γὰρ εὖ οἶδά γε, ἃ γὰρ ἐφ᾽ ἑτέροις ἐστίν, ὡς ἂν
βούλωνται πρᾶξαι, λεπτὴν καὶ ἄδηλον ἔχει τῷ κιν-
δυνεύοντι τὴν ἀσφάλειαν), ἀλλ᾽ ὅτι καὶ τὴν πατρίδα
ἐνθένδε ἑκάστης ἡμέρας ἀφορῶ, εἰς ἣν τοσαύτην
εὔνοιαν ἐμαυτῷ σύνοιδα, ὅσης παρ᾽ ὑμῶν εὔχομαι
τυχεῖν. Ὅπως οὖν, ὦ ἄνδρες Ἀθηναῖοι, μηκέτι πλείω
χρόνον τοῖς παροῦσι κακοῖς συνέχωμαι, ψηφίσασθέ
μοι ταῦτα, ἃ καὶ ἄλλοις τισὶν ἤδη, ἵνα μήτε ἀνάξιον
ὑμῶν μηδέν μοι συμβῇ, μήτε ἱκέτης ἑτέρων ἀναγ-
κασθῶ γενέσθαι· οὐδὲ γὰρ ὑμῖν τοῦτο γένοιτ᾽ ἂν
καλόν. Ἐπεὶ εἴ γέ μοι τὰ πρὸς ὑμᾶς ἀδιάλλακτα
ὑπάρχει, τεθνάναι με κρεῖττον ἦν.

Which is:

But though I could say much about this, I will not write
about it. For I have learned by experience that not having

imbecillum esse experientia didici, ad maiorem vero moesti-
tiam inferendam vehementissimum omnium. Quoniam autem omnibus accusatis reconciliati estis, id quod bene factum dixerim, et mihi velim reconciliemini, viri Athenienses.
Nam neque vos ulla adfeci iniuria — deos testor et heroas,
mihi autem testis est omnis anteacta vita, cui magis iustum
est ut fidem habeatis quam culpae mihi nunc iniuria illa-
tae — neque ego pessimus minimeve eorum fide dignus vide-
bor, qui circumventi sunt calumnia. Atqui discessus meus
immerito vos mihi redderet iratos: neque enim spe vestri
destitutus discessi, neque quod alio animum applicuerim
meum, sed primum quia ignominiam carceris moleste animo
ferebam, deinde quoniam propter aetatem imbecillo corpore
miseriam perferre non poteram. Item non existimabam nolle
vos vacare me vituperio, quod nullo vobis emolumento fuit,
me vero perdidit. Ad haec, in vobis nec ullis aliis animum
fuisse meum, multis poteritis signis perspicere. Nam et urbem petii, non in qua res maximas essem ipse acturus, sed in
quam et maiores nostros profectos cognoveram, quo tempore
illis de Persarum rege periculum imminebat, et cuius plurimam erga vos benevolentiam esse perspexeram: haec autem
est Troezeniorum civitas, cui opto ut dei potissimum, ob ipsius erga vos benevolentiam et collatum in me beneficium,
sint omnes benevoli, tum ipse, servatus a vobis, queam referre gratiam. Caeterum, cum in hac nonnulli, ut mihi grati-
ficarentur, increpare vos conarentur, idque mei animi ignora-
tione, ego eos pro viribus, ut bene dicerent, quod meum erat,
admonui; qua potissimum causa puto eos omnis admiratos
publice me honorasse. Sed cum viderem benevolentiam quidem hominum magnam, sed vires in praesentia imbecillas, in

any crime on my conscience is of little value, but is the most significant cause of increased pain. But since you have been reconciled with all the accused, which I would say is a good thing, I wish, gentlemen of Athens, you would be reconciled with me as well. I have not done you any harm—I call to witness the gods and heroes, and my whole career testifies to this, and it is right for you to place more reliance on it than on charges now wrongfully laid against me; nor will I be seen to be the worst or the most untrustworthy of those who have been the victims of slander. Yet my departure could not justifiably arouse your anger against me;[357] I did not leave because I had lost faith in you or because I was looking in other directions, but in the first place because I could not bear the disgrace of prison and also, owing to my age and poor health, I could not endure the suffering. In addition I did not think you unwilling for me to be exempt from abuse, which did you no good and destroyed me. Furthermore, you will be able to tell from many indications that I was devoted to you and not to others, since I sought a city not as a place where I would perform great acts but as one to which our ancestors had gone at a time when danger from the Persian king threatened them, a city whose great goodwill toward you I had noted—that is the city of Troizen, to which I pray in particular that all the gods may show favor on account of its goodwill to you and the kindness conferred on me; I pray also that I myself, having been preserved by you, may be able to display my gratitude. However, since some people there tried to criticize you in order to win my favor, and did so without knowing my intentions, I advised them as best I could, as was my duty, to be polite; and that I think is the principal reason why they all admired me and honored me publicly. But when I realized that there was much goodwill but for the time being not much power, I set off to the

Neptuni templum profectus, in Calaurea insula me contineo, non solum tutelae gratia, quam mihi esse spero ob reverentiam numinis — neque enim certo scio: nam quae in aliorum arbitrio et voluntate posita sunt, tenuem ac incertam praebent periclitanti tutelam —, sed etiam quia patriam prospicio inde quotidie, erga quam tantae meae mihi conscius sum benevolentiae, quantam consequi opto a vobis. Quapropter, viri Athenienses, ne diutius hisce detinear malis, ea mihi decernite, quae olim aliis, tum nequid indignum vobis mihi eveniat, tum etiam ne supplex esse aliis cogar: nam nec vobis quidem id decori fuerit. Quod si redeundi vobiscum in gratiam nulla mihi spes sit reliqua, mori me esset melius.

5   Vides, quantis semper malis versatus fuerit miser. Qua re non miror a satyro scriptum: 'Diis ille adversis genitus fatoque sinistro.' Quid, quod illo etiam tot iam secula mortuo, suum adhuc fortuna, licet semper varia sit atque instabilis, servare tenorem videtur? Nam abhinc fere triennium desyderanti tibi orationes Demosthenis brevi me informatas mea cura publicaturum recepi. Sed tot id tentanti mihi acciderunt impedimenta, ut persaepe excudi coeptas intermiserim, Carteromacho etiam nostro demirante illudque Iuvenalis saepe repetente: 'Diis ille adversis genitus fatoque sinistro,' cum etiam admodum quam pauca earum orationum exempla imprimenda curaverim; idque coactus, quod in nullo ante accidit volumine excuso in thermis nostris. Quorum omnium est mihi optimus testis Angelus Chabrielus patritius Venetus, excellentis vir ingenii et in utraque lingua doctissimus Demosthenisque studiosissimus, qui a me hoc opus quotidiano fere, ut ait ille, convitio, ut iam excudendum curarem, efflagitabat.

temple of Neptune and confined myself to the island of Calauria, not just for reasons of safety, which I hope to have,
thanks to respect for the deity—but I cannot be sure, since
whatever depends on the arbitrary will of others creates slen-
der and uncertain protection to those in danger—but also
because I look out from there every day toward my country.
I hope to enjoy from you goodwill as great as that which I
am conscious of feeling toward the city. So, gentlemen of
Athens, in order that I am not detained any longer in this
bad situation, decree for me what you have done in the past
for others, lest anything happen to me which would be unworthy of you, or I am compelled to beg help from others,
since that would not be honorable for you either. But if I
have no hope left of regaining your favor, it would be better
for me to die.

You see what troubles the poor man always faced; so I am not   5
surprised by the satirist's line: "He was born with the gods against
him and with a sinister destiny."[358] Again, though he has been
dead for many centuries, his fortune, though always variable and
unstable, seems to retain its character. For about three years ago,
when you wanted Demosthenes' speeches, I promised to publish
them soon, printed by myself. But I encountered so many obstacles to my attempts that I often interrupted the printing after it
had begun. Our friend Forteguerri[359] was surprised and frequently
quoted Juvenal's "He was born with the gods against him and with
a sinister destiny" at a stage when I had printed just a few copies
of the orations; and that I had done under pressure, which never
happened previously with any book printed in our workshop.[360]
For all this the best witness is Angelo Gabriele, a Venetian patrician, a man of outstanding intellect, expert in both languages and
very keen on Demosthenes, who begged me insistently to attend
to the printing, with almost daily reproaches, as he says.

6   Quanquam et illud servasse videtur fortuna: ut, quemadmodum felix ille semper fuit eloquentia et aeternitate scriptorum
suorum, ita nescio quo modo pulcherrimus liber hic omnium,
quos imprimendos vel Latine vel Graece curavimus, exit in publicum ex aedibus nostris. Quamobrem, si serius ad te venit quam et
tu volebas et ipse desyderabam, non mihi velim imputes, sed Demosthenis infortunio, quem summo cum labore et industria fecisse
quae fecit omnia, legimus. Rursus, si pulcherrimis characteribus et
perquam decenti forma habituque necnon castigatissimus exit in
manus hominum ὡς κατὰ τὴν παλιγγενεσίαν, non tantum in-
dustriae nostrae et assiduis curis adscribas, quam illius gratiae et
felicitati, quam semper in suis habuit lucubrationibus.

7   Has vero Demosthenis orationes, Clari doctissime, nomini tuo
nuncupatas ex Neacademia nostra emittimus ob multas causas;
sed praecipua est singularis benevolentia in te mea ob miram probitatem tuam ac doctrinam bonarumque literarum cognitionem;
tum quia in inclyta ista urbe alumna virorum nobilium Epidauro,
cui nunc Rhacusae est nomen, et Latinas et Graecas literas profiteris, instituisque iuventutem istam eloquentiae studiosam arte
dicendi, quod duce Demosthene et te interprete quam facillime
consequetur. Id quod eo etiam feci libentius, quoniam, si cuipiam
reipublicae Demosthenis orationes die noctuque volvendas accurate existimo, isti existimo. Nam, etsi viros omni virtute praeditos
et prudentissimos habet, quales vidi ipse Venetiis Danielem Res-
tium, secundum apud Venetos fungentem legationis officio, et Pe-
trum Mentium, Restii collegam, tamen praeceptis quam optimis
oratorum omnium Demosthenis facile principis, quanta tyrannis
et Philippis habenda sit fides, non obscure cognoscet. Nam cum
aliis plurimis rempublicam Atheniensium admonet divinus orator
cavendum esse a tyrannis, quod sint natura rerumpublicarum ini-
micissimi, ut lupi ovium, tum his verbis in prima pro Olynthiis
oratione: Καὶ ὅλως ἄπιστον οἶμαι ταῖς πολιτείαις ἡ

Yet fate seems to have kept one thing in reserve: just as he was 6
always sublime for his eloquence and the immortality of his writings, so somehow, of all the Latin or Greek books we have printed
this is the most beautiful issued to the public from our house.[361]
So if it reaches you later than you wanted and I had desired, I
hope you will not put it down to me but to the ill fortune of Demosthenes, of whom we read that everything he did was achieved
with great labor and effort. Similarly, if it reaches the public with
a beautiful typeface, very elegantly presented and designed and
carefully edited, as if enjoying a resurrection, you should not as-
cribe this so much to our efforts and thorough care as to the author's graceful and felicitous style, displayed always in his writings.

These orations of Demosthenes we issue from our Neacademia 7
dedicated to you, most learned Clario, for many reasons, the principal one being my goodwill toward you on account of your splendid integrity, learning and knowledge of literature; secondly because you teach Greek and Latin in that famous city Epidaurus,
the birthplace of noble men, which is now called Ragusa, and you
teach the art of public speaking to young people studying rhetoric,
which they acquire easily with Demosthenes as their model and
you to expound him. I have done this all the more willingly because, if there is any city where I think Demosthenes' speeches
should be read with attention by day and by night, I think that is
it. For although it has men of all talents and great wisdom, whom
I have met in Venice, such as Daniele Resti, now serving a second
term as ambassador in Venice,[362] and Pietro Menzio,[363] Resti's colleague, nevertheless from the outstanding teachings of easily the
best of all the orators, the city will clearly recognize how much
trust can be placed in tyrants and men like Philip. For along with
much other advice the divine orator tells the Athenian state to be
wary of tyrants because they are natural enemies of republics, as
wolves are of sheep, and he has this to say in his first *Olynthiac*:[364]
Καὶ ὅλως ἄπιστον οἶμαι ταῖς πολιτείαις ἡ τυραννίς, ἄλλως

τυραννίς, ἄλλως τε κᾂν ὅμορον χώραν ἔχωσι. Hoc est: 'Et omnino tyrannis infida res est rebuspublicis, praesertim si vicinam illi regionem habuerint.' Et in secunda contra Philippum: Οὐ γὰρ ἀσφαλεῖς ταῖς πολιτείαις αἱ πρὸς τοὺς τυράννους αὗται λίαν ὁμιλίαι. Hoc est: 'Non enim tutae sunt rebuspublicis hae nimiae cum tyrannis consuetudines.' Et paulo post:

Ἐν δέ τι κοινὸν ἡ φύσις τῶν εὖ φρονούντων ἐν ἑαυτῇ κέκτηται φυλακτήριον, ὃ πᾶσι μέν ἐστιν ἀγαθὸν καὶ σωτήριον, μάλιστα δὲ τοῖς πλήθεσι πρὸς τοὺς τυράννους. Τί οὖν ἐστι τοῦτο; Ἀπιστία. Ταύτην φυλάττετε, ταύτης ἀντέχεσθε· ἐὰν ταύτην σώζητε, οὐδὲν δεινὸν μὴ πάθητε. Τί οὖν ζητεῖτε, ἔφην, ἐλευθερίαν; Εἶτ᾽ οὐχ ὁρᾶτε Φίλιππον ἀλλοτριωτάτας ταύτῃ καὶ τὰς προσηγορίας ἔχοντα; Βασιλεὺς γὰρ καὶ τύραννος ἅπας ἐχθρὸς ἐλευθερίᾳ καὶ νόμοις ἐναντίος.

Hoc est:

Commune vero quoddam natura prudentum possidet in se tutamen, quod bonum omnibus est et salutare, maxime autem populis adversus tyrannos. Quodnam igitur illud est? Incredulitas. Hanc custodite, hanc complectimini; si hanc servaveritis, nihil adversi patiemini. Quid igitur quaeritis, inquam, libertatem? Nonne videtis Philippum alienissimas ab ea vel appellationes habentem? Omnis enim rex et tyrannus inimicus est libertati et contrarius legibus.

8   Habes igitur tandem, mi Clari, ab Aldo tuo, quas iandiu desyderasti, Demosthenis orationes; habet urbs Epidaurus quem debeat librum ad suam utilitatem nocturna versare manu, versare

τε κἂν ὅμορον χώραν ἔχωσι. Which is: "And in general tyr-
anny is not to be trusted by republics, especially if their territory is
close by." And in his *Second Philippic*:[365] Οὐ γὰρ ἀσφαλεῖς ταῖς
πολιτείαις αἱ πρὸς τοὺς τυράννους αὗται λίαν ὁμιλίαι. That
is: "These unduly close relations with tyrants are not safe for republics." Shortly after that:[366]

Ἐν δέ τι κοινὸν ἡ φύσις τῶν εὖ φρονούντων ἐν
ἑαυτῇ κέκτηται φυλακτήριον, ὃ πᾶσι μέν ἐστιν ἀγαθὸν καὶ σωτήριον, μάλιστα δὲ τοῖς πλήθεσι πρὸς
τοὺς τυράννους. Τί οὖν ἐστι τοῦτο; Ἀπιστία. Ταύτην
φυλάττετε, ταύτης ἀντέχεσθε· ἐὰν ταύτην σώζητε,
οὐδὲν δεινὸν μὴ πάθητε. Τί οὖν ζητεῖτε, ἔφην, ἐλευθερίαν; Εἶτ᾽ οὐχ ὁρᾶτε Φίλιππον ἀλλοτριωτάτας
ταύτῃ καὶ τὰς προσηγορίας ἔχοντα; Βασιλεὺς γὰρ
καὶ τύραννος ἅπας ἐχθρὸς ἐλευθερίᾳ καὶ νόμοις
ἐναντίος.

Which is:

Sensible people have one thing in common in their nature as
a protection, which is good for all and keeps them safe, especially the masses against tyrants. So what is it? Mistrust.
Preserve that, do not lose sight of that. If you maintain it
you have nothing to fear. What is your aim, I ask? Liberty?
Do you not see that Philip's titles are utterly inconsistent
with it? Every king and tyrant is an enemy of freedom and
an opponent of law.

So at last, my dear Clario, you have from your friend Aldus the   8
speeches of Demosthenes which you have wanted for so long; the
city of Epidaurus has the book which for its own good it ought to
turn the pages of by day and by night.[367] And all other republics

diurna; habent et caeterae respublicae, quemadmodum se prudenter regere gubernareque atque a tyrannis reddere tutas queant;
habet studiosissimus quisque, a quo una cum Graeca lingua et
eloquentiam optime discere et utilissimum in sua republica praestare se possit. Vale.

Venetiis mense Octobri M.D.IIII.

: XXXIII :

Ἄλδος τοῖς σπουδαίοις εὖ πράττειν.

1 Καλὸν τὸ σπουδάζειν ἐπὶ λόγοις οὐκ ἀρνησαίμην ἄν, εἴ
τις ἀσπάζοιτ᾽ ἐν τούτῳ καὶ τὰ θεῖα. Ἐφῷ οὖν ὁμοῦ
γενήσεθ᾽ ἑκάτερον, ἰδοῦ ἡμῖν ἡ πρόξενος, λέγω δὴ ταυ-
τηνὶ τὴν βύβλον. Μὴ τοίνυν ὀκνεῖτε ὁμιλεῖν αὐτῇ ὀση-
μέραι, καὶ ταῦτα ὀρθρευόμενοι. Ζητητέα γὰρ τὸ πρῶτον
ἡ τοῦ θεοῦ βασιλεία. Ἔρρωσθε.

have a means to direct their affairs with prudent governance and keep themselves free from tyrants. Every scholar has a source from which, apart from the Greek language, he can acquire true eloquence and perform great services to his state. Farewell.

Venice, October 1504.

: XXXIII :

Hours in Praise of the Most Blessed Virgin
Seven Penitential Psalms
Athanasian Creed
Sacrifice in Praise of the Most Holy Virgin[368]
(*July 1505*)

Aldus to students, greetings.

I would not deny that an interest in literature is a good thing if 1 one also embraces religious matters. In order that both may go together here is an aid, I mean this book. So do not hesitate to look at it daily, and indeed at dawn. The kingdom of God is to be sought first and foremost.[369] Farewell.

: XXXIV :

A

Aldus lectori s.

1 Registrum cum Graeco et Latino simul, ut vides, informandum
curavimus. Sed non sis nescius, lector carissime, posse te Latinum
a Graeco commodissime separare pro arbitrio tuo; item, in quater-
nione Dd in tribus ultimis chartis Latinis et semis, statim post
iambos Gabriae sequi Latinum. Nec te perturbet, si, Phurnuto
insertae, Graecum a Graeco disiungunt: fieri enim aliter haud potuit. Causam tu ipse cognosces perfacile. Quod si minus placuerit,
potes, ut dixi, Latinas chartas extrahere tuo arbitratu. Nos eas
inseruimus propter literarum Graecarum rudes, qui Graeco e
regione Latinum esse operae pretium ducunt, ut pagina paginae
respondeat et versui versus. Vale.

B

Aldus lectori s.

2 Haec Gabrii trimetra cum scazonte, ultimo epigrammate, nacti
correctius exemplum, iterum imprimenda curavimus, ut perperam
excusa ante hisce queas corrigere. Vale.

: XXXIV :

Aesop's Fables *and related texts*[370]
(October 1505)

A

Aldus to the reader, greetings.[371]

As you see, we have arranged the Greek and Latin index together. 1
But, dearest reader, you should not fail to notice that you can, if
you wish, very easily separate the Greek from the Latin;[372] and in
the last three-and-a-half pages of quire Dd the Latin follows immediately after Gabrias' iambics.[373] And don't worry if, inserted in
Phornutus,[374] they separate one Greek text from another. There
was no other way to do it. You will easily see why.[375] But if you
don't like it, you can, as I said, remove the Latin pages at will. We
included them for beginners in Greek who reckon it worth having
the Latin face the Greek, with page and verse matching. Farewell.

B

Aldus to the reader, greetings.[376]

These trimeters by Gabrias, with an epigram in scazons at the 2
end, we found in a better copy and have seen to a reprint, so that
from it you may correct what was faulty in the previous impression. Farewell.

: XXXV :

Aldus Pius Manutius Ioanni Lascari oratori regio s. p. d.

1 Non sum nescius, inclyte ac doctissime Lascaris, capturum te incredibilem voluptatem videndis hisce rhetoricis libris excusis editisque cura nostra in manus hominum: primum, quia quam maxime cupis ut propagetur augeaturque Graeca lingua, quae, vel incursione barbarorum vel iniuria temporum prope extincta, nunc reviviscit; deinde beneficio studiosorum, quando nihil magis desyderas, quam quod in commune omnibus prosit. Cuius rei sum vel ipse testis, a te in hac mea dura curarumque et laborum plena provincia vel consilio vel re semper adiutus, et olim alibi, et nunc Venetiis iam quinquennium, ubi pro Christianissimo Galliarum rege integerrime simul et prudentissime legatum agis. Nam non solum facis mihi copiam librorum tuorum, quorum plena tibi bibliotheca, sed me etiam hortaris assidue, ut maturem optimos quosque libros excusos publicare.

2 Quamobrem placuit eos sub tuo nomine emittere ex aedibus nostris; atque eo magis, quod Sopatri excellentissimi rhetoris praecepta de componendis declamationibus, quae hisce libris inserta visuntur, e Graecia in Italiam advexisti, quemadmodum et plerosque alios lectu dignissimos, e quorum numero sunt Antipho, Denarchus, Andocides, Lycurgus, Isaeus, ex decem illis clarissimis oratoribus, qui Demosthenis temporibus floruere. Quorum Antipho ob vim miram in persuadendo πειθὼ Ἀντιφῶντος

: XXXV :

The Greek Rhetoricians, Volume 1
(November 1508)

Aldus Pius Manutius to Janus Lascaris, the king's
ambassador, warmest greetings.

I am aware, distinguished and learned Lascaris, that you will be   1
utterly delighted to see these works of oratory, printed and edited
by us, reaching the public. Firstly because of your great desire for
the Greek language to be propagated and supported, since it is
now reviving after being almost extinguished by barbarian invasions or the ravages of time; secondly because of its service to
students, since your greatest desire is for whatever serves the common interest of all. I myself can testify to this, since I have always
been helped by your advice or practical support in this difficult
profession of mine, full of worries and exertion, both elsewhere in
the past[377] and now for the last five years in Venice, where you
fulfill most honorably and intelligently the office of ambassador for
the Most Christian King of France. Not only do you make your
books available—your library is fully stocked—but you give me
regular encouragement to make haste with the printing of all the
best works.

So we decided to publish these from our house, dedicated to   2
you, especially as you brought from Greece to Italy the textbook
on the composition of declamations by the excellent rhetor Sopater, which is to be found included here.[378] Similarly you brought
most of the others, which are well worth reading, among them
Antiphon, Deinarchus, Andocides, Lycurgus, Isaeus, members of
the group of ten famous orators who flourished in Demosthenes'
day. Among them Antiphon was known as "persuasion Antiphon"

dicebatur; Denarchus autem, quia proxime ad vim Demosthenis accedebat, κρίθινον Δημοσθένη vocabant, quasi hunc triticeum, illum ordeaceum dixeris. Nisi forte κρίθινος Δημοσθένης dictus est, quod infeliciter eum imitaretur: nam Plotium Gallum, qui puero Marco Tullio rhetoricam Romae docuit, ordearium rhetorem appellatum a M. Coelio scribit Tranquillus, ut inflatum ac levem et sordidum.

3   His adduntur Syrianus, Marcellinus, Sopatrus, diligentissimi doctissimique interpretes rhetoricorum Hermogenis, quos mihi, ut imprimendos curarem, tradidisti — id quod recepi me facturum perbrevi, et facturus sum —; necnon et Nonni poetae duodequinquaginta libri heroico carmine de gestis Liberi patris in India, quae Διονυσιακά Graece inscribuntur.

4   Praeterea quid convenientius, quam viro doctissimo, eique regio oratori clarissimo, doctissimos dicendi magistros dedicare? Adde quod sic faves studiosis omnibus, ut semper atrium tuum amplissimum plenum sit utriusque linguae peritissimorum hominum, atque bona etiam eorum pars tecum vivat. Verum certe est Euripidis illud:

Δεινὸς χαρακτὴρ κἀπίσημος ἐν βροτοῖς
ἐσθλῶν γενέσθαι, κἀπὶ μεῖζον ἔρχεται
τῆς εὐγενείας τοὔνομα τοῖσιν ἀξίοις.

Atque etiam illud Horatii nostri:

Fortes creantur fortibus et bonis.
Est in iuvencis, est in equis patrum
    virtus, neque imbellem feroces
        progenerant aquilae columbam.

Es enim tu non solum ex antiqua illa Graecia ingeniorum doctrinarumque omnium parente oriundus, sed etiam ex stirpe

on account of his extraordinary ability to convince;[379] but Deinarchus, whose powers were very close to those of Demosthenes, they called "the straw Demosthenes,"[380] as if you were to term one of them the "man of grain" and the other the straw man. Unless perhaps he was known as the straw Demosthenes because he was an incompetent imitator, since Suetonius records[381] that Plotius Gallus, who taught rhetoric in Rome when Cicero was a boy, was described as a straw rhetor by Marcus Caelius because of an inflated, superficial and crude style.

To those texts are added Syrianus, Marcellinus, Sopater, thorough and learned commentators on the textbook by Hermogenes which you provided for us to print[382] — which I promised to do very soon, and will do,[383] together with forty-eight books in hexameters by the poet Nonnus on the subject of Bacchus in India, which have the Greek title *Dionysiaca*.

In any case what could be more appropriate than to dedicate expert masters of public speaking to a scholar who is also the king's distinguished envoy?[384] In addition your patronage of all scholars is such that your great antechamber is always full of experts in both languages, a good many of whom reside with you. Euripides was certainly right with:

> To be born of noble parents is a special mark,
> notable among men, and for the deserving,
> the fame of nobility grows greater.[385]

So too this by our own Horace:

> Brave men are created by the brave and good;
> cattle and horses have the qualities of their fathers,
>   and savage eagles do not produce
>   the peace-loving dove.[386]

In fact you are not only a native of that ancient land of Greece, mother of all intellectual and scientific life, but a member of the

nobilissima et imperatoria Lascareorum; ex qua familia quatuor imperatores admodum celebres fuisse traduntur, duo scilicet Theodori, duo item tibi cognomines Ioannes, sed et doctissimus Graecorum omnium aetatis nostrae necnon gloria decusque Graeciae. Debent igitur tibi plurimum tui Graeci, debent Latini, quibus etiam exemplo prodes — nam eorum linguam non minus calles quam Graecam —; debent manes autorum, quos in lucem tanquam ab inferis revocasti. Gaudeant, qui nunc sunt bonarum literarum studiosi, te patrono literatorum, ac precentur ut, quemadmodum desyderas, favere nostrae queas provinciae; cui qui favet, studiosis omnibus favet, profuturus mirum in modum non modo huiusce aetatis hominibus, sed et universae posteritati.

5   Ipse autem interea, quantum in me fuerit, non desistam unquam ab inceptis, sed, Iesu Deo optimo maximo annuente, pergam in dies alacrior, nullo incommodo evitato, nullis laboribus. Quod si non pergimus interdum ut coepimus, fit vel aliqua iusta causa, vel quia maius quiddam movemus, impensius vacaturi illustrandis bonis literis, eruendisque e situ et tenebris antiquis autoribus, more saltantium, cum multis passibus retrocedunt, fortius saltaturi. Vale, Mecoenas aetatis nostrae, 'Mecoenas atavis edite regibus.'

Venetiis mense Novembri M.D.VIII.

noble and imperial house of Lascaris. From that family there are said to have been four quite famous emperors, two of them called Theodore and two sharing your name John[387] — and you are the most learned of the Greeks of our age, to the glory and honor of Greece. Your fellow Greeks therefore owe a great deal to you, as do the Latins, to whom you serve as an example, since you are no less competent in their language than in Greek, as do the shades of the authors whom you have brought back as it were from the underworld to the light of day. Today's students of good literature should rejoice in your patronage of the educated and pray that you are able, in accordance with your wishes, to assist our profession; he who assists it assists all students, and will confer wonderful benefits, not just on the present generation, but on posterity as a whole.

In the meantime I myself will, so far as my abilities permit, 5 never give up the enterprise I have started; but with the favor of Jesus, the best and greatest God, I will press on with increasing energy, not avoiding any difficulty, any hard tasks. If from time to time we do not make such progress as before, that happens for some good reason or because we are preparing for some bigger task, so as to have more time for the enhancement of literary studies and the rescue of ancient authors from rotting in darkness, just as dancers take several steps back before more vigorous movement. Farewell, Maecenas of our age, "Maecenas, descendant of a family of kings."[388]

Venice, November 1508.

: XXXVI :

Aldus Pius Manutius Romanus Iacobo Antiquario Perusino s. p. d.

1 Optima quaeque difficillima factu esse, cum plurimis aliis tum vel eo verum dixerim, quod, ex quo Plutarchi moralia coepi studiose conquirere et colligere undique, ut excusa typis publicarem in manus literatorum, tot mihi impedimento fuerunt, tot alia ex aliis incommoda acciderunt, ut saepe coeptum opus intermittere coactus fuerim. Sed quoniam labor omnia vincit improbus, en tandem absolutum opus. In quo tibi dedicando habeo, mi Antiquari, caussas plurimas, vel mirae probitatis tuae, vel multae doctrinae, vel humanitatis egregiae, vel tui erga me mutui amoris, vel in primis morum sanctissimorum, quibus ita abundas, ut vel maior sis quam fore nos sanctissima Plutarchi praecepta iubent. Quid igitur convenientius quam homini omnium moribus ornatissimo libros de moribus dedicare?

2 Vidi ipse Mediolani hospes tuus plenum te virtutum omnium, miratusque sum non te solum sanctissimum, sed et adolescentem Antiquarium, nepotis tui ex fratre filium, in quo tanta apparebat modestia, tantus amor erga bonas literas — erat enim iam et Latine et Graece doctus —, ut futurus mihi brevi videretur optimus pariter et doctissimus tuique simillimus. Quid, quod ministros tuos ac totam familiam modestiae plenam ac sanctam herique similem admirabar?

3 Unde verissimum illud quod dicitur adfirmaverim: qualescunque patres familiarum, qualescunque heri, nobiles, principes summique civitatis viri fuerint, talem familiam fore, taleis ministros,

: XXXVI :

Plutarch, Moralia
(*March 1509*)

Aldus Pius Manutius of Rome to Jacopo
Antiquario of Perugia,[389] *warmest greetings.*

The best things are the most difficult to achieve. I would say this   1
is true for many other reasons and especially the following: since I
began serious efforts to collect and assemble from all sources Plutarch's *Moral Essays*,[390] in order to make them available in print for
the educated, there were so many obstacles and such a series of
difficulties that I was often forced to interrupt the work that had
been begun. But since unremitting labor overcomes everything,[391]
here at last is the finished product. I have many reasons for dedicating it to you, dear Antiquario, your admirable honesty, great
learning, outstanding kindness, goodwill toward me, which is re-
ciprocated, and especially your saintly way of life, so abundantly
clear that you are superior to what the highly moral teachings of
Plutarch require of us. What better therefore than to dedicate
works on moral questions to the man most distinguished of all for
his morals?

As your guest in Milan I saw you were endowed with every   2
virtue; I admired not just your saintliness but also that of your
young nephew Antiquario, your brother's son, who displayed such
modesty and love of good literature—for he already knew Latin
and Greek—that he looked to me as if he would soon be very expert and learned, just like you. I also admired your staff and the
whole household, entirely modest and saintly, like its master.

So I would affirm the truth of the saying: whatever the qualities   3
of heads of families, masters, noblemen, princes, heads of state,
such will be the qualities of a household, the staff and servants,

servos, civitates ipsas populosque futuros. Quam sententiam M. Tullius in libris de legibus eleganter, ut omnia, dicit his verbis:

> Nec tantum mali est peccare principes—quanquam est magnum per seipsum malum—quantum illud, quod permulti etiam imitatores principum existunt. Nam licet videre, si velis replicare memoriam temporum, qualescunque summi civitatis viri fuerint, talem civitatem fuisse; quaecunque mutatio morum in principibus extiterit, eandem in populo secuturam. Idque haud paulo est verius quam quod Platoni nostro placet, qui musicorum cantibus ait mutatis mutari civitatum status. Ego autem nobilium vita victuque mutato mores mutari civitatum puto. Quo perniciosius de republica merentur vitiosi principes, quod non solum vitia concipiunt ipsi, sed ea infundunt in civitatem, neque solum obsunt quod illi ipsi corrumpuntur, sed etiam quod corrumpunt, plusque exemplo quam peccato nocent.

Quamobrem omneis homines, qui aliis praesunt quibusque λαοί τ᾽ ἐπιτετράφαται καὶ τόσσα μέμηλε, optimos esse velim, mi Antiquari, et tui simillimos; brevi certe fieret, ut cuncti mortales beatam vitam agerent, fugarentur e terris summo omnium consensu scelera et vitia omnia, et, ut ait Ovidius,

> fraudesque dolique
> insidiaeque et vis et amor sceleratus habendi,

atque horum in locum subirent virtutes sanctissimae, probitas et, ut idem ait, 'verum rectumque fidesque.' Sed perpauci sunt aetate nostra boni viri.

4   Quo fit, ut tanto magis tecum esse, tecum vivere semper velim, quem virum optimum integerrimumque cognovi et sermone

the states and peoples themselves. This view is expressed elegantly, as always, by Cicero in his books *On the Laws*:[392]

> There is not so much evil in the misdemeanors of rulers— though they are in themselves a serious evil—as in the fact that a great many people imitate rulers. It can be seen, if one looks back through history, that whatever the character of the leading men in the state, such was the character of the state; whatever change[393] takes place in the behavior of the rulers, the public will follow suit. This is a great deal nearer the truth than what our Plato believes—that after a change of music the condition of cities is changed.[394] But I think the character of states alters as the way of life and behavior of the nobles alters. So bad rulers do all the more damage to states because they are both cultivating vice in themselves and spreading it through the state; they are harmful not just through being corrupt themselves but also because they do more damage by example than by their own misdeeds.

So I would wish all men who have command over others, to whom peoples have been entrusted and such great affairs are a concern,[395] to be of excellent character, my dear Antiquario, and very like yourself; certainly the whole of humanity would soon live a blessed existence, by general consensus crime and all vices would be banished and, as Ovid says,

> fraud, deceit,
> deviousness, violence and the accursed love of possessions.[396]

In their place would enter saintly virtues, honesty and as the same author says, "Truth, decency and trust." But there are very few good men in our generation.

For this reason I would be all the keener to be with you, to live 4 with you always. I have come to know you as an excellent and ab- solutely honest person, both through daily conversation which

quotidiano, qui vitam hominis facile patefacit—nam, quod a So-
lone dictum ferunt: οἷος ὁ βίος, τοιοῦτος καὶ ὁ λόγος, καὶ
οἷος ὁ λόγος, τοιαῦται καὶ αἱ πράξεις—et re ipsa. Merito igitur Galeacius primo, deinde Lodovicus, illustrissimi Mediolani
duces, faciebant te plurimi; merito etiam in ista urbe omnes uno
ore efferunt te in coelum laudibus. Puderet me, optime Antiquari,
privatim ad te de te haec scribere; sed eae sunt epistolae meae,
quae in fronte librorum cura nostra excusorum praeponuntur, ut,
etsi ad privatum aliquem scribi videntur, publice tamen scribantur
legendae doctis omnibus, in quorum manus pervenerint. Quare
velim mihi ignoscas, Antiquari humanissime, si hoc meo testimonio, quod scio esse verissimum, de sanctissimis moribus tuis, de
integerrima vita, de summa probitate, de summa virtute tua, cupio
Antiquarium meum cognosci non solum a studiosissimo quoque
huius aetatis, sed et a posteris, quandiu scripta haec nostra legen-
tur habebunturque in manibus literatorum una cum Plutarchi
moralibus; praeterea tantam inter nos amicitiam intercedere, ut
tribus aut quatuor paribus amicorum, quae antiquitas celebrat,
Antiquarii et Aldi mutua benevolentia et summa amicitia quartum
quintumve par adiungatur.

5   Libuit hic subiungere hendecasyllabos, quos, cum veni ad te
Mediolanum, lusisti extempore prae summo gaudio adventus nostri, ut faciant et hi fidem mutui amoris nostri.

> Aldus venit en, Aldus ecce venit,
> nostrum sinciput occiputque nostrum,
> mel, sal, lac quoque corculumque solus,
> Graios altera et altera Latinos
> qui apprendendo manu, reduxit omneis
> in verum modo limitem, superbos
> victores superans Olympiorum.

soon reveals a man's way of life — for they report a saying of Solon: "a way of life is matched in speech, and speech is matched in actions"[397] — and by practical experience. It was therefore quite right that first Galeazzo, then Lodovico, distinguished rulers of Milan, held you in the highest esteem; it is also right that everyone in the city is unanimous in lauding you to the skies. I would be ashamed, excellent Antiquario, to write to you privately in such terms; but my letters prefacing books printed by us are such that even if they seem to be addressed to an individual, in fact they are composed to be read by the whole scholarly public into whose hands they find their way. So I should like you to forgive me, out of your great kindness, Antiquario, if through this statement — which I know to be absolutely true in regard to your saintly character, decency, honesty, virtue — I wish my friend Antiquario to be known, not just to all scholars of the present generation, but by posterity, as long as these writings of ours are read and circulate among the educated alongside Plutarch's *Moral Essays*. I should also like it to be known that our friendship is such that the mutual esteem and close friendship of Antiquario and Aldus may be added to the three or four pairs of friends celebrated in antiquity, as a fourth or fifth pair.

It is a pleasure to append here the hendecasyllables which you 5 tossed off extempore when I came to Milan, as an expression of delight at our arrival, so that they too may attest our mutual affection:

Aldus has come! Look, here is Aldus:
he alone is our brains, our head,
he is honey, salt, milk, our sweetheart.
He takes the Greeks in one hand,
the Latins in the other
and puts them back on the right path,
outdoing proud Olympic victors.

Nunc o, nunc, iuvenes, ubique in urbe
flores spargite: vere nanque primo
Aldus venit en, Aldus ecce venit!

6   Sed iam indicem eorum, quae hisce Plutarchi opusculis habentur, lege, ac vale.
Venetiis mense Martio M.D.IX.

: XXXVII :

Aldus Pius Manutius Romanus Marco Musuro Cretensi
in urbe Patavio Graecas literas profitenti s. p. d.

1   Si quisquam est, cui dicandi sint libri Graeci excusi cura nostra,
Musure doctissime, is tu es: nam non solum profuisti semper et
prodes assidue huic nostrae durae provinciae, sed profiteris etiam
in clarissimo gymnasio Patavino Graecas literas tanta frequentia
studiosorum literarum Graecarum, ut mirentur omnes plurimum;
unde paucis admodum annis multi te docente periti Graecae linguae evaserunt. Quam quidem rem et Latinis literis, quae a Graecis fluxerunt, et ipsis liberalibus disciplinis, quae a Graecis auctoribus traditae sunt, magnum adiumentum brevi allaturam esse, vel
hinc colligi potest, quod aetate nostra iam fere omnes, spreta barbarie, non minus Graece quam Latine discere aggrediuntur, non
immemores Horatiani illius: 'Vos exemplaria Graeca nocturna versate manu, versate diurna' necnon et illius in officiis M. Tullii
ad Marcum filium: 'Ego autem ad meam utilitatem semper cum
Graecis Latina coniunxi; neque id in philosophia solum, sed etiam
in dicendi exercitatione feci. Idem tibi censeo faciendum, uti par

Now, now, young people, put out flowers
all over the city; for at the start of spring
Aldus has come, look, Aldus has come!

But now read the list of what is included in these opuscula by   6
Plutarch. Farewell.

Venice, March 1509.

: XXXVII :

The Greek Rhetoricians, Volume 2
(May 21, 1509)

*Aldus Pius Manutius of Rome to Marcus Musurus of Crete,
professor of Greek in Padua, warmest greetings.*

If there is anyone to whom Greek texts printed by us should be   1
dedicated, it is to you, most learned Musurus. Not only have you
always been helpful, giving regular assistance to this difficult enterprise of ours, but you also lecture on Greek literature in the distinguished university of Padua to such a large audience of students of
Greek literature that everyone is full of admiration; as a result
within quite a short time many under your tuition have emerged
as experts in the Greek language. This will soon bring great benefit for Latin literature, which originated from Greek, and for the
liberal arts transmitted by Greek authorities, as can be inferred
from the fact that now practically everyone, despising barbarous
habits, is just as keen to learn Greek as Latin, mindful of Horace's
words: "You must study Greek models at night and study them by
day,"[398] and of Cicero's words to his son Marcus in *De officiis*:[399]
"But I have always combined Greek and Latin, to my advantage,
and I have done this not only in philosophy but also in the practice of public speaking. I think you should do the same, so as to be

sis in utriusque orationis facultate.' Id quod tu praeter caeteros facis, Marce Musure, tanquam ad te Marcum filium ille scripserit: nam tanta felicitate cum Latinis Graeca coniungis, ut non solum utriusque linguae evaseris peritissimus, sed iam doctissimus quoque philosophus, nec qualem barbari, sed qualem docti solent appellare philosophum.

2   Dedicamus igitur tibi hos Syriani, Sopatri ac Marcellini in Hermogenis rhetorica et Aphtonii progymnasmata commentarios; de quorum doctrina ac copia potuissemus non nihil scribere, ut adhortaremur studiosos ad studendum more nostro, si fuisset nobis quietus animus. Nam hoc tempore dicere illud vere possumus:

Vicinae ruptis inter se legibus urbes
arma ferunt, saevit toto Mars impius orbe.

Vale.

Venetiis duodecimo calendas Iunias M.D.IX.

∺ XXXVIII ∺

Aldus Caesari Aragonio s. p. d.

1   Manuel Chrysoloras, qui primus iuniorum reportavit in Italiam literas Graecas easque ipsas Florentiae multos, ut aiunt, annos professus est, rudimenta grammatices Graecae linguae et docte et breviter composita edidit. Ea nos hortatu Marci Musuri Cretensis, viri doctissimi, qui nunc publice profitetur Venetiis frequenti semper ac gravi auditorio literas Graecas, imprimenda curavimus. Tum

equally fluent in both languages." In this, Marcus Musurus, you excel all others, as if Cicero had been writing to you as his son Marcus. Your combination of Greek and Latin is so fortunate that you have become thoroughly expert in both languages and in addition a most learned philosopher, not the type so called by the barbarians,[400] but the type so called by the educated.

So we dedicate to you these commentaries by Syrianus, Sopater 2 and Marcellinus on Hermogenes' rhetorical works and on Aphthonius' *Progymnasmata*. About their erudition and comprehensiveness we could have written something, to encourage people to study them, as is our custom, if our state of mind had been calm; for at present we can truly say:

Neighboring cities war against each other, breaking
legal agreements, wicked Mars rages all over the world.[401]

Farewell.
Venice, May 21, 1509.

: XVIII :

Chrysoloras, Erotemata
(1512)

Aldus to Cesare d'Aragona,[402] warmest greetings.

Manuel Chrysoloras,[403] the first person in modern times to bring 1 back to Italy a knowledge of Greek literature, who lectured in Florence for many years (so they say), composed and published a basic, well informed and succinct grammar of the Greek language. Encouraged by the learned Marcus Musurus, who now lectures on Greek literature in Venice[404] to an audience that is always large and serious, we have seen to the printing of it. Also, we have

alia quaedam addidimus non inutilia iis, qui Graece discere concupiscunt.

2   Quamobrem meas esse parteis duxi, pro mea erga familiam
Aragoniam ac in te praecipue benevolentia, si illa sub tuo nomine
publicarem excusa typis nostris, munerique ad te mitterem, ut ipsis legendis ediscendisque proficias plurimum Graecis literis, quarum es studiosissimus; quando sic iam Latinis profecisti, nondum
annos natus duodecim, ut et carmine et prosa oratione quod legis
intelligas. Incumbe igitur, mi Caesar, incumbe, ut coepisti, bonis
literis; disce omneis, quae regios pueros decent, virtutes. Nam non
dubito, cum ante annos animumque geras curamque virilem, quin
dignissimus futurus sis domo tua illustrissima; quandoquidem,
etsi

παῦροι γάρ τοι παῖδες ὁμοῖοι πατρὶ πέλονται,

οἱ πλέονες κακίους, παῦροι δέ τε πατρὸς ἀρείους,

ut Homerus ait, tamen ea est indoles, id ingenium, ea modestia, ii
mores tui in hac tua tenerrima aetate, ut non modo patris similis,
optimi regis, sed vel eo melior, id quod paucis admodum datum
est, futurus videare. Vale.

added some material which will be useful to those wishing to learn Greek.

So I thought it a duty, in the light of my friendship with the 2 d'Aragona family and with you in particular, to dedicate to you these texts that we have printed, and to send them to you as a gift, so that by reading and mastering them you can make great progress in Greek studies, which you are so keen on; for your progress in Latin has been such that, though you are not yet twelve years old, you understand what you read in verse or in prose. Settle, my dear Cesare, settle down to the study of literature, as you have begun; acquire all the virtues suitable for the children of rulers. For I have no doubt that since you possess the mind and heart of an adult years in advance,[405] you will be fully worthy of your distinguished family. Although

few sons are like their fathers,
most are inferior, few are better than their fathers,[406]

as Homer says, still your character, intelligence, modesty, and behavior at your very tender age are such that you look as if you will not merely resemble your father,[407] an excellent king, but even outdo him—which is given to very few. Farewell.

: XXXIX :

A

Aldus lectori s.

1 Hoc libello et Graece et Latine habentur haec, videlicet: De Graecarum proprietate linguarum, ex scriptis de arte Ioannis grammatici. Plutarchi de proprietate linguarum, quae apud Homerum:
sunt autem duo tractatus, quorum alter, qui falso Eustathio attri-
buitur, mendosus est, Latinumque e regione correctum habet, alter in medio est primi quinternionis emendatus, Plutarchique inscribitur, Latinum autem non habet, quia quod contra alterum est,
etiam hunc interpretatur. De Graecarum proprietate linguarum,
ex iis quae a Corinthio decerpta. Correctio praeterea quorundam
erratorum, quae vel inter excusionem facta sunt vel ante in exemplaribus fuerant.

2 Traducere autem in Latinum has Graecarum linguarum pro-
prietates fuit certe labor Herculeus atque ita taedii plenum, ut
persaepe his traducendis doluerim, saepiusque Terentiani illud
succurrerit:

fronte exile negocium
et dignum pueris putes,
adgressis labor arduus
nec tractabile pondus est.

3 Sed quid facerem? Primum receperam me id in fronte libri
facturum, deinde utilissimum fore existimabam Graecarum literarum studiosis, quorum causa nullum unquam quamvis magnum

: XXXIX :

Constantine Lascaris, The Eight Parts of Speech
(New edition,[408] October 1512)

A

Aldus to the reader, greetings.

In this pamphlet there are Greek and Latin texts as follows. *On the*   1
Characteristics of Greek Dialects, from the textbooks of John the
Grammarian.[409] [pseudo-] Plutarch, *On the Features of the Dialects in
Homer*: this consists of two tractates, of which one, wrongly attributed to Eustathius, is full of error, and has a corrected version on
the facing pages; while the other, not corrupt, is in the middle of
the first quire, and is attributed to Plutarch; it is not accompanied
by a Latin version, but the one facing the preceding text explains
this one very well. [There follows] *On the Characteristics of the Greek
Dialects*, excerpted from the Corinthian.[410] In addition, it corrects
some errors which occurred in the course of printing or were already present in the manuscripts.

To translate these features of Greek dialects into Latin was   2
certainly a Herculean task and so tedious that I very often found
these translations painful, and frequently recalled Terentianus'
words:[411]

A task seemingly trivial,
one you might think suitable for children,
but for those who tackle it,
hard work and an awkward burden.

But what was I to do? In the first place I had made a promise   3
at the beginning of the volume, and then I thought it would be
useful for students of Greek literature, on whose behalf I shall

laborem evitaturus sum. Te igitur, carissime lector, hortor ac rogo
ut id studiose legas: plurimum, mihi crede, proficies, et debebis
laboribus nostris. Vale.

B

Aldus lectori s.

4   Quoniam hae duae pagellae in medio huiusce quaternionis va-
cuae et non scriptae superfuissent, nisi quid aliud in ipsis excudendum curassem (nihil enim erat e regione, quod interpretari oporte-
ret, ut in reliquis factum vides), placuit ut in ipsis et iis, quae id
genus sequuntur in medio duorum, qui deinceps sequuntur, quaternionum, errata corrigenda adnotarentur, quae in his de Graecarum proprietate linguarum tractatibus partim inter impressionem,
partim exemplarium depravatorum culpa facta animadvertimus;
idque celeriter. Vix enim credas quam sim occupatus. Non habeo
certe tempus non modo corrigendis, ut cuperem, diligentius qui
excusi emittuntur libris cura nostra summisque die noctuque laboribus, sed ne perlegendis quidem cursim; id quod si videres, mise-
resceret te Aldi tui, quae tua est humanitas, cum saepe non vacet
vel cibum sumere vel alvum levare. Interdum ita distinemur, utraque occupata manu atque coram id expectantibus impressoribus
quod habetur in manibus, tum importune rusticeque instantibus,
ut ne nasum quidem liceat emungere. O provinciam quam durissi-
mam!

5   Divinabam equidem id futurum, vix eam aggressus, cum in
fronte eius libri, quae κανονίσματα appellantur, κίχλα χέζει
αὐτῇ κακόν scripsimus, quod sic nobis malum creaturi essemus,
ut turdus sibi. Sed cacaverim, si sic iuvero. Nec id accidit adiuto-
rum defectu—sunt mihi sescenti—sed culpa: ea est haec nostra
provincia. Parce igitur, carissime lector, quoties erratum quid
vides, sisque aequus iudex tantorum laborum; quanquam veniet,

never shun any task however great. So, dear reader, I encourage and invite you to read it carefully; believe me, you will benefit greatly and owe much to our labor. Farewell.

B

Aldus to the reader.

Since there are two pages which would have been left blank 4 without text if I had not found something else to print on them (there was nothing on the facing page requiring translation, as you see from the other pages), it was decided to make a note of errors to be corrected on these pages and the similar ones which follow in the next two quires — errors we had noticed in the texts about dialect features, partly arising during the printing, partly resulting from corrupt manuscripts. We did it in a hurry. You can scarcely believe how busy I am. I certainly do not have time, not merely for the careful correction I would like to make of the printed volumes issued by me after great labor night and day, but even for a cursory reading of them. If you could witness this, out of the kindness of your heart you would take pity on your friend Aldus, since he often does not have time to eat or to relieve himself. Sometimes we are so hard pressed, with both hands full and the printers in front of us waiting for what we hold in our hands, pressing us insistently and crudely, that it is not even possible to wipe our nose. What a hard profession it is!

I reckoned it might be so almost from the outset, when at the 5 beginning of the book called *Canonismata* we wrote, "The thrush shits to its own disadvantage," because we would be creating trouble for ourselves as the thrush does.[412] But shit I would, if that is how I can help.[413] This does not arise from lack of helpers — mine are innumerable — but through my fault, such is our profession. So, dear reader, when you see a misprint, be forgiving and be a fair-minded judge of great labors. Yet I hope there will come a

spero, tempus, idque brevi, quo decies et ad unguem castigatos suppeditemus libros studiosis. Nunc, quandiu argentea atque aurea vasa defuerint, Samiis, ut aiunt, delectemur.

6   Ad rem revertar. Inter errores, qui corrigendi sunt, quaedam obiter dicturi sumus, quae, ut puto, non displicebunt, ut vel in erroribus prosim. Corrigenda autem sunt haec.

Vale, lector, et nos de his laboribus ama, ut, puto, facis.

: XL :

Aldus Manutius Romanus Andreae Navagerio patritio Veneto s. p. d.

1   Sunt iam quatuor anni, Navageri carissime, cum statui duram hanc provinciam nostram intermittere, quod viderem totam fere Italiam ardere crudelissimo bello, tum quia cogebar abesse Venetiis, ut agros et pretiosa praedia nostra, quae amisimus, non nostra quidem culpa, sed horum infelicium temporum, recuperaremus. Vivi enim et nos pervenimus, quibus dicatur durum illud: 'Haec mea sunt, veteres migrate coloni.' Verum, cum nihil proficeremus atque integrascere mala et incendia belli viderentur, quae propediem extinctum iri sperabamus, revertimur Venetias, quas Athenas alteras hoc tempore possumus dicere cum propter alios plurimos singulari doctrina praeditos viros, tum propter Musurum nostrum,

time, and soon, when we can supply scholars with books precisely corrected ten times over.[414] For now, as long as silver and gold vessels are lacking, let us use Samian ware, as they say.[415]

Returning to the matter at hand: among the corrigenda I am 6 going to make some *obiter dicta* that I think will not displease you; I would make myself useful even in the *errata*. These are the corrigenda: [. . .].[416]

Farewell, reader, and love us for our labors, as I think you do.

: XL :

Pindar, Odes
Callimachus, Hymns
Dionysius Periegetes, Description of the World
Lycophron, Alexandra
(*January 1513*)

*Aldus Manutius of Rome to Andrea Navagero,
patrician of Venice,*[417] *warmest greetings.*

It is four years, my dear Navagero, since I decided to interrupt this 1 demanding profession of ours,[418] because I saw most of Italy consumed in fierce warfare, and I had to be away from Venice in order to recover land and valuable properties which we had lost, not by our own fault, but because of the current situation. We too have come to the point in our lives when we have heard the harsh words: "This is mine, you previous owners of the farm are to go away."[419] But as we were making no progress and the evils and destruction of the war seemed to be renewed,[420] — we had hoped they would soon be extinguished — we are returning to Venice, which in these days we can call a second Athens because of a great many other men of exceptional learning and because of our friend

cuius hortatu et tuo et Iucundi nostri iucundissimi et caeterorum, qui bonis literis magnopere delectantur, mutavi sententiam atque ad labores redii eos, quos quam durissimos, iam viginti annos expertus, vixque aequos noveram viribus nostris. Sed quoniam iam pridem mihi imperavi nulla unquam evitare incommoda, nullas impensas, nullos labores, dum prosim hominibus, summisi caput cervice parata ferre iugum.

2   Quamobrem optimos quosque libros tam Graecos quam Latinos, id quod saepe alias memini polliceri, emittere est animus excusos cura nostra in manus studiosorum. Sum praeterea aggressurus et Hebraicos, propter libros sacros nostros, qui ex Hebraicis Graeci et e Graecis Latini facti sunt, ut cum illis conferri possint et siqui sunt errores — aiunt enim esse quam plurimos — tollantur, idque ad utilitatem et gloriam Christianae religionis. Faveat igitur Deus optimus maximus, δοτὴρ ἐάων.

3   En exit tibi primus in publicum ex aedibus nostris, mi Navageri, tuus Pindarus tanquam dux, habens secum comites Callimachum, Dionysium de situ orbis, Lycophronem; et exit quidem sub tuo nomine, cum pro mea erga te incredibili benevolentia, quod sis apprime doctus et, quod paucis admodum datum est, acutissimo homo ingenio acerrimoque iudicio. Sunt enim multi ingeniosi quidem, sed vel parvo vel nullo iudicio; contra nonnulli acri quidem iudicio, sed minimo ingenio. Tu aeque et ingenio et iudicio vales plurimum: testimonio sunt tua scripta absolutissima vel carmine vel prosa oratione; nam et hac et illo certas cum antiquitate, quemadmodum et Petrus Bembus noster, decus eruditorum aetatis nostrae et magnae spes altera Romae. Sed haec parcius, ne videar assentari, id quod a me maxime est alienum; Deus est mihi testis, nec dicere me quicquam nec scribere unquam nisi quod sentio quodque verum mihi esse videtur.

Musurus. Through his encouragement and yours, and that of our delightful friend Giocondo[421] and all the other real enthusiasts for literature, I changed my mind and went back to the job which after twenty years of experience I knew was very hard and scarcely compatible with my strength. But as I had long ago told myself never to shirk difficulty, expense and labor, provided I help the world, I bowed my head, prepared to accept the yoke on my neck.[422]

So it is my intention to print and make available to scholars all 2 the best books in Greek and Latin, as I recall having promised on many other occasions. I am also about to tackle Hebrew on account of our sacred texts, which were rendered from Hebrew into Greek and from Greek into Latin, so that a comparison of them can be made and any errors (there are said to be a great many)[423] removed, to the benefit and glory of the Christian religion. So may God, the best and greatest, favor us, as the giver of good things.[424]

Here now, first to reach the public from our publishing house, 3 dear Navagero, is your Pindar, as it were the leader, with as companions Callimachus, Dionysius on geography and Lycophron; and he appears dedicated to you, because of my unbelievable goodwill toward you, since you are exceptionally learned and a person of the most acute and sharp judgment, which is given to very few. There are in fact many people admittedly clever but possessed of little or no judgment, and others are sharply critical but possessed of very little ingenuity whereas you are equally formidable in intellect and judgment, as is shown by your polished writing, whether in verse or in prose; in both you rival the ancients in the same way as our friend Pietro Bembo, eminent among the scholars of our generation and the other hope of the great city of Rome.[425] But not too much of this, in case I give the impression of adulation, which is not at all in my character; God is my witness that I never say or write anything except what I believe or what seems to me to be true.

Ἐχθρὸς γάρ μοι κεῖνος ὁμῶς Ἀΐδαο πύλῃσιν,
ὅς χ᾽ ἕτερον μὲν κεύθῃ ἐνὶ φρεσίν, ἄλλο δὲ εἴπῃ.
Αὐτὰρ ἐγὼν ἐρέω ὥς μοι δοκεῖ εἶναι ἀληθῆ.

4   Tum etiam volui ut sub tuo nomine exiret Pindarus ex Academia nostra, quia sic delectaris hoc poeta, ut saepe eum tua manu accurate descripseris, puto, ut tibi magis fieret familiaris, tum ut edisceretur a te facilius et teneretur memoria tenacius. Id quod describendo Thucy⟨di⟩dem fecit Demosthenes, qui, ut Lucianus ait πρὸς ἀπαίδευτον, octies illum descripsit, idque ad suam ipsius utilitatem. Nam haud facile dixerim, quantum suam adiuvet memoriam, qui vel notet in margine singula quaeque scitu et memoratu digna quae legerit, vel describat sua manu integros libros, quos sibi velit fieri familiareis, Graecos praesertim, cum propter alia multa tum propter accentus et orthographiam, quae siquis aut ignorat aut negligit, non habetur doctus. Quare meo quidem iudicio non hortandi solum sunt iuvenes, ut sua manu sibi describant quibus studeant libros, sed etiam compellendi, etsi omneis non queant, at optimum quenque et candidissimum.

5   Commentaria autem in Pindarum et caeteros, quos ei adiunxi comites, necnon in Hesiodum, Sophoclem, Euripidem, Aeschylum, Theocritum, Oppianum, brevi daturi sumus uno volumine. Quibus est animus facere indicem eorum omnium, quae scitu digna in iis ipsis habentur commentariis. Quam quidem rem in omnibus libris, qui ex aedibus nostris exibunt in manus hominum, facturi sumus, si saxum, quod tot annos volvo alter Sisyphus, in montis cacumen perduxero. Nunc vero premuntur torcularibus horum oratorum orationes, videlicet: Aeschinis, Lysiae, Dinarchi, Andocidae, Isaei, Antiphontis, Gorgiae, Demadis, Alcidamantis, Lesbonactis, Antisthenis. Post hos dabuntur, Deo volente, Platonis opera, tum Xenophontis et deinceps caeterorum illustrium.

For a man who hides one thing in his mind and says another
is as abhorrent to me as the gates of Hades.
But I will speak as the truth appears to me.[426]

My other reason for wishing to issue Pindar from our Academy   4
and dedicated to you is that you enjoy the poet so much, to the
extent of often transcribing him in your own hand, to make him
more familiar, I imagine, also to make him easier to learn by heart
and have fixed in the memory. That is what Demosthenes did by
his transcriptions of Thucydides; as Lucian, *Against an Ignoramus*
says,[427] he made eight copies, and it was for his own personal
benefit. I cannot easily describe how much it helps the memory to
note in the margin details worth knowing and remembering from
the text that one has read, also to copy in one's own hand complete texts which one wishes to make familiar, especially Greek
texts on account of their accents, spelling and many other points;
if one is ignorant or neglectful of these one is not considered
learned.[428] In my own opinion therefore the young should not just
be encouraged to write out in their own hand the texts they are
studying, they should be compelled, even if they cannot manage
all, at least to transcribe those which are best and purest.

Soon we shall offer in one volume commentaries on Pindar and   5
the other authors that I added as his companions, also on Hesiod,
Sophocles, Euripides, Aeschylus, Theocritus and Oppian. It is my
intention to make an index of all matters worth knowing that are
found in these commentaries.[429] This we will do in all books to
emerge from our house and reach the public, if like a second Sisyphus I bring up to the top of the hill the rock which I have been
pushing for so many years. At present the speeches of the following orators are in the press, namely Aeschines, Lysias, Deinarchus,
Andocides, Isaeus, Antiphon, Gorgias, Demades, Alcidamas, Les-
bonax, Antisthenes. After them, God willing, Plato's works will be
offered, then Xenophon and after him the rest of the famous

Tu, mi Navageri, interea tuum Pindarum lege, et nos, ut amas, ama. Vale.

: XLI :

Aldus Manutius Romanus Ioanni Baptistae Egnatio Veneto s.

1   Etsi bella et arma, mi Egnati, semper fuerunt calamitas ac pernicies cum aliarum plurimarum rerum tum praecipue studiorum et bonarum literarum, id quod adeo verum esse constat, ut nulla egeat demonstratione; tamen temporibus nostris, quibus non solum Italiam, sed totum fere terrarum orbem videmus ardere bello, vel cupiditate et avaritia hominum vel, quod magis credo, vitiis et peccatis nostris — solet enim Deus tribus hisce malis potissimum punire scelera hominum: bello, fame, pestilentia; idque simul plerunque: nam bellum fames, famem pestilentia sequitur, unde natum proverbium apud Graecos: λιμὸς μετὰ λοιμόν — temporibus, inquam, nostris una cum armis sic vigent studia bonarum literarum, ut etiam floreant; idque, quod magis mirum est, Venetiis praecipue, licet multos iam annos assiduo bello vexentur.

2   Quoniam igitur tu in hac inclyta urbe ingenio, eloquio et doctrina es praestantissimus plurimumque et faves et prodes provinciae nostrae, has Isocratis orationes diligentius recognitas tibi dicamus more nostro, qui, cum aliter benevolentiam nostram in amicos et amantissimos nostri ostendere non possimus, hoc epistolarum genere, et debere nos illis et non esse immemores ipsorum in nos officiorum, publice non solum aetatis nostrae studiosis, sed, si victura nostra haec sunt, vel posteris testamur.

writers. In the meantime, my dear Navagero, read your Pindar, and love us, as you do. Farewell.

: XLI :

The Greek Orators, Volume 1
(April 1513)

Aldus Manutius of Rome to Giovanni Battista Egnazio,[430] *greetings.*

Wars and hostilities, dear Egnazio, have always brought disaster 1 and destruction to much else but especially to education and literature — that is so well established as not to need demonstration. But in our own time, when we see not just Italy but practically the whole world engaged in war because of human greed and avarice or, as I prefer to think, because of our faults and sins — God usually punishes human crimes mainly by these three evils, war, famine, plague, and often together, since famine follows war and plague famine, which led to a proverb among the Greeks, "famine after plague"[431] — in our time, I say, the study of literature is so vigorous during the wars that it is even flourishing — and more surprisingly in Venice in particular, although the city has been troubled by continuous warfare these many years.

Since therefore you are remarkable in this distinguished city for 2 your intelligence, eloquence and learning, and you give great support and assistance to our enterprise, we dedicate to you, in accordance with our custom, these orations of Isocrates, carefully edited. Since we have no other way to show our goodwill toward our friends and devoted admirers, we testify by this kind of letter that we owe a debt to them and are not unmindful of their own good offices toward us; we do so publicly, not just to scholars of our own time, but if our works are to live, also to posterity.

3   Addidimus hisce Isocratis orationibus, Musuri nostri hortatu, Alcidamantis orationem contra dicendi magistros, Gorgiae de laudibus Helenae, Aristidis de laudibus Athenarum. Quod ideo factum est, quia, cum de iisdem et Isocrates scripserit, operae pretium videbatur, si de eadem re diversos, eosdemque doctissimos, legendos authores studiosis simul traderem. Addidimus insuper Aristidis de laudibus urbis Romae orationem, nostra in eam urbem benevolentia, ut, ubi Athenae laudantur, et Roma laudetur, cum de utriusque urbis laudibus idem author et docte et accurate scripserit. Vale.

Venetiis mense Aprilis M.D.XIII.

: XLII :

Aldus Manutius Francisco Faseolo iurisconsulto ac senatus
Veneti a secretis magno s. p. d.

1   Memini legere duos duntaxat cognomento magnos ob eorum clarissima gesta appellatos apud veteres, alterum apud Graecos Alexandrum Macedonum regem, apud Romanos alterum Cn. Pompeium. Tum multis post seculis Carolus ille Gallorum rex ob excellentiam rerum gestarum magnus et tunc dici meruit et nunc dicitur. Sunt et nostro tempore qui magni cognomento appellantur, vel regni et principatus amplitudine vel dignitate et excellentia magistratus, et hi quidem perpauci, ut Assyriae rex Solitanus, Rhodi princeps ἔρεισμα Χριστιανῶν, Turcarum dominus, clarissimi quidam apud regem Christianissimum. In Italia, idque

To these orations of Isocrates we have added, on the suggestion 3
of our friend Marcus Musurus, Alcidamas' speech against the
teachers of rhetoric, Gorgias in praise of Helen, and Aristides in
praise of Athens. This has been done since Isocrates also had written on the same themes and it seemed worthwhile to give students
the chance to read different but very expert authors on the same
subject. We have appended in addition Aristides' oration in praise
of Rome because of our affection for that city, so that where Athens is praised, Rome may be too, since the same author wrote with
learning and accuracy about the merits of both cities. Farewell.

Venice, April 1513.

: XLII :

The Greek Orators, Volume 2
(May 6, 1513)

*Aldus Manutius to Francesco Fasolo, lawyer and grand
chancellor of the Venetian senate,*[432] *warmest greetings.*

I remember reading that in antiquity only two people were called 1
"the Great" in virtue of their achievements, one among the Greeks,
Alexander, king of Macedon, the other among the Romans,
Gnaeus Pompeius. Then, many centuries later, Charles, the king
of France, earned the title on account of his outstanding achievements and is now so called.[433] In our own day as well there are
those who are called great, from the extent of their kingdom or
principality or the honesty and excellence of their administration,
and they are very few, such as the Assyrian king Solitanus,[434] the
prince of Rhodes,[435] a bastion of Christianity, the sultan of the
Turks, and some eminent personages at the court of the Most
Christian King.[436] In Italy, in Venice no one is called great except

Venetiis, cognomento magnus nemo, nisi qui primus a secretis senatus est, quem magnum cancellarium appellant; cuius tanta est dignitas, ut alterum a principe in urbe caput esse videatur, eiusque funus princeps ipse cum omni senatu, officii et honoris gratia, ad aedem usque comitetur.

2   Hic tu, Francisce, creatus es. Nec mirum; eras enim et ante magnus maiorum splendore: magnus quidem, ut taceam caeteros, Matthaeo abavo, quem in historiis Sabellicus rerum in bello Genuensi magnitudine gestarum laudibus extollit; magnus item huius filio Antonio, qui Venetorum Patavinorumque finium arbiter fuit atque Patavii a thesauris primus creatus est; magnus Andrea patre, viro doctissimo, qui inter discipulos illos Victorinae Academiae, Vallam, Omnibonum, Guarinum et alios, qui Latinae linguae elegantiam et eruditionem tot seculis sepultam suscitarunt, a Platina connumeratur, quique a Christophoro Mauro duce in classe, a decemviris in senatu, ut inter primos ab epistolis esset, vocatus est; magnus utroque patruo, quorum alter, Aloisius, Constantinopoli pro patria mortuus est, alter autem, cui nomen Angelo, episcopus, ad regem Polloniae ac Daciae missus, ut una in Turcas expeditionem facerent, voti compos rediit, ob eamque causam Romae a thesauris pontificis publicique cubiculi apostolici praeses ac gubernator urbis Romae simul creatus est.

3   Sed tu maiorum tuorum omnium maximus, qui, quanquam extra eum ordinem penitus esses, ex quo ea omnino electio fieri debere videbatur, atque ex usu forensi, genere inviso, tantae tamen, praeter facundiam sermonisque leporem, praeter vehementiam et eloquii gravitatem, praeter illam tuam tibi innatam oratoriam dicendi artem, quibus virtutibus in foro regnare merito dicebaris, tantae, inquam, modestiae tantaeque innocentiae fuisti adeoque in pauperes liberalis et pius, ut, magnis illius ordinis reiectis

the chief secretary to the Senate, who is termed the great chancellor. Such is his standing that he looks like a second ruler after the
doge, and the doge himself with all the senate takes part in his
funeral all the way to the church in recognition of his office and
his honor.

You, Francesco, have been elected to this office, and no wonder; 2
you were already great through the splendor of your ancestors.
Though I will not mention them all, you are eminent thanks to
your great-great grandfather, whom Sabellico in his history praises
for his achievements in the war against Genoa;[437] thanks also to
his son Antonio, whose arbitration fixed the boundaries of Venice
and Padua and who was elected treasurer of Padua;[438] thanks to
your father Andrea,[439] a man of great learning who is listed by
Platina[440] as one of the famous pupils of Vittorino's academy
(Valla, Ognibene, Guarino and others,[441] the restorers of the elegance of the Latin language and knowledge of it, when it had been
buried for centuries)—he was appointed by the Doge Cristoforo
Moro[442] to the fleet and by the Council of Ten to the Senate to be
one of the principal secretaries; thanks also to two uncles, one,
Alvise, who died for his country at Constantinople,[443] the other,
Angelo by name, a bishop, who was sent to the king of Poland and
Dacia to arrange a joint mission against the Turks and returned
successful, for which he was simultaneously appointed in Rome
president of the Apostolic Camera, and governor of the city of
Rome.[444]

But you far excel all your ancestors. Although you were cer- 3
tainly not a member of the class from which the election apparently had to be made, and your experience was in the law, a profession not well regarded, you possessed eloquence and charming
style, powerful and weighty delivery, an innate gift for oratory,
qualities through which you were rightly called king of the courts;
in addition, I emphasize, your modesty and honesty, generosity
and kindness to the poor were such that powerful competitors

competitoribus, numerosissimo ex comitiis suffragiorum concursu, praeses omnibus, qui a secretis sunt, crearere, magnusque cancellarius appellatus sis. Tuis nimirum virtutibus factum. Quod siquis te rogaret, quonam modo tot ac tanta adeptus fueris, posses et tu quod Alexander ille Magnus respondere: μηδὲν ἀναβαλλόμενος.

4   Tot itaque ac tantis tuis impulsus laudibus, tum quia tua potissimum opera, tuo studio, Venetiae hoc tempore Athenae alterae vere dici possunt propter literas Graecas, quarum studiosi undique concurrunt ad Marcum Musurum, hominem huius aetatis eruditissimum, quem tu publico stipendio conducendum curasti, cuique, quae tua est in doctissimum quenque benevolentia, faves plurimum; Aeschinis, Lysiae et caeterorum, qui in fronte libri excusi visuntur, orationes sub tuo nomine, qui et haberis et es magnus illustrisque orator, exire ex aedibus nostris volui in manus studiosorum. Id quod eo gratius tibi futurum existimavi, quoniam quas plerique horum scripserunt orationes, multis seculis abditae latuerunt. Latebant autem in Atho, Thraciae monte; eas Lascaris is, qui abhinc quinquennium pro Christianissimo rege Venetiis summa cum laude legatum agebat, doctissimus et ad unguem factus homo, in Italiam reportavit. Miserat enim ipsum Laurentius ille Medices in Graeciam ad inquirendos simul et quantovis emendos pretio bonos libros; unde Florentiam et cum iis ipsis orationibus et cum aliis tum raris tum pretiosis voluminibus rediit.

5   Debemus quidem Lascari, qui summo studio conquisitos tot bonos libros ad nos e Graecia advexerit; sed longe magis Laurentio Medici, cuius iussu opibusque et liberalitate regia id factum est. Fuit enim semper familia Medicum liberalissima ac fautrix literatorum et bonorum omnium. Quanquam miserrimis hisce temporibus nostris debet ei ipsi Laurentio plurimum ipse terrarum orbis, quod Leonem X pontificem maximum genuerit, ἀγαθὸς

from the association were rejected by a very large vote at a meeting, and you were appointed chief secretary and grand chancellor. That is no wonder in view of your merits. If someone asked you to account for so many great achievements, you too could reply as Alexander the Great did: "By not postponing anything."[445]

Inspired by your many meritorious acts, I wanted our house to 4 issue to the public the orations of Aeschines, Lysias and the others named on the title page of the printed volume, with a dedication to you, since you are, and are known to be, a great and distinguished orator. It is principally due to your energy and enthusiasm that Venice can now deservedly be called a second Athens on account of Greek literature. Students from everywhere flock to study under Marcus Musurus, the most learned man of his generation, whose appointment with a stipend from the state you arranged and to whom you give great support, since you are well disposed to all the best scholars. I reckoned you would appreciate the book all the more because the speeches written by most of these orators have lain hidden and unknown for many centuries. But they were hidden on Athos, a mountain in Thrace. They were brought back to Italy by Lascaris, a scholar and a man of great accomplishments,[446] who five years ago served with great distinction as envoy of the Most Christian King in Venice. The famous Lorenzo de Medici had sent him to Greece[447] to look for good books and buy them at any price; from there he returned to Florence with these very orations and other rare and precious volumes.

We owe a debt to Lascaris, who energetically collected so many 5 good books and brought them from Greece for us; but far greater is our debt to Lorenzo de Medici, since this came about through his instructions, his wealth and his regal generosity. In fact the Medici family was always very generous and supportive of the educated and of all good men. Yet in these dreadful times we live in the world owes a great debt to Lorenzo himself as the father of Pope Leo X, the good son of a good father, or rather, which is

ἀγαθόν, ac potius, quod rarissimum, πατρὸς ἀρείω. Hoc enim pontifice tot rapinae, tot caedes, tot hominum scelera cessabunt, et bella in primis, malorum omnium causa; hoc pacis filio renovabitur mundus; hic ille est, quem afflicti, oppressi, submersi promissum expectabamus; hic vir, hic est, 'aurea condet Secula qui rursus Latio regnata per arva Saturno quondam'; hic ille Leo, de quo scriptum est: 'Vincet leo ex tribu Iuda.'

> Di patrii indigetes et Romule Vestaque mater,
> quae Thuscum Thyberim et Romana Palatia servas,
> hunc saltem everso iuvenem succurrere seclo
> ne prohibete! Satis iampridem sanguine nostro
> Laomedonteae luimus periuria Troiae.

Ad propositum revertar. Non enim dubito quin Iesus Deus optimus maximus sua clementia ex hac familia Medicum creari voluerit ποιμένα λαῶν, qui afflictis rebus succurrat ecclesiae et Christianorum suorum.

6   Treis illustrium oratorum fuisse copias legimus: ex prima Themistoclem, Periclem et illius aetatis caeteros nulla scripta posteris reliquisse; ex secunda Demosthenem, Aeschinem, Lysiam, Isocratem et alios plureis, quorum decas illustris, non habendis solum, sed etiam scribendis orationibus, tum doctissimis lucubrationibus, et sui temporis homines et posteros iuvando, claruisse. Ex hac vero copia sunt decem illi oratores, quorum vitas scripsit Plutarchus eo libello, cuius titulus βίοι τῶν δέκα ῥητόρων. Sunt autem scripti, ut alius alium aetate antecessit, hoc ordine: Antiphon, Andocides, Lysias, Isocrates, Isaeus, Aeschines, Lycurgus, Demosthenes, Hyperides, Deinarchus. M. Tullius in libro de claris oratoribus addit his Demadem et Phalereum Demetrium. Ubi enim de Isocrate, Lysia et Demosthene scripsit, haec subiungit:

very rare, better than his father.[448] Under his papacy the frequent incidence of brigandage, murder and human crimes will cease, and war especially, the cause of all evil; the world will be renewed by this son of peace; he is the promised man whom we, the afflicted, the oppressed, the downtrodden, awaited; he is the man "who will once again establish a golden age in Latium, in territory once ruled by Saturn."[449] He is the lion of whom it is written, "A lion of the tribe of Juda will triumph."[450]

> Gods of our homeland, Romulus and mother Vesta,
> who preserve the Etruscan Tiber and the Roman Palatine,
> at least do not stop this young man from helping a world
> that has been convulsed. Long ago we paid in our own blood
> sufficiently for the perjury of Laomedon's Troy.[451]

Let me come back to the point. I have no doubt that Jesus, the best and greatest God, out of his clemency wished a Medici of this family elected as a shepherd of the peoples,[452] to bring aid for the afflictions of the Church and his Christians.

We have read that there were three groups of famous orators. 6 From the first Themistocles, Pericles and the others of that generation left no writings for posterity.[453] From the second Demosthenes, Aeschines, Lysias, Isocrates and several others, an illustrious group of ten, were famous not just for delivery of speeches but for writing them and for very learned treatises that helped their contemporaries and posterity. From this group come the ten orators whose biographies Plutarch composed in his short work, *Lives of the Ten Orators*,[454] written in the following order as one succeeded another: Antiphon, Andocides, Lysias, Isocrates, Isaeus, Aeschines, Lycurgus, Demosthenes, Hyperides, Deinarchus. Marcus Tullius in his work on famous orators adds to them Demades and Demetrius of Phalerum. Having written about Isocrates, Lysias and Demosthenes he adds:

Huic Hyperides proximus et Aeschines fuit et Lycurgus et Deinarchus et is, cuius nulla extant scripta, Demades, aliique plures. Haec enim aetas effudit hanc copiam; et, ut opinio mea fert, succus ille et sanguis incorruptus usque ad hanc aetatem oratorum fuit, in qua naturalis inesset, non phucatus nitor. Phalereus enim successit eis senibus adolescens, eruditissimus ille quidem horum omnium, sed non tam armis institutus quam palaestra; itaque delectabat magis Athenienseis quam inflammabat.

Haec ille, ubi nulla extare scripta Demadis dicit. Hoc tamen libro est Demadis oratio ὑπὲρ τῆς δωδεκαετίας. De iis ipsis et Fabius meminit libro x, quos etiam inter se doctissime comparat. Sed hae duae oratorum copiae Athenis fuerunt. Tertiam fortuna Asiae dedit: fuerunt ex ea Polemon, Herodes, Aristeides et alii.

7   Tu vero, Francisce, decus et praesidium literatorum, magnos hos oratores magnus ipse orator accipe in aedibus tuis, lecturus eos assidue una cum doctis, quos apud te domi habes; et Aldo tuo in dura hac et laborum plena provincia fave, ut tuus est mos. Fac valeas.

Pridie nonarum Maii M.D.XIII.

Close to him were Hyperides, Aeschines, Lycurgus and Deinarchus, and Demades, none of whose works survive, and several others. That period produced a great crop; and in my opinion the sap and blood of oratory remained pure down to the time of that generation of orators. There was a natural elegance in it, not cosmetic. When these men were old they were succeeded by the young man from Phalerum, much the most accomplished of them all, but equipped more for a display at school than for the battleground. So he charmed the Athenians rather than rousing them.[455]

That is his comment, where he says that no works of Demades survive. But in this volume there is Demades' speech *On the Twelve-year Period*.[456] These same people are also mentioned by Quintilian in Book X[457] with a very well-informed comparison of them. But these two groups of orators lived in Athens; destiny gave the third to Asia; its members were Polemon, Herodes, Aristides and others.[458]

But you, Francesco, ornament and defender of the literary 7 world, yourself a great orator, receive in your home these great orators, to read them attentively in the company of the scholars you have at home; and support your Aldus in this difficult and toilsome enterprise, as is your custom. Take care of your health.

May 6, 1513.

: XLIII :

Aldi Pii Manutii ad Leonem X pontificem maximum pro
republica Christiana proque re literaria supplicatio.

1   Est vetus proverbium, beatissime pater, languescere et alia membra,
cum caput doleat. Verissimum id quidem in aegris corporibus, sed
multo verius in moribus summorum virorum et principum, qui
caput sunt populorum: nam longa experientia compertum est,
qualescunque principes fuerint, talem civitatem futuram; quaecunque mutatio morum in principibus extiterit, eandem in populo
secuturam. Quamobrem, cum primum creatus es pontifex maximus, tantam ceperunt voluptatem Christiani omnes, ut dicerent,
praedicarent, affirmarent alter alteri, cessatura brevi mala omnia,
quibus opprimimur, futura bona, quae seculo aureo fuisse commemorant; quandoquidem principem, pastorem, patrem nacti sumus,
qualem expectabamus, quo nobis miserrimis, his temporibus maxime, opus erat. Audivi ipse meis auribus illis ipsis diebus, ubicunque fui, omneis haec eadem uno ore dicere et praedicare. Nec vana
fides: multa enim sunt, quae ut tantae hominum expectationi respondeas promittunt. Primum est quam optime semper et sanctis-
sime anteacta vita tua a teneris usque ad pontificatum. Secundum,
familia Medicum clarissima, altrix semper magnorum virorum.
Δεινὸς χαρακτὴρ κἀπίσημος ἐν βροτοῖς Ἐσθλῶν γενέσθαι.
Hinc, ut taceam caeteros, ortus est pater ille tuus Laurentius, vir
optimus ac tanta prudentia, ut non solum pacis patriae sed et totius Italiae author fuerit, quandiu vixit. Qui utinam et nunc viveret! Bella enim, quibus paulo post eius mortem coepit ardere et

: XLIII :

Plato, Complete Works
(*September 1513*)

Aldus Pius Manutius to Pope Leo X,[459] *a petition on behalf of
the community of Christians and of literature.*

It is an ancient proverb, most blessed father, that when the head is   1
in pain, the other parts of the system suffer.[460] This is certainly
true of bodies that are ill, but even more so of the behavior of
leading men and princes, who are in charge of their peoples. By
long experience it has been found that whatever the character of
the princes, such will be the character of the state; whatever
change takes place in the behavior of princes,[461] it will find its way
down to the people. So as soon as you were elected pope, all
Christians felt such pleasure that they said, they declared, they
asserted to each other that soon all the troubles by which we are
oppressed would cease, there would be blessings recorded to have
existed in the golden age. For we have acquired a prince, a pastor,
a father of the kind we were waiting for, who was essential for us
in our distress, especially in these days. During those days I myself
overheard, wherever I was, everyone saying and declaring the same
thing. Nor was faith misplaced;[462] there are many signs to suggest
that you can match men's great expectations. One is your past life,
from tender years up to the pontificate, always conducted in the
best and most saintly fashion. Another is the Medici family, ever
the nurse of great men. "It is a special mark, notable among men,
to be of noble birth."[463] From that family came — I need not mention the others — your father Lorenzo, an excellent man of great
prudence, so that throughout his lifetime he ensured peace both
for his country and the whole of Italy. Would that he were still
alive today.[464] The wars by which Italy began to be consumed

nunc maxime ardet Italia, ardet et tota fere Europa propter Italiam, vel nunquam fuissent, vel accensa, statim, ut quam plurimi
opinantur, heros ille gravis pietate, gravis et meritis, sua prudentia
extinxisset, quemadmodum saepe ab illo factum meminimus. O
ter quater damnosam, o semper dolendam, semper deflendam
mortem! Sed ad haec omnia una consolatio est, quod, sicut paulo
post mortem patris tui tanta incendia belli exorta sunt, sic te, illius
filio, creato pontifice maximo, brevi tua opera, tuo unius studio
penitus extinguentur.

2   Tertium est aetas tua: non enim sine numine divum factum est,
ut tu, nondum annum agens trigesimum octavum, pontifex maximus crearere, posthabitis tot magnis patribus, tot summa veneratio-
ne dignis senibus. Quoniam enim composituro res Christianae
religionis et correcturo mores hominum, qui ubique terrarum sunt,
longa vita opus erat, te eum fore Deus voluit, iuvenem integerrima
vita et moribus ornatissimum, qui haec omnia faceres longa die,
nullis succumbendo laboribus, nullis vigiliis:

Οὐ χρὴ παννύχιον εὕδειν βουληφόρον ἄνδρα,
ᾧ λαοί τ᾽ ἐπιτετράφαται καὶ τόσσα μέμηλε.

3   Additur et illud, quod maximi faciendum est: tantum terrarum,
tantum maris, tot varios populos ante vel Romanis illis rerum do-
minis nedum nobis incognitos inveniri aetate nostra et subiici
Christianis regibus, ita ut, te rectore Romanae ecclesiae, speran-
dum sit unum futurum ovile sub uno pastore, eodemque optimo
et pientissimo. Quapropter nunquam satis laudari potest Emanuel,

shortly after his death and is now entirely consumed, by which almost all of Europe is consumed because of Italy, either would not have occurred, or once started, as most people believe, would have been checked at once by that heroic figure with his solid sense of duty and solid merits, thanks to his prudence, by means of which we remember he often had success. His death is a triple, a quadruple disaster, ever to be regretted, ever to be lamented. But there is one consolation for all this: just as so many wars flared up soon after your father's death, so, now that you his son have been elected pope, they will soon be completely extinguished through your efforts and your single-handed action.

Thirdly there is your age. It cannot have come about without 2 divine influence[465] that you were elected pope when you were not yet in your thirty-eighth year, in preference to so many great prelates, so many elderly and deservedly much-venerated figures. Since long life was essential for the man who would bring harmony to Christian affairs and improve the morals of mankind all over the world, it was God's wish that you should be that man, young, of blameless life and admirable character, to perform this whole task in the fullness of time without shrinking before any labor, any all-night exertion.

> A man who provides counsel, to whom peoples are entrusted
> and has so many concerns, must not sleep all night.[466]

In addition the following fact must be treated as of the great- 3 est importance: so much land, so much of the seas, so many diverse peoples, unknown to the Romans as lords of creation[467] and equally to ourselves, are being discovered in our own day and being made subjects of Christian kings, that one must hope, under your direction of the Roman Church, that there will be a single flock under a single shepherd, himself the best and most pious. So Manuel, the undefeated king of Portugal,[468] can never be

rex Lusitaniae invictissimus, qui multos iam annos nunquam desi-
nit validissima classe novas terras, nova regna disquirere,

victorque beatos
per populos dat iura viamque affectat Olympo.

Solvens enim Olyssippone ac praeteriens circulum Cancri Aequinoctiique et Capricorni, proxime Antarcticum, tum vertens
cursum, rursus circulum Capricorni Aequinoctiique transiens, totam Africam ac bonam totius Asiae partem circuiit, itinere ad
centies ac quadragies et amplius centena millia passuum, devenit-
que in locum aromatum quam ditissimum, Callicutium appellatum, atque inde nuper ad dexteram, relicta Taprobane insularum
maxima, devenit ad urbem nomine Malacen, populosissimamque
ac ditissimam et plenam mercium, eamque difficillimo praelio vic-
tor tandem expugnavit. At illi, cognitis sacris nostris, visis Christianorum moribus, certatim baptizantur. O felicissimum regem! o
heroem semper mirandum, colendum, extollendum in coelum laudibus et nobis et posteris seculorum omnium! Atque utinam caeteri Christianorum reges idem facerent, nec inter se crudeliter
bella gerendo, seipsos ac potius miseros populos absumerent!

Quicquid delirant reges, plectuntur Achivi.

Nam paucis annis omnes homines ubique terrarum Deum verum
cognoscerent, in Iesum Deum optimum maximum constanter cre-
derent eumque solum supplices adorarent. Sed cognoscent, cre-
dent, adorabunt te pontifice. Cum enim tu, pater, amare inter se
filios tuos, nedum proiicere tela manu, coegeris, afflictisque populis succurreris, restituta pace, curabis debellandos Christiani nominis acerrimos inimicos; curabis homines, ubicunque terrarum in-
cogniti lateant, disquirendos, ad eosque subactos mittes apostolos

sufficiently praised for having not ceased over many years to seek out new lands, new kingdoms, with a very powerful fleet:

> in victory he hands down laws
> to blessed peoples and makes his way toward Olympus.[469]

Setting out from Lisbon, crossing the tropic of Cancer, the equator, the tropic of Capricorn, close to the Antarctic, then changing course, again crossing the tropic of Capricorn and the equator, he circumnavigated the whole of Africa and a good part of Asia in a journey of fourteen thousand miles and more, and arrived at a place rich in perfumes called Calcutta. From there he recently headed off to the right and passing the very large island of Ceylon reached a city called Malacca, densely populated, rich and a center of trade; after a very difficult battle he was finally victorious and captured it.[470] But those people, on learning about our religion and witnessing the conduct of Christians, compete to obtain baptism. What a fortunate king! What a hero, ever to be admired, venerated, praised to the skies by us and posterity for all time. Would that all the other Christian kings did the same instead of fighting each other in cruel wars, destroying themselves and still more so their suffering subjects.

> Whatever madness kings commit, the Achaeans suffer.[471]

Within a few years the human race throughout the world would recognize the true God, would have a firm faith in Jesus, the best and greatest God; to him alone they would pray and offer worship. But with you as pope they will recognize Him, they will have faith, they will worship. For when you, father, compel your children to love each other and not to fire weapons,[472] when you help populations in distress by restoring peace, you will see to the pacification of Christianity's fiercest enemies; you will seek out men, in whatever corner of the earth they hide unknown, and when they have submitted, you will send your apostles to preach the

tuos ad praedicandum illis Euangelium, ut, sacris Romanae ecclesiae instituti, soli Deo nostro serviant. En potes iam ab Indis incipere, potes ab aliis populis, quos in oceano occidentali Hispani superioribus annis invenere.

4   Nec minor gloria servatur tibi, beatissime pater, instaurandis bonis literis, suppeditando optimos quosque libros studiosis, et qui nunc sunt et qui post aliis erunt in annis, propagandis bonis artibus et disciplinis. Tentarunt hoc olim plurimi ex veteribus, et Graeci et Latini et barbari; et quia mirum in modum profuere, consecuti sunt ex ea re gloriam sempiternam. Tentarunt et nonnulli ex iunioribus, non solum privati ac mediocris fortunae homines, sed et pontifices maximi, imperatores, reges atque alii illustres; et ut taceam caeteros, nonne plurimum iuvit rem literariam Nicolaus V pontifex maximus? nonne et parens tuus Laurentius? Qui si diutius vixissent, multa essent in manibus, quae non habentur; tum quae habentur, facta fuissent eorum cura longe meliora. Debes tu igitur, illius magnus successor, huius dignus filius, quod efficere illi morte praeventi non potuerunt, perficere.

5   Ego autem iandiu hoc saxum volvo. Qua in re mihi quidem videor esse alter Sisyphus, quod nondum illud volvendo perduxerim in apicem montis, aliis autem, iisque eruditis, Hercules, quod, nullis cedens malis, nullis succumbens laboribus, iam plus unus ipse iuverim rem literariam, quam simul omnes, quotquot fuere multis seculis. Ita me amant de tantis laboribus, ut nunc coram nunc accuratis literis laudando obtundant. Sed non ego credulus illis: nullum enim adhuc dedi librum, in quo mihi satisfecerim. Nam tanta erga bonas literas benevolentia est mea, ut emendatissimos simul et pulcherrimos esse cupiam libros, quos emittam in

Gospel to them, so that they can be instructed in the rites of the
Roman Church and serve our God alone. Look: you can now begin with the Indians, with the other peoples whom the Spanish
discovered in previous years in the Western Ocean.[473]

No less glory is reserved for you, most blessed father, for the   4
restoration of literature, by the supply of all the best books for
students, both those of today and those who will come in future
years, and by support of the liberal arts and disciplines. In the past
many of the ancients attempted this, Greeks, Romans and barbarians,[474] and because they were admirably successful, they achieved
eternal fame for that achievement. Some people have attempted
more recently, not only private individuals of modest means but
popes, emperors, kings and other famous men; if I may omit the
others, did not Pope Nicholas V[475] gave great help to the literary
world? And also your father Lorenzo? If they had lived longer,
much that we do not possess would be available; and what we do
possess would be in far better condition thanks to their efforts. So
it is your duty as the great successor of the one and worthy son of
the other to bring to completion what they, cut off by death, could
not do.

But I have been rolling this boulder for a long time.[476] In this   5
matter I feel like a second Sisyphus, because I have not yet pushed
it up to the top of the mountain; yet to others — and they are educated — I look like Hercules because I do not give way in the face
of any troubles or succumb in the face of any toil, and by my
single-handed efforts have done more to help the world of letters
than everyone else put together, however numerous they were over
the course of many centuries. On account of such great labors
they now deafen me with their praise, either on meeting me or in
elegant letters. But I do not believe them,[477] because I have never
yet produced a book with which I felt satisfied. My love of literature is such that I want the books which I put into the hands of
the educated to be very accurate and very beautiful. So whenever a

manus studiosorum. Quamobrem, quotiescunque vel mea vel eorum incuria, qui mecum corrigendis libris incumbunt, aliquo in
libro quamvis parvus error committitur, etsi opere in magno fas est
obrepere somnum—non enim unius diei labor hic noster, sed
multorum annorum, atque interim nec mora nec requies—, sic tamen doleo, ut, si possem, mutarem singula errata numo aureo.

6   Damus igitur nunc, beatissime pater, quaecunque extant Platonis opera, idque sub tuo nomine felicissimo. Quod ob eam quoque
causam fecimus, quia, cum Marsilius Ficinus, domus tuae alum-
nus, Platonis opera Latina a se facta Laurentio parenti tuo dicave-
rit, quod sic foverit semper doctissimos quosque utriusque linguae, ut Florentia et esset et haberetur vivente Laurentio Athenae
alterae, nos quoque tibi, illius filio eidemque pontifici maximo,
tum decori et praesidio expectato huius aetatis eruditorum, eiusdem authoris libros, eosque Graecos atque Atticos, qualeis ipse
composuit, merito dedicare voluimus. Simulque ea in re morem
gessimus quibusdam amicis nostris, amantissimis bonarum literarum, qui, etsi id mea sponte eram facturus, tamen amice me mo-
nuerunt, ut nulli magis divini hominis lucubrationes quam tibi,
summo divinarum rerum antistiti, nuncuparentur, sperantes eam
rem Academiae, quam tot annos parturimus, mirum in modum
profuturam, ut scilicet nos foveas, provinciamque hanc nostram,
maximi cuiusque principis favore ac auxilio dignissimam, amplec-
taris, ac potius eam ipsam Academiam, sempiternum bonum hominibus, tu pontifex maximus in urbe Roma cures instituendam.
Quorum unus ac praecipuus est Musurus Cretensis, magno vir
iudicio, magna doctrina, qui hos Platonis libros accurate recognovit cum antiquissimis conferens exemplaribus, ut una mecum,
quod semper facit, multum adiumenti afferret et Graecis et nostris

misprint, however trivial, occurs in one of my books due to my own lack of attention or that of the men who have the task of correcting books with me, although it is reasonable that sleep should creep up in the course of a big job[478] (our task is not for a single day but for many years and "there is no rest or respite"[479] in the meantime), I feel so upset that I would redeem each error, if I could, with a gold coin.

Now therefore, most blessed father, we issue the extant works 6 of Plato, most fortunate in being able to dedicate them to you. Another reason for so doing is that Marsilio Ficino, a protégé of your family, dedicated his Latin version of Plato to your father Lorenzo[480] because he had always been so supportive of all the most learned students of both languages, with the result that in Lorenzo's lifetime Florence was, and was acknowledged to be, a second Athens. We too with good reason wished to dedicate the same author's works, in Greek and in Attic as he composed them, to you, his son and pope, who bring distinction and long-awaited support for scholars of the present generation. Thereby we have simultaneously done a favor to some friends, great lovers of literature; although I was going to do it of my own free will, they courteously advised me that the writings of a superhuman person should not be dedicated to anyone other than yourself, as the supreme authority in matters of divinity. They hoped that this could be of splendid benefit to the Academy which we have been creating for so many years; that you might of course help us, and support this enterprise of ours, which fully deserves the favor and assistance of every great ruler; or rather that you as pope might see to the establishment of this very Academy in the city of Rome, a permanent boon for mankind.[481] One leading member of it is Musurus the Cretan, a man of great judgment and great learning, who has carefully edited these works of Plato, collating the oldest manuscripts[482] so that, in conjunction with myself, as always, he has conferred a great benefit on the Greeks and on our people. For

hominibus. Quapropter non minus quam nos pacem desyderat; aeque ac nos et ipse, ut tuo sumptu, tuis opibus fiat Academia, rogat: id quod ex eius docta et eleganti ac gravi elegia Graece composita, quae statim post Latinum indicem librorum Platonis sequitur, facile est cognoscere.

7   Gratissimum praeterea futurum tibi Platonem hunc nostrum nobis persuademus, cum aliis plurimis, tum etiam quia, cum multis iam seculis in plura dissectus membra vagaretur, nunc, illis in unum corpus diligenter collectis, integer habetur cura nostra, idque per ordines quaternarios novem, quemadmodum in vita Platonis Diogenes Laertius, Thrasyllum secutus, memoriae prodidit. Sed de Platone hactenus.

8   Tu modo, beatissime pater, qui Iesu Christi Dei optimi maximi locum tenes, cuique commissa est cura populorum, curabis pro viribus, quae tua est probitas, tua prudentia, tua pietas, pacem, quam solam moriturus Christus tanquam testamento reliquit hominibus, habendam passim Christianis tuis, qui nunc, inter se eheu bella gerentes crudelissima, validas Christianorum vireis infesto ferro absumunt, quo graves Turcae melius perirent; curabis, inquam, tu, communis omnium pater, summa tua authoritate sanguinolentos filios tuos componendos, haec iterum atque iterum repetens:

    Neu, iuvenes, neu tanta animis assuescite bella;
    proiice tela manu, populus meus!

Atque interim non minus quam nos speramus, quod et Graece et Latine sis apprime doctus, favebis nobis, tandiu ac tantum pro re lite⟨ra⟩ria laborantibus. Nam, etsi maximum videmur attulisse adiumentum utriusque linguae studiosis, tamen tanto maius allaturi sumus, te amplexante provincia⟨m⟩ nostram, quanto maior est Aldo Leo X pontifex maximus.

this reason he desires peace as much as we do. He too, just like me, asks that an Academy be created at your expense and through your resources; this is easily understood from his learned, elegant and serious elegiac poem in Greek which follows the Latin index of Plato's works.[483]

We are in any case persuaded that this Plato of ours will be 7 most welcome to you for many other reasons and because, as his text circulated, it was for many centuries divided into several sections, whereas now they have been carefully put together in one corpus; thanks to our attention the corpus is available complete in nine groups of four works, as Diogenes Laertius in his life of Plato records,[484] drawing on Thrasyllus. But so much for Plato.

As for you, most blessed father, who are the vicar of Jesus 8 Christ, the best and greatest God, and to whom the care of nations is entrusted, thanks to your honesty, your prudence, your piety, you will use your abilities to ensure for your Christians everywhere peace, which Christ, when about to die, left as his sole legacy to mankind. Now, alas, they wage ferocious wars against each other and diminish with hostile armaments the powerful forces of Christianity. It would be better that the troublesome Turks perished by them. You as the common father of all will, as I say, by means of your great authority, make your bloodthirsty sons agree, with frequent repetition of these lines:

No, young men, do not accustom yourselves to such wars;
my people, cast away your weapons.[485]

And in the meantime you, as a great expert in Greek and Latin, will support us in no smaller measure than we hope, since we have labored so long and so hard for literature. For although we are seen to have given great help to students of both languages, still we will make a greater contribution if you encourage our enterprise, greater to the same degree that Pope Leo X is greater than Aldus.

: XLIV :

Aldus Pius Manutius Alberto Pio Carporum principi ac Caesareae
maiestatis apud ponteficem maximum oratori s. p. d.

1 Optima quaeque difficillima factu esse, cum aliis plurimis, tum
praecipue in dura hac provincia nostra emittendorum librorum
utriusque linguae in manus studiosorum sum saepe expertus: alia
enim ex aliis impedimenta et incommoda non cessant obstare iam
multos annos, ne, ut cupimus, prodesse possimus bonarum literarum studiosis, ut nuper accidit. Differ[r]ebam edere Alexandri
Aphrodisiei in topica Aristotelis commentarios superiore anno
excusos cura nostra, expectans quos in ea ipsa topica Graece scrip-
serat commentarios Franciscus Victorius Bergomas, philosophus
et medicus quam doctissimus, in quibus et stylo et doctrina certare videbatur cum eo ipso Alexandro et caeteris Graecis, qui vel
Platonem vel Aristotelem doctissime interpretati sunt, ut una cum
Alexandri commentariis publicarentur; quod opus ad circiter
quinquaginta quaterniones excreverat. Sed fortuna tot labores et
tam doctas lucubrationes invidit nobis. Nam, paucis ante diebus
quam haec ad te scriberem, domus, quam ille habitabat, tam re-
pentino celerique incendio tota absumpta est, ut et ii quos dixi
commentarii et tota eius bibliotheca optimorum plena librorum
utriusque linguae miserabiliter arserint; in quibus erant et in totum Platonem tot annotationes, ut iam pro iustis haberi commentariis possent; erant et in Galenum et caeteros medicos aliae, ex
quibus non unum sed multa confici volumina potuissent.

: XLIV :

Alexander of Aphrodisias, Commentaries on the Topics of Aristotle
(February 15, 1514)

Aldus Pius Manutius to Alberto Pio, prince of Carpi and his imperial majesty's envoy to the pope, warmest greetings.

All the best things are very difficult to achieve for many reasons, as   1
I have often found, and especially in this difficult profession of
ours, the provision of books in both languages for students. One
difficulty and inconvenience after another has continuously ob-
structed us now for many years, so that we cannot help students
of literature as we wish — as happened recently. I delayed the publication of Alexander of Aphrodisias' commentaries on Aristotle's
Topics, which I had printed last year, because I was waiting for the
commentaries on those same *Topics* written in Greek by Francesco
Vittori of Bergamo,[486] a philosopher and doctor of great learning,
in which he appeared to match for style and learning Alexander
himself and the other Greeks who had written learned interpreta-
tions of Plato or Aristotle. This was to be published along with
Alexander's commentary; the work had grown to fill about fifty
quires. But fate has denied us those great labors and learned ob-
servations. For a few days before writing this to you the house he
lived in was completely destroyed by fire so suddenly and quickly
that the commentary I mentioned and the whole of his library, full
of the best books in both languages, disastrously went up in
flames. Among them were such extensive notes on the whole of
Plato that they could already have been treated as a proper commentary. There were additional notes, both on Galen and the
other doctors, from which not just one, but many volumes could
have been produced.

2   Sed quoniam superanda omnis fortuna ferendo est, tum quia ἐλπίδες ἐν ζωοῖσιν, non solum aequo fortique animo fert quam fecit iacturam, sed brevi in illa ipsa topica commentarios vel cum usura, hoc est non solum Graece sed et Latine se daturum confidit et pollicetur, tum alia multa suo tempore dignissima cognitu. Et si, nondum triginta annos natus, vel tantundem vixerit, non dubito quin sit et quae pollicetur daturus omnia et superaturus nostram caeterorumque amicorum expectationem; quemadmodum et Patavii fecit, ubi adolescens summa cum laude et frequentia auditorum publice professus est philosophiam. Iesus igitur Deus optimus maximus, cuius et est et semper fuit reverentissimus, dignos illius inceptus fortunet, ut spero futurum ob miram ipsius iustitiam et probitatem. Quod si incendio nuper afflictus est, nil aliud dixerim quam solere Deum sic experiri constantiam servorum suorum, ut de Iobo legimus, qui, etsi vir erat omnium optimus Deique observantissimus, nihil non mali tamen et calamitatis perpessus est. Talis et Homeri Ulysses:

> πολύτροπος, ὃς μάλα πολλὰ
> πλάγχθη, ἐπεὶ Τροίης ἱερὸν πτολίεθρον ἔπερσεν,
> πολλῶν δ' ἀνθρώπων ἴδεν ἄστεα καὶ νόον ἔγνω,
> πολλὰ δ' ὅ γ' ἐν πόντῳ πάθεν ἄλγεα ὃν κατὰ θυμόν,
> ἀρνύμενος ἥν τε ψυχὴν καὶ νόστον ἑταίρων.

Et ut idem Latine subiunxerim:

>   qui domitor Troiae, multorum providus, urbes
> et mores hominum inspexit, latumque per aequor,
> dum sibi, dum sociis reditum parat, aspera multa
> pertulit, adversis rerum immersabilis undis.

Talis et Vergilii pius Aeneas:

But since all misfortune has to be overcome by endurance[487]   2
and since there is hope among the living,[488] he not only bears his
loss with fortitude but is confident in his promise to provide soon
commentaries on these same *Topics*, and with interest: that is, not
just in Greek but in Latin too, to be followed in due course by
much else thoroughly worthy of attention. Indeed, while he is not
yet thirty, if he lives as long again, I have no doubt that he will
produce everything that he promises and will surpass our and his
friends' expectations, just as he did in Padua, where as a young
man he lectured on philosophy to a large audience to great ac-
claim. May Jesus therefore, the best and greatest God, of whom he
is and always has been the most devoted worshipper, promote his
worthy beginnings, as I hope will come to pass on account of his
admirably just and honest character. If he has recently suffered
because of the fire, I would merely say that God regularly tests the
resolve of his servants, as we read of Job, who, though he was the
best of men and most devoted to God, suffered every trial and disaster. So also did Homer's Ulysses:[489]

πολύτροπος, ὃς μάλα πολλὰ
πλάγχθη, ἐπεὶ Τροίης ἱερὸν πτολίεθρον ἔπερσεν,
πολλῶν δ' ἀνθρώπων ἴδεν ἄστεα καὶ νόον ἔγνω,
πολλὰ δ' ὅ γ' ἐν πόντῳ πάθεν ἄλγεα ὃν κατὰ θυμόν,
ἀρνύμενος ἥν τε ψυχὴν καὶ νόστον ἑταίρων.

If I may add the same in Latin:

who as captor of Troy
and a man of much forethought, inspected the cities
and characters of men; over the broad sea he suffered greatly
while ensuring for himself, for his companions,
a return home, not submerged by adverse waves of trouble.[490]

Such also was Vergil's pious Aeneas:[491]

> multum ille et terris iactatus et alto,
> multa quoque et bello passus.

Quaenam igitur vox in malis dignior viro forti? quam vel illa:

$$\tau\acute{\epsilon}\tau\lambda\alpha\theta\iota\ \delta\acute{\eta},\ \kappa\rho\alpha\delta\acute{\iota}\eta\cdot\ \kappa\alpha\grave{\iota}\ \kappa\acute{\upsilon}\nu\tau\epsilon\rho\rho\nu\ \ddot{\alpha}\lambda\lambda\rho\ \pi\sigma\tau\mbox{'}\ \ddot{\epsilon}\tau\lambda\eta\varsigma$$

vel illa:

> O socii — neque enim ignari sumus ante malorum —
> o passi graviora, dabit deus his quoque finem.
> Vos et Scyllaeam rabiem penitusque sonanteis
> accestis scopulos, vos et Cyclopea saxa
> experti; revocate animos, moestumque timorem
> mittite: forsan et haec olim meminisse iuvabit.
> Per varios casus, per tot discrimina rerum
> tendimus in Latium, sedes ubi fata quietas
> ostendunt; illic fas regna resurgere Troiae.
> Durate et vosmet rebus servate secundis.

3   Hercules praeterea ille, sceleratorum omnium hostis acerrimus ac domitor, qui a depellendis malis ἀλεξίκακος cognomento appellatus est, adversa omnia invictissimo animo tulit; quamobrem meruisse coelum fingitur a poetis. Quid, quod ipse Christus Deus optimus maximus, cum in humanis ageret, labores et mala pati voluit? Idem et nobis suo exemplo censuit faciendum; quem eius discipuli et alii innumerabiles, per labores, per erumnas constantissime imitati, in divorum coetum tandem recepti, bono et quiete fruuntur sempiterna. Quibus ergo, ut sunt casus humani, adversa contingunt, boni ac pii potius Deoque acceptissimi habendi quam secus: nam, quos Deus amat, corrigit et castigat.

   much buffeted on land and on the high seas,
suffering much in war as well.

So what more noble utterance could there be from a brave man
than

   Stand firm, my heart, you have suffered even worse in the
      past — ?[492]

Or

   Companions who have suffered worse — for we are conscious
   of previous misfortunes — god will grant an end to this as well.
   You came close to the fury of Scylla and the thunderous roar
   of her cliffs, you also reached the rocks of the Cyclops;
   retrieve your spirit, cast out gloomy fear;
   perhaps in time it will be a pleasure even to recall all that.
   With various adventures and through so many difficulties
   we are heading for Latium, where the fates show us
   a peaceful home; there Troy has a right to be restored.
   Be patient and preserve yourselves for better things.[493]

In addition the celebrated Hercules, determined adversary and   3
scourge of malefactors, who earned the title *alexikakos*[494] by repel-
ling the wicked, endured all reverses with indomitable spirit; for
this, according to the fictions of poets, he earned a place in heaven.
Similarly Christ himself, the best and greatest God, was willing to
suffer toil and evil while he lived among men. By his example he
declared we should do the same. His disciples and innumerable
others, resolutely following him in their labors and hardships,
were in the end received into the community of the blessed and
enjoy eternal felicity and peace. Those who suffer the reverses of
human existence are therefore to be accounted good, pious and
very dear to God rather than the opposite; for God corrects and
chastises those whom he loves.[495]

4   Id quod adeo verum est, ut maxime timendum sit iis, qui lon-
gissimo vitae cursu nihil unquam adversi experti, felices videntur:
nam, quo diutius ne minimis quidem incommodis afficiuntur,
tanto maiora illos mala infortuniaque expectant. Quemadmodum
Policrati Samiorum tyranno accidit, cui tam feliciter omnia succe-
debant, ut, cum annulum quam gratissimum sibi in mare abiecis-
set, ut illius saltem desyderio tristaretur, continuo capto pisce, qui
annulum devoraverat, illum recuperavit. Τέρμα δ᾽ ὁρᾶν βιότοιο
Σόλων: hic enim ipse, qui fortunatus praeter caeteros omnes semper fuerat, cui ne volenti quidem adversi quicquam accidere poterat, ab Oronte, Darii regis praefecto, in Mycalensis montis vertice
cruci affixus, Samiis dura tandem servitute liberatis laetissimum
diu spectaculum fuit. Cum igitur alia ex aliis nobis adversa contingunt, salutis est signum et summae Dei in nos benevolentiae.
Quare non est unquam cedendum malis, sed eundum contra audentius: sic tollimur humo, sic itur ad astra, sic dii immortales
evadimus. Hoc idem et illa innuunt:

Τῆς δ᾽ ἀρετῆς ἱδρῶτα θεοὶ προπάροιθεν ἔθηκαν
ἀθάνατοι· μακρὸς δὲ καὶ ὄρθιος οἶμος ἐπ᾽ αὐτὴν
καὶ τρηχὺς τοπρῶτον· ἐπὴν δ᾽ εἰς ἄκρον ἵκηται
ῥηϊδίη δ᾽ ἤπειτα πέλει, χαλεπή περ ἐοῦσα.

Et quanquam mirum est, quam fortiter ferat quae sibi ex crudeli
illo incendio evenere incommoda Victorius noster — et vere Victorius, cum sic facile vincat affectus animi, ut ne minimum quidem
signum ex tanta iactura in eo sit moeroris, eaque nos conditione
nasci dicat, ut nihil, quod homini accidere possit, recusare debea-
mus —, etsi mira est, inquam, illius in tantis malis tolerantia, tamen sint haec illi, vel mihi potius, qui magis amicorum quam
propriis moveor incommodis, qualiacunque duri solatia casus.

This is so certain that those who never experience any setback   4
in the course of a long life should be very nervous; for the longer
they avoid being affected by even the slightest trouble, the greater
the evil and misfortune that awaits them. That is what happened
to Polycrates, tyrant of Samos,[496] when he threw his most prized
ring into the sea so that he might at least experience sadness
through regretting its loss. He recovered it at once when the fish
which devoured it was caught. Look to the end of life, said Solon.[497] That same Polycrates, who had always been the most fortunate of men, to whom nothing unfavorable could happen even
when he wished it, was crucified by Orontes,[498] King Darius' governor, at the top of Mount Mycale, and was for a long time a most
welcome spectacle for Samians finally freed from harsh servitude.
So when one trouble after another afflicts us, it is a sign of sal-
vation and God's unsurpassed goodwill toward us. Hence one
should never give way in the face of troubles, but advance to meet
them with greater courage.[499] That is how we are raised from the
ground, how we head toward the stars,[500] how we become divine
and immortal. The same idea is hinted at in these lines:[501]

> The immortal gods placed much sweat in the path
> of virtue, long and steep is the path toward it,
> and initially it is rough. But when one reaches the peak,
> then it is easy, though it was hard.

And although it is remarkable how bravely our friend Vittori puts
up with the troubles caused by that cruel blaze — he is truly victorious if he can so easily overcome his feelings that he shows not
the least sign of distress at so great a loss, and he says that our
human condition is such that we must not reject anything that can
befall a man — although, as I say, his endurance in such difficulties
is remarkable, let these words be some modest consolation to him
for his hard luck[502] and more so to myself, since I am more troubled by my friends' misfortunes than my own.

5   Equidem quanto illum amore prosequar, non facile dixerim, cum ob peracre eius ingenium, flagrans studium, eximiam doctrinam, singulare iudicium, divinam prope memoriam, quae simul omnia non alii cuiquam hac aetate video contigisse — vix enim singula singulis invenias — ; tum praecipue, quia non solum optimus homo est, sed et Christi cultor optimus. Qui si fuisset temporibus Socratis, vel unus facile potuisset eorum opponi calumniae, qui dicebant philosophos negare esse deos, Socratemque ipsum, qui Apollinis oraculo, quod tunc verissimum habebatur, sapientissimus est iudicatus, ἄθεον iuventutisque corruptorem esse praedicabant. Sunt tamen et nunc nonnulli, qui hoc idem existiment, quod videant quosdam, qui profitentur se esse philosophos et non sunt, pessime vitam agere et scatere vitiis, ob eamque causam dicere non esse Deum vel, si sit, nullam illi rerum humanarum esse curam, tum animos hominum una cum corporibus interire. Sed tota errant via. Mea quidem sententia sunt primum viri quam optimi veri philosophi, expertesque vitiorum omnium. Ex quibus te unum esse, possum esse ipse optimus testis, qui te a puero institui et erudivi; quanquam et me et caeteris deinceps longe melior et doctior tuis evasisti praeceptoribus: πολλοὶ γὰρ μαθηταὶ κρείττονες διδασκάλων. Sunt, inquam, primum optimi viri veri philosophi; deinde non modo ipsi Deum esse credunt, ab eoque uno et mundum et quae in eo sunt omnia perpetuo regi et gubernari, sed id ipsum et docent alios sedulo et memoriae produnt. Id quod ex apologia Socratis facile est cognoscere, in qua divinus ille philosophus et gratissimus omnium discipulus Plato adversus illam ipsam improborum et malevolorum calumniam Socratem inducit disputantem. Sed γλαῦκας εἰς Ἀθήνας, qui haec ad te.

6   De Victorio autem nostro an vera scripserim, et ex doctis eius lucubrationibus brevi, ut spero, cognosces, et coram aliquando.

Indeed I cannot easily express my affection for him, for his ac- 5
tive intelligence, enthusiasm for work, great learning, outstanding
judgment and almost divine memory, the combination of which I
do not see in anyone else in this generation (one can scarcely find
these qualities singly in an individual); and in particular he is not
just an excellent man but an excellent Christian. If he had lived in
the days of Socrates he by himself could easily have been put forward to contest the slander of those who said that philosophers
deny the existence of the gods, and who claimed that Socrates
himself, who was judged to be the wisest of men by the oracle of
Apollo, then held to be infallible, was an unbeliever and corruptor
of youth. But there are still some people holding that same opinion, because they see that certain persons who claim to be philosophers and are not, live very bad lives and have many vices, conse-
quently denying the existence of God or, if he exists, that he has
any concern for humanity, and saying that men's souls die with
their bodies.[503] But they are utterly wrong. In my opinion true
philosophers are above all excellent men and free from all vices. I
can be an excellent witness to the fact that you are one, since I
have educated and instructed you from your childhood onward—
though you have emerged far better and more learned than me
and your other teachers; many pupils are better than their masters.[504] As I say, true philosophers are above all excellent men; and
they do not just have a personal belief in God—that by him alone
the world and everything in it is ruled and governed for all time—
but assiduously impart this fact to others and put it on record.
That is easy to see from Socrates' *Apology*, in which that divine
philosopher, his favorite pupil Plato, presents Socrates arguing
against that very slander of the wicked and malevolent. But it is
"Owls to Athens" if I say this to you.[505]

Whether I have given a true account of our friend Vittori you 6
will soon, I hope, be able to tell from his writings and at some

Interea hosce Alexandri commentarios sub tuo nomine a nobis editos in manus hominum, siquid occupatissimo tibi maximae molestiarum et turbulentissimae tempestates nostrorum temporum tribuent otii, cum ipsorum doctrina et excellentia studiose leges, tum etiam quia Musurus noster eos cum antiquis conferens exemplaribus accuratissime recognovit. Dabuntur deinceps, Deo volente, caetera omnia in Aristotelem, ut olim memini polliceri, cum primum absoluti fuerint Strabo, Athenaeus, Pausanias, Xenophon, quos multorum rogatu nunc imprimendos curamus. Dabuntur et alia suo tempore; nam, etsi

vicinae ruptis inter se legibus urbes
arma ferunt, saevit toto Mars impius orbe,

tamen quieturi nunquam sumus, nisi pollicita praestiterimus, saxumque illud gravissimum, quod tot annos assidue volvimus, in montis apicem perduxerimus.

Vale, decus ingens principum et gloria huius aetatis philosophorum.

Venetiis XV Februarii M.D.XIIII.

: XLV :

Ἄλδος ὁ Μανούτιος τοῖς ἀναλεξομένοις εὖ πράττειν.

1 Ἐπειδὴ ἐπὶ τουτουῒ τοῦ Σουΐδα οὐχ ἡ αὐτὴ τάξις θεωρεῖται τῶν γραμμάτων, ἥτις καὶ ἐπὶ τοῦ ἀλφαβήτου, ἀλλ᾽ ἄλλη τις καὶ διάφορος, δοκῶ μοι ὠφέλιμόν τι

point from meeting him. In the meantime here are the commentaries of Alexander, issued by us for the public and dedicated to
you. If the extreme turbulence and convulsions of our times allow
you any leisure in the midst of your many duties, you will read
them attentively for their learning and quality—and also because
our friend Musurus has collated them very carefully with ancient
manuscripts.[506] There will follow, God willing, all the rest dealing
with Aristotle, as I recall promising long ago, as soon as Strabo,
Athenaeus, Pausanias and Xenophon are ready; these we are now
printing, many people having requested them.[507] Other texts will
be offered in due course; for although

> neighboring cities are at war, having broken their treaties,
> and wicked Mars savages the whole world,[508]

still we shall never relax until we have fulfilled our promises and
pushed to the top of the hill that heavy boulder which we have
been rolling continuously for so many years.

Farewell, great glory of princes, ornament of today's philosophers.

Venice, February 15, 1514.

: XLV :

Suidas, Lexicon[509]
(February 1514)

Aldus Manutius to readers, greetings.

Since in this text of Suidas the sequence of the letters is seen not 1
to be the same as in the alphabet, but in an alternative and different order, I think I will be doing something helpful for students if

ποιήσειν τοὺς σπουδαίους, εἰ νῦν ὑποθήσομαι, τίνα τρόπον ἐνταῦθα ἔπονται ἀλλήλοις τά τε γράμματα καὶ αἱ
δίφθογγοι· καὶ πρῶτον μὲν τὰ τῆς ἀλφαβήτου ὁμοῦ
ἅπαντα, ὡς ἕπεται ἀλλήλοις ἐφεξῆς, ἔπειτα δὲ ἰδίᾳ ἕκαστα τῶν εἰρημένων, ὧδε.

: XLVI :

Aldi Pii Manutii ad Ioannem Iacobum Bardellonum
in Hesychii dictionarium praefatio.

1 Si caeteri studiosi, nobilitatis Mantuanae decus Bardellone, sua
sponte ac gratis, ut ipse facis, iuvarent me edendis publicandisque
bonis libris, qui tanquam *κατὰ παλιγγενεσίαν* reviviscant mea
cura et laboribus, brevi quamplurimi, qui desyderantur, exirent in
publicum: ut de Hesychio factum est, quem cum penes te tantum
esse duceres, et vere fortasse—nemo enim est, quod sciam, qui
extare alium audiverit—, eum ad me misisti, ut daretur imprimen-
dus impressoribus nostris, nihil prorsus aliud spectans quam, quae
tua est liberalitas, qui tuus amor erga literatos viros, ut fiat communis studiosis omnibus, etiam posteris; nec imitaris invidos
quosdam, qui, dum se solos esse doctos volunt, bonos libros in-
vident aliis, sed, tui omnes quam simillimos fore cupiens—es
enim et Graece et Latine doctissimus mathematicarumque disciplinarum longe peritissimus—, bibliothecam tuam plenam optimorum librorum omnibus benignus impertis.

I now explain the sequence of letters and diphthongs in this text—firstly all the letters of the alphabet together, how they follow in a sequence, then each of the aforesaid variants individually, as follows.[510]

: XLVI :

Hesychius, Lexicon
(August 1514)

*Aldus Pius Manutius' preface to Hesychius' dictionary,
addressed to Gian Giacomo Bardellone.*[511]

Bardellone, glorious member of the Mantuan nobility, if other intellectuals gave me free and willing help as you do in editing and publishing good books, which thanks to my care and efforts are reborn by a kind of reincarnation, then a great many that are still awaited would appear. This is the case with Hesychius. When you reckoned it was unique and in your possession—and perhaps you were right, since to the best of my knowledge no one has heard of the existence of another copy[512]—you sent it to me, so that it could be entrusted to our printers, with no other motive—such is your generosity and your goodwill toward the educated—than that it should be available to all students, including those of the future. You do not behave like certain jealous men who try to be unique as scholars and withhold good books from other people; instead, in your desire that everyone should resemble you—for you are an expert in Greek and Latin and have unrivaled competence in mathematical disciplines—you kindly grant everyone access to your library, which is well stocked with the best books.

2   Ecce, quod iussisti, factum est diligenter. Agimus igitur tibi quas possumus gratias et nostro et studiosorum nomine, qui hoc ipso libro usuri sunt. Utentur autem eo omnes quicunque, capti amore bonarum literarum, non cessant exemplaria Graeca nocturna versare manu, versare diurna, idque ob plurimam, quae in eo est, dictionum copiam.

3   Omnes enim, quae in variis dictionariis habebantur, dictiones primum Diogenianus, homo doctissimus, de quo in praefatione, quae statim sequitur, Hesychius meminit, deinde Hesychius ipse, cuius Suidas in dictione Ἡσύχιος facit mentionem, in unum diligentissime collegit. Sed illud admodum dolendum est, quod, nescio cuius iniuria, proverbiorum argumenta, quae praetermissa a Diogeniano Hesychius adiunxerat, tum plurium dictionum, et quae rariores sunt, authoritates, quas is ipse Hesychius studiose addiderat, sublatae sunt summo studiosorum incommodo et iactura.

4   Hunc autem librum sub tuo nomine in publicum exire voluimus, Bardellone doctissime, ut et tibi deberent hoc munere studiosi. Quem eo gratiorem tibi futurum existimamus, quod eum Musurus, compater utriusque nostrum, quantum per occupationes licuit, diligenter recognovit, fecitque, licet cursim, πατρὸς ἀρείω: quamplurima enim in eo loca emendata sunt, id quod facile cognoscet, qui exemplar ipsum cum novo hoc conferet. Vale.

Venetiis mense Augusto M.D.XIIII.

As you can see, your instructions have been carried out care- 2
fully. We therefore offer thanks as best we can, in our own name
and that of students who will use this volume. And it will be used
by everyone who, captivated by the love of literature, does not
cease to peruse Greek books night and day,[513] and this they will do
because of the great number of entries in it.

All the words included in various dictionaries were carefully 3
collected and put together, first by the learned Diogenian, about
whom Hesychius himself speaks in the preface that follows immediately, then by Hesychius himself, who is recorded by Suidas
in the entry "Hesychius." But it is rather regrettable (I do not
know who is to blame) that the subject matter of the proverbs,
omitted by Diogenian and added by Hesychius, and the authorities for many words, including the rarer ones, which Hesychius
himself had carefully added, have been removed, a great loss and
inconvenience to scholars.[514]

Most learned Bardellone, we wished this book to appear with a 4
dedication to you, so that students should feel indebted to you as
well as for this gift. We believe it will be all the more welcome to
you because Musurus, a good friend to both of us, checked it carefully, as far as his commitments allowed, and made it, admittedly
working in haste, "better than its father,"[515] since a vast number of
passages have been emended, as will easily be recognized if one
compares the manuscript itself with this new text.[516] Farewell.

Venice, August 1514.

: XLVII :

Aldus Pius Manutius Iano Vyrthesi Pannonio s. p. d.

1 Quantum gratuler tibi, Iane, quantum Hungaris tuis, quantum ipsi Hungariae, non facile dixerim, quod tantum iam profeceris Graecis literis nondum annum audiens Musurum Cretensem, idque Venetiis, ut primus Graecas Musas Attice loquentes brevi relaturus in patriam videare.

Macte nova virtute, puer; sic itur ad astra.

2 Nosti suscepisse te onus grave et Venetiarum et Musuri, quorum alter te scientia augere potest, alterae exemplis. Nosti illud Homeri:

αἰσχρόν τοι δηρόν τε μένειν κενεόν τε νέεσθαι.

Nosti quam excitet te ad virtutem Thomas cardinalis et legatus a latere domini nostri ac Strigoniensis archiepiscopus maxime venerandus, avunculus tuus, qui illud Aeneae ad Ascanium tibi dicere vere potest:

Disce, puer, virtutem ex me verumque laborem.

Nosti quam excitet te et Philippus Cyulanus a secretis regis, homo gravissimus atque optimus, qui, dum summa fide et integritate oratorem agit apud Venetos, te, quoties ad eum officii gratia salutatum vadis, id quod saepe facis, assidue monet inquiens: 'Iane,

: XLVII :

Athenaeus, The Learned Banqueters
(*August 1514*)

Aldus Pius Manutius to Janus Vyrthesis from Hungary,[517]
warmest greetings.

I cannot easily express my congratulations to you, Janus, to your   1
fellow Hungarians, to Hungary itself, on your great progress in
Greek after less than a year of attendance at the lectures of Musurus the Cretan here in Venice. It looks as if you will soon be the
first to take back to your country Greek Muses speaking Attic.

A blessing boy, on your youthful virtue; in this way men
reach the stars.[518]

You know that you have taken on a serious task in Venice and   2
with Musurus; he can elevate you by means of his knowledge, she
by her example. You know the line from Homer:

It is shameful for you to stay a long time and depart empty-
handed.[519]

You know how much you are encouraged[520] by your uncle, cardinal
Thomas, envoy *a latere* of our lord the pope and the most venera-
ble archbishop of Esztergom,[521] who can truly say to you what
Aeneas said to Ascanius:

Boy, learn about virtue and true labor from me.[522]

You know also how you are stimulated by Philip Gyulai,[523] secretary to the king, a serious and excellent man, who, as envoy to
Venice of great reliability and honesty, always advises you when
you go to make a formal visit, as you often do, "Janus,

pauci, quos aequus amavit
Iuppiter aut ardens evexit ad aethera virtus:

cura, precor, ut sis unus ex paucis et avunculi cardinalis simillimus. Perge, fili, ut coepisti'; et id genus alia plena patriae dilectio-
nis. Nosti praeterea, quam excitet te Ianus ille Quinquecclesiensis
episcopus, gloria et decus ingens Pannoniae (nam et tibi nomen
est Iano), in cuius sepulchro elegans illud distichum legitur:

Hic situs est Ianus, patrium qui primus ad Istrum
duxit laurigeras ex Helicone deas.

Retulit vir ille nunquam satis laudatus in patriam primus Latinas
Musas; tu et Latinas et Atticas Musuro doctore relaturus videris.
Neque enim dubito quin, quae gloriose coepisti, sis perfecturus,
tum quia bene coepisti (dimidium facti, qui coepit, habet: ἀρχὴ
γὰρ ἥμισυ παντός), tum etiam quia iam plurimum profecisti.

3   Quamobrem impulsus ego acri ingenio, frequenti studio, miro
amore erga bonas literas, sanctissimis moribus tuis, hosce Athenaei libros de coenis doctorum hominum, plenos variarum et mi-
rabilium scituque dignissimarum rerum, sub tuo nomine exire volui ex aedibus nostris in manus studiosorum, quo fias alacrior ad
sacra studia literarum. Hi enim libri, praeter variam ac miram rerum, quas continent, cognitionem, ut piscium, herbarum, arbo-
rum et aliorum pene innumerabilium, iuvabunt te et studiosos
caeteros corrigendis aliis libris ex plurimis, quos citat, authoribus.
Cuius rei facere fidem potest locus apud Theophrastum de historia plantarum libro quarto, ubi de malis Medicis ac Persicis tractat: qui, cum sit mutilatus et corruptus et in eo libro, quem e

Few are those whom a fair-minded
Jupiter favored or whom glowing virtue propelled to the
stars.[524]

I beg you to take care to be one of the minority and very like your
uncle the cardinal. Continue, my son, as you have begun." And
he has plenty more of this type of advice, full of fatherly affection. You know also what encouragement you receive from Janus,
bishop of Pécs,[525] an ornament and great glory of Hungary (you
too are called Janus); on his tomb the following elegant couplet
can be read:

Here lies Janus, who first brought to his native Danube
the laurel-bearing goddesses of Helicon.

No praise can do justice to him; he was the first to bring the Latin
Muses to his country; you look as if, thanks to the teachings of
Musurus, you will bring back both the Greek and the Latin. For I
have no doubt that you will complete what you have so gloriously
begun, partly through a good start (he who begins is half way to
completion;[526] the beginning is half of the whole[527]), partly because you have already made great progress.

So, impelled as I was by the keen intelligence, the regular study, 3
the great love of good books, the saintly character you display, I
wanted these books by Athenaeus about the banquets of scholars,
full of a variety of astonishing and important facts, to reach the
public from our house with a dedication to you, to enhance your
support for the sacred study of letters. These books, apart from
the wonderful variety of factual knowledge they contain, for instance about fish, plants, trees and almost innumerable other subjects, will help you and scholars in general to correct other texts
thanks to the numerous quotations. This can be shown from a
passage in Book IV of Theophrastus, *Historia plantarum*,[528] where
he deals with Persian and Median fruits. Since it is mutilated and

Graeco in Latinum non minus eleganter quam docte traduxit Theodorus Gaza, et in eo, qui Graece cura nostra habetur impressus, facile ex eo corrigi potest, quod in tertio libro δειπνοσοφιστῶν citat Athenaeus. In Graeco enim impresso et in traducto per Theodorum, post καὶ σχεδὸν ἴσον deest τῷ τῆς δάφνης, et post ἀδράχνης deest καὶ καρύας. Est enim ἀδράχνη absque ν potulaca arbor absque r; ἀνδράχνη autem cum ν portulaca herba cum r: id quod et Plinius testatur. Et post εὔοσμον δὲ πάνυ deest καὶ αὐτό. Item post πεπωκὼς θανάσιμον φάρμακον deest δοθὲν γὰρ ἐν οἴνῳ, διακόπτει τὴν κοιλίαν, καὶ ἐξάγει τὸ φάρμακον. Praeterea illud in impresso: ὅταν δὲ ἀδρόν * τι διαφυτεύηται, legendum est ὅταν δὲ ἀδρὸν ᾖ, διαφυτεύεται, absque asterisco. Deesse autem τῷ τῆς δάφνης et δοθὲν γὰρ ἐν οἴνῳ, διακόπτει τὴν κοιλίαν, καὶ ἐξάγει τὸ φάρμακον, confirmatur ex his Virgilii versibus in secundo *Georgicon*:

> Media fert tristes succos tardumque saporem
> felicis mali, quo non praesentius ullum,
> pocula siquando saevae infecere novercae
> miscueruntque herbas et non innoxia verba,
> auxilium venit et membris agit atra venena.
> Ipsa ingens arbor faciemque simillima lauro;
> et si non alium late iactaret odorem,
> laurus erat; folia haud ullis labentia ventis;
> flos apprima tenax. Animas et olentia Medi
> ora fovent illo, et senibus medicantur anhelis.

Totum enim accepisse videtur ex Theophrasto. Hanc arborem Athenaeus probat esse citrium multis rationibus, et addit, quo modo in Media primum inventum sit pomo eius arboris venena exagi ex membris, nec obesse ea quicquam posse iis, qui comederint citrium.

corrupt both in the text which Theodore Gaza translated in elegant and learned style from Greek into Latin and in the Greek text we printed, it can easily be corrected from Athenaeus' quotation in Book III of *The Learned Banqueters* (*Deipnosophistae*).[529] In the Greek as printed and in the translation by Theodore the words τῷ τῆς δάφνης are missing after καὶ σχεδὸν ἴσον, and so are καὶ κάρυας after ἀδράχνης. For ἀδράχνη without *nu* is the tree *potulaca* without *r*; ἀδράχνη with *nu* is the plant *portulaca* with *r*, as is also confirmed by Pliny.[530] And after εὔοσμον δὲ πάνυ the words καὶ αὐτὸ are missing. Again, after πεπωκὼς θανάσιμον φάρμακον the words δοθὲν γὰρ ἐν οἴνῳ διακόπτει τὴν κοιλίαν καὶ ἐξάγει τὸ φάρμακον. In addition where the printed text has ὅταν δὲ ἁδρὸν* τι διαφυτεύηται, one should read ὅταν δὲ ἁδρὸν ᾖ, διαφυτεύηται, without the asterisk. The loss of τῷ τῆς δάφνης and δοθὲν γὰρ . . . φάρμακον is confirmed by these verses of Vergil in *Georgics* II:[531]

Media produces the bitter juices and lingering taste
of the citron. If ever malign stepmothers poison
drinks with a mixture of herbs, adding a dire incantation,
no more helpful relief exists than this,
expelling sinister poisons from the limbs.
The tree itself is huge and in appearance very like the bay tree,
and if it did not spread a different scent far and wide it would be
laurel. The leaves do not move in any wind, the flower clings
tenaciously. With this the Medes take care of their breath
and the smell of the mouth, and cure the elderly short of breath.

He appears to have taken it all from Theophrastus. Athenaeus shows by many proofs that this tree is the lemon, and adds how it was first discovered in Media that poisons are removed from the limbs by its fruit and no harm comes to those who have eaten a lemon.

4   Haec diximus verbosius, ut cognosceres, quam utiles futuri sint tibi et caeteris studiosis hi Athenaei libri, quos Musurus noster sic accurate recensuit collatos et cum multis exemplaribus et cum epitomate, ut infinitis pene in locis eos emendaverit, carminaque, quae veluti prosa in aliis legebantur, in sua metra restituerit. Adde quod primus et secundus liber, qui in aliis deerant, ex epitomate additi sunt cum bona parte tertii libri: erat enim hic sine capite; quo factum est, ut iidem fere hi existimari possint, qui erant integri, quoniam ea est materia, ut non multa subtrahi ex iis potuerint.

5   Habes igitur integros Athenaei libros. Dabuntur, ut spero, et alii, qui desyderantur, authores vel brevi (faveat Deus): quamobrem omnia tibi abunde erunt, ut Musas Atticas in patriam tuam gloriosus referas. Vale.

Venetiis mense Augusto MDXIIII.

I have stated this at some length so that you could see how use- 4
ful these books by Athenaeus will be for you and other scholars.
Our friend Musurus has checked them so carefully with many
manuscripts and the epitome that he emended an almost infinite
number of passages and restored the original meter of the poems,
which elsewhere were read as if they were prose.[532] In addition
Books I and II, missing in other copies, have been supplied from
the epitome, together with a good part of Book III, the beginning
of which was missing.[533] As a result these books can be regarded
as not much different from the complete books; the subject matter
is such that not a great deal could be removed.

So you have Athenaeus complete. Other texts in demand will, I 5
hope, be made available soon (may God favor us); as a result you
will have an abundant supply of everything, in order to make a
glorious return to your country with the Attic Muses. Farewell.

Venice, August 1514.

APPENDICES

: I :

Marsilius Ficinus Florentinus Aldo Romano s. p. d.

1 Gratias ago benivolentie et diligentie tue. Doleo autem me minus posse meam his temporibus diligentiam adhibere. Esse multa ex scribentium vitio in libris istis errata facile credo. Nam acceptis litteris tuis statim post initium Iamblichi duo errata deprehendi, neque id quidem mirum. Nam codices quos habetis non ego quidem recognovi, tunc in Parmenidis Dionysiique commentariis occupatus, sed mei quidam admodum negligentes, quorum negligentiam postquam ad vos missi sunt animadverti. Grecos equidem libros a Medicibus accepti commodo. Hi nunc nec haberi facile nec forte inveniri possunt. Synesium pre ceteris arbitror esse mendosum, non solum ex scribentium vel amicorum vitio, sed quia exemplar habui mendarum plenum. Denique hec omnia me olim in ceteris occupatissimo nescio quomodo edita sunt. Ego vero isthec tempestate hac curare non possum. Preter enim id quod valitudinarius sum, nec in urbe nec in suburbiis habitare tuto possum nec meos qui in civitate sparsi sunt libros colligere. Tres enim furie Florentiam iamdiu miseram assidue vexant, morbus pestilens et fames atque seditio, atque id quod acerbius est, una cum ceteris mortalium dissimulationibus dissimulata pestis.

APPENDICES

Marsilio Ficino on textual errors in
his translations of Iamblichus and other Platonica

Marsilio Ficino of Florence to Aldus of Rome, warmest greetings.

I am grateful for your kindness and attention. But I regret not be-   1
ing able at present to give as much attention myself. I can well
believe that those copies are full of errors through the fault of the
scribes, since immediately after reading your letter I noticed two
mistakes after the beginning of Iamblichus.[1] In fact I was not the
person who checked the manuscripts you now have, being occupied at the time with the commentaries on Parmenides and Dionysius, but it was some rather careless members of my circle,
whose negligence I spotted after the books had been sent to you.
The Greek texts I have were on loan from the Medici. They are
not now easy to get hold of and perhaps are impossible to find.[2]
The Synesius, I think, is more faulty than the rest, which is not
just the fault of the scribes or friends, but because the exemplar I
had was full of mistakes. Then all these texts were published
somehow when I was very busy with other projects, and I cannot
deal with them at present. Apart from the fact that my health is
poor I cannot live safely in the city or the suburbs, nor can I collect books of my own which are scattered round the town. Three
Furies have for some time been afflicting Florence continually —
the plague, famine and sedition —,[3] and what is worse, along with
all the other forms of human hypocrisy, concealment of the plague.

2   Lego quod in Synesio emendas; emendationem tuam probo.
Quapropter cetera fidei tue credo iudicioque committo. Denique
si ad me ut nunc unum ita deinceps plures quinterniones miseris,
ego quoque pro viribus emendabo, et quando totum opus impressum fuerit, mittam emendationum indicem, quem vos post codices imprimetis antequam libri ipsi vendantur.

3   Vale feliciter et Hieronymo Blondo nostre dignitatis studios-
simo me nomine dicito salutem et gratias agito.
       Kalendis Iuliis MCCCCLXXXXVII.

: II :

A

Ἐπίγραμμα εἰς Ἀριστοφάνην

1   Βίβλοι Ἀριστοφάνους, θεῖος πόνος, αἷσιν Ἀχαρνεὺς
      Κισσὸς ἐπὶ χλοερὴν πουλὺς ἔσεισε κόμην·
      Ἤνιδ᾽ ὅσον Διόνυσον ἔχει σελὶς, οἷα δὲ μῦθοι
      Ἠχεῦσι, φοβερῶν πληθόμενοι χαρίτων.
      Ὦ καὶ θυμὸν ἄριστε καὶ Ἑλλάδος ἤθεσιν ἶσα
      Κωμικὲ, καὶ στίξας ἄξια καὶ γελάσας.

I have read your corrections in Synesius and approve of your 2
emendations; so I submit the rest to you and leave it to your judgment. Finally, if for the future you send me some quires of ten
leaves like the one you have sent, I will do my best to check them,
and when the whole text is printed I will give you a list of errata,
which you will print after the main body of the text before the
books themselves are put on sale.

All good wishes, and pass on my greetings and thanks to Gi- 3
rolamo Biondo,[4] who has great regard for my reputation.

July 1, 1497.

: II :

Musurus on Aristophanes
(1498)

A

Epigram on Aristophanes

Books of Aristophanes, a divine work, over which the ivy of 1
Acharnai flutters in profusion with luxuriant foliage.[5] See how
much of Dionysus the page offers, how the stories speak loud and
clear, brimming with awe-inspiring charm.[6] O best in spirit and
writer of comedy to match the character of Hellas, who pilloried
and laughed at worthy targets.

B

Μάρκος Μουσοῦρος ὁ Κρὴς τοῖς
ἐντευξομένοις, εὖ πράττειν.

2   Ἄχρι μέντοι παρόντος, ὦ φιλέλληνες, Ἄλδος ἔπραξεν
ἡμῖν Ἑλληνικῶν εὐπορεῖν βιβλίων, ἀφ᾽ ὧν ἔστι τὴν μὲν
φύσιν τῶν ὄντων κατανοεῖν, τὰς δὲ περὶ τὸ ἦθος ἀρετὰς
καὶ κακίας διαιρεῖν, καὶ τίνι συλλογιζομένους μεθόδῳ
τἀληθὲς μετέρχεσθαι προσήκει, μανθάνειν· ἃ γὰρ τῶν
Ἀριστοτέλους συγγραμμάτων καὶ ἐς ἡμᾶς σωθέντα δια-
τελεῖ, δαπάνης φεισάμενος οὐδεμιᾶς ἐνετύπωσεν, ἐφ᾽ ᾧτε
δεξιὸς τοῖς εἰλικρινοῦς παιδείας ἐφιεμένοις τό γε ἐς αὐτὸν ἧκον γενέσθαι. Νῦν δὲ θεωρῶν καὶ σκοπῶν τοῖς φι-
λοσοφοῦσι μετὰ τὴν τῶν λεπτῶν καὶ μετεώρων ἀνάγνω-
σιν ἐνδεῖν τινα καὶ ψυχαγωγίαν, δι᾽ ἧς τὴν διάνοιαν
ἔχοιεν ἂν ἀπειρηκυῖαν ἀνεῖναι, παιδιὰν ἡμῖν οὐ πάντως
ἀσπούδαστον ἐπενόησε, μηδοτιοῦν προϊεμένοις καιροῦ,
τὰς Ἀριστοφάνους θυμέλας οὐ μόνον ἀγομένων Διονυ-
σίων Ἀθήνησιν, ἀλλ᾽ αἰεὶ προχείρους καὶ πανταχοῦ
θεᾶσθαι παρασκευάσας. οὕτως ἡ τἀνδρὸς χορηγία πολυ-
τελής, τοῦ γε μὴν κωμικοῦ τί ἂν τις ὑπερλαλοίη; ὃς τῷ
μὲν χαρίεντι τῶν λόγων καὶ τῇ ἐς τὸ τέρπειν καὶ ἥδειν
ἀστειότητι τοὺς φιλομαθοῦντας ἐπάγεται, ἐξ ὧν δὲ τοὺς
μὲν ἀρετῆς ἀντιποιουμένους εὐλογεῖ, τοὺς δὲ φαύλης τυ-
χόντας ἀγωγῆς, καὶ διὰ τοῦτο τὸν τρόπον ἀποβάντας οὐ
μάλα σπουδαίους ὁτὲ μὲν τῇ παρ᾽ ὑπόνοιαν ἐλέγχει δρι-
μύτητι, ὁτὲ δ᾽ ἀποκαλύπτως ὡς αὐτός φησιν Ἡρακλέους ὀργὴν ἔχων ἔπεσι μεγάλοις καὶ σκώμμασιν οὐκ

B

Preface

Marcus Musurus the Cretan to readers, greetings.[7]

Up till now, lovers of Greece, Aldus has certainly ensured for us   2
a plentiful supply of books from which one may gain understanding of the nature of things, know how to distinguish moral virtues and vices, and learn by which logical method it is correct to approach the truth. With no expense spared he printed those works of Aristotle that have been preserved right down to our own day,[8] so as to favor, as far as lay in his power, lovers of true culture. And now, on reflection, seeing that the philosophers are in need of some enjoyment after their reading of subtle and abstruse matter, so that they can give relaxation to their exhausted intellects, he has devised an entertainment for us which is not entirely without a serious element, since we do not waste any opportunity: he has produced Aristophanic drama, not confined to the festival of the Dionysia at Athens but to be permanently available and for spectators everywhere. Such is his lavish provision; but as to the author of comedy himself, what should one say on his behalf? He attracts students by the grace of his language, by his pleasing and enjoyable wit. He praises those who strive after virtue. Those who receive a bad education, and as a result turn out not at all honorable in character, he sometimes exposes with subtle acerbity,[9] at other times without disguise, as he himself says, with the spirit of Hercules,[10] in grandiose verse and with jokes that are not vulgar. He

ἀγοραίοις, μετὰ παρρησίας διαβάλλων οὐδὲ στρατηγοῦ
ἀπέχεται ἁμαρτάνοντος, τί μὲν αἱρετὸν καὶ φευκτὸν ταῖς
προσεσχηκόσιν αὐτῷ τὸν νοῦν εἰσηγεῖται· εἰ δέ τις μὴ
πάρεργον ἔνια τῶν εἰρημένων ἐπιλέγοιτο, πάσης ἡμᾶς
ἐλευθεροῖ τερατείας μὴ δεδιέναι τὰ τῷ σύρφακι δήμῳ
φοβερὰ νουθετῶν. Καὶ μὲν δὴ τοὺς ὑποδεδυκότας αὐτόν,
παμμιγεῖ ὀνομάτων ποικιλίᾳ πρὸς πᾶν ὁτιοῦν συντελούν-
των ἐκ περιουσίας οὕτω πλουτίζει ὥστ᾽ εἴ τις πρὸς τοὺς
πλησιάζοντας διαλεγόμενος τὸν Ἀριστοφάνους ἐπιτη-
δεύειν χαρακτῆρα φιλοτιμοῖτο, ἐμφιλοχωρούντων ἐναύλῳ
τῇ μνήμῃ τῶν Ἀττικοῦ ἀποπνεόντων θυμοῦ ῥημάτων, ἐν
ἥπατι τῆς Ἑλλάδος τραφῆναι καὶ παιδευθῆναι δοκεῖν·
ὡς μὲν οὖν εὔχρηστός ἐστι, τὸν ποιητὴν οὐ δεῖ συν-
ιστᾶν τῷ λίθον ποτὶ τὰν σπάρτον ἄγοντι· ἐπεὶ οὐδ᾽ ἡμῖν
τοῦτο πρόκειται, μηδ᾽ οὕτω μαινοίμην ὡς μὴ συνειδέναι
ἐμαυτῷ πολλοῦ δέοντι ἢ ὥστε τὸν Ἀριστοφάνην ἐγκω-
μιάζειν ὁπότε οὐδ᾽ ἂν αὐτὸς ἑαυτὸν τῆς ἀξίας ἐγγὺς
ἐξαρκέσειεν ἐπαινέσαι.

3   Τὰ δ᾽ ὑπομνήματα ταυτὶ καὶ πόνου πολλοῦ καὶ χρόνου
ἐδεῖτο μακροῦ, εἴ τις αὐτὰ πρὸς τὸ βέλτιον ἐγχειροίη
μεθαρμόσασθαι σχῆμα, ὧν θατέρου μὲν ἐπεκρατήσαμεν
καίτοι κρείττονος ἢ φέρειν. περὶ στενὸν δέ μοι κομιδῇ τὰ
τοῦ χρόνου συνέβη, οὐδὲ μόνον τὰς ἐξηγήσεις συνείρειν
ἠργολαβήσαμεν πεφυρμένας τέως ὡς ἴστε που καὶ αὐτοὶ
ἀλλὰ καὶ τυπωθείσας ἤδη ἐπετετράμμεθα διορθοῦν, αἱ
δὲ τῶν χαλκογράφων ἁμαρτίαι κάρηνά εἰσι λερναῖα τῆς
παλιμφύους ὕδρας πολυπλοκώτερα καὶ τῆς Ἰόλεω ἐπι-
κουρίας δεόμενα, ὅσῳ δ᾽ ἐξεκόπτομεν τοσῷδε πλείους

criticizes freely and does not even spare a military commander who was at fault.[11] To those willing to listen to him he shows what they should do and not do. If one gives careful consideration to some of his remarks, he makes us immune to all extravagantly pompous claims with his advice not to fear what frightens the common herd. Furthermore, for those who really get to grips with him, the vast variety of vocabulary appropriate to every subject brings such abundant enrichment that anyone having a conversation and aiming to follow Aristophanes' usage, with words redolent of Attic thyme,[12] firmly rooted in a well-tuned memory, would appear to have been born and bred in the heart of Greece.[13] Since he is so valuable, one should not compare the poet to the man who makes the stone true to the plumb line.[14] That is not our aim either. I hope I would not be so stupid as to fail to realize that I myself am far from being able to write an encomium of Aristophanes, given that he too would not be remotely equal to the task of praising himself in the terms he deserves.

Those commentaries took a lot of effort and a long time, if one 3 was to try to put them into better shape; the first difficulty we overcame, even though it was more than one could bear, but the time turned out to be very limited.[15] We did not simply have to put the explanations in order—they were previously in confusion, as you too may know—but we were given the task of correcting them when they had already been printed. The mistakes of the compositors are more complex than the heads of the resurgent Hydra of Lerna and need the assistance of an Iolaos,[16] and the more we cut them back, the more the occasion arose to change

ἡμῖν ἀνεφύοντο τοῦτο μὲν μεταβάλλειν, τὸ δὲ προσ-
τιθέναι τὸ δ' ἀφαιρεῖσθαι τῶν στοιχείων ἀφορμαί. Ἡμῖν
μὲν οὖν ὁ πίθος κεκύλισται ἐς ὠφέλειαν, εἰ μὲν τῶν καθ'
ἡμᾶς Ἑλλήνων οὐκ ἂν ῥᾳδίως ἔχοιμεν εἰπεῖν· πλὴν γὰρ
ὀλίγων τῶν ἀπὸ τῆς προτέρας εὐδαιμονίας ὥσπερ τι
ζώπυρον σωζομένων εἰς τοὺς λοιποὺς μάτην ἄν τις ἐπη-
ρεάζοι περὶ τἀναγκαῖα κατατεινομένους καὶ χαλεπῶς
ὃν τελοῦσι φόρον τῷ βαρβάρῳ ποριζομένους, τῶν δ'
Ἰταλῶν ὅσοις λίαν Ἀττικῶς τῆς γλώττης ἔχειν ἐσπούδασται, καὶ πάνυ ἀκριβῶς οἶδα· τοῖς γε μὴν ὑπὸ τῆς εὐτυ-
χοῦς τῶν Ἐνετῶν ἀριστοκρατουμένοις συγκλήτου, καὶ
αὐτῶν δὴ τῶν Εὐπατρίδων τοῖς γενναιοτέροις τὸ ἦθος,
εἴημεν ἂν εἰκότως κεχαρισμένοι.

4   Τῆς γὰρ Ἀθηναίων πολιτείας, ἧς ἡ βασιλὶς αὕτη τῶν
πόλεων ἔστιν οὗ κατ' ἴχνη χωρεῖ, τὰς Ἀριστοφάνους
κωμῳδίας εἰκόνας εἶναι, παρὰ πάντων σχεδὸν ὡμολόγηται. Ὑμέτερον δ' ἂν εἴη τὸν ἡμῶν κάματον τίθεσθαι
παραπολὺ μήτ' ἐκφαυλίζοντας εἴ τί που ἔλαθεν ἡμᾶς
παραδραμόν, μηδ' ἀργυραμοιβικῶς ἐξ ἅπαντος ἀνιχνεύ-
οντας· ἀλλὰ τῆς μὲν ῥαγείσης νευρᾶς κατὰ τὸν ἐν-
δήμειον τέττιγα τὴν ἐμμελῆ κροῦσιν εὐγνωμόνως ἀνα-
πληροῦντας· πάσης δ' ἀνωτέρω μικρολογίας τῶν ἤδη
τυπωθέντων ἐμφορουμένους, οὕτω δὲ τοὺς ἐπιστάτας τῆς
βιωφελοῦς ταυτησὶ μηχανῆς διεγείραντες ἀκμαιοτέρους
ἢ πρὸ τῆς ἐπιβολῆς πρὸς τὸ καὶ μείζω καὶ πλείω τούτων ὑμῖν ἐκπορίσαι καίπερ οἴκοθεν ὡρμημένους ποιή-
σετε· αἰνουμένας δὲ τέχνας ἐπιδιδόναι πεπαροιμίασται.

Ἀπὸ Ἐνετιῶν.

this, to add that, to delete some letters. At any rate our pot has been fashioned on the wheel[17] so as to give benefit—but whether it is so for today's Greeks I could not say with confidence. Leaving aside the few surviving, like a spark remaining from their previous happy state, it would be pointless to criticize all the others, who struggle to obtain the necessities of life and have difficulty in paying their taxes to the barbarian. But for those Italians who have made great efforts to acquire the language of Athens I am absolutely sure of the benefit. By those admirably governed by the blessed senate of Venice, and among them the nobler members of the patrician class, we should be deservedly appreciated.

It is almost universally agreed that Aristophanes' comedies are a   4
mirror of the Athenian state, in whose tracks this imperial city follows in some respects.[18] You should value our labors seriously and not belittle them for any faults that have slipped in unnoticed—or look for them everywhere in the manner of money changers—but like the local cicada, when a string is broken, you should complete the harmonious melody with goodwill.[19] Being above all pedantic criticism, you should enjoy to the full what has now been printed. In this way you will encourage the masters of this life-enhancing invention and make them, dependent as they are on their own resources,[20] more active than they were before this undertaking, so as to supply you with better and more numerous books than these. It is proverbial that arts which are praised make progress.[21]

From Venice.

C

Σκιπίωνος Καρτερομάχου τοῦ Πιστωριέως.

5   Ὅσσῳ τῶν προτέρων πλείους ποτὲ τἀνδρὸς ἐφεῖντο,
     Τόσσῳ παυρότεροι εἶχον Ἀριστοφάνην·
     Νῦν δ᾽ ὀλίγου παρὰ μὲν πᾶσιν, καὶ πᾶσιν ὀπηδεῖ·
     Μηδένα τῶν πάντων, πῶς γάρ, ἀναινόμενος.
     Αὐτὰρ ἐπεὶ πάντες τὸν ἐρώμενον ἔσχετ᾽ ἐρασταί,
     Χρή γ᾽ Ἄλδῳ πολλὰς εὐθὺς ἔχειν χάριτας·
     Ἄγνωστον δ᾽ αὐτῷ καὶ πλείονας ὅστις ὀφείλει,
     Ἢ ἡμεῖς, ἢ καὶ αὐτὸς Ἀριστοφάνης.

: III :

Μάρκου τοῦ Μουσούρου

1   Ὡς μὲν Ἐνετίῃσι τὸ παρὸν ἐνετυπώθη βιβλίον καὶ ὅτι
     παρ᾽ Ἄλδῳ, καὶ ὡς οὐκ ἄνευ προνομίου, καὶ ὅτι Μουνι-
     χιῶνος φθίνοντος τρίτῃ χιλιοστῷ ῦ ἐννενηκοστῷ θ᾽ ἀπὸ
     τῆς θεογονίας ἔτει, ταῦτα δὴ οὔτε πρὸς ἐμοῦ λέγειν, οὔτε
     τῶν φιλολόγων οὐδεὶς ἄν ποτε τῆς τοιαύτης ἀπειροκα-
     λίας οὐδὲν ἀπόναιτ᾽ ἂν ἀγαθόν.

2   Εἰ δέ τις τῶν ἀκριβῶς τοῖς τῶν πέλας ἐλλείμμασιν
     ἐπεξιόντων ἀκηδῶς ἔχει πρὸς ἣν ἔκκεινται τάξιν αἱ παρ᾽
     ἡμῶν ἐπιστολαί, ἐνθυμείσθω καὶ ἡμᾶς οὐκ ἂν οὕτως
     αὐτὰς ἀγνοήσαντας διαθέσθαι, ὡς ὁ χρόνος ἀπῄτει καθ᾽
     ὃν τῶν ἐπιστειλάντων ἕκαστος ἤνθησεν, εἴ γε πασῶν

C

By Scipio Carteromacus of Pistoia.

In previous generations the more people desired to have the 5
man, the fewer possessed Aristophanes. But now for a small price
he is available to everyone and helps everyone, not refusing anyone
at all—how could he? And since all you lovers have your beloved,
you must at once thank Aldus warmly. He does not know who
helps more people than we do, or indeed Aristophanes himself.

: III :

Musurus on the Epistolographi graeci
(1499)

Marcus Musurus:

That this book was printed in Venice and by Aldus, not without 1
copyright privilege, on the twenty-eighth day of Mounichion[22] in
the year 1499 from the birth of Jesus[23]—these facts are not for me
to point out. Nor should any scholar ever be so lacking in taste as
not to derive some benefit.

But if anyone investigating closely the shortcomings of his 2
neighbors is unhappy with the order of the letters as published by
us, let him take note that we too would not have arranged them
thus, in disregard of the correct date at which each writer flourished, if we had disposed of all the letters at the outset of the en-

ηὐπορῦμεν εὐθὺς ἀρχομένης τῆς πραγματείας. Ὡς γὰρ
εἴχομεν ἐπιχειρήσαντες ὀλίγαις οὔσαις, τὰς ἑκάστοτε
μνηστευομένας ἡμῖν ὁποιασοῦν ἀξιῶσαι προειλόμεθα
λήξεως ἢ τὴν ἐκ τούτων ὠφέλειαν ἀφελέσθαι τοὺς φιλο-
λόγους.

3   Ἔτι κἀκεῖνο πάντας εἰδέναι βουλοίμην, μάλιστα μὲν
ἡμῖν τοῦ ἄριστα διορθώσεως τὴν πραγματείαν ἕξειν
μελῆσαν, εἰ δέ τί που παρέδραμεν, ἢ διεστραμμένον
εἶναι γράμμα ἤ τι τοιοῦτον, οἷον οὐδὲ τοῖς ἄκρῳ φασὶ
δακτύλῳ τῆς Ἑλληνικῆς γευσαμένοις φωνῆς ἐμποδὼν
ἂν πρὸς τὴν ἔννοιαν τοῦ κειμένου γιγνέσθαι. Ἐν μέντοι
τοῖς Ἀλκίφρονος ἔστιν οὗ τῆς ἐννοίας διημαρτῆσθαι,
μηδὲν ἡμῶν παρὰ τὰ ἐν ἀντιγράφοις ἀνηκέστως οὖσι
διεφθαρμένοις ῥιψοκινδύνως καινοτομεῖν τολμησάντων.
Ὅθεν οὐδ' ἐκεῖνό γ' ἄν, εἰ καὶ μάλα φορτικὸν εἰπεῖν, ὑπο-
στειλαίμην, μηδένα τῶν καθ' ἡμᾶς τὰ τοιάδε μεταχειρι-
ζομένων ἐπὶ τοῖς αὐτοῖς οἷς ἡμεῖς ἐνετύχομεν ἀντιγράφοις ὑγιέστερον ἂν ταύτην ἐπανορθῶσαι τὴν βίβλον. Εἰ
δ' ὁμοίως ἡμῖν οὐ φθονῶ ὥστε τὸν ἐφ' ἅπασι σκωμμά-
των εὐποροῦντα Μῶμον ἐνταῦθα μηδὲν ἔχειν μωμήσα-
σθαι τέλεον, ὃ δικαίως ἂν ἡμῖν προστριβείη ἐκτὸς εἰ μὴ
τυχὸν αὐτά γε ταῦτα τὰ κατὰ τὴν κορωνίδα δυσχεραί-
νοι στωμύλα.

terprise. Since we had begun the task with a small number, we preferred to assign each successive additional collection that appealed to us to whatever place was available, rather than deprive students of the benefit to be had from them.[24]

In addition I would like everyone to know that we were concerned to take the greatest care to correct the material as best we could; and if by any chance anything slipped through, that should be a character upside-down or something of that sort, such that it would not be an obstacle to understanding of the text even for people whose fingers, as they say, have barely sampled the Greek language.[25] But in the letters of Alciphron there are passages which make no sense, and we did not dare to make any bold emendations to correct the impossibly corrupt text.[26] So once again, even if it is a presumptuous remark, I would not refrain from saying that no one else of the present generation working on such texts, if presented with the manuscripts that we happened upon, could have produced this edition in a more correct form. On the other hand I do not envy myself. Momus[27] has no valid criticism here, though he is eloquent in ridicule of everything, no criticism that could be flung at me, except perhaps for these concluding ramblings.

: IV :

Gulielmus Grocinus Britannus Aldo Manutio Romano s. p. d.

1 Rediit in Britanniam nuper amicus meus summus, idemque tuus, Alde humanissime, Thomas Linacrus saluus (est deo gratia) et incolumis. Is cum tua singularia in se merita abunde mihi exposuisset, facile perfecit, ut te uel hoc solo nomine mirifice diligerem, perinde gratum existimans quicquid in eum contuleris officii, ac si in me ipsum contulisses. Debent enim τὰ τῶν φίλων κοινά. Quamquam (neque enim dissimulare fas est) non nihil iam in meipsum profiteor esse a te et priuatim et publice collatum. Adeo me tibi iam triplici nomine, uel amici, uel meo, uel (quod omnia complectitur) publico debere prae me fero.

2 Atque, ut de publico in omnes beneficio pauca commemorem, id mihi uidetur eiusmodi, ut haud sciam quid potissimum mirer aut laudem, ingenium an iudicium, fiduciam an industriam, foelicitatem and benignitatem. Non enim potuisses neque sine summo ingenio mirum illud artificium ad imprimendas praesertim graecas literas excogitatum assequi; neque sine acerrimo iudicio in deligendis authoribus, quorum impressa uolebas opera, idque contra Ciceronis censuram, Aristotelem Platoni anteponere—in quo etiam ego tuae nimirum accedo sententiae, ut qui inter summos philosophos Aristotelem et Platonem tantum interesse arbitror, quantum (pace omnium dixerim) inter πολυμαθῆ καὶ πολυμυθῆ—; neque sine incredibili fiducia rem tantam praesertim in maximis difficultatibus temporum aggredi; neque sine mira diligentia, inchoa-

: IV :

William Grocyn's letter to Aldus
(August 27, [1499])[28]

William Grocyn of Britain to Aldus Manutius of Rome, warm greetings.

Aldus, kindest of men: My best friend—and yours too—Thomas 1
Linacre, recently returned to Britain safe and sound, thanks be
to God. When he told me of your extraordinary services to him,
he easily ensured that I should feel marvelous affection for you
on this account alone, since I reckon I should be grateful for any
services done to him as though they were also done for me. For
"all things ought to be common among friends."[29] Yet I confess (since it's wrong to disguise it) that you have already conferred both a private and a public benefit on me. Indeed I declare
that I am your debtor thrice over, for a friend, for myself, and for
the public—the last category comprehending them all.

Let me say a few words about the public benefits conferred on 2
everyone. The case is such that I do not know what I admire the
most or what I should most praise: your ingenuity or good judgment, your confidence or your industry, your good fortune or your
goodwill. You could not have devised without the highest degree
of ingenuity that marvelous technique for printing Greek letters.[30]
Nor without the finest judgment [could you have succeeded] in
choosing the authors whose works you wanted to print, even put-
ting Aristotle ahead of Plato, despite the considered opinion of
Cicero.[31] (In this matter I too certainly take your view, since I feel
that the difference between these two greatest of philosophers is
simply—forgive me, everyone—the difference between a polymath
and a "polymyth."[32]) Nor without incredible confidence could you
have undertaken so great a project, especially amid the very great
difficulties of our times. Nor without a wondrous amount of effort

tam inter tot impedimenta persequi. Denique quid uideri potest, aut foelicius quam posse, aut benignius quam uelle literatissimos quosque tuo demereri obsequio?

3   Quocirca cum tuum istud tam late pateat munus amplissimum, ut orbem terrarum propemodum obstrinxeris memoria beneficii sempiterna, cumque praeterea huc accesserit tuum in nos, nos inquam diuisos toto orbe Britannos, priuatum munus, idemque cum ipso publico munere coniunctissimum, fatear necesse est nos (si modo grati esse uolumus) non solum cum caeteris omnibus, sed etiam plusquam caeteros omnes tibi debere. Et quamquam maior est magnitudo beneficii tui, quam ut parem tibi pro eo gratiam referre possimus, nos tamen nunquam pudebit accepti, magis quam te poenitebit collati. Quod ne fiat summopere curabimus.

4   Noster item Linacrus nuntiauit mihi te rem multo magis admirandam moliri, iamque statutum habere, ut libros sacros Veteris quidem Testamenti trifariam, latine, graece, et hebraice, Noui autem bifariam graece et latine imprimas, opus plane arduum et christiano uiro dignissimum. In quo, si modo perficere licebit, non modo caeteros omnes, qui unquam in hoc genere floruerunt, sed etiam te ipsum longo interuallo superabis. Age igitur, mi Alde, auspicare tandem opus quod cogitas, et quod iandiu parturis, aliquando parias. Non enim adduci possum, ut credam, posse opus tam diuinum secundis carere successibus. Nam quod ad nos attinet, nihil plane praetermittemus, quod huic rei futurum adiumento uidebitur. De iis, quae tibi a nobis priuatim debentur, noli laborare. Curauimus ut prope diem satis tibi fiat. Vale.

Ex urbe Londino VI Calen. Septembr.

could you have continued what you had begun amid so many obstacles. Finally, what could be thought more fortunate than the ability, or more benevolent than the wish, to earn the repect of all learned men?

On this account, since the extraordinary extent of your public services is so obvious that you have obliged almost the whole world to remember them forever, and since moreover you have added to them in our own case — we Britons separated from the whole world[33] — a private service, one closely connected with that public service, I confess that, so long as we wish to show our gratitude, we must be under obligations to you not only along with the rest of the world, but even more than the rest. And although the service you have done us is greater than we can repay, we shall never be ashamed of receiving great benefits any more than you will regret having conferred them. We shall try very hard that the latter may not happen.

Our Linacre tells me you are planning a still more remarkable work, and have already set it on foot: the printing of the Scriptures, the Old Testament in Latin, Greek and Hebrew, and the New in Greek and Latin — a most arduous work and one most worthy of a Christian man. In this, if you are but permitted to finish it, you will surpass not only all those who have ever shone in this branch of learning, but by a great stride outdistance even yourself. Go on, then, my Aldus, with this plan, and set to work; bring to birth at last what has cost you so prolonged a labor; for I cannot be brought to believe that so divine an undertaking can fail of success. As for ourselves, we shall omit nothing which is likely to be useful in the matter; and as to what we privately owe you, do not trouble yourself. We have taken care that you shall be satisfied at an early day. Farewell.

From the city of London, August 27.

: V :

Νεακαδημίας Νόμος

1 Ἐπειδὴ πολλὰ καὶ ὠφέλιμα τοῖς περὶ παιδείαν ἐσπου-
δακόσι παραγίνεσθαι πέφυκεν ἐκ τῆς ἑλληνικῆς ὁμιλίας, δέδοκται κοινῇ τοῖς τρισὶν ἡμῖν, Ἄλδῳ τῷ Ῥωμαίῳ,
Ἰωάννῃ τῷ Κρητὶ, καὶ τρίτῳ ἐμοὶ Σκιπίωνι τῷ Καρτερο-
μάχῳ, νόμον θέσθαι, μὴ ἄλλως ἐξεῖναι ἀλλήλοις ὁμιλεῖν,
εἰ μὴ τῇ Ἑλλάδι φωνῇ. Εἴ τις δὲ ἄλλως διαλέγοιτο ἐν
ἡμῖν, ἢ ἐξεπίτηδες, ἢ μὴ προνοούμενος, ἢ καὶ αὐτοῦ τοῦ
νόμου ἐπιλαθόμενος, ἢ κατ' ἄλλην τινὰ τύχην. ζημιούσθω
ἀργυρίδιον ἕν, ὁποσάκις ἂν τύχῃ τοῦτο ποιῶν· σολοι-
κισμοῦ δὲ μὴ κείσθω ζημία, εἰ μὴ ἄρα τις ἐπιτηδεύων
ἐξαμάρτοι καὶ τοῦτο.

2 Καταβαλέτω δὲ ὁ ἐξαμαρτὼν τὸ ἐπιτίμιον εὐθὺς, μηδ'
ἀναβαλέσθω ἔστ' αὔριον, ἔστ' ἔννηφιν. μὴ ἀποτίσας δὲ,
διπλάσιον ὀφειλέτω μὴ δοὺς δὲ καὶ τοῦτο, τετραπλάσιον,
καὶ κατὰ λόγον ἀεὶ τῆς ὑπερθέσεως, εἰσπραττέσθω.

3 Ὀλιγωρῶν δὲ τοῦ νόμου, ἢ καὶ τοῦ ἐκτίνειν ὑπεριδὼν,
τοῦ κοινοῦ τῶν Ἑλληνικῶν ἀπελαυνέσθω, καὶ τῆς τῶν
σπουδαίων ὁμιλίας ἀπαξιούσθω, καὶ τὸ ἀπὸ τούτου
ἀποφρὰς νομιζέσθω τὸ τοῦ τοιούτου ἀπάντημα.

4 Ἐμβεβλήσθω δὲ τὸ καταβαλλόμενον ἀργυρίδιον ἑκάστοτε εἰς βαλάντιόν τι, ἢ καὶ νὴ Δία πυξίδα, εἰς τοῦτο
μόνον ἐκτετορνευμένην, αὕτη δὲ παραδεδόσθω εἰς φυλα-
κὴν, ἢ ἡμῶν τινι, ἢ τῷ χειροτονηθέντι ὑφ' ἡμῶν, ᾡτινιοῦν,

: V :

Statutes of the New Academy
(1502?)

Whereas many benefits can accrue to people with a serious inter- 1
est in education from speaking Greek, it has been jointly determined by the three of us, Aldus the Roman, John the Cretan[34] and
thirdly myself, Scipione Forteguerri, to pass a law that they should
not speak to each other except in Greek. If any of us, whether
deliberately or without thinking, talks in another language, forget-
ting this[35] law or for some other reason, he shall be fined one small
coin for each occasion on which he happens to do this. But there
shall not be a penalty for solecism, unless someone does that too
deliberately.

The guilty party shall pay the fine at once without postpone- 2
ment to the following day or the day after that. If he does not pay,
he shall owe twice the amount; if the does not pay that either, he
shall owe four times the amount, and shall always be charged according to the length of the delay.

For disregard of the law or failure to pay he shall be expelled 3
from the community of the Grecians and declared unworthy to
associate with serious people; and thereafter an encounter with
such a person shall be deemed unlucky.[36]

Each coin paid shall be put in a purse or by Zeus a casket 4
crafted for this purpose alone, which shall be handed over for safe
keeping either to me or to someone elected by us, any person

καὶ ἀξίῳ κριθέντι, ἐπικεκλεισμένη πρότερον ἐπιμελῶς, καὶ ἐπεσφραγισμένη ἐς τὸ ἀσφαλέστατον. Ὅταν δὲ ἀνοιχθῆναι δοκῇ, εἰς τὸ μέσον προτεθείσθω, καὶ διηριθμήσθω τὸ νόμισμα, καὶ εἰ μὲν ἱκανὸν ᾖ εἰς συμποσίου τιμήν τε καὶ δαπάνημα, ἐγκεχειρίσθω Ἄλδῳ τῷ κυρίῳ, ἀφ' ὧν ἡμᾶς ἐκεῖνος ἑστιάτω λαμπρῶς, καὶ οὐ κατὰ τοὺς ἐντυπωτὰς, ἀλλ' ἀνδράσι πρεπόντως τοῖς τὴν νεακαδημίαν ὀνειροπολοῦσιν ἤδη, καὶ πλατωνικῶς μικροῦ δεῖν κατασκευάσασιν αὐτήν. Εἰ δὲ μήπω ἱκανὸν τ' ἀργύριον εἰς τὸ συμπόσιον, ἀναποτεθείσθω πάλιν εἰς τὴν πυξίδα, καὶ ἀναφείσθω ἕως οὗ τοσοῦτον ἐνείη τε, καὶ ἐγγένοιτο, ὅσον ἐξαρκεῖν εἰς τὴν ἑστίασιν.

5 Ἐξέστω δὲ μηδένα ἡμῖν συμπότην παραλαβεῖν, πλὴν εἰ ἄρα τῶν φιλελλήνων τινὰ, οὐκ ἀνάξιον τοῦ χοροῦ τοῦτ' ἔστιν οὐκ ἄμουσον, οὐκ ἄμοιρον τῶν ἑλληνικῶν, καὶ τὸ μέγιστον, τῆς Νεακαδημίας οὐκ ἀλλότριον, οὐκ ἄπειρον, οὐδ' ἀμύητον τῶν ἡμετέρων· εἰ δέ τις ξένος ἢ τῶν ἔξωθεν (οἷα φιλεῖ) ἀφίκοιτο ποτε, καὶ ἐπιδημοίη ἐνταῦθα κατά τινα χρείαν, εἰ μὲν πεπαιδευμένος καὶ τῶν ἑλληνικῶν ἐπιστήμων, καὶ αὐτὸς ἔνοχος ἔστω τοῖς ἀναγεγραμμένοις, ἀντιτείνων δὲ τῷ νόμῳ ἢ ἐναντιούμενος, μηδεμιᾶς τυχὼν συγγνώμης, μηδὲ ἀπολογίας τινὸς, ἐρήμην εὐθὺς καταδεδικάσθω, καὶ τῆς Νεακαδημίας ἐκδεδιώχθω ἀνάξιος ὢν, καὶ τοὐντεῦθεν μηκέτι εἰσδεδέχθω ἐν ἡμῖν, εἰ μὴ μετανοῶν ἐφ' οἷς ἥμαρτε, τοῖς ἅπαξ κατασταθεῖσιν ἐμμένειν ὑποστῇ, καὶ ὥσπερ ἐγγυητὰς καταστήσῃ. Εἰ δ' αὖθις μὴ εἰδὼς τὰ ἑλληνικὰ, ὡς μήπω τούτων ἡμμένος εἰ μὴ ἐπὶ τοσοῦτον, ὥσθ' ἑλληνίζειν δύνασθαι, ἀλλ' ἐν

judged worthy. It shall first be locked and carefully sealed for
safety's sake; and when it is to be opened it shall be displayed to all
and the money counted; and if there is enough for the cost and
outlay of a party, it shall be handed to Aldus as master, and from
it he shall entertain us handsomely, not in the style for the typesetters but for men who are already quite properly dreaming of the
New Academy and have all but established it after the fashion of
Plato. But if the money is not yet enough for a party, it shall be
put back in the casket and left until there is enough in it, so that it
is sufficient for an entertainment.

It shall not be possible for us to bring a guest unless he is one 5
of the philhellenes, not unworthy of the group, that is, not uncultivated, not uninterested in things Greek, and above all not alien
to the New Academy, nor ignorant of or uninitiated in our affairs.
If a visitor or someone from elsewhere should arrive, as happens,
and stay here on business, if he is cultivated and knows Greek, he
too shall be subject to the stated regulations, and shall not be par-
doned for opposition to the rules or obstruction nor given a defense, but shall immediately lose his case by default. He shall be
expelled as unworthy of the New Academy and not be readmitted
thereafter to our company unless he repents of his misbehavior
and agrees to abide by the rules once they have been established,
providing as it were guarantees. If on the other hand there is[37]
someone not knowing Greek, or not sufficiently to be able to
speak it,[38] but still receiving instruction in such matters and keen

τοῖς τοιούτοις ἔτι παιδευομένος, ἢ καὶ παιδεύεσθαι προ-
θυμούμενος, καὶ οὗτος ἐν ἡμῖν ἐξετασθεὶς ἐθιζέσθω καὶ
αὐτὸς κατὰ μικρὸν τὰ ὅμοια ἡμῖν ἑλληνίζειν· ἀτακτήσας
δὲ, ἢ καὶ νὴ διὰ καταγελάσας τῆς διατριβῆς, ἀποκεκλεί-
σθω τοῦ λοιποῦ, μηδ' αὖθις τῆς συνουσίας ἀξιούσθω,
μηδ' ἂν πάνυ δέοιτο.

6   Εἰσηγήσατο τὸν νόμον Σκιπίων Καρτερόμαχος, φυλῆς ἀναγνωστίδος· ἐπεψήφισαν Ἄλδος Ῥωμαῖος, ὁ τῆς
Νεακαδημίας ἀρχηγέτης, καὶ Ἰωάννης Κρὴς, φυλῆς δι-
ορθωτίδος, πρυτανεύοντες· ἐπεχειροτόνησαν δὲ οἱ Νεακα-
δημαικοὶ πάντες, ὧν Βαπτιστὴς πρεσβύτερος, φυλῆς
ἱεροπρεπίδος, καὶ Παῦλος Ἐνετὸς, φυλῆς εὐγενετίδος, καὶ
Ἱερώνυμος Λουχαῖος ἰατρὸς, φυλῆς θεραπευτίδος, καὶ
Φράγκισκος Ῥόσηττος Βηρωναῖος, φυλῆς διδασκαλίδος,
καὶ ἄλλοι συχνοὶ μαθητιῶντες ἤδη, καὶ τῆς Νεακαδημίας ἐπιθυμοῦντες, ὀνόματι μόνον προσαγόμενοι.

7   Εἴη δὲ εὐτυχεῖν ταύτην εἰς ἅπαντα, καὶ τοὺς αὐτῆς
ἐχομένους.

to be educated, he too shall adapt himself to our ways and little by little shall become accustomed to speak Greek as we do. But if he misbehaves or scorns our procedures, he shall be excluded thereafter and not deemed worthy of our company again, even if he urgently requests it.

The statute was proposed by Scipione Forteguerri of the tribe[39] 6 of readers. It was put to the vote by Aldus of Rome, founder of the New Academy, and John the Cretan of the tribe of correctors, presiding officers. All the New Academicians voted in favor, among them Battista the Elder of the tribe of priests,[40] Paul of Venice, of the tribe of nobles,[41] Girolamo Lucchaio, doctor of the tribe of healers, and Francesco Rosseto of Verona, of the tribe of teachers, and many others anxious to learn and desirous of the New Academy, attracted by the mere name.

May it and those attached to it flourish in all respects. 7

: VI :

A

Aldus Romanus Accursio Mainero Avenionensi iure
consulto ac legato Christianissimi Gallorum regis
apud Venetos, oratori prudentissimo, s. p. d.

1 Bessarionis cardinalis, Graeci hominis, quam doctissimos libros
adversus calumniatorem Platonis in aedibus nostris summa cura
nuper informatos tibi, viro doctissimo et doctrinae Platonis perstudioso, nuncupamus donoque mittimus. Placituros enim tibi
summopere certo scimus, tum quia Platonem tuentur, tum etiam
quod tanti viri aurea documenta ingeniose et breviter complectun-
tur. Nam, praeter doctissimas disputationes et caetera, quae ad
doctrinam faciunt, toto hoc libro dispersa, operae pretium inibi est
legere, quonam modo se ipsum quisque, tum domum et familiam,
hinc res publicas sapienter regere et gubernare possit. Nihil enim
fere a Platone tractatum est vitae hominum conducibile, quod hoc
volumine adductum brevissime non habeatur. Quare inter summas occupationes tuas, Christianissimi regis legatus, dum remit-
tere relaxareque animum voles, has Bessarionis utilissimas lucubrationes legendas damus, simulque ut sint Aldi tui apud te assiduum
monimentum et pignus amoris. Vale.

: VI :

Aldus' preface to Bessarion's In calumniatorem Platonis
(*July 1503*)

A

*Aldus of Rome to Accursio Maino of Avignon, jurisconsult and
envoy of the most Christian king of France in Venice,
ambassador of great wisdom, warmest greetings.*

We are dedicating to you, and sending as a gift, since you are a   1
man of great learning and keen student of Plato, the extremely
erudite books by Bessarion the Greek cardinal, which we have just
produced with the utmost care in our house.[42] We are quite certain that they will give you pleasure, both because they defend
Plato and because with subtlety and brevity they cover the golden
teachings of such a great man. For apart from the learned discus-
sions and all the other matters relating to his teaching which are
scattered throughout this book, it is worth reading there how any
man may prudently conduct and rule himself, his house and his
family, and beyond that the state. For of all Plato's proposals for
the benefit of humanity practically none is missing from this volume, and they are presented with great brevity. So in your busy
round of duty as ambassador of the most Christian king, when
you wish to relax and refresh your mind, we offer you these very
valuable essays by Bessarion as reading matter, to be at the same
time a lasting souvenir from your friend Aldus and a proof of his
esteem. Farewell.

B

2   Excusa iam parte libri tertii, allatum ad me est hoc Bessarionis opus manu scriptum perquam diligenter et emendate, ubi etiam Graecum inierat totum manu ipsius Bessarionis; quo multa correximus, quae perperam Romae impressa fuerant, accentusque addidimus. In eo opere est argumentum libro tertio praeponendum, quod in libris Romae impressis non haberi demiror. Id, ne periret, hic ego imprimendum curavi.

: VII :

Σκιπίων Καρτερόμαχος Ἄλδῳ τῷ Ῥωμαίῳ, εὖ πράττειν.

Τὰ τίμια ὅσῳ μικρότερα, τοσούτῳ καὶ χαριέστερα δοκεῖ τοῖς πολλοῖς. ὡς γάρ φησι τὸ ἐπίγραμμα, χάρις βαιοῖσιν ὀπηδεῖ. τὸ οὖν ἐπιγραμμάτων βιβλίον ἐπιγραφόμενον τῶν ποιητικῶν ἁπάντων τὸ τιμιώτατων, εἰς βραχύτατον ὡς οἷόν τ' ἦν, συναγαγὼν σὺ τῇ τυπώσει, χαριέστατον ἅπασι παρεσκουάσω, ὡς μηδένα ἂν εἶναι τὸν μὴ τῷ τοιούτῳ ἐπιμανησόμενον. οὐ γὰρ τοσοῦτον τῶν ἐμπεριειλημμένων τὸ φίλτρον προσάξεται αὐτούς, ὅσον τὸ εὐμεταχείριστον. πλεῖστα τοίνυν ὠφελήσας αὐτὸς τοὺς φιλοκάλους εἰς τὴν τῶν βιβλίων κτῆσιν, πῶς ἂν καὶ εἰς τὴν χρῆσιν ἤδη αὐτῶν ὠφελοῖντο προσεπινε-

B

When part of Book III had already been printed, a manuscript   2
copy of this work by Bessarion, very carefully and accurately written, reached me. It included[43] the whole of the Greek also, in
Bessarion's own hand.[44] From it we corrected much that had been
badly printed in Rome and added the accents. In this work there is
a summary to be prefixed to Book III; to my great surprise this is
not included in the Roman edition.[45] To ensure that it is not lost I
have had it printed in this volume.

: VII :

*Letter of Scipione Forteguerri to Aldus
printed on the last page of the 1503 edition
of the* Greek Anthology

Scipio Carteromachus to Aldus the Roman, greetings.

The smaller valuable objects are, the more attractive they seem to
most people. For as the epigram says, "Elegance keeps company
with miniature things."[46] So you have collected together in a
printed version as minute as possible the book entitled "epigrams,"
the most valuable of all poetic works. You have made it most ap-
pealing to everyone, and there could not possibly be any person
who failed to be madly attracted by such a product. The charm of
its contents will not contribute as much as its handiness. Therefore, having given so much help to men with good taste in the
acquisition of books, you have in addition found a way to facilitate

νόηκας, μὴ τῷ τῶν κρατουμένον ὄγκῳ βαρούμενοι τῶν ἀναγινωσκομένον τῆς διανοίας ἀπασχοληθεῖεν. ἔρρωσο.

: VIII :

1 Aesop. Habentur hoc volumine haec, videlicet: Vita et fabellae Aesopi cum interpretatione latina, ita tamen ut separari a graeco possit pro uniuscuiusque arbitrio, quibus traducendis multum certe elaborauimus. Nam quae ante tralata habebantur infida admodum erant, quod facillimum erit conferenti cognoscere. Gabriae fabellae tres et quadraginta ex trimetris iambis, praeter ultimam ex scazonte, cum latina interpretatione. Quas idcirco bis curauimus informandas, quia priores, ubi latinum a graeco seiungi potest, admodum quam incorrecte excusae fuerant exempli culpa. Quare nacti emendatum exemplum, operae pretium uisum est iterum excudendas curare, ut ex secundis prima queant corrigi. Phurnutus seu, ut alii, Curnutus de natura deorum. Palaephatus de non credendis historiis. Heraclides Ponticus de allegoriis apud Homerum. Ori Apollinis Niliaci hieroglyphica. Collectio prouerbiorum Tarrhaei et Didymi, item eorum, quae apud Sudam, aliosque habentur per ordinem literarum. Ex Aphthonii exercitamentis de fabula. Tum de formicis et cicadis graece et latine. De fabula ex imaginibus Philostrati graece et latine. Ex Hermogenis exercitamenta de fabula Prisciano interprete. Apologus Aesopi de cassita apud Gellium.

Venetiis apud Aldum mense Octobri MDV.

their use, lest readers should be distracted from the contents of the text by the weight of the volumes being handled. Farewell.

: VIII :

The title page of Aldus' Aesop
(*October 1505*)

Aesop. This volume contains the following, namely: A life and the   1
Fables of Aesop with a Latin translation, but arranged so that it may be separated from the Greek as each person chooses; we have surely spent a great deal of effort in translating them. The previous translation was quite unfaithful, which will be readily apparent upon comparison. Forty-three fables of Babrius in iambic trimeter, except the last which is in scazons, with a Latin translation. We have printed these twice because the first time, where the Latin can be separated from the Greek, it was rather incorrectly printed owing to a faulty exemplar. Hence, coming across a corrected copy, it seemed worthwhile to edit it a second time, so that the first text could be corrected from the second. Phornutus or, as some say, Curnutus, *On the Nature of the Gods*.[47] Palaephatus, *On Not Believing Stories*. Heraclides Ponticus, *On Allegories in Homer*. Horopollo's *Hieroglyphica*. [Lucilius of] Tarrha's *Collection of Proverbs*, Didymus' similar collection from the *Suda*, and others in alphabetical order. *Lessons on the Fable* from Aphthonius. Then, *On Ants and Cicadas* in Greek and Latin.[48] *On the Fable* from Philostratus' *Icones* in Greek and Latin. *Lessons on the Fable* from Hermogenes, translated by Priscian. Aesop's *Apology for the Lark*, from Gellius.[49]

Venice, from Aldus, October 1505.

: IX :

Aldus studiosis s.

1 Erasmus Roterodamus, homo et Graece et Latine doctissimus, Hecubam et Iphigeniam in Aulide, Euripidis tragoedias, carminibus nuper quidem Latinas fecit, sed admodum quam fideliter et erudite. Quamobrem curavi eas excudendas characteribus nostris, tum doctissimi viri rogatu et amici mei summi, tum quia vobis utilissimum fore existimabam et intelligendis Graecis et interpretandis. Quo fit, ut vobis plurimum gratuler. Deerant olim boni libri, deerant docti praeceptores; eorum enim, qui callerent utranque linguam, mira paucitas. Nunc est, Deo gratia, et bonorum librorum copia et doctorum hominum, tam in Italia quam extra, ita ut de conducendo tractet iam rhetore Thule. Non poenitet igitur me magnorum laborum, quos iam multos annos edendis bonis autoribus vestra et bonarum literarum caussa perfero; immo plenus gaudii — cur enim dissimulem? — sic mecum saepe: 'Eia, Alde, βάλλ᾿ οὔτως!' Quod si maius quiddam, ut spero, praestare potuero, felices quidem vos eritis, sed feliciores posteri; ipse autem sublimi feriam sydera vertice. Valete.

: IX :

Aldus' preface to Erasmus' translation of Euripides
(December 1507)

Aldus to students.

Erasmus of Rotterdam,[50] a man very expert in Greek and Latin, 1
has quite recently translated Euripides' tragedies *Hecuba* and *Iphige-
neia in Aulis* into Latin, in verse, but pretty faithfully and in scholarly style. So I have had them printed in our type, partly at the
request of the learned scholar who is my close friend, partly because I thought it would be a great help to you in understanding
and translating Greek. The result is that I am very happy for you.
In the past there was a lack of good books, a lack of learned teachers, since there were surprisingly few who excelled in both languages. Now, thanks be to God, there are many good books and
learned scholars in Italy and abroad, so that Thule is negotiating a
contract for a teacher of rhetoric.[51] So I do not regret my great
efforts, which I have now performed for many years in editing
good authors for your sake and for that of literary studies. In fact
I am full of joy — why should I conceal the fact? — and often say to
myself, "Now, Aldus, carry on like this!" If I can produce something more important, as I hope, you will certainly be delighted,
but posterity will be the greater beneficiaries; for myself, "with my
head I shall touch the stars."[52] Farewell.

: X :

Μ. ΜΟΤΣΟΤΡΟΤ.

1 Θεῖε Πλάτων, ξυνοπαδὲ θεοῖς καὶ δαίμοσιν ἥρως
  Πασσυδίῃ μεγάλῳ Ζηνὶ παρεσπομένοις,
  Ἅρμα κατ᾽ οὐρανὸν εὐρὺν ἀελλοπόδων ὅτε πώλων
  Κεῖνος ἐλᾷ πτηνῷ δίφρῳ ἐφεζόμενος,
  Εἰ δ᾽ ἄγε νῦν κατάβηθι λιπὼν χορὸν οὐρανιώνων   5
  Ἐς γᾶν ψυχοφυῶν εἰρεσίῃ πτερύγων,
  Καὶ λάζευ τόδε τεῦχος, ὁ Σωκρατικὴν ὀαριστὺν
  Ἀμφὶς ἔχει καὶ σῆς κεδνὰ γένεθλα φρενός.

2 Ὧι ἐνὶ κοσμοτέχνης ὀκτὼ πτύχας Οὐλύμποιο
  Ἐξ ἰδίων ἕλκων ἀρχέτυπον πραπίδων,   10
  Δείματο καρπαλίμως, ὑπάτην σελάεσσιν ἀπείροις
  Δαιδάλλων, τήν περ κλείομεν ἀπλανέα.
  Τὰς δ᾽ ἀρ ὑφεξείης μονοφελλέας ἐξετόρευσεν
  Αὐτόθεν ἀκροτάτης ἀντία κινυμένας.
  Ἡ σφέας ἁρπάζουσα παλιμπλάγκτοιο κελεύθου   15
  Σύρει ἀναγκαίῃ, ταὶ δὲ βιαζόμεναι
  Οὐκ ἀέκουσαι ἕπονται, ὁμῶς ἐὸν οἶμον ἑκάστη
  Ἔμπαλιν ἐξανύει βάρδιον ἢ τάχιον.

3 Ὧι ἐνὶ κυδρὸς ἔρως ἀπὸ γαίης ὑψόσ᾽ ἀείρων,
  Ἱμέρῳ ἄμμε φλέγει κάλλεος οὐρανίου.   20
  Ὧι ἐνὶ σὺ ψυχᾶς φύσιν ἄφθορον, οὐδ᾽ ἀμενηνοῦ
  Σκήνευς ὀλλυμένου δεῖξας ἀπολλυμένην.

: X :

Musurus' poem on Plato, in the Complete Works
(1513)

By Marcus Musurus.[53]

Divine Plato, companion hero of gods and divinities who at full   1
speed follow great Zeus when he, sitting in his winged chariot,
with storm-swift steeds drives across the breadth of the heavens,[54]
please now leave the celestial company and with the energy of
spiritual wings descend to earth. Accept this volume, which contains separately Socratic discourse and the noble creations of your
mind.[55]

In it the architect of the cosmos,[56] deriving a pattern from his   2
own intellect,[57] swiftly constructed the eight layers of Olympus,
crafting a superior one with innumerable bright lights, which we
call the unmoved one. Then without delay he constructed the others in sequence with their individual light,[58] moving in opposite
direction to the furthest one. It grips them and sweeps them forc-
ibly along their reverse path, and they under pressure follow not
unwillingly, but each alike[59] performs its own journey again at a
greater or lesser speed.

In it glorious love raises us high above the earth and fires us   3
with desire for heavenly beauty.[60] In it you show the indestructible
nature of the soul, not destroyed as a weak vessel that perishes.[61]

Ἄλλοτε διογενῶν πόλιν οὐρανογείτονα φωτῶν
Κτίζεις, οἷσι μέλει πότνα δικαιοσύνη
Ἠδὲ καὶ εὐνομίη κουροτρόφος, οὐδ' ἀπ' ἐκείνου   25
Νόσφιν ἀπετραπέτην ἄστεος ὄσσε πάλιν
Αἰδὼς καὶ νέμεσις· τίς ἕκαστά κε μυθολογεύοι
Ὅσσα θεοπνεύστοις ταῖσδ' ἐνέθου σελίσι;
4   Τάς γε λαβὼν ἀφίκοιο πόλιν βασιληΐδα πασέων,
Ὅσσας οὐρανόθεν δέρκεται ἠέλιος,   30
Ῥώμην ἑπτάλοφον γαίης κράτος αἰὲν ἔχουσαν.
Ἧς διὰ μεσσατίης Θύμβρις ἑλισσόμενος,
Κοίρανος ἑσπερίων ποταμῶν, κερατηφόρος εἶσιν
Οὖθαρ πιαίνων βώλακος Αὐσονίης.
Ἐλθὼν δ' οὐ Σικελῶν ὀλοόφρονα κεῖθι τύραννον   35
Ὠμοφάγον Σκύλλης λευγαλέης τρόφιμον,
Ὑβριστὴν μουσέων Διονύσιον, ἀλλά γε δήεις
Ὧι τόθ' ὅμοιον ἰδεῖν φῶτα μάτην ἐπόθεις,
Ἀμφότερον σοφίης τε πρόμον καὶ ποιμένα λαῶν
Ὁππόσοι Εὐρώπην ναιετάουσιν ὅλην,   40
Λαυριάδην ἐρατῆς Φλωρεντίδος ἀστέρα πάτρης
Λαμπρὸν, ἀτὰρ Μεδίκων τῶν ὀνομαστοτάτων,
Τηλεθόον καλὸν ἔρνος ἀειθαλὲς ἀγλαόκαρπον
Τὸ πρὶν Ἰωάννην, νῦν δ' ἄρ' ἀπειρεσίων
Γαιάων ἐσσῆνα Λεόντα, κράτιστον Ὀλύμπου   45
Κλειδοῦχον, τοῦ νεῦμ' ὡς Διὸς ἁζόμεθα.
Πᾶς ὃν ἄναξ σέβεται γουνούμενος, οὐδέ τις αὐτῷ
Τολμᾷ σκηπτούχων ἀντιφεριζέμεναι·
Εἰσβὰς δ' ὀλβιόδαιμον ἀνάκτορον, εὐθὺς ἐραστὰς
Σεῖο, Πλάτων, πολλοὺς ὄψεαι ἐν μεγάροις   50

At other times you establish an almost heavenly city of divinely born mortals, whose concern is for Justice as their overlord, with good laws that support their young, while Respect and Retribution do not avert their eyes from that community.[62] Who could recount in full all that you have included in these divinely inspired pages?

May you then go to the city which rules over all that the sun   4
looks down upon from heaven, Rome of the seven hills with eternal power on earth. Making its circuitous way through the middle of it the Tiber, lord of western rivers, a horned god,[63] enriches the fertile soil of the Ausonian land.[64] On arrival there you will not find a brutal Sicilian tyrant, the ferocious protégé of dreadful Scylla, Dionysius the enemy of the Muses,[65] but someone like the mortal whom you hoped to see in the past, a man who is both a leader in wisdom and a shepherd of his peoples living throughout Europe—the son of Lorenzo, the bright star of his beautiful Florentine homeland, from the most distinguished family of the Medici,[66] a noble scion, luxuriant, ever-flourishing, of finest fruit. Formerly Giovanni, now Leo, lord of unlimited lands, mighty keeper of the keys of Olympus, his nod we revere as that of Zeus.[67] Every ruler kneels before him respectfully; none of the kings dares oppose him. Entering the divinely blessed palace you, Plato, will immediately see many of your admirers in the halls, devotees of all kinds of virtue, pleasing and trusted companions of

Παντοίαις ἀρεταῖσι μεμηλότας, ἠδ᾽ ὀαριστὰς
Τερπνοὺς καὶ πινυτοὺς Ζηνὸς ἐπιχθονίου.
Πάντοθεν οὓς αὐτὸς μετεπέμψατο, καί σφισι χαίρει,
Τιμήεντα διδοὺς καὶ πολύολβα γέρα.
5 Ἔξοχα δ᾽ αὖ περὶ κῆρι φιλεῖ δύο, τὸν μὲν ἀφ᾽ ἱρῆς   55
Ἑλλάδος οὐχ ἕνα τῶν, οἳ πελόμεσθα τανῦν,
Ῥωμαῖοι Γραικοί τε καλούμενοι, ἀλλὰ παλαιοῖς
Ἀτθίδος ἢ Σπάρτης εἴκελον ἡμιθέοις·
Λασκαρέων γενεῆς ἐρικυδέος ἄκρον ἄωτον.
Καὶ τριπροσωποφανοῦς οὔνομ᾽ ἔχοντα θεοῦ.   60
Ὅς μ᾽ ἔτι τυτθὸν ἐόντα πατὴρ ἅτε φίλτατον υἱὸν
Στεργόμενος περὶ δὴ στέρξεν ἀπὸ κραδίης.
Καί μοι στεῖνος ὁδοῦ πρὸς Ἀχαιΐδα μοῦσαν ἀγούσης
Δεῖξεν ἀριγνώτως μοῦνος ἐπιστάμενος.
Τὸν δ᾽ ἕτερον τριπλαῖσι κεκασμένον εὐεπίῃσι,   65
Καὶ πλασθέντα τριῶν χερσὶ σοφαῖς χαρίτων,
Βεμβιάδην ἥρωα, πατὴρ δὲ συνίστορα πάντων
Θῆκεν ἀπορρήτων οὔατα τοῦδε μέγας,
Πάντα οἱ ἐξαυδῶν μελεδήματα πορφύροντος
Θυμοῦ, ἀναπτύσσων τ᾽ ἦτορ ἔνερθεν ὅλον.   70
Κεῖνοι δή σ᾽ ἐσιδόντες ἀγινήσουσιν ἐς ὦπα
Πατρὸς, ὁ δ᾽ ἀσπασίως δέξεται, ἀλλὰ σύ περ,
Ἧι θέμις, ἀχράντου δράξαι ποδός, Ἵλαθι, λέξας,
Ὦ πάτερ, ὦ ποιμὰν, ἵλαθι σαῖς ἀγέλαις·
Δέχνυσο δ᾽ εὐμενέως δῶρον τό περ Ἄλδος ἀμύμων   75
Δεψηταῖς ἐρίφων γραπτὸν ἐν ἀρνακίσι,
6 Πρόφρων σοὶ προΐησι διοτρεφές· αὐτὰρ ἀμοιβὴν
Τῆσδ᾽ εὐεργεσίης ἤτεε κεῖνος ἀνήρ,

earthly Zeus. He personally has summoned them from far and wide, takes delight in them, and gives them highly prized and valuable honors.

But for two of them he has special affection, one from holy 5 Greece—not from our contemporaries who are called *Romaioi* and *Graikoi* but the equal of ancient demigods of Attica or Sparta, the leading light of the glorious Lascaris family, and bearing the name of the two-faced divinity.[68] When I was still young he was like an affectionate father to a son and loved me with all his heart. He alone knew how to point out clearly for me the narrow path that led toward the Achaean Muse.[69] The other is distinguished by his eloquence in three languages, fashioned by the hands of the three Graces, the heroic son of Bembo.[70] His great father made him listen to acquire knowledge of all the secrets of this author, declaring all the concerns of a reflective spirit and revealing all the innermost feelings of his heart. They on seeing you will take you to the presence of the father, who will be gracious in his reception; and for your part you must grasp his immaculate foot, as is proper, saying, "Father, be kind, shepherd, be kind to your flocks. Receive with goodwill the gift which the excellent Aldus devotedly offers you, a divine gift, written on soft goatskin from young animals.[71] To you, cherished by Zeus, he gives it willingly."

He begs nothing in return for his act of generosity, not gold 6 and silver, nor that you should send him a chest full of purple gar-

Οὐχ ἵνα οἱ χρυσόν τε καὶ ἄργυρον, οὐδ᾽ ἵνα πέμψῃς
Ἐμπλείην ῥηγέων λάρνακα πορφυρέων.　　　　　　80
Ἀλλ᾽ ἵν᾽ ἀποσβέσσῃς μαλερὸν πῦρ ἀλλοπροσάλλου
Ἄρηος, τῷ νῦν πάντ᾽ ἀμαθυνόμενα
Ὄλλυται. οὐκ ἀΐεις ὡς Εὐγανέαις ἐν ἀρούραις
Πάντα πλέω λύθρου, πάντα πλέω νεκύων;
Παίδων δ᾽ οἰμωγὴν καὶ θηλυτερῶν ὀλολυγὴν　　　85
Ὤικτισε μὲν Κύκλωψ, ᾤκτισε δ᾽ Ἀντιφάτης·
Φλὸξ δ᾽ ὀλοὴ τεμένη τε θεῶν οἴκους τε πολιτῶν
Δαρδάπτει μογερῶν τ᾽ ἀγρονόμων καμάτους.
Ὄσσων δ᾽ αὖθ᾽ Ἥφαιστος ἐφείσατο, ταῦτ᾽ ἀλαπάζει
Βάρβαρος, οὐ στοργὴν οὐδ᾽ ἐλεητὺν ἔχων.　　　90
Παῦσον ἄναξ χάρμην ἐμφύλιον, ἔνθεο σοῖσιν
Ὑιάσιν εἰρήνην καὶ φιλότητα, πάτερ,
Σχέτλιος ἦν τεταγὼν Ἄρης πολυβενθὲς ἐς ἄντρον
Ὦσε λίθοις φράξας πῶμα κατωρυχέσιν.
Ἀλλὰ σύ μιν μοχλοῖσιν ἀνέλκυσον, ἠδὲ λόγοιο　　95
Δεῖξον ἰδεῖν θείου λάτρισιν ἀρτεμέα,
Εἰρήνην πολύκαρπον εὔφρονα βοτρυόδωρον,
Εἰρήνην κόσμῳ παντὶ ποθεινοτάτην·
7　Αὐτὰρ ἀριθμηθέντας ἐπιπροΐαψον ἅπαντας
Τουρκογενῶν ἀνόμοις ἔθνεσιν αἰνολύκων.　　　100
Οἳ χθόνα δουλώσαντες Ἀχαΐδα, νῦν μεμάασι
Ναυσὶ διεκπεράαν γῆν ἐς Ἰηπυγίην,
Ζεύγλαν ἀπειλοῦντες δούλειον ἐπ᾽ αὐχένι θήσειν
Ἄμμιν, ἀϊστώσειν δ᾽ οὔνομα θειοτόκου.
Ἀλλὰ σὺ δὴ πρότερος τεῦξον σφίσιν αἰπὺν ὄλεθρον　105
Πέμψας εἰς Ἀσίης μυρία φῦλα πέδον,

ments. Instead, you should extinguish the destructive fire of unpredictable Ares by which everything now is ground down into destruction. Have you not heard how in the Euganean fields everything is full of gore, every place is covered with corpses.[72] The groans of children and the laments of women were pitied by Antiphates.[73] Dreaded fire takes hold of the temples of the gods, the homes of citizens, the labors of wretched farmers. And whatever Hephaestus has spared is attacked by the barbarian who has neither love nor pity.[74] Put a stop, my lord, to civil war; father, instill in your sons peace and friendship, which ruthless Ares seized and pushed into a deep cavern, closing the entrance with a pile of boulders.[75] Please use levers to bring it out again and display peace safe and sound to servants of the Divine Word, peace that brings many crops, goodwill and the gift of the grape, peace that is seriously missed by the whole world.

But rally and dispatch them all against the lawless tribes of   7
Turkish wolves who have enslaved the land of Achaea and now are keen to cross in their ships to Iapygia,[76] threatening to impose the yoke of slavery on our necks and abolish the name of the Virgin.[77] But you must first devise their complete destruction by sending countless nations to the lands of Asia—the violent Enyo[78] of

Χαλκεοθωρήκων Κελτάων θοῦριν Ἐνυὼ
Ἵππους κεντούντων πρώοσιν εἰδομένους·
Αἰθώνων μετέπειτα σακέσπαλον ἔθνος Ἰβήρων,
Καὶ μέλαν Ἑλβετίης πεζομάχοιο νέφος·   110
Γερμανῶν τε φάλαγγας ἀπείρονας ἀνδρογιγάντων
Τοῖς δ' ἐπὶ Βρεττανῶν λαὸν ἀρηϊφίλων·
Πάσης τ' Ἰταλίης ὅσ' ἀλεύατο λείψανα πότμον
Οὐδὲ διερραίσθη δούρασιν ἀλλοθρόων.
Ἄλλοι μὲν τραφερῆς δολιχὰς ἀναμετρήσαντες   115
Ἀτραπιτοὺς, ἀν' ὄρη καὶ διὰ μεσσόγεων,
Καὶ ποταμῶν διαβάντες ἀεὶ κελάδοντα ῥέεθρα,
Δυσμενέεσσι γένους κῆρα φέροιεν ἐμοῦ,
Θωρηχθέντες ὁμοῦ σὺν Παίοσιν ἀγκυλοτόξοις
Τοῖς θαμὰ Τουρκάων αἵματι δευομένοις.   120
Αὐτὰρ χιλιόναυς Βενέτων ἁλὸς ἀρχιμεδόντων
Οὐλαμὸς, ὠκυάλοις ὁλκάσι μαρνάμενος,
Καὶ νέες Ἱσπανῶν μεγακήτεες, οὔρεσιν ἶσαι,
Αἳ κορυφὰς ἱστῶν ἐντὸς ἔχουσι νεφῶν,
Εὐθὺς ἐς Ἑλλήσποντον (ὑπὲρ καρχήσια δὲ σφέων   125
Αἰὲν ἀειρέσθω σταυρὸς ἀλεξίκακος)
Ὁρμάσθων· ἦν γάρ τε πόλει Βυζαντίδι πρώτῃ
Νόστιμον ἀστράψῃ φέγγος ἐλευθερίης,
Αὐτήν κεν θλάσσειας ἀμαιμακέτοιο δράκοντος
Συντρίψας κεφαλήν· τἆλλα δὲ τοῖο μέλη   130
Ῥεῖ ἀλαπαδνὰ γένοιντο· λεὼς ὅτι θάρσος ἀείρας
Γραικὸς ὁ δουλείᾳ νῦν κατατρυχόμενος,
Ἀρχαίης ἀρετῆς, ἵν' ἐλεύθερον ἦμαρ ἴδηται
Μνήσεται οὐτάζων δήϊον ἐνδομύχως.

bronze-clad Celts spurring on their horses that resemble head-lands;[79] after them the shield-bearing race of fierce Iberians and the black cloud of infantry from Helvetia, the limitless phalanxes of giant Germans, after them the race of warlike Britons, and all the remnants of Italy that have avoided doom, not torn apart by the supremacy of foreigners. Another force should make long marches by land, in the mountains and inland, crossing the ever noisy river streams, in order to bring disaster to the enemies of my race; let them wear their armor alongside the archers of the Paio-nes,[80] who are often soaked in the blood of Turks. And let a squadron of a thousand Venetian ships that are masters of the sea, fighting with swift merchantmen that are towed behind, along with the giant ships of the Spaniards, the size of mountains, the top of whose masts reaches into the clouds, let them head at once for the Hellespont, and above their mastheads let the cross be raised as protection against evil. For if the light of freedom returns first to shine on the Byzantine city, you could destroy and crush the very head of the dreaded serpent. His other limbs would easily weaken because the Greek nation, now oppressed in slavery, will acquire confidence and recall its ancient virtues in order to set eyes on freedom and mortally wound the enemy. And when they kill

Αὐτὰρ ἐπεὶ κτείνωσιν ἀλάστορας ἢ πέραν Ἰνδῶν   135
Φεύγοντας κρατερᾷ γ᾽ ἐξελάσωσι βίῃ,
Αὐτῆμαρ σὺ θεοῖς ἐπινίκιον ὕμνον ἀείδων,
Καὶ μεγάλης χαίρων εἵνεκε καμμονίης,
Ἀνδράσι νικηταῖς στεφανηφόρα κράατ᾽ ἔχουσιν
Ἀσίδος ἀφνειῆς πλοῦτον ἀπειρέσιον,   140
Τουρκάων ἄφενός τε ῥυηφενίην τε καὶ ὄλβον
Ἑξηκονταετὴς ὃν συνέλεξε χρόνος,
Χερσὶ τροπαιούχοις διαδάσσεαι ἀνδρακάς· οἱ δ᾽ αὖ
Σκυλοχαρεῖς πάτρης μνησάμενοι σφετέρης,
Μέλψονται καθ᾽ ὁδὸν παιήονα, καὶ πρύλιν ὅπλοις   145
Ὀρχήσονται ὅλᾳ ψυχᾷ ἀγαλλόμενοι.
Καὶ τότε δὴ ποτὶ γαῖαν ἀπ᾽ οὐρανοῦ εὐρυόδειαν
Πτήσεται Ἀστραίου πρέσβα Δίκη θυγάτηρ,
Μήκετι μηνίουσα βροτοῖς. ἐπεὶ οὐκ ἔτ᾽ ἀλιτρὸν
Ἀλλ᾽ ἔσται χρυσοῦν πᾶν γένος ἡμερίων   150
Σεῖο θεμιστεύοντος ὅλῃ χθονί· καὶ μετ᾽ ὄλεθρον
Δυσσεβέων, οὔσης πανταχοῦ ἠρεμίης.
8   Καὶ τὰ μὲν εἴθε γένοιτο, μαθήμασι νῦν δὲ παλαιῶν
Ἑλλήνων, ὦ ἄναξ ἄρκεσον οἰχομένοις.
Θάρσυνον δ᾽ Ἑκάτοιο φιλαγρύπνους ὑποφήτας,   155
Δώροις μειλίσσων καὶ γεράεσσι θεῶν.
Παντοδαπούς τε πάτερ ξυναγείρας ἢ μὲν Ἀχαιῶν
Ἠδὲ πολυσπερέων υἱέας Ἑσπερίων,
Πρωθήβας, καὶ μήτε φρενῶν ἐπιδευέας ἐσθλῶν
Μήτε φυῆς μήτ᾽ οὖν αἵματος εὐγενέος,   160
Ἐν Ῥώμῃ κατάνασσον, ἐπιστήσας σφίσιν ἄνδρας
Οἳ σώζουσι λόγων ζώπυρον ὠγυγίων.

the wretches or drive them in headlong flight beyond India by force of arms, on that day you will sing a joyful hymn of victory to the gods. Rejoicing at their great and steady courage you will distribute to victorious men, their heads garlanded, the limitless riches of wealthy Asia, the wealth, affluence and resources of the Turks, acquired in a period of sixty years.[81] With triumphant hands you will reward each man. They in their delight at the booty and thinking of their country will sing a paean on their way and dance in armor, hearts filled with delight. At that point lady Justice, daughter of Astraeus, will fly down from heaven to the broad earth, no longer angry with mortals, since the whole ephemeral race will no longer be accursed but golden, as you hold sway over the entire earth and there will be peace everywhere after the destruction of the impious.

May that come to pass; and now, my lord, give support to the study of the ancient Greeks, which has disappeared. Give encouragement to the wakeful representatives of the far-darting god,[82] mollifying him with gifts and divine honors. Assembling, father, a variety of young men, sons of Achaeans and the populous nations of the West—in their first youth, not lacking in good qualities or character or indeed noble blood—establish them in Rome and set in authority over them men who preserve the spark of primeval

8

Ναίοιεν δ' ἀπάνευθε πολυσκάρθμοιο κυδοιμοῦ
Νηϊάδων προχοαῖς γειτονέοντα δόμον.
Τῷ δ' Ἀκαδημείης ὄνομ' εἴη κυδιανείρης   165
Ζήλῳ τῷ προτέρης, ἥν ποτ' ἐγὼ νεμόμην,
Κούροις εὐφυέεσσιν ἐπισταμένως ὀαρίζων
Τούς γ' ἀναμιμνήσκων ὧν πάρος αὐτοὶ ἴσαν.
Ἀλλ' ἡ μὲν δὴ ὄλωλε, σὺ δ' ἦν καινὴν ἀναφήνῃς,
Ἔνθεν ἄρ' εὐμαθίης πυρσὸς ἀναπτόμενος,   170
Βαιοῦ ἀπὸ σπινθῆρος, ἀναπλήσει μάλα πολλῶν
Ψυχὰς ἠϊθέων φωτὸς ἀκηρασίου.
Ἐν Ῥώμῃ δέ κεν αὖθις ἀνηβήσειαν Ἀθῆναι
Ἀντί τοι Ἰλισσοῦ Θύμβριν ἀμειψάμεναι.
Ταῦτά τοι ἐκτελέσαντι κλέος πάτερ οὐρανόμηκες   175
Ἐσχατιὰς ἥξει μέσφ' ἐς Ὑπερβορέων.
Ποία γάρ ποτε γλῶσσα τεὴν, ποῖον στόμα φήμην,
Ἢ ἀγορητάων ἢ καὶ ἀοιδοπόλων,
Οὐκ ἂν ἐφυμνήσειεν; ἀμαυρώσει δὲ τίς αἰὼν
Τηλεφανῆ τοίης πρήξιος ἀγλαΐην;   175 [180]
Ταῦτα τεοῦ γενετῆρος ἀοίδιμον ἠδὲ προπάππων
Πάντας ἐπ' ἀνθρώπους οὔνομα θῆκαν ἄναξ.
Τῶν δὲ σέθεν προτέρων βάξις κακὴ ἀρχιερήων
Κακκέχυται, ἅτε δὴ πάμπαν ἀρειμανέων
Καί τε φιληδούντων ἀνδροκτασίαις ἀλεγειναῖς   185
Καὶ κεραϊζομένοις ἄστεσι τερπομένων.
9 Τοῖα σὺ παρφάμενος, πείσεις σπεύδοντα παρορμῶν,
Θεῖε Πλάτων, ἐπεί οἱ πάτριόν ἐστιν ἔθος,
Εἰρήνην φιλέειν, ἑκὰς Αὔσονος ὠθέμεν αἴης
Ῥίμφα ταλαύρινον βαρβαρόφωνον ἄρη,   190

thought. Let them live far from disturbance and commotion in a house close to the fountain of the Naiads.[83] Let it have the glorious title of Academy in emulation of a predecessor which I once directed, discoursing knowledgeably to noble youths and reminding them of what they had once known.[84] That Academy is no more, but if you create a new one, then from it a blazing beacon of learning will arise from a tiny spark and will infuse the souls of a great many young men with pure illumination. Athens would then be rejuvenated in Rome, exchanging the Ilissus for the Tiber; that achievement, father, will bring you heavenly glory reaching as far as the Hyperboreans on the edge of the world. What tongue, what lips, whether of orators or poets, would not celebrate your reputation? What length of time will obliterate the universally visible glory of such an act? This, my lord, has made the name of your father and your ancestors famous among all mankind. But evil repute has attached to the high priests who preceded you because they were quite crazed with warlike instinct, took pleasure in dire slaughter of men and delighted in the destruction of cities.[85]

Rejecting such acts, divine Plato, you will encourage[86] a man 9 who is active, and will persuade him to love peace dearly, since that is the custom of his fathers, to banish swiftly far from the Ausonian land the war caused by heavily armored barbarians, and

Ἠδ᾽ Ἑλικωνιάδων Ἑλλήνιον ἄλσος ὀφέλλειν
Ὀρπήκεσσι φυτῶν ἄρτι κυϊσκομένων.
Ναὶ μὰν εὐμεγέθους σέο μορφῆς ἐκπρεπὲς εἶδος
Καί τε θεοῖς ἱκέλην ἀθανάτοισι φυὴν,
Καὶ γεραροὺς ὤμους, βαθυχαιτήεντά τε κόσμον,   195
Παλλεύκου κορυφῆς κεῖνος ἀγασσάμενος,
Αἰδεσθείς τε σέβας πολιῶν καὶ σεμνὰ γένεια,
Οὐ νηκουστήσει σῶν ὑποθημοσυνῶν,
Πειθοῖ θελξινόῳ κηλούμενος. Ἀλλά τοι ὥρα
Πτηνὸν ἐλῶντι θεῶν ἄρμα καθιπτάμεναι.   200

Τέλος

cherish the Hellenic grove of the Muses of Helicon, whose plants
are just beginning to grow young shoots. Certainly he will admire
the handsome aspect of your substantial figure, a physique like
that of the immortal gods, majestic shoulders,[87] a white head with
fine flowing hair; he will show respect to your white hair and
decorous beard; charmed by your convincing persuasion, he will
not ignore your counsel. Now is the time for you to drive[88] the
winged chariot of the gods and fly down.

THE END

Note on the Text

꙳꙳

The Latin and Greek texts of Prefaces 1–47 are based on those printed in volume 1 of Orlandi (incorporating the corrigenda in 2:417). The order followed is the chronological order of the prefaces, whose dates sometimes differ from the date of publication of the volume in which they occur. Where the preface is undated, the date of the imprint in which it appears, as in Ahmanson-Murphy, has been used. Full bibliographical details of the editions where the prefaces occur may be found in Ahmanson-Murphy (see the Concordance, below).

The following corrections to Orlandi's text have been suggested *obiter* in the Notes to the Translation; they are listed here separately for the convenience of the reader. Readings in boldface have been introduced into the present text in place of those in Orlandi's text.

3.3. nam] *perhaps* etiam *should be read* (n. 32)

6.8. magni verbi] *perhaps* magni libri *or* magni de verbo libri (n. 87)

6.9. ἀνόμαλα] *emended to* **ἀνώμαλα** (n. 89)

7.2. eo maxime] *perhaps* eo magis *should be read* (n. 106)

8.2. ex] *emended to* **et** (n. 129)

21.2. quando] *emended to* **quantum** (n. 231)

22.6. voluntate] *emended to* **voluptate** (n. 243)

25.1. *perhaps* καὶ ⟨διὰ⟩ ταῦτα *should be read* (n. 261)

25.2. *perhaps* τε *should be read for* δέ, *or the latter simply deleted* (n. 266)

25.3. θυμοῦ] *corrected to* **θύμου** (n. 268)

27.2. Caza] *emended to* **Gaza** (n. 284)

28.3. ἐπεκάθηντο *should be* **ὑπεκάθηντο** (n. 293)

28.10. *reading* bonorum, *as in modern texts, for* Aldus' deorum (n. 314)

28.11. earum] *perhaps* eorum *should be read* (n. 321)

28.13. quos] *emended to* **quis** (n. 329)

32.4. reddet] *emended to* **redderet** (n. 357)

36.3. imitatio] *emended to* **mutatio** (n. 393)

39.1. Corintho] *emended to* **Corinthio** (n. 410)

39.5. creaverim] *emended to* **cacaverim** (n. 413)

43.1. imitatio] *emended to* **mutatio** (n. 460; cf. n. 393)

Appendix 6.2. inierat] *emended to* **inerat** (n. 43)

Appendix 10.2. *corrected to* **μονοφεγγέας** (n. 58)

Appendix 10.2. *corrected to* **ὁμῶς** *in line 17* (n. 59)

Appendix 10.9. παρορμέων] *emended to* **παρορμῶν** (n. 88)

Appendix 10.9. ἐλῶντι *corrected from* ἐῶντι

The textual sources for Appendices I to X are as follows:

I. Ficino to Aldus on textual errors in his translations of Platonica. From P. O. Kristeller, *Supplementum Ficinianum*, vol. 2 (Florence: Olschki, 1937): 95–96.

II. Musurus on Aristophanes. Text from Aldus' 1498 edition, f. 2r–v, reproduced online in the Digitale Bibliothek of the Bayerische Staatsbibliothek, Munich (Münchener Digitalisierungs Zentrum).

III. Musurus on the *Epistolographi graeci*. From the 1499 edition, reproduced online in the Digitale Bibliothek of the Bayerische Staatsbibliothek, Munich (Münchener Digitalisierungs Zentrum).

IV. William Grocyn's letter to Aldus. From the 1499 edition of Firmicus Maternus (Pr 16). Digital images available through the Vatican Library Digitization Project at: http://digi.vatlib.it/view/Inc.II.515/0753 (ff. 368v–69r)

V. *Statues of the New Academy*. From a digital image published by the Vatican Library Digitization Project; the physical source is a leaf in a printed book, Stamp. Barb. AAA.IV.13, inserted inside the rear binding. Digital image available at: http://digi.vatlib.it/view/Stamp.Barb.AAA.IV.13/

VI. Aldus' preface to Bessarion's *In calumniatorem Platonis*. From Orlandi, p. 78, Text L = Ahmanson-Murphy 58.

VII. Letter of Scipione Forteguerri to Aldus in the 1503 edition of the *Greek Anthology*. From the 1503 edition held by the Biblioteca Nazionale

Centrale of Florence (Ald. I.1.2). Reproduced online by ProQuest LLC
in the collection "Early European Books."

VIII. The title page of Aldus' Aesop. Text adapted from that in
Ahmanson-Murphy 77.

IX. Aldus' preface to Erasmus' translation of Euripides. From Orlandi,
p. 93, Text LXII = Ahmanson-Murphy 79.

X. Musurus' poem on Plato, in the *Complete Works* (Venice: Aldus, 1513),
online with the Hathi Trust Digital Library.

CONCORDANCE

Wilson	Ahmanson-Murphy	Orlandi	Renouard 1834
I	I	I	pp. 1–4, no. 1
2	2, 10	II	pp. 257–58, no. 3
3	4	III	pp. 7–9, no. 5
4	5	IV	pp. 4–5, no. 2
5	7	V	pp. 5–7, no. 3
6	8	VI	pp. 9–10, no. 1
7	11	VIII	pp. 10–11, no. 1
8	12	VII	p. 11, no. 2
9	13	IX	p. 11, no. 3
10	18	XI	pp. 13–14, no. 7
11	20	XII	pp. 11–12, no. 4
12	21	XIII	p. 16, no. 1
13	22	XIV	pp. 16–17, no. 3
14	24	XVI	pp. 18–19, no. 1
15	26	XIX	p. 21, no. 4
16	27	XVII	pp. 20–21, no. 3
17	39	XXIV	pp. 262–63, no. 15
18	41	XXXII	pp. 38–39, no. 15
19	42	XXXIV	pp. 32–33, no. 1
20	45	XXXVII	pp. 33–34, no. 4
21	48	XXXVIII	pp. 34–35, no. 6

Wilson	Ahmanson-Murphy	Orlandi	Renouard 1834
22	50	XL	pp. 35–36, no. 8
23	55	XLVI	pp. 43–44, no. 10
24	59	XLIX	p. 40, no. 4
25	61	LI	p. 41, nos. 7–8
26	64	LII	p. 45, no. 1
27	63	XLVIII	pp. 45–46, no. 2
28	65	XXVI	pp. 26–27, no. 2
29	67	LIII	p. 46, no. 4
30	68/1	LIV	pp. 46–47, no. 6
31	68/2	LV	pp. 46–47, no. 6
32	69	LVI	pp. 47–48, no. 7
33	74	LVIII	p. 49, no. 3
34	77	LX	pp. 49–50, no. 6
35	83	LXV	pp. 54–55, no. 4
36	84	LXVI	pp. 55–56, no. 1
37	87	LXIX	pp. 54–55, no. 4
38	88	LXX	p. 59, no. 2
39	90	LXXI	p. 58, no. 1
40	92	LXXII	pp. 64–65, no. 9
41	95/3	LXXV	pp. 60–61, no. 2
42	95/1	LXXVI	pp. 60–61, no. 2
43	97	LXXVIII	p. 62, no. 4
44	100	LXXIX	pp. 62–63, no. 5
45	101	LXXXI	p. 70, no. 11
46	104	LXXXIV	pp. 66–67, no. 3
47	105	LXXXV	pp. 67–68, no. 4

Notes to the Translation

ꙮ

ABBREVIATIONS

Ahmanson-Murphy   *A Catalogue of the Ahmanson-Murphy Aldine Collection at UCLA*, compiled, or with contributions by, Nicolas Barker [et al.] (Los Angeles, 1989).

Barker 1992   Nicolas Barker, *Aldus Manutius and the Development of Greek Script and Type in the Fifteenth Century*, 2nd ed. (New York, 1992).

CAG   *Commentaria in Aristotelem Graeca* (Berlin, 1882–1909).

DBI   *Dizionario biografico degli italiani* (Rome, 1960–).

Diels-Kranz   H. Diels and W. Kranz, *Die Fragmenta der Vorsokratiker*, 6th ed., 3 vols. (Berlin, 1965).

Hankins 1990   J. Hankins, *Plato in the Italian Renaissance*, 2 vols. (Leiden, 1990).

ODNB   *Oxford Dictionary of National Biography*, 60 vols. (Oxford, 2004).

Orlandi   *Aldo Manuzio editore: Dediche, prefazioni, note ai testi*, introduction by Carlo Dionisotti, ed. and trans. G. Orlandi, 2 vols. (Milan, 1975).

Otto   A. Otto, *Die Sprichwörter und sprichwörtlichen Redensarten der Römer* (Leipzig, 1890).

PG   *Patrologiae cursus completus . . . series graeca*, ed. J. P. Migne, 161 vols. (Paris, 1857–87).

PL   *Patrologiae cursus completus . . . series latina*, ed. J. P. Migne, 221 vols. (Paris, 1844–64).

Renouard 1834   A. A. Renouard, *Annales de l'Imprimerie des Aldes, ou Histoire des trois Manuci*, 3rd ed., 3 vols. in 1 (Paris, 1834).

Sicherl 1997   Martin Sicherl, *Die griechischen Erstausgaben des Aldus Manutius: Druckvorlagen, Stellenwert, kultureller Hintergrund* (Paderborn, 1997).

Tosi   R. Tosi, *Dictionnaire des sentences latines et grecques* (Grenoble, 2010).

Wilson 1992   N. G. Wilson, *From Byzantium to Italy: Greek Studies in the Italian Renaissance* (Baltimore, 1992).

Wilson 1996   N. G. Wilson, *Scholars of Byzantium*, 2nd ed. (London, 1996).

Pr = Preface, numbered as they appear in this volume.

PREFACES

1. Constantine Lascaris (1434–1501) was a refugee from Constantinople who found employment in Milan as tutor to Ippolita, daughter of the ruler Francesco Sforza (1460–64). While in Milan he composed his grammar, first printed in Milan in 1476 (there is a facsimile reprint with a preface by J. J. Frankel [Amsterdam, 1966]). Thanks to the patronage of Cardinal Bessarion, from 1468 until his death from the plague in 1501, he held a chair in Messina. See Wilson 1992, 120–23; T. Martínez Manzano, *Constantino Lascaris: semblanza de un humanista bizantino* (Madrid, 1998).

2. The result of the French invasion under Charles VIII in 1494. The logic of the writer's thoughts is not entirely clear, either here or at the end of the paragraph.

3. Valerius Maximus, 1.1. ext. 3.

4. G. Giusti and G. Capponi, *Dizionario dei proverbi italiani* (Milan, 1956), 76, citing "A colpa vecchia pena nuova" and "Peccati vecchi, penitenza nuova."

5. *De officiis* 1.105. In the sentence quoted Cicero has *quidam* instead of *nonnulli*.

6. Vergil, *Aeneid* 1.199.

7. The first edition had been followed by reprints in 1480 (Milan) and 1489 and 1491 (Vicenza).

8. Identified as Vatican City, Biblioteca Apostolica Vaticana, MS Vat. gr. 1401. But other sources may also have been used for this edition; see Martínez Manzano, *Constantino Lascaris*, 208–9.

9. Pietro Bembo (1470–1547) became the preeminent exponent of Ciceronian Latin. An authoritative account of his significance in the history of Italian literature is given by C. Dionisotti in *DBI* 8 (1966): 133–51. Aldus' continuing relations with Gabriele are shown by the dedication of the 1501 reprint of the grammar to him and by his interest in the 1504 Demosthenes. Gabriele was also the dedicatee of Bembo's dialogue *De Aetna* of 1496 (published in this I Tatti series, no. 18, translated by Betty Radice). During their stay in Messina in 1492–94, Bembo composed his *Oratio pro litteris graecis*; see the *editio princeps* by N. G. Wilson (Messina, 2003). This text, written in a competent imitation of classical Attic Greek, is a rhetorical exercise in which Bembo imagines himself addressing the Venetian senate and advocating the study of Greek.

10. This preface introduces the second part of the volume and appeared with minor modifications in reprints of the Lascaris grammar and in Aldus' Latin grammar.

11. Almost all early Greek types, including the four used by Aldus, were made unnecessarily complex by the inclusion of many abbreviations, chiefly for the syllables that occur in grammatical inflections. Aldus' influence was so great that these annoying and aesthetically unpleasing conventions remained in use until the nineteenth century, whereas the simpler uppercase type devised by Janus Lascaris in Florence in the early 1490s was not adopted.

12. A pseudonymous moralizing composition consisting of seventy-one hexameter verses. For the numerous editions and translations of this popular work in the Renaissance, see Hankins and Palmer, *The Recovery of Ancient Philosophy*, 49–51.

13. A similar pseudonymous composition, consisting of 230 hexameters. In the 1501 and 1512 editions, the text varies and a reference to Isocrates is

given; it is to his essay *Ad Nicoclem* 43, which cites Hesiod, Theognis, and Phocylides as good sources of advice on questions of ethics.

14. Aldus' past career had been as a tutor, initially perhaps in Rome, then in Ferrara and Carpi.

15. In the Vulgate, Job 5:7 reads, *Homo nascitur ad laborem*, "Man is born unto trouble."

16. The thought here is an adaptation of Sallust, *Catiline* 1.1.

17. A quotation, with some textual modification, from Gellius, *Noctes Atticae* 11.2.6.

18. *de re dicere* literally means "to talk about the matter in hand," which is not exactly what Aldus meant to say, and so I have paraphrased.

19. This text serves as the colophon of the volume.

20. This is a note at the end of a supplementary bifolium and is followed by the list of misprints.

21. At this date the epyllion *Hero and Leander* was believed to be the work of one of the earliest Greek poets, who allegedly pre-dated Homer and Hesiod. It was Henri II Estienne and J. J. Scaliger who established that the poem is a product of the early Byzantine period; see A. Grafton, *Joseph Scaliger*, vol. 2 (Oxford, 1993), 65, 691–92.

22. Similarities between Ovid and Musaeus can be explained as resulting from dependence on a common source of Hellenistic date.

23. *Heroides* 18–19.

24. *Olynthiac* 1.20.

25. The volume also contains Porphyry's *Isagoge* to Aristotle's logic (CAG IV.1).

26. Bassiano, about thirty-seven miles southeast of Rome, was Aldus' birthplace. The verses are not metrically impeccable. In the first line, Aldus elides the inflection of φίλοι, which is a breach of metrical rules; in the third line, the particle ἄρα is simply a space filler; in the sixth, the enclitic particle μοι eliminates the required diaeresis. Such faults are regularly found in humanists' attempts to compose verse in the meters of classical Greek, whereas they normally achieved a high standard in Latin.

27. The commentators named are Alexander of Aphrodisias (fl. ca. 200 CE), Ammonius (fl. ca. 500 CE), and his pupil John Philoponus.

28. Lachesis, Clotho, and Atropos were the three Fates who governed human life.

29. Alberto Pio (1475–1531) had been Aldus' pupil in the 1480s, and the two maintained close links right up until the publisher's death, as is shown by the dedication of several Aldine volumes.

30. *De senectute* 3.

31. Ibid, 26. Solon's verse γηράσκω δ'αἰεὶ πολλὰ διδασκόμενος (fr. 18) is cited or alluded to by many ancient authors, also by Bessarion in a letter to Lorenzo Valla (letter 24, ed. L. Mohler, *Kardinal Bessarion als Theologe, Humanist, und Staatsmann*, 3 vols. [Paderborn, 1923–42], 3:471). See Tosi, 1474–75 (no. 2035).

32. *nam* in the Latin does not create a logical connection with what precedes, and *etiam* seems to be required. Is this a *lapsus calami* on the part of Aldus or a misprint?

33. *Tusculan Disputations* 1.22.

34. *princeps* here creates wordplay not reflected in the translation; just above, the same epithet had described Aristotle.

35. *Odes* 1.1.2.

36. He had died on November 17, 1494. A fellow student of Aldus in Ferrara ca. 1480–81, he had given him hospitality at his court in Mirandola.

37. Ermolao (1453/54–93) was a member of an important Venetian family and made his name as a translator of and lecturer on Aristotle. He later worked on the Elder Pliny and Dioscorides. See E. Bigi in *DBI* 6 (1964): 96–99. With the benefit of hindsight, it is a little odd to see him classed with such an outstanding figure as Poliziano (1454–94), who however thought him his equal. For Poliziano's contribution to Greek studies, see Wilson 1972, 101–13.

38. This promise was only partly made good; in 1503 he issued Ammonius and some other texts, in 1504 Philoponus, and in 1514 Alexander of Aphrodisias.

39. In due course, but perhaps not before 1502, Aldus formed his scholarly associates into a group, which he called the New Academy (*Neacademia*), whose "statutes" were printed up about this time; see Appendix V.

40. A student of logic and supporter of Aristotelianism; see G. Ballestreri in *DBI* II (1969): 735–36.

41. See Cicero, *Orator* 31.

42. Theodore Gaza (ca. 1400–1478) was one of the most influential Byzantine refugees in Italy; Aldus (Pr 27.2, below) calls him the leading scholar of his generation. He was particularly famous for his Latin versions of various works by Aristotle, which Aldus published in 1504. See Wilson 1972, 78–80, and essays III, IV, and V in John Monfasani, *Greeks and Latins in Renaissance Italy: Studies on Humanism and Philosophy in the 15th Century* (Aldershot, 2004).

43. Attic style was the ideal to which most writers in Greek had aspired from the second century CE onward; this fashion for adhering as closely as possible to the vocabulary and syntax of the leading Athenian authors of the classical period lasted right up to the end of the Byzantine period.

44. A quotation from Horace, *Ars poetica* 269, which Aldus was very fond of.

45. Porphyry (234–ca. 305) was a disciple of Plotinus and a prolific writer of philosophical treatises and commentaries. The most popular, alluded to here, was the *Isagoge* to Aristotle's *Organon*, which Aldus printed in the first volume of his edition of Aristotle; see Pr 3, above.

46. *Barbarismus*, originally a Greek term, was much used by grammarians to describe incorrect usage of words; it was often distinguished from *soloecismus*, incorrect syntax.

47. Apollonius, the leading grammarian of the second century CE, was known as Dyscolus ("difficult"). He was the father of the more famous Herodian, as stated by Aldus below.

48. Priscian (fl. ca. 500–ca. 530) was the leading Latin grammarian of late antiquity. Despite the fact that he spent much of his career in Constantinople, his works enjoyed very wide circulation in western Europe in the Middle Ages. Aldus' quotations are to be found in the edition by M.

Hertz, *Grammatici latini* (Leipzig, 1855), 1:1, line 9, and 2, line 21; he also refers to Book XVIII of the *Institutiones*.

49. Aldus' statement that very few of the numerous works by Apollonius and Herodian have come down to us remains valid. But a small fragment of Herodian's Καθολικὴ προσῳδία was discovered in some palimpsest leaves of Vienna, Österreichische Nationalbibliothek, MS hist. gr. 10 by H. Hunger and published by him in *Jahrbuch der Österreichischen Byzantinistik* 16 (1967): 1–33.

50. These manuscripts have not been identified, and it is not certain that any of them are still extant.

51. It was a common topos among humanists to report the recovery of ancient texts in such terms. Poggio described his discovery of seven orations of Cicero in the colophon of MS Vat. lat. 11458, fol. 94r: *cum latentes comperisset in squalore et sordibus;* see also his famous letter to Guarino of Verona from the Council of Constance in 1416, in *Epistolae Familiares*, ed. H. Harth, 2:153–56, at 155 (IV.5), where he reports finding a complete Quintilian, *plenum tamen situ et pulvere squallentem . . . in teterrimo quodam et obscuro carcere*.

52. The difficult path leading to virtuous success was a topos in ancient thought, first found in Hesiod, *Works and Days* 289, and often presented in the story of Heracles at the crossroads. Many Latin authors convey the idea in aphorisms using the word *arduus*. See Otto, 36.

53. *Ad Demonicum* 18.

54. Battista Guarino (1434–1505) was the son of the famous humanist schoolmaster Guarino of Verona and succeeded his father in the chair of Greek at Ferrara in 1460. His important treatise *A Program of Teaching and Learning* of 1459 can be consulted in the edition by Craig W. Kallendorf, in *Humanist Educational Treatises*, in this I Tatti series, no. 5 (2002).

55. An unusual way of referring to the *Works and Days*.

56. 630a.

57. *Ad Nicoclem* 43.

58. Phocylides is mentioned alongside Hesiod and Theognis in that passage of Isocrates.

59. The *Disticha* (or *Dicta*) *Catonis* in four books, dating from the third century CE, were very popular in the Middle Ages (ed. M. Boas [Amsterdam, 1952]). Maximus Planudes (ca. 1255–ca. 1305) was exceptional among Byzantine intellectuals for his knowledge of Latin and translated a number of texts into Greek; see Wilson 1996, 230–41.

60. Francesco Roscio is known to have been a student in Padua ca. 1492–93; he is mentioned in Aldus' preface to the Ovid edition of 1503. He has been tentatively identified as Francesco Roseti (or Rossetto), a member of Aldus' "New Academy."

61. In view of Planudes' dates, the manuscript cannot have been more than two hundred years old. Whether it served indirectly as the basis for Aldus' edition is unclear. The manuscripts used for Theocritus in this volume are analyzed by Sicherl 1997, 341–47.

62. Oedipus' solution of the riddle of the Sphinx had become proverbial.

63. I take this to be Aldus' Latin title for Theocritus' *Idylls*.

64. The first printed editions of Quintilian and Pliny the Younger had appeared in 1470 and 1471, respectively; further editions soon followed, but to claim that they all presented an improved text is probably exaggerated.

65. The author of a commentary on Juvenal, who had contacts with many leading humanists and taught in Florence and Rome (d. 1474). See P. Viti in *DBI* 52 (1999): 466–70.

66. A collection of short, specialized grammatical treatises.

67. This means that the business had been founded as far back as 1490, and it is remarkable that its first products did not appear until 1495.

68. This proverb is not found in the ancient collections, but Erasmus, *Adagia* 1.1.55, has it, doubtless from here.

69. Quoted by Servius on Vergil, *Aeneid* 6.205.

70. Pliny the Elder, *Natural History* 16.93.247.

71. Diogenianus 4.66. Also cited in Aulus Gellius, *Noctes Atticae* 2.22.24. Aldus modifies the wording slightly.

72. The northeast wind.

73. *Meteorologica* 364b12–14, *Problemata* 940a18.

74. This word may have been coined by Michael Apostoles, one of the Byzantine refugees, the copyist of many extant manuscripts. It is found in a letter he sent to Cardinal Bessarion in 1467. But he could possibly have derived it from Isidore of Pelusium, *Letter* 1.127 (PG 78:268B).

75. It is important to bear in mind that, contrary to what was assumed for a long time, the wonderful collection of Greek and Latin manuscripts donated by Bessarion to Venice in 1468 was not ordinarily accessible to the public at this date. It is odd that Aldus was not influential enough to gain access.

76. Originally the goat that suckled the infant Zeus; rationalized versions of the myth made her a nymph. Her horn of plenty, the proverbial symbol of abundance, may have derived from a separate myth.

77. In midsummer, at a festival in honor of Adonis, Athenian women sowed seeds in pots placed on the roof; germination followed rapidly.

78. An allusion to the sophistic paradox in Plato, *Euthydemus* 298d.

79. This and the next form cited are highly dubious.

80. Martial 9.11, lines 13–14, 16–17; his complaint, however, is about metrical license in Greek poetry, not dialectal or irregular inflection and word formation.

81. Guarino Favorino of Camerino (1445/50–1537), from 1514 a Benedictine monk, had studied under Poliziano and Janus Lascaris. He became tutor to Giovanni de' Medici, the future Pope Leo X, had a career in the Curia, and was appointed to a chair of Greek in Rome. His chief work was a Greek dictionary (Rome, 1523), the first serious lexicon, which enjoyed a lasting reputation. See M. Ceresa in *DBI* 45 (1995): 474–77.

82. Carlo Antinori (d. 1503) was another of Poliziano's pupils.

83. Eustathius, archbishop of Thessalonica (ca. 1115–95/96), was best known for his extensive commentaries on Homer, which contain a great deal of linguistic and lexicographical information.

84. Which of the various Byzantine dictionaries meant is not made clear. The lexicon ascribed to St. Cyril of Alexandria was probably the most popular in Byzantium, and the lexicon compiled by Zonaras also

survives in numerous copies; Aldus might also be referring to the so-called *Etymologicum Magnum*.

85. See n. 37 above.

86. Urbano da Belluno (1443–1524), after many years of travel, had opened a school in Venice. The grammar mentioned here was issued by Aldus in 1498 and enjoyed great success.

87. Aldus' Latin is odd here; instead of *magni verbi* one would expect *magni libri* or *magni de verbo libri*. There may be a misprint here. But A. Lentz, *Herodiani technici reliquiae*, vol. 2 (Leipzig, 1867), cxi, lists Παρεκβολαὶ ἐκ τοῦ μεγάλου ῥήματος, cited by Choeroboscus.

88. George Choeroboscus, a Byzantine grammarian once thought to have been active in the late sixth century, is now dated to the second half of the eighth century at the earliest; see W. Bühler and C. Theodoridis, "Johannes von Damaskos *terminus post quem* für Choiroboskos," *Byzantinische Zeitschrift* 69 (1976): 397–401, and C. Theodoridis, "Der Hymnograph Klemens terminus post quem für Choiroboskos," ibid. 73 (1980): 341–45.

89. The correct spelling of the Greek term is ἀνώμαλα.

90. A mistake by Aldus; there were no enclitic nouns.

91. A sixth-century grammarian of whose work only a small amount survives.

92. Author of a lexicon of Attic usage, compiled in the reign of Hadrian (117–138 CE); the fragments were edited by H. Erbse, *Untersuchungen zu den attizistischen Lexika* (Berlin, 1950).

93. The *obelus* was a horizontal stroke written in the left-hand margin; it was one of the critical signs devised by the Alexandrian scholars of the Hellenistic period, used to mark lines of Homer that were thought to be inauthentic. For an illustration of their use, see plates I–II in L. D. Reynolds and N. G. Wilson, *Scribes and Scholars*, 4th ed. (Oxford, 2013).

94. *Ars poetica* 351–53.

95. This epigram displays some Doric forms, e.g., λῆς, in place of the Attic-Ionic that was standard in the genre. γνῶς' is a dubious form, and

the elision is a metrical liberty; at least one of the particles in the third line is superfluous; in the last line the particle is a line filler.

96. A patronymic referring to Theocritus.

97. The second half of the pentameter is obscure. I take Τὰν to be intended as a pronoun agreeing with βίβλον, which has to be inferred from the context. The future participle is mysterious: "for study" must be Aldus' intention, since πράττω in late Greek had that meaning.

98. Apollo and the Muses.

99. The tradition about Peisistratus circulated widely in antiquity. Aldus is most probably citing it from Cicero, *De oratore* 3.137. What Peisistratus actually did remains uncertain; see R. Pfeiffer, *History of Classical Scholarship*, vol. 1 (Oxford, 1968), 6 and n. 3.

100. The leading critic of antiquity (ca. 216–144 BC), head of the Alexandrian Library from ca. 153, and author of many treatises (now lost, but the source of much material that has come down to us in the scholia to Homer and other authors). The *obelus* was one of a number of critical signs used in his editions of classical texts; see n. 93 above. The source for the statement that financial inducements led to the production of forgeries is unclear; a similar assertion is made by Galen about the early history of the Library, but Aldus was probably unaware of that.

101. A reminiscence of Vergil, *Georgics* 1.115–16.

102. Aldus evidently regarded the *Organon*, published in the previous volume, as belonging to a different category from the rest of Aristotle's works; this is implied by the order in the 1498 catalog of Aldine imprints (see Tav. IX in Orlandi, between pp. 22 and 23), where Aristotle's works *in logica* are listed separately from his works *in philosophia*. Renouard 1834 (10), by contrast, believed that the phrase "complete the first" (*primum absolvimus*) meant that this volume formed the second half of Pr 3, also dedicated to Alberto Pio. This seems unlikely. For the date, see Ahmanson-Murphy 11.

103. This is the first mention of a plan to form what became the "New Academy," or Neacademia, a few years later. See Appendix V.

104. See n. 46 above.

105. *unguiculis* is literally "fingernails." The Latin phrase is a proverbial expression, which Aldus may have derived from Cicero, *Epistulae ad familiares* 1.6.2.

106. *eo maxime*] The Latin is odd; one expects *eo magis*, and I have translated accordingly.

107. See n. 36 above.

108. Or Gianfrancesco Pico della Mirandola, 1469–1533, nephew of the more famous Giovanni Pico della Mirandola (1463–94). A scholar of wide interests, he advised Aldus to publish Poliziano's works, and Aldus dedicated to him the Greek grammar of Urbano.

109. Philosopher and rhetorician, born ca. 317 CE; his extant writings include paraphrases of Aristotle.

110. An aphorism that Aldus may have found in the *Suda* entry on Philo (φ 448).

111. Taken from Diogenes Laertius, 5.1–33 and 3, respectively.

112. A sixth-century CE commentator, some of whose works Aldus issued in 1504 (Pr 26, below).

113. A spurious work; the printer's copy for this text survives in Cambridge, MA, Harvard University, Houghton Library MS. Gr 17; see Sicherl 1997, 31–113. The main corpus of Galen's writings was first issued in Greek by Aldus' successors in 1525.

114. Aldus was evidently unaware of the *Characters*, of which 1–15 were first edited by Willibald Pirckheimer in 1527.

115. Thomas Linacre (ca. 1460–1524), an expert in medicine who had already spent some time in Italy studying under Poliziano, Demetrius Chalcondyles, and others. A number of Greek manuscripts that he had collected were purchased after his death for the library of the newly founded Corpus Christi College in Oxford. See V. Nutton, *ODNB* 33 (2004), 803–6.

116. Gabriele Braccio set up as a printer in 1498, apparently in rivalry to Aldus, and issued two slim volumes, one containing Aesop, the other spurious letters attributed to Phalaris, the tyrant of Acragas (Agrigento),

and other notable figures of antiquity. Braccio also produced a volume of Ficino in Latin.

117. A Roman critic named by Horace, *Ars poetica* 438.

118. Justin Dekadyos (b. ca. 1470) edited the Greek Psalter printed by Aldus in 1498.

119. Niccolò Leoniceno (1428–1524), an expert in medicine who taught in Ferrara for many years, beginning in 1464. See Wilson 1992, 118–20, and P. Pellegrini, *DBI* 78 (2013): 409–14.

120. Lorenzo Maioli (or Maggioli) (d. 1501) was an Aristotelian philosopher who taught in Ferrara. His pupils included Giovanni Pico della Mirandola and Alberto Pio. Aldus published a volume of his writings in 1497.

121. Ovid, *Metamorphoses* 15.234–36.

122. Vergil, *Eclogues* 9.51.

123. Martial 9.49.9.

124. A reminiscence of Vergil, *Georgics* 2.490, followed here by an allusion to Aldus' favorite tag from Horace (see n. 44 above).

125. *Remedia amoris* 94.

126. Vergil, *Aeneid* 5.815; but Vergil wrote *multis* instead of *cunctis*.

127. A reminiscence of Theocritus 4.41.

128. Under this title, Aldus, following the practice of Theodore Gaza, comprehends the various zoological writings of Aristotle, including the *Historia animalium*, *De partibus animalium*, *De anima*, *Parva naturalia*, and other works. Gaza had published under the title *De animalibus* a collection containing, in Latin translation, the *Historia animalium*, the *De partibus animalium*, and the *De generatione animalium*. The collection, dedicated to Pope Sixtus IV, was first printed in 1476 and reprinted in 1492, 1495, and 1498. Aldus himself republished the Gaza version in 1503/4; see Pr 27, below.

129. *ex* seems to be a misprint for *et*.

130. This flattering judgment is not shared by modern readers; it is influenced by similar judgments expressed in antiquity, e.g., by Cicero,

Academica priora 2.119; these are generally thought today to apply to Aristotle's lost works that were intended for circulation to a wider public and doubtless written with more attention to stylistic considerations. A number of humanists in the Renaissance tried to revive Aristotle's reputation for eloquence, including Petrarch (in *On His Own Ignorance* [1368]) and Leonardo Bruni (in the latter's *Life of Aristotle* [1429]). Also influential was the elegant Latin of Gaza's version of the *De animalibus*, which enjoyed great critical favor among humanists by resorting to paraphrase, gloss, and sheer invention; see S. Perfetti, "*Cultius atque integrius:* Teodoro Gaza, traduttore umanistico del *De partibus animalium,*" *Rinascimento*, ser. 2, 35 (1995): 253–86. See also n. 132 below.

131. Girolamo Donà (ca. 1457–1511), a member of a Venetian patrician family, had an active career as scholar, public servant, and ambassador. See *DBI* 40 (1991).

132. Aldus here claims that all the best Western scholars use Gaza's translation of Aristotle's *De animalibus* as a crutch to learn Greek and advises Alberto Pio to do the same; the claim was repeated on the title page of the 1513 edition. For this surprising but not wholly implausible claim, see Perfetti, "*Cultius atque integrius.*" From other sources it is known that a text used frequently as the basis for teaching oneself Greek was the Psalms. See N. G. Wilson in C. Caruso and A. Laird, eds., *Italy and the Classical Tradition* (London, 2009), 64.

133. For the date, see Ahmanson-Murphy 12.

134. The wording recalls Horace, *Ars poetica* 78, which refers to controversy among grammarians.

135. Francesco Cavalli of Brescia (d. 1540) was a scientist who made contributions to biology; he taught at the University of Padua; see M. Palma in *DBI* 22 (1979): 724–25. The work mentioned in the next sentence was not published by Aldus, but by Giovanni and/or Albertino Rosso in 1499–1500.

136. The manuscripts used for the edition of Aristotle are discussed by M. Sicherl 1997, 31–113.

137. The volume also contains the *Problemata* of Alexander of Aphrodisias, as indicated below in the preface. The *Mechanics* and *Problems* are

now considered spurious works of Aristotle. For the date, see Ahmanson-Murphy 9.

138. Plato, *Republic* 473cd.

139. Probably an allusion to the attack on hypocritical philosophers in Juvenal 2.8ff. In place of the words *at cetera non nobis sed satyro liceant*, one copy of this volume in the Beinecke Library of Yale University has *ut ait satyrus clunem agitant*, a quotation from Juvenal 2.20–21, which Aldus presumably decided was too bold to print. This interesting discovery of the original wording by Professor Randall McLeod was communicated to me by Professor J. N. Grant.

140. *Phaedo* 67b.

141. An allusion to Vergil, *Aeneid* 6.129–30.

142. A reference to the book by Cavalli; see above, n. 135.

143. Quoted from Juvenal, 10.360–62.

144. See n. 15 above.

145. See above, n. 52.

146. "Double" because the second part of the volume is a Latin-Greek dictionary; the main part is a reprint of Crastonus' dictionary, with a few minor revisions by Marcus Musurus.

147. Aldus here confuses the lexicographer Pausanias, of whose work only fragments survive, with the author of the guidebook to Greece, which was edited by Musurus and issued by Aldus' successors in 1516.

148. In fact, the Aristophanes included only nine plays, omitting the *Lysistrata* and *Thesmophoriazusae* (see Pr 13 below).

149. A promise not made good until 1525.

150. *Ars amatoria* 1.444.

151. *Works and Days* 354–55.

152. This text introduces the second part of the volume.

153. *Georgics* 2.103–8.

154. The list, here omitted, follows.

155. Aldus had been a member of the court circle of Ercole d'Este in Ferrara when his addressee was aged about thirteen.

156. Giovanni Pico della Mirandola, a close friend of Poliziano and protégé of Lorenzo de'Medici, was famous for his exceptional knowledge of Western and non-Western theologies. There was an ancient belief, recorded by Seneca, *Letter* 42.1, that a single phoenix was born every five hundred years.

157. A pupil of Poliziano; he arranged the publication of his master's *Stanze per la giostra* (Bologna, 1494) and in 1498 collaborated with Crinito in overseeing the Aldine edition of Poliziano's works.

158. Mentioned above; see n. 86.

159. For the manuscripts used by Aldus, see Sicherl 1997, 53–62.

160. Leonardo Bruni (1370–1444) had translated the *Nicomachean Ethics* by 1416, Books I and III of the *Oeconomica* in 1420–21, and the *Politics* in 1438. His version of the *Oeconomica* has been traced in no fewer than 256 extant copies (J. Hankins, *Repertorium Brunianum: A Critical Guide to the Writings of Leonardo Bruni* [Rome, 1997], 253), and would have been readily available. Aldus must mean that he tried to find the Greek text behind Bruni's Book II (= Book III in Susemihl's edition). Since Bruni's version was in fact based on a medieval Latin version of which the Greek original is still lost, it is not surprising that Aldus could not locate it.

161. An allusion to Vergil, *Eclogues* 1.66.

162. *etiam* is difficult; perhaps "anyway." But did Aldus mean *iam*, "already"?

163. Bruni's version of Book III was not based on the lost Greek text but was a revision of two medieval Latin versions. See H. Goldbrunner, "Durandus de Alvernia, Nicolaus von Oresme und Leonardo Bruni. Zu den Übersetzungen der pseudo-aristotelischen Ökonomik," *Archiv für Kulturgeschichte* 49 (1967): 200–39.

164. Aldus refers to what is Book II in modern texts of the pseudo-Aristotelian *Economics*, which Bruni did not include in his Latin version.

165. These moralizing verses, cited by Stobaeus 4.34.8 and attributed to the Alexandrian satirist Sotades (third century BCE), are regarded as

spurious by modern scholars. How Aldus came across them is not clear; the text he prints is incorrect in some details.

166. Horace, *Ars poetica* 269, Aldus' favorite allusion; first at n. 44 above.

167. Another reminiscence of Horace, *Odes* 1.1.2 (cf. n. 35).

168. Most of what is known about Clario derives from this preface; but from a letter he wrote in 1510, it emerges that he and Aldus had quarreled.

169. All the authors listed here, with the exception of the last, date from late antiquity. Eustratius, metropolitan of Nicaea (fl. ca. 1080–20) wrote a commentary on the *Nicomachean Ethics* 1 and 6, and on *Analytica priora* 2, which was printed by Aldus' successors in 1536. Aldus appears to confuse him with the better known Byzantine scholar Eustathius; or is this an uncorrected misprint?

170. Paul of Aegina (d. after 642 in Alexandria) wrote an *Epitome of Medicine* in seven books. It was printed by Aldus' successors in 1528.

171. In this list, the absence of Archimedes is notable. It is not clear which work by Porphyry is referred to.

172. See n. 41 above.

173. Dubrovnik, known as Ragusa to Italians, was an important staging post on the route by which Venetians traveled to Crete and Greece.

174. *Institutio oratoria* 1.1.12–14.

175. *ediscendum* is ambiguous; it could mean "learn by heart," and Orlandi took that view.

176. *coniunctionem studiorum amorisque nostri* is an expression found in a letter of Cicero to Varro, *Ad familiares* 9.8.1 (254 in Shackleton Bailey's edition).

177. Aldus had no knowledge of the *Thesmophoriazusae*, preserved only in the Ravenna manuscript and the late copy descended from it (Munich, Bayerische Staatsbibliothek, cod. gr. 492). The manuscripts used for the edition are discussed by Sicherl 1997, 114–54. The two plays omitted were first printed by Bernardo Giunta (Florence, 1515).

178. The edition also contains scholia by Thomas Magister, Jean Tzetzes, Demetrius Triclinius, and others, collected and edited by Aldus' colleague Marcus Musurus. See Appendix II for Musurus' own preface.

179. See n. 42 above.

180. No source for this anecdote has been found, but it is difficult to see why Aldus should have invented it.

181. Terence was one of the staple authors in the medieval and Italian humanist school curriculum in western Europe. Cicero quotes him often and praised him in some hexameter verses cited by Suetonius, *De poetis*.

182. See M. Sicherl, "Die Aldina der griechischen Epistolographen," in Zeidberg, *Aldus Manutius*, 81–91, and Appendix III, below. The edition was in two volumes: Musurus' preface stood at the beginning of volume 1 and Aldus' at the beginning of volume 2.

183. On Codro Urceo (Antonio Cortesi Urceo), see L. Gualdo Rosa in *DBI* 29 (1983): 773–78. He had studied with Battista Guarino in Ferrara, and from 1482 held a chair in Bologna in grammar, rhetoric, and poetics, where his pupils included Filippo Beroaldo and Copernicus. He also composed a supplement to make good the lacuna at the end of Plautus' *Aulularia*. In a letter to Aldus he complained of the high prices of the Greek editions; see Wilson 1992, 128.

184. Aldus did not manage to print them, except for a few letters of St. Basil; see Sicherl 1997, 282–83.

185. See above, n. 131.

186. Vergil, *Aeneid* 6.95.

187. Ovid, *Metamorphoses* 7.20.

188. For Aldus' Greek type, see Barker 1992. His Hebrew type was used for his *Introductio perbrevis in Hebraicam linguam*, an appendix to his 1501 edition of Lascaris' Greek grammar and his own Latin grammar. There also survives a proof sheet with the opening words of Genesis in all three languages (Paris, Bibliothèque Nationale de France, MS gr. 3064, f. 86r). See M. Davies' correspondence in *The Library*, ser. 7, 5.3 (2004): 316.

189. In fact, they depend on a common source. The syntax of the Latin seems faulty here; one might expect "quod <videbis si>."

190. Though the names of many plants in Latin and other languages appear in the famous illustrated manuscript, Vienna, Österreichische Nationalbibliothek, med. gr. 1 (ca. 512 CE), this manuscript does not present the text in its original form.

191. The works of Firmicus Maternus and Manilius are in Latin, while the *Phaenomena* of Aratus appears in both the original Greek and in the ancient Latin translations known collectively as the *Aratea*; Aratus' text was also accompanied by some scholia on the text in Greek, attributed to a certain Theon (possibly Theon of Alexandria). To the original Greek text of pseudo-Proclus' *Sphaera* was added the Latin translation of Thomas Linacre. The volume contains two prefaces by Aldus. The first is a dedication of the Firmicus Maternus text to Guidobaldo da Montefeltro (duke of Urbino, 1482–1502); it will be translated in a future I Tatti collection of Aldine prefaces, *The Latin Classics*, by John N. Grant. The second preface, included here, stood at the head of the last part of the volume containing Proclus' *Sphaera* in Greek, accompanied by Linacre's Latin version.

192. Aldus' famous device, as used in his books from 1502 (*Poetae Christiani veteres*), combined the design of dolphin and anchor with the motto *Festina lente* ("Make haste slowly"); see A. Henkel and A. Schöne, *Emblemata* (Stuttgart-Weimar, 1967/1996), nos. 615–16, 683–84. For the history of the device, see L. Donati, "Le marche tipografiche di Aldo Manuzio il Vecchio," *Gutenberg-Jahrbuch* (1974): 129–32, and E. Wind, *Pagan Mysteries in the Renaissance*, revised and enlarged ed. (New York, 1968), 98–99, illustrated in fig. 52; on the proverb, see Tosi, 542–43 (no. 696).

193. See above, n. 115.

194. The elder son (d. 1502) of Henry VII, king of England.

195. The translations were never completed.

196. A reference to leading representatives of scholasticism, such as Duns Scotus and William of Ockham, whose philosophy still held sway in some Italian universities.

197. An allusion to the story of Telephus, who was wounded by Achilles. An oracle informed him that the wound could be healed by Achilles' spear.

198. Grocyn (1449? — 1519), another English student of Demetrius Chalcondyles and Poliziano, had introduced the study of Greek during his residence in Oxford in 1491–93. Some of his manuscripts were acquired by Linacre and then passed to Corpus Christi College, Oxford. On him, see J. B. Trapp's entry in *ODNB* 24 (2004), 56–58; for the letter to Aldus included in this imprint, see Appendix IV; it is discussed by Burrows, "A Memoir of William Grocyn," 349–53.

199. This looks like a proverb, but I have failed to trace its source.

200. See above, n. 9.

201. See above, n. 16.

202. Not located.

203. Twice in Milan (1476, 1480) and once in Vicenza (1489), apart from Aldus' edition of 1495 (Pr 1, above).

204. In August 1501; his will is dated the fifteenth.

205. This note to the reader was first printed in Aldus' edition of Prudentius, Prosper of Aquitaine, and John Damascene (January 1501); the latter text contained John's Greek poetry with a Latin translation. See Orlandi, 35–36.

206. The Latin is obscure here. For an explanation, see R. Flogaus, "Aldus Manutius and the Printing of Greek Liturgical Books," in *The Books of Venice*, ed. L. Pon and C. Kallendorf (Venice, 2008) = *Miscellanea Marciana* 20 (2005–7), 212–20.

207. In the 1512 reprint, the word "all" is added here.

208. In Greek, δύσκολος (see n. 47 above).

209. An expert in Aristotelian and scholastic philosophy; *inter alia* he edited Duns Scotus (Venice 1492).

210. Scipione Forteguerri (1466–1519) (Carteromachus is a rendering of his name into Greek), who had been a pupil of Poliziano, was invited to Venice by Aldus in 1494 and became an important member of the publisher's circle. His inaugural lecture on the value of Greek studies appeared in 1504; in the same year he left for Rome. See F. Piovani, *DBI* 49 (1987): 163–67.

211. Cebes was a long-standing friend of Socrates, but the short text that goes under his name probably dates from the first century BCE and shows the influence of Stoic and Cynic philosophy. The *Picture* was among the most popular texts of the Renaissance (see Hankins and Palmer, *The Recovery of Ancient Philosophy*, 9); Aldus here printed the Greek text with the Latin translation of Lodovico Odassi (1497).

212. This paragraph is an addition of 1512; it had been printed in the list of contents in the original edition.

213. An ambition that was not realized.

214. Taberio, who had edited Lucan in 1486, held a chair in Brescia until 1502 and apparently died soon after.

215. In fact, a very small proportion of the text is preserved in its full original form. See the edition of the *Ethnica* by M. Billerbeck (Berlin–New York, 2006–).

216. ε 3048.

217. These texts appeared in 1502 and 1503.

218. Caprioli (d. 1519) was the author of a successful history of Brescia, where he held public office. See M. Giansante, *DBI* 19 (1976): 218–19.

219. Arduenna is the name for the Ardennes. Toup suggested that Arados, an island off the coast of Phoenicia, is meant. I have wondered if Arindela, a town in Palestine, is the right reading. In either event, it is not clear what humorous point is being made.

220. Not included in the ancient collections of proverbs.

221. Renier had been a pupil of Urbano da Belluno, and the inaugural lecture of Forteguerri, issued by Aldus in 1504, is dedicated to him.

222. See above, n. 74.

223. Aldus' edition includes the life of Thucydides by Dionysius of Halicarnassus.

224. *Adversus indoctum* 4.

225. See Pr 25 and n. 269.

226. Janus Lascaris (ca. 1445–1534), no relation to Constantine, held a chair in Florence and was sent by Lorenzo de Medici to Greece to collect

manuscripts for his library. After Lorenzo's death, he edited several important Greek texts, printed for him by Lorenzo de Alopa in Florence, using for the most part a much more elegant and legible Greek type than Aldus. But when the French invaded Italy, he entered their service for a number of years and was employed as ambassador on various missions. From 1513 he was in Rome, having been invited there by Pope Leo X. See Wilson 1992, 98–100.

227. Musurus (ca. 1470–1517) was an exceptionally gifted scholar; on him see Wilson 1992, 148–56, and Ferreri, *Marco Musuro*.

228. The pocket edition in small format for literary texts was one of Aldus' greatest contributions to publishing.

229. It is not obvious why Aldus conveyed this information in Greek, unless he wished to deflect criticism for having failed to make good the promise given at the end of the preface to Thucydides. The title page to this edition promises the texts *cum commentariis*, but no such appear in the volume; the scholia on Sophocles were first printed in Rome, under Leo X's patronage, in 1518, edited by Janus Lascaris and Marcus Musurus.

230. This remark suggests that Aldus had found a manuscript that presented the text in the recension of Demetrius Triclinius (fl. ca. 1300–1320); thanks to his knowledge of meter, Triclinius had been able to emend some corrupt passages.

231. Aldus' *quando* must be a misprint for *quantum*, which I have restored.

232. Calpurnio (1443–1503) was the holder of a chair in Padua from ca. 1486 and was primarily a Latinist. But he also had quite a collection of Greek texts; see D. Marcotte, "La bibliothèque de Jean Calphurnius," *Humanistica Lovaniensia* 36 (1987): 184–211.

233. First found in ps.-Plato, *Axiochus* 366c, attributed there to the Sicilian poet Epicharmus; common also in its Latin form, *manus manum lavat*; see Otto, 210 (no. 1037).

234. The printer's copy was Nuremberg, Stadtbibliothek, MS Cent. V. App. 10, first identified by B. Mondrain, "Un nouveau manuscrit d'Hérodote: le modèle de l'édition aldine," *Scriptorium* 49 (1993): 263–75.

Aldus was able to consult a manuscript belonging to the superior "Florentine" family, whereas the so-called "Roman" tradition offers Book I (*Clio*) in somewhat abridged form, and Valla had depended on it, using Vatican City, Biblioteca Apostolica Vaticana, MS Vat. gr. 122 as his main source. His Latin version, commissioned in the 1450s by Pope Nicholas V, had been printed several times before the Aldine edition.

235. Among those who in antiquity had accused Herodotus of untruthfulness was Cicero in *Laws* 1.5.

236. Zenobius 4.62 is the source for this passage, including the story about Idomeneus.

237. *Iliad* 2.405.

238. *Hymns* 1.8.

239. This notion may be derived from Lactantius, *Divinae institutiones* 1.11.38, or Poliziano, *Miscellanea* 1.35.

240. Titus 1:12. Aldus refers to the famous logical problem known as the Liar's Paradox, or *pseudomenon*. The oldest known version of the paradox was attributed to Eubulides of Miletus in the fourth century BCE.

241. The text of the *Hymns* was transmitted with some marginal scholia.

242. *Institutio oratoria* 10.1.73.

243. *voluntate* is a misprint for *voluptate*.

244. For instance, Erasmus in his later *De duplici copia*.

245. Demetrius Chalcondyles (1423–1511) published the first editions of Homer (Florence, 1488), Isocrates (Milan, 1493), and the *Suda* (Milan, 1499). He taught Greek in Padua, Florence, and Milan.

246. It is not entirely clear what Aldus is referring to; perhaps he had in mind the losses that began to be sustained when the western Roman Empire fell.

247. The story is told by Plutarch, *Caesar* 49 and others, but modern scholars are not all agreed on the extent of the damage suffered by the library in Alexandria.

248. This remark appears to be an allusion to Cicero, *De officiis* 1.26.

249. The fall of Constantinople had occurred in 1453, exactly fifty years earlier.

250. In fact, only seventeen were printed; the *Electra* was omitted.

251. This promise was not kept, despite what appears on the title page: *Euripidis tragoediae septendecim, ex quibus quaedam habent commentaria* (Seventeen tragedies of Euripides, with commentaries on some of them).

252. The text published by Aldus is today attributed to Ammonius' Christian student, John Philoponus (= *CAG* IV.5). The volume also contains logical works by (pseudo-) Ammonius, Leon Magentinus, and Psellus. The *De interpretatione*, a study of propositions, was the second volume of Aristotle's *Organon*.

253. Competition and the absence of enforceable copyright agreements caused Aldus great difficulty. Earlier this year he had felt obliged to issue his *Monitum in Lugdunenses typographos* (Orlandi, 1:170–72) in an attempt to deal with unwelcome competition from printers in Lyon; among other works, they pirated his 1503 edition of Aristotle and Theophrastus in the translation by Gaza (Pr 27, below).

254. Cf. Romans 8:31.

255. I.e., on Aristotle's logical treatise, the *Categories*.

256. Leon Magentinos (fl. 13th century), Byzantine scholar, based on Lesbos in Asia Minor, author of several commentaries on Aristotle's logical works.

257. Michael Psellos (1018–78?), Byzantine polymath, now best known for his *Chronographia*, a fascinating history of his own times, written by a powerful establishment figure. The *Paraphrasis* printed here by Aldus was of Aristotle's *De interpretatione*.

258. Guidobaldo da Montefeltro (1472–1508), son of Federico da Montefeltro. The latter was a famous Renaissance example of the virtuous prince and commander, often praised by humanists for his virtue. Guidobaldo is best known from the idealized portrait of his court in Castiglione's *Courtier*, first published in 1528 by Aldus' heirs.

259. Pollux 1.1, the dedicatory letter to the son of the emperor Marcus Aurelius (161–180).

260. Herodian wrote a history of the Roman Empire covering the years 180 to 238. Before the Greek was printed, the Latin version by Poliziano had been readily available.

261. Perhaps the Greek should be supplemented καὶ ⟨διὰ⟩ ταῦτα.

262. Guido had succeeded Federico in 1482; he was twice ousted briefly by Cesare Borgia in 1502–3, as is mentioned below.

263. Euripides, *Hecuba* 379–81.

264. An adaptation of *Iliad* 2.371–72.

265. See above, n. 138.

266. In the Greek at this point Aldus' particle δέ has been replaced by τε.

267. The famous concluding remark in a story told by Herodotus, 6.128–29.

268. This judgment is taken from the *Suda* ξ 47. Aldus should have printed θύμου (paroxytone).

269. George Gemistos, called Plethon (ca. 1360–1452), best known as a philosopher with controversial views about the relative merits of Plato and Aristotle, also wrote a brief summary of Greek history from the battle of Mantinea, at which Epaminondas died, to the death of Philip of Macedon. It was compiled from Diodorus Siculus and Plutarch and meant to supplement the *Hellenica* of Xenophon.

270. The name of the eighth month in the ancient Athenian calendar, which was wrongly supposed by many humanists to correspond to November.

271. Both texts may be found in CAG XIII.3, though Aldus gives variants only for the first.

272. Aldus was not aware that the epithet also applied to lay members of a parish who gave help to a church.

273. Aldus was not able to print this text, which first appeared in Venice in 1536, edited by Trincavelli.

274. The manuscripts used by Aldus so far have not been identified.

275. A half-line from verses composed by Aldus and printed in Pr 29B.

276. Aldus once again quotes Horace, *Odes* 1.1.2.

277. On Gaza, see note 42, above.

278. Lang (1468–1540), trusted advisor of Maximilian I, emperor from 1493 to 1519, had become provost of Augsburg in 1500. He subsequently was made a cardinal (in 1512) and archbishop of Salzburg (in 1519). He was strongly anti-Lutheran. There is a drawing of him by Dürer in the Albertina collection in Vienna.

279. Johannes Spiesshammer (1473–1529) was the emperor's librarian and held a chair at the University of Vienna.

280. Practically nothing is known of this man, apart from his association with the imperial court and with the Neo-Latin poet Nicolò d'Arco, whose works he edited.

281. In classical Latin, the adjective *divus* applied to a Roman emperor indicated that he was no longer living.

282. Vergil, *Aeneid* 9.641, which Aldus was fond of quoting.

283. *Odyssey* 17.218.

284. Aldus' *Caza* appears to be a misprint for *Gaza*.

285. This note was added at the end of the volume before a list of errata. It was omitted in the 1513 edition.

286. I must admit to feeling uncertain about the meaning of the Latin here.

287. Zanobi Acciaiuoli (1461–1519), a pupil of Ficino and Poliziano, became a Dominican monk of San Marco in Florence in 1495. When his friend Giovanni de' Medici became pope in 1513, he moved to Rome, and in 1518 he was made Prefect of the Vatican Library. On him, see A. L. Redigonda in *DBI* 1 (1960), 93–94.

288. The Latin version printed by Aldus was the work of Alamanno Rinuccini, completed in 1473 and dedicated to Federico da Montefeltro.

289. The tract *In Hieroclem*, of which more below. It is an early work, written before his appointment as bishop of Caesarea in 313.

290. *Letter* 53.1–4.

291. Described by Herodotus 3.17.2, 3.18, 3.23.4.

292. Sossianus Hierocles was a pagan governor of Bithynia, responsible for a persecution of Christians in 303; his book *Philalethes* ("Lover of truth") is not extant.

293. *Vita Apollonii* 3.16.1. There is an error in Aldus' Greek; the verb is ὑπεκάθηντο. In the passages cited below there are further mistakes.

294. Ibid. 6.4.2.

295. *quaecumque* is a literal rendering of ὁπόσα; both are syntactically puzzling.

296. 15.5.

297. *Natural History* 36.58.

298. 17.1.46 (816).

299. 3.18.

300. *Vita Apollonii* 2.18.

301. Aldus' Latin is faulty here, because he renders some difficult Greek literally.

302. Stephanus Byzantius, ι 64.

303. Aldus is here quoting Genesis 2:10–31.

304. *Hebraicae quaestiones in Genesim* 2.11.

305. *In Danielem*, prologue (PL 25:494 B).

306. 15.6.

307. 1.53.

308. 13.44.3, 14.5.1.

309. 1.3.2.

310. The identity of Moiragenes is uncertain; see E. L. Bowie, in *Aufstieg und Niedergang der Römischen Welt* II 16.2 (Berlin, 1978), 1678–79.

311. *Divinae institutiones* 5.3.22–26.

312. The gloss is Aldus'.

313. Diels-Kranz 59 A 97, a paradox culled from the report of Cicero, *Academica* 2.31.100.

314. Reading *bonorum*, as in modern texts, instead of the *deorum* printed by Aldus.

315. 1.1.

316. A Trojan mentioned in the *Iliad*, who wounded Patroclus and was eventually killed by Menelaus.

317. The lexica indicate that this usage is not confined to Philostratus.

318. 1.1.

319. Ibid.

320. 1.7.

321. 1.21.3. Should *earum* be *eorum*?

322. 1.24.2.

323. 2.36.1.

324. μ 449.

325. κ 1405.

326. This story is no. 39 in the scholia of pseudo-Nonnus on Gregory of Nazianzus, *Oration 4*, ed. J. Nimmo Smith (Turnhout, 1992), 106. Her apparatus reveals that for the mysterious Dius the Armenian version has *Hesiodus historicus*.

327. *plantae* would normally refer to a shoot, but that is not what the Greek says and is not plausible; perhaps in Latin of this date the meaning had altered.

328. 8.7.39.

329. The Latin attributed to Rinuccini cannot be translated, and I have assumed that we must read *quis* for *quos*.

330. 993 b 12–14.

331. This was not published.

332. Vergil, *Aeneid* 6.129.

333. Printed in Greek with an anonymous Latin translation.

334. One of the manuscripts available to Aldus was Vatican City, Biblioteca Apostolica Vaticana, Pal. gr. 90, but it was not the copy used in the printing shop; see N. Gertz, in *Scriptorium* 35 (1981): 65–70.

335. Pr 29 B and C appear at the end of the volume, before and after the index. The list of errata is omitted.

336. The figure of 3,047 should refer to the number of lines, not poems.

337. The Latin is not easy; Orlandi took the meaning to be "only now are they published," which would make sense. But if *premo* means "print," *adhuc* is out of place, and I have preferred to take the verb in its more usual sense.

338. Aleandro (1480–1542) had studied under Musurus and later collaborated in the Aldine edition of Plutarch's *Moralia*. He spent the years from 1508 to 1516 in Paris and for much of the later part of his career was in the service of the Church. Created cardinal in 1538, he was deeply involved in the religious controversies of the time. See G. Alberigo in *DBI* 2 (1960): 128–35.

339. This pronouncement by the Roman poet is reported by Aulus Gellius, 17.17.1.

340. *equestri* in the sense of "poetic" is unusual and must derive from pseudo-Acro's scholia on Horace, *Odes* 2.12.9–11.

341. The Greek term was ἐγκύκλιος παιδεία and referred to a general education.

342. The dedicatee of an edition of Cicero's letters *Ad familiares* issued by Paolo Manuzio in 1533.

343. *bonorum* is ambiguous; it could also be taken as neuter, meaning "⟨the path leading to⟩" blessings. But the contrast with *infideles* here suggests "Christians."

344. Luke 1:31 and 1:13.

345. The technical term for the four-lettered Hebrew word for God.

346. Vergil, *Aeneid* 9.641.

347. Florence, 1488; this was the *editio princeps*.

348. Chalcondyles' edition also included Dio Chrysostom's *Oration* 36 (51).

349. Taken literally this sentence implies that students sometimes attempted to learn texts by heart because they were unable to acquire their own copy.

350. On him see above, Pr 13, n. 167. K. A. Kapparis, *Apollodoros "Against Neaira" [D. 59]* (Berlin, 1999), 72 and 76, states that the Aldine edition is based on MS B (Monacensis gr. 85), which is misleading, since it does not show signs of having served as copy for the printer.

351. Vergil.

352. See above, n. 72.

353. 7 ext.1.

354. This and the following quotations are taken from the *Argumenta orationum Demosthenicarum* by Libanius (314–ca. 393), the leading rhetorician of his day, ed. R. Foerster, vol. 8 (Leipzig, 1915), 601ff.

355. *Demosthenes* 20, 26, 28–29.

356. *Letter* 2.15–21.

357. *reddet* is probably a misprint for *redderet*.

358. Juvenal 10.129.

359. On Scipione Forteguerri, see above, n. 210. He lectured publicly on Demosthenes and collaborated with Aldus in producing this edition of his works.

360. *thermis* is obscure; was the building a former bath house? For this and a more speculative explanation, see Fletcher, *New Aldine Studies*, 60–61.

361. It might be supposed that Aldus made this boast because he was using a fresh typeface for the first time, but, despite his remark just below, this is not so; see Barker 1992, 43–64. He is presumably referring to the layout and generous margins.

362. Little is known of this man; he is mentioned along with Daniele Clario in the preface to the 1501 edition of Sedulius, Iuvencus, and Arator.

363. Menzio (Petar Menčetić, 1451–1508) was a literary figure of some note in Dubrovnik.

364. 1.5.

365. 6.21.

366. 6.24–25. The Aldine punctuation of the second question leaves something to be desired.

367. Horace, *Ars poetica* 269, once again.

368. Liturgical works in honor of Mary, printed in Greek. The first three items in the volume were first printed by Aldus in an edition of 1497, but without the short preface.

369. Cf. Matthew 6:33.

370. For the contents, see Appendix VIII.

371. This text is printed on the last page of the first of the two parts of the volume (f. 4 of quire omicron).

372. The meaning of this is not clear. The volume (as usually arranged) prints first the Greek text of the several works; then, in Latin, the life of Aesop by Maximus Planudes, Aesop's fables, and Babrius' fables; then, some other fables in both Latin and Greek together. The Latin texts are unpaginated and have a separate pattern of signatures. Aldus probably expected the reader to purchase the quires unbound and then rearrange them for ease of study. See Appendix VIII, where further light is shed on the design of the volume; also Ahmanson-Murphy 77 and 77a. Some copies exist with the Latin pages rearranged to face the Greek, e.g., the copy at the University of Illinois Library (Urbana-Champaign), visible online at the library's website.

373. This refers to the last leaves of part B of the volume. The correct form of Babrius' name was not known. Orlandi prints it as Gabrius (as at the beginning of the text on folio D3), but on the title page and preface it is Gabrias.

374. This was the name by which Cornutus was known; Aldus also calls him Curnutus (see Appendix VIII). The text occupies pages 59–81 of

part A of the volume. The Latin text of Aesop is on folios B5–D7 in part B.

375. Orlandi notes here that the description appears to be inaccurate.

376. This text is on the verso of folio D10 in part B.

377. They had corresponded in 1501, but *alibi* is puzzling; possibly he means *alibi* in its less usual sense of "in another matter."

378. The manuscript of Sopater brought by Janus Lascaris from Greece is now Laurentianus 58.21; the printer's copy used by Aldus is Paris grec 2924. See Sicherl 1997, 319–22.

379. I have not traced the source of this remark (it is not in the *Suda* entry), but he is described *inter alia* as πιθανός, "persuasive," by Hermogenes, *De ideis* 2.11, p. 401.1 Rabe.

380. Ibid.; I translate "straw" for reasons of idiom; the Greek has "barley."

381. *De grammaticis et rhetoribus* 26.2.

382. The printer's copy has not survived; see Sicherl 1997, 313.

383. These texts appeared in the second volume of the set in May 1509 (see Pr 37, below).

384. *oratori* has this additional meaning, creating a play on words which cannot be reproduced in English.

385. *Hecuba* 379–81, which Aldus had quoted before; see above, n. 263.

386. *Odes* 4.4.29–32.

387. Three of these rulers belong to the period of exile in Nicaea after the capture of Constantinople by the Crusaders in 1204: Theodore I (1204–22), Theodore II (1254–58), and John IV (1258–61). The fourth is presumably John II of Trebizond (1280–97).

388. Horace, *Odes* 1.1.1.

389. Antiquario (1444/45–1512) spent most of his career in Milan, serving as secretary to successive rulers of the Sforza family; he was also a correspondent of Poliziano. Aldus had visited him in Milan ca. 1506.

390. This assertion appears to be somewhat misleading, as the edition was based mainly on a Milan manuscript, Biblioteca Ambrosiana C 195 inf.; see Sicherl 1997, 357–59.

391. An allusion to Vergil, *Georgics* 1.145–46.

392. 3.31–32.

393. *imitatio* in the Latin is a misprint for *mutatio*, and I have translated accordingly.

394. *Republic* 424bc.

395. *Iliad* 2.25.

396. *Metamorphoses* 1.129–31.

397. This may be an allusion to a remark attributed to him in Diogenes Laertius 1.58.

398. See above, n. 44.

399. 1.1, but not quoted very accurately.

400. I.e., a scholastic philosopher.

401. Vergil, *Georgics* 1.510–11. The battle of Agnadello had taken place on May 14, 1509, and it was a disastrous defeat for Venice.

402. Cesare (1501–20) was the son of Federico I, king of Naples. He was educated at the court of Mantua. Aldus met him in Ferrara ca. 1510.

403. Chrysoloras (ca. 1350–1415), a Byzantine diplomat, was employed by Florence to teach Greek from 1397 to 1400. Aldus' following statements are not quite accurate: (1) he fails to mention the unsuccessful attempt to establish a chair of Greek in Florence in 1360, when Leonzio Pilato was employed briefly on the recommendation of Boccaccio; (2) Chrysoloras' stay in Florence lasted only three years. See Wilson 1992, 8–12.

404. Musurus had just moved to take up the chair in Venice.

405. Vergil, *Aeneid* 9.311.

406. *Odyssey* 2.276–77.

407. His father Federico I (1452–1504) had reigned in Naples from 1496 to 1501, when he abdicated and retired to France.

408. The texts that follow are an introduction to the addenda prepared for this edition and a comment on the errata sheet added at the end. For the first edition, see no. 17, above. The date is from the colophon.

409. On John Philoponus, see above, n. 27.

410. *Corintho* is a misprint for *Corinthio*; Gregory Pardos, metropolitan of Corinth (ca. 1070–1156), was a prolific author and wrote a treatise on the dialects of the classical language, which enjoyed wide circulation.

411. Terentianus Maurus 63–66 (p. 326, ed. Keil). This grammarian flourished ca. 200 CE and wrote his work in verse.

412. See above, n. 68. *Canonismata* is a Byzantine term for grammatical rules; one would expect here the title to be quoted as *Thesaurus Cornu Copiae*.

413. *creaverim* is a misprint and defies satisfactory translation. Aldus must have meant to write *cacaverim*.

414. An allusion to Horace, *Ars poetica* 294.

415. I.e., earthenware, a semiproverbial expression; see Otto, 305 (no. 1577).

416. The corrigenda are here omitted.

417. Navagero (1483–1529) edited some Latin authors for Aldus and had a considerable reputation as a Latin poet. After the publisher's death, he was appointed librarian of the Libreria Nicena, i.e., Bessarion's collection, and official historian of the Venetian Republic. In his final years he served as an ambassador in Spain and France. See I. Melani, *DBI* 78 (2013): 32–35.

418. Aldus had suspended operations in May 1509 and only resumed late in 1512.

419. Vergil, *Eclogues* 9.2–4.

420. *integrascere* is a very rare word, cited in the *Oxford Latin Dictionary* only from Terence, *Andria* 688.

421. Giovanni da Verona (1433–1515), architect and Latinist (he edited Vitruvius and made a discovery of Pliny's *Letters*), epigrapher and military engineer. He is thought to have designed the Fondaco dei Tedeschi

in Venice and was certainly involved in the redesigning of St. Peter's in Rome. See P. N. Pagliara in *DBI* 56 (2001): 326–38.

422. An allusion to Juvenal 6.207.

423. Aldus could have been made aware of this through conversation with Erasmus, who in 1505 had edited one recension of Lorenzo Valla's notes on the New Testament and would later produce his own edition of the New Testament in Greek (*Novum instrumentum omne*, Basel, 1516) with the printer Froben.

424. An adaptation of a Homeric phrase; cf. *Odyssey* 8.325.

425. Cf. Vergil, *Aeneid* 12.168. Bembo was the greatest master of Latinity in the Ciceronian style and perhaps in his lifetime more famous for that than for his works in Italian. He succeeded Navagero as the official historian of Venice.

426. *Iliad* 9.312–14.

427. *Adversus indoctum* §4. Cf. Pr 20.4.

428. Cf. H. W. Chandler, *A Practical Introduction to Greek Accentuation*, 2nd ed. (Oxford, 1881), xxiii. "In England at all events, every man will accent his Greek properly who wishes to stand well with the world. He whose accents are irreproachable may indeed be no better than a heathen, but concerning that man who misplaces them, or, worse still, altogether omits them, damaging inferences will certainly be drawn, and in most instances with justice."

429. Aldus failed to fulfill either of these projects, the second of which was extraordinarily ambitious, since indexes to the ancient and medieval commentaries on classical authors did not figure in scholarly publications until relatively recent times. One of the first attempts to provide such guidance was J. C. G. Ernesti's *Lexicon technologiae Graecorum rhetoricae* of 1795, followed two years later by a companion volume for Latin.

430. Battista Egnazio (Giovanni Battista Cipelli) (1478–1553) was a historian and Latinist who succeeded Raffaele Regio in the chair of Latin in 1520; he was a prominent figure in Venetian public life. A member of the Neacademia, he continued his association with the press after Aldus' death. See E. Mioni in *DBI* 25 (1981): 698–702.

431. The two are often mentioned in association by Greek writers from Hesiod, *Works and Days* 243, onward.

432. Fasolo, elected in 1511, was the author of legal and literary works but had not made his career in the chancellery. See F. Piovan in *DBI* 45 (1995): 256–59.

433. I.e., Charlemagne.

434. The reference is unclear, but the first Safavid shah of Iran, Ismael I (1487–1524), may be meant. *Solitanus* (*sultanus*, *soldanus*) is a generic term for a Muslim ruler.

435. The Grand Master of the Knights of St. John.

436. I.e., of France.

437. In 1379, when the Genoese occupied Chioggia, which was Fasolo's birthplace. The humanist Marcantonio Sabellico (ca. 1436–1506) became librarian of San Marco and official historiographer of the Republic.

438. Apparently a reference to a boundary dispute of 1398.

439. A lawyer (d. 1466) who had a distinguished career in Chioggia and Venice; in 1464 he was sent by the Doge to meet Pius II at Ancona with a view to joining the projected crusade.

440. Bartolomeo Platina (1421–81) wrote an account of Vittorino da Feltre's famous school at Mantua and became librarian of the Vatican.

441. Aldus is inaccurate here; neither Valla nor Guarino was a product of the school, and Ognibene da Lonigo became the head of it after the founder's death.

442. Doge from 1462 to 1471.

443. Probably during a Venetian attack on the Dardanelles in 1465.

444. Angelo Fasolo (1426–90). His diplomatic mission was undertaken for Pope Pius II; he achieved further promotion under Paul II and was a close associate of Sabellico and a collector of manuscripts. See Paolo Cherubini in *DBI* 45 (1995).

445. This dictum is found in a scholium on *Iliad* 2.435–36.

446. Cf. Horace, *Satires* 1.5.32–33.

447. Janus Lascaris (see n. 225); he traveled to Greece in 1491–92.

448. Cf. *Odyssey* 2.277. Leo had just been elected pope (March 11, 1513).

449. Vergil, *Aeneid* 6.792–94.

450. Apocalypse 5:5.

451. Vergil, *Georgics* 1.498–502.

452. A Homeric formula, e.g., *Iliad* 1.263.

453. Cf. Quintilian 12.10.49.

454. *Moralia* 832B–852E.

455. Cicero, *Brutus* 36–37.

456. Modern scholars are agreed that it is spurious.

457. In fact, in Book XII (not X): 10.20–26.

458. Leading figures of the Second Sophistic, in the second century CE. Contrary to Aldus' implication, Herodes Atticus was Athenian, not from Asia Minor.

459. Giovanni de' Medici (1475–1521) had been elected on March 11, 1513, a few months before the composition of this letter.

460. Otto, 75 (no. 346), cites Augustine, *Enarrationes in Psalmos* 29 verse 14 (PL 36:223): *proverbium est antiquum et verum: ubi caput, et cetera membra.* This may be the source of Aldus' remark, but in Augustine the context is a discussion of resurrection.

461. *imitatio* can hardly be translated; *mutatio* should be read. Cf. above, n. 393.

462. Vergil, *Aeneid* 4.12.

463. Part of one of Aldus' favorite quotations, from Euripides, *Hecuba* 379–81.

464. His death in 1492 was seen as unleashing the great turbulence that soon followed, for example in Francesco Guicciardini's *Storia d'Italia* 1.1, who credits Lorenzo with maintaining the peace through a balance of power.

465. Cf. Vergil, *Aeneid* 5.56.

466. *Iliad* 2.24–25. Cf. n. 395 above.

467. Vergil, *Aeneid* 1.282.

468. Manuel I, king from 1495 to 1521. During his reign, a maritime route to India was explored by Vasco da Gama and a trading empire founded in the Indian Ocean.

469. Vergil, *Georgics* 4.561–62. Modern editions have "willing" peoples, not "blessed."

470. This account of Portuguese exploration is grossly oversimplified.

471. Horace, *Epistles* 1.2.14.

472. Cf. Vergil, *Aeneid* 6.835.

473. I.e., the Central and South American peoples discovered by Columbus and his successors on behalf of the king of Spain.

474. Who are these *barbari*? Could this be a reference to Charlemagne?

475. Tommaso Parentucelli (1397–1455), elected in 1447, was a notable patron of scholars and collector of manuscripts. He commissioned many translations of Greek texts.

476. Cf. Terence, *Eunuchus* 1085, an allusion to the story of Sisyphus.

477. Cf. Vergil, *Eclogues* 9.34.

478. Cf. Horace, *Ars poetica* 360.

479. Vergil, *Georgics* 3.110; *Aeneid* 5.458, 12.553.

480. In 1484.

481. Having failed to obtain support for the Academy in Germany, Aldus had recently turned for help to Lucrezia Borgia, duchess of Ferrara since 1503; this is made clear in his preface to the poetical works of the Strozzi. Again he was unsuccessful. But Leo did found a Greek academy in Rome, headed by Lascaris, with its own printing press; the latter printed its first Greek book in 1515, the year of Aldus' death.

482. It is most unlikely that Musurus collated any of the oldest manuscripts. This remark is sales patter typical of publishers. The printer's copy for the edition has not survived. See further, Sicherl 1997, 279–80; C. Brockmann, *Die handschriftliche Überlieferung von Platons Symposion*, Serta Graeca 20 (Wiesbaden, 1992), 185–90; S. Martinelli Tempesta, *La tradizione testuale del Liside di Platone* (Florence, 1997), 182–89.

483. Appendix X.

484. 3.56–61, the so-called Tetralogies of Plato, an ordering ascribed to Claudius Thrasyllus of Alexandria (d. 36 CE). Ficino had followed a personal and rather idiosyncratic ordering of the dialogues in his 1484 edition of the complete Plato in Latin; see Hankins 1990, 1:308–11.

485. Vergil, *Aeneid* 6.834–35; but Vergil wrote *sanguis* instead of *populus*.

486. Vittori (1483/84–1529), nicknamed Francesco della Memoria, was registered as a doctor in Bergamo in 1507. From 1523 he held a chair of medicine at Padua.

487. Vergil, *Aeneid* 5.710.

488. See above, Pr 29 B.

489. *Odyssey* 1.1–5.

490. The versification here is competent but at the expense of some freedom in the translation of the Greek.

491. *Aeneid* 1.3–4.

492. *Odyssey* 20.18.

493. *Aeneid* 1.198–207.

494. "Averter of evil"; the epithet is found in Lucian, *Alexander* 4, and elsewhere.

495. Cf. Hebrews 12:6, Apocalypse 3:19.

496. The story is told by Herodotus 3.40–43.

497. A famous aphorism; see, e.g., *Palatine Anthology* 9.366.6.

498. Here there is a misprint or a slip by Aldus; the name was Oroites. See Herodotus 3.125.

499. Another reminiscence of *Aeneid* 6.95; see above, n. 186.

500. *Aeneid* 9.641.

501. Hesiod, *Works and Days* 289–92.

502. Cf. *Aeneid* 6.377.

503. A position associated with the Epicurean school of philosophy.

504. Menander, *Monostichoi* 651.

505. A well-known proverb (Zenobius 3.6), the equivalent of "coals to Newcastle." It is first found in Aristophanes, *Birds* 301. See Tosi, 1404–5 (no. 1928).

506. It is not known which manuscripts Musurus was able to consult.

507. Aldus managed to print Athenaeus; the other texts appeared after his death.

508. Vergil, *Georgics* 1.510–11. The quotation is followed by yet another allusion to the story of Sisyphus.

509. The work is variously known as the *S(o)uda*, which is the title apparently guaranteed by the manuscripts and used by a twelfth-century commentator on Aristotle, or Suidas, which is given as if it were the author's name by other Byzantine writers from the thirteenth century on. See Wilson 1996, esp. 145–47.

510. In the *Suda*, the order of the entries reflects changes that had taken place in the pronunciation of vowels and diphthongs by the tenth century.

511. Bardellone (1472–1527) was a prominent figure at the court of Mantua and a friend of Ariosto.

512. The manuscript, now Venice, Biblioteca Marciana, Marc. gr. 622, is indeed the unique copy of this text. It was produced ca. 1430, probably in Constantinople.

513. See above, n. 44.

514. The history of Greek lexica is extremely complex; see K. Alpers, in *Hesychii Alexandrini lexicon*, vol. 3 (Berlin, 2005), xv–xxiii.

515. *Odyssey* 2.277.

516. Modern scholars are agreed that Musurus' emendations prove him to have been an exceptionally gifted textual critic. See Wilson 1992, 148–56.

517. Very little is known of this man, also known as Vértessy.

518. Vergil, *Aeneid* 9.641; see nn. 191 and 466.

519. *Iliad* 2.298.

520. The phrasing here is perhaps influenced by Vergil, *Aeneid* 3.342–43.

521. Thomas Bakács, bishop of Gnor (1487–97), later of Eger and Esztergom (d. 1521). He had been appointed cardinal in 1500.

522. Vergil, *Aeneid* 12.435.

523. Philip Gyulai Móré, the Hungarian envoy to Venice, had studied in Bologna. He became bishop of Pécs in 1524 and died at the battle of Mohács in 1526. He appears to have initiated the study of Roman inscriptions found in Hungary.

524. Vergil, *Aeneid* 6.129–30.

525. Janus Pannonius (1434–72), educated at Ferrara under Guarino, became bishop of Pécs in 1461 and a few years later was employed on diplomatic missions. He won great fame for his Latin poetry.

526. Horace, *Epistles* 1.2.40.

527. Plato, *Laws* 753e.

528. 4.4.2–3.

529. 83DE.

530. *Natural History* 13.120 is the source of this discussion. Modern texts give the form ἀνδράχλη, *arbutus*.

531. 2.126–35.

532. Though Aldus is right to praise Musurus for his work as a textual critic, the suggestion that he consulted many manuscripts is highly dubious. J. Irigoin, "L'edition princeps d'Athénée et ses sources," *Revue des études grecques* 80 (1967): 418–24, revised version in *La tradition des textes grecs* (Paris, 2003), 683–92, observed that the Greek note on the title page, probably drafted by Musurus, refers to a single exemplar.

533. Subsequent research has not led to the discovery of a more complete text.

APPENDICES

1. Marsilio Ficino (1433–99), the famous Platonic philosopher and translator of Plato and Plotinus, sent a collection of Neoplatonic texts he had translated into Latin around 1488 to Aldus to be printed (Ahmanson-Murphy 17, published September 1497). For the circumstances see P. O. Kristeller, *Supplementum Ficinianum* (Florence: Olschki, 1937), 1:cxxxii–cxxxiv. The commentaries on the *Parmenides* and [pseudo-] Dionysius the Areopagite mentioned below were finished by the end of 1492, so presumably the copies Aldus was trying to correct were made before that time.

2. The Medici library, kept in their palazzo on the via Larga (now via Cavour), had been dispersed when Piero de'Medici had been expelled from Florence in 1494.

3. Ficino refers to the political instability associated with the city government, then dominated by the apocalyptic preacher Girolamo Savonarola, with whom he was not (by this date) in sympathy.

4. The merchant-printer Girolamo Biondo (or Biondi), a Florentine who worked in Venice as a publisher, not to be confused with the son of Flavio Biondo the historian, *doctor utriusque iuris* in 1459. This Girolamo Biondo published Ficino's *Epistolae* in Venice in 1495.

5. An allusion to the earliest of the surviving plays, *Acharnians*, produced in 425 BCE.

6. Dionysus, the patron god of Athenian dramatic festivals, is here presumably understood as representative of the vigor inherent in living beings rather than as the god of wine.

7. The autograph of this letter was published by Nicolas Barker. It is preserved in the John Rylands Library in Manchester, bound into a copy of the Aristophanes (shelf-mark R213276, formerly Christie 35.h.5). See Barker 1992, 119–20, with plates on 123–25.

8. Musurus is aware that Aristotle wrote many books for circulation to a wide, nonspecialist public. These were much appreciated for their elegant style, but they gradually lost their popularity after his specialist writings

had been rediscovered in the first century BCE and as a result are no longer extant. See n. 130 above.

9. A reference to the results of dubious educational practice as seen in *Clouds*.

10. An allusion to the poet's boast at *Wasps* 1030.

11. This may be a reference to the violent attacks on Cleon in the *Knights*, but there is also satire of Lamachus in the *Acharnians*, and the verb μελλονικιάω at *Birds* 639 reflects dissatisfaction with Nicias.

12. The scent of Attic thyme became a cliché to describe the style of writers of the Second Sophistic and later Atticists, who imitated as best they could the great Athenian authors of the classical period. It is used contemptuously by Lucian, *De historia conscribenda* 14, about a contemporary historian.

13. This passage is striking proof that educated Greeks were still trying to use the classical language in conversation, a fact that Italian students probably found puzzling, since their aim in studying the ancient texts was quite different.

14. Musurus cites what is said to have been a Dorian proverb, known from various patristic and other authors (*Corpus paroemiographorum Graecorum*, ed. E. L. Leutsch and F. G. Schneidewin, vol. 2 [Göttingen, 1851], 775, no. 3.15, in their *Mantissa Proverbiorum*). It usually referred to the process of achieving precise alignment in building a wall. Its application here is not immediately clear; from the context one is inclined to suggest that Musurus sees the builder as the practitioner of a humble manual craft, in contrast to the poet, who can teach so much.

15. The commentaries written in the margins of the medieval manuscripts and containing a fair amount of valuable material from monographs by ancient scholars were transmitted in two recensions. The later of the two was the work of Demetrius Triclinius (fl. ca. 1320), who simplified and abridged much of the contents but added his own commentary on metrical matters. Musurus did his best to conflate the two recensions, and he is justified in claiming that great effort was required.

16. Iolaos, a Boeotian hero particularly revered in Thebes, was Hercules' companion and helper in some of his twelve labors, including the decapitation of the many-headed Lernaean Hydra.

17. This expression looks like a proverb, but it is not found in the ancient collections.

18. Whatever the Venetian establishment may have claimed, the government of the city was not democratic as Athens had been; conceivably, the point is that Athens had a seaborne empire.

19. I have not traced the fable or proverb that appears to be alluded to here, and "local" is a tentative translation.

20. This phrase is not found in the autograph draft.

21. If this assertion was proverbial, once again it does not appear in the ancient collections. Perhaps he was thinking of Cicero's *honos alit artes* in Tusculans 1.4.

22. The tenth month in the ancient Athenian calendar; Musurus was correct in thinking that it corresponded roughly to April.

23. The Greek word here is "theogony." The numerals indicating 400 and 9 are abbreviated in the standard Byzantine style by letters of the alphabet.

24. Presumably, he means that a fresh start would have led to unwelcome delay (not to mention additional expenses for typesetting).

25. A proverbial expression in both Greek and Latin; the closest parallel to its use in a literary context is in an epigram in the Greek Anthology (15.13). See Tosi, 1255–56 (no. 1709).

26. The printer's copy for this text has not survived.

27. The personification of faultfinding. Hesiod, *Theogony* 214, made him a child of Night; Leon Battista Alberti wrote a novel in four books entitled *Momus*, published in this I Tatti Library (no. 8, 2003).

28. On the circumstances, see Pr 16. The translation borrows a few lines from that of M. Burrows, "A Memoir of William Grocyn," 353.

29. Erasmus included this saying in his *Adagia* (*Collected Works of Erasmus*, vol. 31, ed. R. A. B. Mynors [Toronto, 1982], 29), published by Al-

dus in 1508, where he attributes it to Pythagoras, while naming other sources, including Euripides, Plato, Terence, and Cicero.

30. I.e., the Greek fonts used at the Aldine press.

31. *Tusculan Disputations* 1.22.

32. I.e., a fabulist, a teller of many tales.

33. An allusion to Vergil, *Eclogues* 1.66.

34. John Gregoropoulos, a copyist who was an important member of the Aldine circle.

35. I translate αὐτοῦ as "this," in accordance with medieval and modern usages.

36. The Greek term is equivalent to the Latin *nefastus*, the epithet applied to "unlucky" days.

37. The verb is missing in the Greek but has to be inserted.

38. The words εἰ μὴ disrupt the syntax; whether they are a misprint or not, I cannot translate them.

39. This word is used in imitation of the formal phraseology of ancient Athenian decrees.

40. Giambattista Egnazio (Cipelli) was in orders. See n. 430, above.

41. Paolo (da) Canal (1481–1508) was an aristocrat, and his script has been identified in some extant manuscripts. See F. Lepori, *DBI* 17 (1974), 668.

42. Bessarion's work (first published in Rome, 1469) was a response to George Trapezuntius (1395–1472/73), whose *Comparatio philosophorum Aristotelis et Platonis* of 1458, a shallow and one-sided polemic against Plato, needed to be refuted; see J. Monfasani, *Collectanea Trapezuntiana* (Binghamton, 1984), 600–602. An additional spur to refute it was that it included criticism of George Gemistos Plethon, Bessarion's much-respected teacher, who was accused of being a neo-pagan. See Hankins 1990, 1:236–63.

43. *inierat* is a misprint for *inerat*.

44. Now part of the composite MS Escorial C.III.1 (100), in which Book III occupies folios 152–85. This part of the present manuscript belonged to Diego Hurtado de Mendoza.

45. The Latin text, in a version prepared by Niccolò Perotti and revised by the author himself, was printed by Sweynheim and Pannartz in Rome in 1469. The modern edition of the Greek and Latin texts is by L. Mohler, in volume 2 of his *Kardinal Bessarion als Theologe, Humanist, und Staatsmann* (Paderborn, 1927); see vii–viii, for a list of extant manuscripts.

46. From an anonymous distich preserved in the *Palatine Anthology* 9.784.

47. Now known as the *Compendium of Theology*.

48. An allegory attributed to Aesop, no. 373, in the index compiled by B. E. Perry (*Aesopica* [Urbana, IL], 1952).

49. Aulus Gellius, *Noctes Atticae* 2.29.

50. Erasmus arrived in Venice late in 1507, in order to supervise the printing of the *Adagia*, which appeared in September 1508. His much later account of residence in Aldus' house given in *Opulentia sordida*, one of his *Colloquia*, dating from 1531, is notoriously hostile.

51. Cf. Juvenal 15.112. Thule can stand for any extremely remote place; should one infer that an English or a Scottish university was trying to tempt an Italian humanist to take a chair?

52. Horace, *Odes* 1.1.36.

53. The versification of these elegiacs is reasonably competent. The syntactical structure is often very complex and the vocabulary recherché; a few words are *hapax legomena* or *lexicis addenda*. Not many of the original readers will have been able to understand the text fully. In line 4 the particle μὲν and in line 7 καὶ are space fillers, which do not contribute usefully to the sense.

54. The concept of Zeus rather than Apollo driving a chariot across the sky no doubt derives from *Phaedrus* 246e.

55. Whether Musurus had criteria for distinguishing Socratic from Platonic concepts is uncertain, but he may have had inklings of what is known to modern scholars as "the Socratic problem," and he will have had predecessors; see, e.g., Hankins 1990, 1:321–28, on Ficino, and idem,

"Socrates in the Italian Renaissance," in *Socrates from Antiquity to the Enlightenment*, ed. M. B. Trapp (Aldershot, 2006), 179.

56. κοσμοτέχνης is found in Synesius, *Hymn* 1.425/26 (and the feminine form occurs at 5.30).

57. This appears to be a reference to the concluding sentence of the *Timaeus* (92c7), accepting with Burnet the reading τοῦ νοητοῦ (MSS. FY) rather than τοῦ ποιητοῦ (MSS. AP and Stobaeus).

58. μονοφεγγέας is a necessary emendation in line 13.

59. The correct accentuation of ὁμῶς needs to be restored. The obscure lines relating to the spheres look like a recollection of *Republic* 616d–617b, where Plato describes concentric spheres for the fixed stars and the planets.

60. A reference to the *Symposium*.

61. A reference to the *Phaedo*, and perhaps also to the *Phaedrus* and the *Meno*.

62. Is he thinking of the *Republic* or of the *Laws*?

63. This was a frequent feature of the iconography of rivers that received worship as gods.

64. Ausonia is often used as a synonym of Italy; the Ausones were among the original inhabitants.

65. Plato visited Syracuse when it was ruled by Dionysius I, ca. 388 BCE, and again in 367–365, when his successor was in power. An account of his experiences is given in the pseudo-Platonic *Letters*, included in Aldus' edition.

66. Cardinal Giovanni de Medici, son of Lorenzo, was elected Pope on March 11, 1513, at the age of thirty-seven and took the name Leo. Musurus' language here echoes that of Aldus in Pr 43.

67. Does this expression of respect for papal authority indicate that Musurus was a member of the Uniate church (in communion with the Roman Catholic church) or merely reflect the publisher's faith?

68. On Janus Lascaris, see above, n. 225. "Two-faced" is a necessary emendation of the Greek, because Janus was also the name of the

double-headed Roman god of doors and gates. The Greek as printed
means literally "displaying three persons/faces" and might be appropriate
in a discussion of Trinitarian theology. If the typesetters were members
of the Greek community in Venice, they might easily have imported a
familiar notion into the text; otherwise it must be an oversight of the
author.

69. In Homer the Greeks are called Achaeans. Musurus went to Florence ca. 1486 and studied with Lascaris for several years.

70. Pietro Bembo (1470–1547) had been appointed apostolic secretary by
the newly elected Pope. His three languages were Latin, Greek, and Italian, but the expression *homo trilinguis* more usually indicated competence
in the two classical languages and Hebrew. Bembo's father, Bernardo
(1433–1519), held important offices in Venice and served as ambassador on
various occasions. He was also known as a patron of humanists and a
book collector. In this period he would still have been better known than
his son Pietro.

71. Early printers occasionally produced deluxe copies on vellum, usually
made from the skin of goats rather than sheep. The copy referred to here
is not preserved in the Vatican Library.

72. The area between Rovigo and Padua; but the reference may be to the
battle of Ravenna in the spring of 1512. Venice had suffered seriously in
the war against the League of Cambrai, and Aldus' operations had been
suspended for more than three years. Ares here and Hephaestus below
stand by metonymy for War and (destructive) Fire. Here too Musurus
elaborates on a theme in Aldus' preface.

73. Lines 85–86 seem to be an inaccurate reference to *Odyssey* 10.198–200,
where it is the recollection of the cruelty of Antiphates and the Cyclops
that provokes despair among Odysseus' crew. Perhaps Musurus thought
that the verb ᾤκτισε could convey that meaning, but the sentence would
in any case need to be recast.

74. Probably a scornful reference to northern Europeans, such as the
French; but in many contexts the Turks might be meant and are mentioned below.

75. Here Musurus has in mind the main action in Aristophanes' *Peace*.

76. Puglia. The successful Turkish attack on Otranto in 1480 had been a blow to Western morale, and it was natural to fear that something of the kind might happen again.

77. The following passage rehearses many themes of humanist crusading literature, for which see J. Hankins, "Renaissance Crusaders: Humanist Crusade Literature in the Age of Mehmed II," in idem, *Humanism and Platonism in the Italian Renaissance*, vol. 1 (Rome, 2003), 293–424.

78. A goddess of war, mentioned in Greek poetry from Homer onward.

79. Musurus here borrows with slight adjustment a phrase from Callimachus, *Hymn to Diana* 52; the rare noun originally meant "headland."

80. In classical times this was the name of a tribe living in Macedonia. Musurus may mean the Albanians, who under their leader Skanderbeg had built a reputation as the Christian bulwark against the Ottomans in the Balkans; another candidate might be the Hungarians under Vladislaus II (d. 1516).

81. Since the fall of Constantinople in 1453.

82. An epithet of Apollo in Homer.

83. The Collegio Greco was set up in Rome on the Quirinale in the house of Angelo Colocci, an apostolic secretary. Lascaris organized it and Musurus was the first professor. But its printing press was run by Aldus' former rival Zacharias Callierges. The present-day Fontana di Montecavallo is a more recent construction.

84. A reference to the Platonic doctrine of *anamnesis* ("recollection") expounded in the *Meno*.

85. Alexander VI (1492–1503) and Julius II (1503–13) were particularly open to criticism in this respect.

86. παρορμέων is a mistake for παρορμῶν, and I have emended accordingly.

87. An allusion to the notion that Plato was a nickname derived from his broad physique.

88. ἑῶντι is a mistake for ἐλῶντι.

Bibliography

EDITION

Aldo Manuzio editore: Dediche, prefazioni, note ai testi. Introduction by Carlo Dionisotti. Latin text with Italian translation and notes by Giovanni Orlandi. 2 vols. Milan: Edizioni Il Polifilo, 1975.

STUDIES

Aldus Manutius and Renaissance Culture: Essays in Honor of Franklin D. Murphy. Edited by David S. Zeidberg. Florence: Leo S. Olschki, 1998.

Barker, Nicolas. *Aldus Manutius and the Development of Greek Script and Type in the Fifteenth Century.* 2nd ed. New York: Fordham University Press, 1992.

Burrows, Montagu. "A Memoir of William Grocyn." In *Collectanea: Second Series,* 332–80. Oxford: Oxford Historical Society, 1890.

Davies, Martin. *Aldus Manutius: Printer and Publisher of Renaissance Venice.* Tempe: Arizona Center for Medieval and Renaissance Studies, 1999.

Dionisotti, Carlo. *Aldo Manuzio umanista e editore.* Milan: Il Polifilo, 1995.

Ferreri, Luigi. *L'Italia degli Umanisti 1: Marco Musuro.* Turnhout: Brepols, 2014.

Fletcher, Harry George. *New Aldine Studies: Documentary Essays on the Life and Work of Aldus Manutius.* San Francisco: B. M. Rosenthal, Inc., 1988.

Geanakoplos, Deno John. *Greek Scholars in Venice: Studies in the Dissemination of Greek Learning from Byzantium to the West.* Cambridge, MA: Harvard University Press, 1962.

Hankins, James, and Ada Palmer. *The Recovery of Ancient Philosophy in the Renaissance: A Brief Guide.* Florence: Leo S. Olschki, 2008.

Lowry, Martin. *The World of Aldus Manutius: Business and Scholarship in Renaissance Venice.* Ithaca: Cornell University Press, 1979.

Pagliaroli, Stefano. "L'Accademia Aldina." *Incontri triestini di filologia classica* 9 (2009–2010): 175–87.

Renouard, Antoine Auguste. *Annales de l'Imprimerie des Aldes, ou Histoire des trois Manuci*. 3rd ed. Three volumes in one. Paris: J. Renouard, 1834.

Sicherl, Martin. *Die griechischen Erstausgaben des Aldus Manutius: Druckvorlagen, Stellenwert, kultureller Hintergrund*. Paderborn: F. Schöningh, 1997.

Tessler, Andrea. "La prefazione al Sofocle aldino: Triclinio, Andronico Callisto, Bessarione." In *Letteratura e riflessione sulla letteratura nella cultura classica: Atti del Convegno, Pisa, 7–9 giugno 1999*, edited by Graziano Arrighetti, 345–66. Pisa: Giardini, 2000.

Wilson, N. G. *From Byzantium to Italy: Greek Studies in the Italian Renaissance*. Baltimore: The Johns Hopkins University Press, 1992.

———. *Scholars of Byzantium*. Rev. ed. London: Duckworth, 1996.

Index

❧❦❧

Academy: in Germany (proposed), 360n481; of Musurus, 315; New (Neacademia), 39, 105, 115, 127, 159, 163, 187, 221, 243, 291, 293, 328n39, 330n60, 333n103, 357n430; Platonic, 51; in Rome, 243–45, 360n481

Acciaiuoli, Zanobi, 131, 159, 348n287

Achaeans, 239, 309, 313, 370n69

Acharnai, 273

Achilles, 341n197

Adonis, 29, 35, 331n77

Aegae, 145

Aegina, 177

Aelius Dionysius, 35, 332n92

Aeneas, 249–51, 263

Aeschines, 221, 229, 231, 233

Aeschylus, 67, 221

Aesop, 299, 334n116, 353n372, 354n374, 368n48; *Fables*, 193

Africa, 239

Agnadello, battle of, 355n401

Albanians, 133, 371n80

Alberti, Leon Battista, *Momus*, 366n27

Albertina (Vienna), 348n278

Alcidamas, 221, 225

Alciphron, 283

Aldine press, xiii, 327n29, 330n67. *See also* Manutius, Aldus (Pius)

Aldus (Pius) Manutius. *See* Manutius, Aldus (Pius)

Aleandro, Girolamo, 163, 167, 351n338

Alexander VI, Pope, 371n85

Alexander of Aphrodisias, 11, 17, 53, 69, 247, 327n27, 327n38; *Commentaries on the Topics of Aristotle*, 247–57; *On Aristotle's Meteorologica*, 81; *Problems*, 127–31, 336n137

Alexander the Great, 41, 83, 177, 225, 229

Alexandria, 133, 332n93, 361n484; Library, 113, 333n100, 345n247

Alopa, Lorenzo de, 344n226

Amaltheia, 29, 35, 331n76

Ambrogini, Angelo (Poliziano). *See* Poliziano (Angelo Ambrogini)

Ammonius of Alexandria, 11, 17, 69, 327n27, 327n38; *On Aristotle's De Interpretatione*, 115–17, 125

Anaxagoras, 147

Ancona, 358n439

Andocides, 195, 221, 231

Annaeus Seneca, L., 338n156

Antarctic, 239

Antinori, Carlo, 31, 331n82

Antipater, 177

Publication of this volume has been made possible by

The Myron and Sheila Gilmore Publication Fund at I Tatti
The Robert Lehman Endowment Fund
The Jean-François Malle Scholarly Programs and Publications Fund
The Andrew W. Mellon Scholarly Publications Fund
The Craig and Barbara Smyth Fund
for Scholarly Programs and Publications
The Lila Wallace–Reader's Digest Endowment Fund
The Malcolm Wiener Fund for Scholarly Programs and Publications